THE TEACHINGS
OF
POPE ⌐PAUL VI
1970

1971
Publications Office
UNITED STATES CATHOLIC CONFERENCE
1312 Massachusetts Avenue, N.W.
Washington, D.C. 20005

Authorized reprint of the edition: *The Teachings of Pope Paul VI, 1970,* of the Libreria Editrice Vaticana, Città del Vaticano

Jesus looked at him, and said, " So you are Simon, the son of John? You shall be called Rock ".

JOHN 1, 42

The hour now striking on the clock of history demands great courage indeed from all the Church's children. In a very special way it calls for the courage of truth ...

POPE PAUL VI
to the Consistory
of the Sacred
College of Cardinals
18 May 1970

PREFACE

T *hrough the pages of this little volume we meet Pope Paul VI. We meet him in St. Peter's talking to the faithful who have come to see the Pope; we meet him talking to bishops and cardinals, outlining his plans and hopes for the Church; we meet him talking to men of state and talking to the world, making his own contribution to its affairs as one of its most respected citizens. To all his message is the same: Peace, Unity, Brotherhood.*

The Holy Father considers his audience each Wednesday to be a most important opportunity for his preaching of the Gospel. To anyone who has had the privilege of hearing him, these talks will bring back at once the unmistakable impression of simplicity and candour that his personality evokes. Pope Paul is not a very spectacular person, yet he can make all feel that he is one of themselves. Elevated indeed by his office, at heart he is no more, and no less, than the priest who has been chosen from among his brothers to be Christ's Vicar at this most important time of renewal in the Church. The subjects of these talks range from our choices in life to our search for God in the modern world, and each one contains something for every man.

The year 1970 was the fiftieth anniversary of the Holy Father's ordination to the priesthood. The importance of the priest is consequently one of the major themes that will be found running through the book. Also the reader will notice how the Vatican Council is mentioned on nearly every page, reflecting the Pope's desire to promote in every way the advances and the insights of that great assembly. Another feature is the constant appeal to young people, for whom there is always encouragement coupled with sympathetic guidance. For most people however 1970 will be remembered as the year of the Pope's visit to Asia, the Pacific and Australia. The various addresses which he gave on this journey are included here, as well as his personal reflections before departing from Rome, some of his recollections on returning, as confided to those present at the general audiences around Christmas.

Perhaps the following words from St. Catherine of Siena, quoted by the Holy Father on October 4th when he proclaimed her Doctor of the Church, summarise best the programme of Paul VI for progress both in the Church and in the World: " Not with war, but with peace and quiet, with the humble and continuous prayers, sweat and tears of the servants of God ".

TABLE OF CONTENTS

Preface VII
Pope Reflects on " Time " at Year's Final Audience 3
World Day of Peace—1970 7
Avoid two Dangerous Deviations 11
Pope Paul to Diplomatic Corps 15
Follow the Council to Halt Present Troubles 21
The Law of the Gospel is Love 25
No Watered Down, Camouflaged Catholicism 31
Maria Soledad Torres Acosta enrolled in Calendar of Saints . . . 36
Obedience and Liberty in the Church 42
Liberty and Authority go Hand in Hand 46
The Council can Educate to Good " Spirit " 55
Pope Paul to Parish Priests and Lenten Preachers of Rome . . . 59
Greater Spiritual Intensity Should Mark Lenten Season 67
Christian Perfection Demands an Inquiry into Fundamentals . . 71
Renunciation and Sacrifice: Hallmark of Christian Life 74
Pope Shows Role of Natural Law in Christian Concept of Life . . 78
Pope Details Role of Laity in the Church 83
Answers to Today's Problems lie in the Person, the Words of Jesus 88
The Cross: " Only Hope " for a Sinful World 94
Charity Brings the Church Together 99
All must be Messengers of Peace! 104
Christ's Plan of Redemption requires Personal Initiative 108
What Youth Expects of the " Mass Media " 112
Faith-Principle of Unity and Charity 115
Have Confidence in the Church! 119
Magisterium is the Rule of Faith 130

Table of contents

In Conquest of the Universe Man encounters the Creator . . . 135

Personal Prayer is diminishing 142

Enlightened Renewal of our Veneration for Mary 146

Reform rooted in Love of the Church 154

The Church is suffering 156

Give to the World a Love modelled on that of Christ 161

The Family, a School of Holiness 166

The Voice of the Church Reveals Man to Himself 177

Holiness Through suffering and the Cross 181

We need Firm Faith and Active Charity 189

The Council, the Programme of Pope Paul's Pontificate 193

Paul VI ordains 278 Priests in St. Peter's Square 197

Great Courage demanded from the Members of the Church . . . 202

The Hour of Courage for the Truth has Struck 208

Hope-the driving Force of the Christian 212

Only Jesus can Teach True Meaning of Love 216

Saint John of Avila—a Model for Priests Today 222

A Sense of Community 228

Pope urges " Communion " through " Communication " 232

Message of His Holiness Pope Paul VI for Mission Sunday 238

Justice and Law, Supreme Principles for the Life of the Human
Community 244

Pope Thanks Catholic World 247

Entire Church has Task of Service 251

Pope Paul Appeals for Greater Peace Efforts 255

The " Poor in Spirit " Take First Place 265

Meditate Upon Listen to the Sacred Scriptures as Vatican Council II Directs 270

Pope describes Pastoral Feature of Council 274

Holy Father urges Threefold Fidelity: to the Council, the Church,
to Christ 278

The Way to God—Reason and Faith 282

God is Real Purpose of our Existence 286

Modern Man tempted to Reject God 290

Table of contents

Religious Renewal—a Continual Process Towards Perfection . . 294

" Reject Temptations against the Faith " 298

We must Search for God 302

Reason and Faith needed by Man in searching for God 306

To Seek God is Already to Find 310

Faith Made for Men of Today 315

Replaces General Audience Speech with Confidant Appeal for Peace 319

" You belong to the World by a Special Title ... " 320

St. Teresa—an Exceptional Woman and a Religious 326

Plan for Authentic Christianity 333

St. Catherine-Doctor of the Church 337

Message of His Holiness Pope Paul VI on the 25th Anniversary of
the United Nations 344

Man's Moral Conscience must be strengthened 350

Solidarity and Prayer for Catholic Missions 354

Paul VI condemns Police Torture, Violence and Terrorism . . . 358

Paul VI's Homily at Canonization of the Forty Martyrs 362

The Church in a changing World 369

Paul VI to Priests of Rome 372

Missionary Aspect of Pope's Trip 378

Tourism can become Basis of Fraternity among Men 383

Our Journey is an Apostolic witness 386

Pope Paul's " Day of Peace " Message 389

Brotherly Love and Solidarity can bring about a New World . . . 395

Pope Paul explains Spiritual Purpose of Trip to Far East . . . 406

Pope Paul's Journey as Pastor and Missionary 410

Discusses Apostolic Nature of the Church 414

Asia must not succumb to Godlessness 422

Episcopal Conference in Sidney 428

Spotlight on Youth in Australia 433

Love, which will be forever 437

Pope's Discourse to College of Cardinals 440

Pope reminisces on two Aspects of Recent Journey 445

Wisdom alone liberates the World 448

Table of contents

APPENDIX

Letter of Pope Paul VI on Priestly Celibacy 455

Apostolic Letter issued " Motu Proprio " by Pope Paul VI establishing an Age Limit for the Exercise of Major Functions by Cardinals 461

Apostolic Exhortation to all the Bishops in Peace and Communion with the Apostolic See, on the fifth Anniversary of the Close of the Second Vatican Council 465

SUBJECT INDEX 479

X

THE TEACHINGS
OF
POPE PAUL VI

POPE REFLECTS ON " TIME "
AT YEAR'S FINAL AUDIENCE

Beloved Sons and Daughters!

We have come to the last day of the year. Reflection instinctively and powerfully turns our minds to that very well known and indefinable word: time, to the common yet very mysterious observation that time passes. The original side to this observation is that we are continually measuring this fact in relation to the mobility and contingency of things. We use clocks calendars, and extremely exact means of computing earthly and astronomical time. But we do not give enough attention to the inexorable nature of the phenomenon of the passing of time, which is outside our will and powers; " Time goes on ", Dante says, " and man does not notice " (*Purg.* 4, 9). When we do give attention to this cosmic and historical law, the mind is touched by a fearful sense of how irreversible it is. Time never bends back. " Think how it never relents " (Dante again: *Purg.* 12, 84).

This is a troubling thought indeed for us when we consider its obscurity and fatality. Let us relate it to our personal lives, our destiny, our lot, which come to good fortune or to grief in time. Machiavelli tells us that his Prince (cap. VII), had thought of everything, except that he might die suddenly. This is a matter that arouses endless thought: philosophers and writers have worn the eyes out over it, but have never grown tired.

The influence of Providence

And we Christians? We shall do well to pay great attention to it, because it is something that essentially concerns our frail and ephemeral beings. It makes us look at the scale of values

3

again, to see which are true (and deserve to be grappled to our hearts) and which are not. Remember how in the Gospel Jesus gave us an outline of the rich man full of his possessions, and then let drop the terrible sentence: " You fool, your life will be taken from you tonight; and what will become of the things you have accumulated? " (*Lk.* 12, 20).

Consideration of the precariousness of life, of the domination of life by Saturn, who ate his own children, can lead to taking decisive moral bearings. These can have a hedonistic character (compare Horace's *carpe diem!* pluck the fruit of every. day) and a spiritual character (recall Christ's words: " Walk, while there is still light ... " *Jn.* 12, 35). But these are thoughts which hardly find a place in that tremulous moment when we wait for the end of the civil year and turn the first page of the new calendar—for that hour is dominated by careless festivity.

But a good and pious thought for the last day of December is the thought of thanksgiving. When we sing the Te Deum and remember the events of the last twelve months, we become aware that " all is grace ", that everything has been penetrated and directed by a mysterious and beneficent influence, that of divine Providence. Divine Providence turns all things to our good (*Rom.* 8, 28), by guiding or by permitting. This is one of the best and wisest observations that we can make today about time past. It brings us at this milestone to a meeting with God's indescribable Fatherhood. Our pilgrimage in time sets out from him, is carried through in him, and heads towards him. This is Christian.

Look ahead

If we wish to complete our Christian ideas at this point, we have to take another step forward. It is not enough to look back: we have to look ahead. And not just with plans and projects for the coming year, and certainly not with fantastic horoscopes about the future. We need, rather, to have a view of the main lines of our life projected into the future, the temporal one and the eternal one. This future is what our faith tells us of, even though only in shadow during our mortal life, *in aenigmate*, as St. Paul said (*1 Cor.* 13, 12). This is a fundamental demand in

4

our faith: the thought of the future life ought never leave us. The Gospel message is full of it. The so-called eschatological vision of the last realities, is always present in Jesus' teaching. Indeed it constitutes an essential and terminal element of his message of salvation.

That vision is too often forgotten, even in the minds of many who call themselves Christians. The present moment absorbs our minds. Only the present seems to have any value, both as time and as the framework of the life that is carried on in time. This is one of the consequences of secularization, horizontalism, topicalism, and unbelief.

We have to be very careful here. The Christian too lives in time. He has to take great account of time and all its duties and values. He has to take greater account than others do, for it is in time that the experiment or examination which will settle his future and everlasting destiny is carried on. In time also he has to build up his earthly city, develop it, and make it just and human in its progress and its history. The efforts of believers, who are also citizens of the earth, have to be committed to this task.

But God's kingdom is also proclaimed and begun in time, and will reach it fullness beyond time. We ought always bear in mind how time is thus ambivalent for the Christian. It is a present gift and a promise for the future. Attention to the promise ensures that the present gift will not be undervalued, but will rather be used intensively and enjoyed wisely (cf. *Gaudium et spes*, 39-40).

The journeying Church

A term now in use in our spiritual vocabulary is " the pilgrim Church ". It refers to all of us, and fits in very well with Our exhortation for the end of the year. It is a marvellous expression. It is a true one. The Council often used it in its documents. In one of its most inspired passages, which is full of scriptural references, it speaks expressly of the Church as a pilgrim on the earth, in the world and in time, always in tireless striving for the final revelation of the children of God (*Lumen gentium*, 48-49).

May you always keep before your minds this evaluation of

time, this vision of Christians journeying towards a goal which is beyond time and which is attained over that terrible frontier which temporal death is for us. May these considerations admonish us to cleanse our past lives with salutary recollection, and to accept the coming time as a gift from above and an invitation to go up higher in that time still granted to us in our passage across the fleeting stage of the world (*1 Cor.* 7, 31).

So, a Happy New Year in the Lord, with Our Blessing.

WORLD DAY OF PEACE—1970

*In the Church of the Gesù on January 1st, 1970,
Pope Paul VI delivered his official address for
the third consecutive World Day of Peace, as
follows.*

Sons and Brothers,

We are gathered here to inaugurate the new civil year with the wish, the resolve, and the hope of Peace. With prayer for Peace. There we have an ideal which, more than any other, should be reflected in the reality of human life, because it sums up and favours every good thing to which mankind can aspire in the personal and also in the domestic, social, political, national and international, temporal and other-wordly order. We have need of it always. Indeed, the more our civilization grows and asserts itself, the more it becomes rich, developed and, therefore, complex in knowledge, means, institutions, questions, aspirations, the greater too is the need for order and Peace. This will assure and advance the just and happy complexity of our personal and collective lives on all levels, beginning from the interior level of our conscience (how can one live well, as a human being, as a Christian without peace of conscience?) and rising to the other levels on which we live our lives, amid numerous relationships (which, to be good, must needs be peaceful), amid many problems (which remain unsettled and tormenting, unless solved in Peace), amid thousands of difficulties (which all have to be overcome by Peace), and amid numberless griefs and misfortunes (which can receive from Peace alone their just and efficacious remedy).

Meaning of Peace

We wish to give you the vision of this universality of Peace, as if to find in this great and blessed name the synthesis of Our optimistic conception of the world in which we live, and of time,

7

which, in our conventional calculation, imitative in its own way of that of the sun, begins today a new course, a newer year. Peace is meant to be the sign of the time that is coming, the wish for all that will befall us in the future, the program of our history.

Today We say one thing only: Peace is a duty.

As everyone sees, linking the concept of Peace to that of duty makes our reflection a serious one, and seems to take from the idyllic vision of Peace much of its serenity; certainly it removes any equivocal kinship it may have with weakness and cowardice Because every duty involves an effort which we are not always prepared to make, it demands a power for which we often lack the energy and often too the desire. Yet, having understood in some measure that Peace stands at the apex of the human framework, We repeat: Peace is a duty, a serious duty.

There may perhaps spring spontaneously to our minds an answer which would free us of that seriousness: Yes, it is a duty, but it is not our concern. It concerns Leaders, those responsible for guiding a community, and especially those invested with international responsibility. It is within nations and between nations that conflicts opposed to Peace arise; we, say the private citizens, stand and watch; what can an individual do on his own, or what can a limited extraneous group do to bring Peace to a people's internal relations or to external relations between peoples? It is for statesmen, diplomats and governments, one might say, to make Peace a synonym for comfortable selfish lack of concern.

Peace is everyone's duty

Yes, Peace is a duty of Leaders. But not of Leaders alone. Today, democratically organized society assigns powers and duties to all the members of the community. Even if this were not so, it would still be true that Peace is everyone's duty, because Peace has dominion not in politics alone, but in many lower spheres which, in practice, involve our personal responsibility even more; and also because Peace has its active source in ideas, in minds, in moral attitudes, even more than in exterior activity. Before being a policy, Peace is a spirit. Before being expressed, victorious or vanquisher, in historical happenings and social re-

8

lationships, it is expressed, formed and asserted in our consciences, in that philosophy of life which everyone must acquire as a light for his footsteps along the pathways of the world and in the experiences of daily life.

That means, beloved Brothers and Sons, that Peace demands an education. We affirm it here at the altar of Christ, while celebrating the Holy Hass which recalls His Word and renews in an unbloody and sacramental form His sacrifice which made peace between heaven and earth: here, as disciples, as pupils, ever needing to listen, to learn, to begin anew the apprenticeship of our " metanoia ", that is, of the transformation of our instinctive and, regrettably, traditional mentality.

We must shake the foundations of ingrained prejudices: the idea that force and revenge are the ruling criterion of human relationships; that an injury received calls for another injury, often graver, in return—" an eye for an eye, a tooth for a tooth " (*Mt.* 5, 38);—that self-interest must prevail over the interests of others, without regard for their needs or for common right. We must place at the foundation of our social psychology hunger and thirst for justice, together with that seeking for peace which merits for us the title of children of God (cf. *Mt.* 5, 6, 9).

Christians have great resource

It is no Utopia; it is progress today more than ever before, it is demanded by the evolution of civilization and by the Damoclean sword of an increasingly serious and increasingly possible terror hanging over our heads. Civilization has succeeded in banishing, at least in principle, slavery, illiteracy, epidemics, social classes, etc., evils, that is, which were long established and which were tolerated as if they were unavoidable and were inherent in the sad tragic social life of mankind: civilization must also succeed in banishing war. Mankind's " good manners " demand it. The terrible increasing danger of a world conflagration prescribes it.

Have we, individual weak mortals, no means of averting the the possibility of catastrophic disasters of universal proportions? Yes, we do. We have recourse to public opinion, which in this emergency becomes the expression of mankind's moral conscience;

and we all know how great can be its power for good. We have our individual personal duty to be good. That does not mean to be weak. It means to be capable of breaking the sad logical chain of evil by patience and forgiveness. It means to love, that is, to be Christians.

We Christians have another resource, one that can have the power to move mountains (cf. *Mt.* 17, 20, 21, 21): this is the grafting of divine causality onto the mysterious interplay of natural causality and human freedom. This resource has two sides like a coin: one side is prayer (cf. *Mt.* 7, 7), the other is faith (cf. *Jn.* 1, 6). What will be the result in spiritual power, of prayer made with faith, we shall not always be able to measure by the experimental methods of our material and temporal world. To claim to do so would be to imagine and instrumentalize divine action as though it were a cosmic energy placed at our disposal to be used at will; this is not how the plan of divine mercy works, as it penetrates the events of our temporal world.

Effects not disappointing

But the effects will not be wanting. Prayer made with faith will not be disappointed. It may well be answered in overflowing measure, even if the when and the how remain for the present hidden from us. The Lord, the Lord Himself, has exhorted us to have recourse to this powerful aid, which makes us at one and the same time admit our radical powerlessness to attain salvation on our own, and also the all-powerful goodness of the Father to " deliver us from evil " (*Mt.* 6, 13), and even to turn to our good our very misfortunes and sufferings (cf. *Rom.* 8, 28).

This, after all, is the thought that gathers us here and now to pray with lively faith to Christ " our peace " (*Eph.* 2, 14), Christ, " the Prince of peace " (*Is.* 9, 6), Christ, who at His birth had the Angels proclaim " peace on earth " (*Lk.* 2, 14), Christ, who, after His resurrection, repeats to His followers the happy greeting, " Peace be with you " (*Jn.* 20, 19, 21). May He, apart from any merit of ours, deign to listen to our call: " Guide our feet into the way of peace " (*Lk.* 1, 79).

AVOID TWO DANGEROUS DEVIATIONS

Beloved Sons and Daughters!

It seems to Us a duty to look at the teaching of the recent Council to find a theme for this morning's talk with you. We have an idea, dear visitors, that in your hearts you are curious to know: What is the Pope thinking? Well, here is Our answer: We are still thinking about the Council.

That event did not terminate at the end of its labours, like any historical fact shut away in time. It was the beginning of a renewal in the Church which will have to keep on developing and reach the life of the whole great ecclesial community. The Council left a body of teachings which we ought not forget. We must remember them, get to know them, and put them into practice. The Council must live on in the Church's thinking; it must give it a new mentality, imprint on it new ways of behaving, renew it, spread it, and sanctify it.

Personal Renewal

We are well aware that a whole literature has arisen out of the Council and is still producing new writing. We know well that works and institutions have arisen from the Council, and by virtue of its prescriptions. Everyone knows what big doctrinal developments have derived from the Council and are fostering study and culture. We call upon the Holy Spirit so that this doctrinal and canonical process may go forward happily.

But now We have to ask a question: What can the individual believer do, what ought he do in regard to the Council? What should single ecclesial communities do? The answer to this question leads us to give some special consideration to the moral demands deriving from the Council's teachings and from the very

11

fact that it was celebrated. This means that we all have to ask ourselves what coherent course of action we should foster, both in thought and action, in regard to the Council, assuming that each of us desires to give practical and useful importance to that great event, not only as regards the whole Church, but also as regards our own moral lives and renewal of our concrete and personal profession of Christianity.

Deviations

It will be well to begin our reflection by immediately laying down a line of demarcation to avoid two dangerous deviations. The first is that of believing that the Council began an era of such newness that we are justified in depreciating the Church's tradition, standing apart from it and being intolerant towards it. A state of mind of radical refusal to bear with the Church's past exists in many minds. Men, institutions, customs, doctrines: all are summarily set aside, if they have the mark of the past on them. The implacable critical spirit of these unrestrainable innovators condemns the whole of the Church " system " of yesterday. They can no longer see anything but faults and defects, and inability and ineffectiveness in expressing Catholic life in years gone by. The consequences would give rise to many grave considerations, and darken that historical feeling for the Church's life which is a precious characteristic of our culture. It is replaced by facile sympathy for everything outside of the Church. The adversary becomes likeable and a model; the friend becomes unlikeable and unbearable.

If this course is not modified, it even gives rise to the conviction that it is right to look forward to and form the hypothesis of a Church completely different from our Church of today. A Church, it is said, invented for the new times, where all bonds of troublesome obedience will be done away with, together with all limits upon personal freedom and every form of sacred commitment. This deviation is unfortunately possible; but it is to be hoped that its obvious excesses will reveal the error in it. It is certain that " aggiornamento ", the renewal of the Church fostered by the Council, is not intended to produce such disintegration of tested historical and institutional reality.

Another deviation consists in confusing custom with tradition, and in believing that the Council is to be regarded as finished with and ineffective, that the Church's real enemies are those who promote and adopt the innovations deriving from the Council. Tradition (that is, custom) must prevail, they say. These defenders of unchanging forms in Church practice perhaps make their mistake through excess of love, but they end by expressing this love in polemics with friends belonging to the household, as if these were more unfaithful and dangerous than anyone else.

The voice of the Pastors: Confidence in the Church

So, which is the right road? It it the one which the responsible authority of the Church's Pastors and Our authority lays down for the ecclesial community. The pastoral voice is not silent. The good hear it. They do not disregard it, and they do not neglect it. We are firmly convinced in the Lord that the Church can not only preserve her efficacious means but also carry out her mission of salvation and peace in this hour which is so critical in her own history and so grave for the history of the world, if the pastoral function is exercised freely and lovingly and if the community of clergy and faithful will understand it and support it.

And where is this way leading? The question belongs to the order of ideas which We indicated at the beginning. That is, it is aimed at finding out what moral and spiritual line (not to go any further at present) the Council offers the Church, for it is exactly along this line that the footsteps of pastoral guidance lead.

The Order of Charity

Before We end We will just refer to a few preliminary criteria. For example, consistency, which is so obvious and wholly necessary. The Christian must restore his spiritual and moral unity. It is not enough just to say that one is a Christian; we must live as Christians. This is the ancient and fundamental maxim which the Apostle enunciated: " Justus ex fide vivit ". The just man, that is, the genuine Christian, derives the rule, style and strength of his life from the faith. He not only lives *with* faith, but also *according to* it. This is a basic principle. We can speak about it on

13

other occasions. This is the axis of the renewal which the Council desired.

We might add two other fundamental criteria, but will simply mention them, so as not to tire you any further with this discourse. Here they are: Christ must be put at the top, at the centre, at the source of our lives, of our thought and our conduct. He should be our Master, our example, the bread of our personal lives. And we must go into the communitarian notion of Christian living, including the interior and personal part of it; that is, we must enter the order of charity. Charity is the distinguishing mark of those who follow Christ. Let us never forget that (cf. *Jn.* 13, 35).

May Our Apostolic Blessing render fruitful in you these fleeting hints.

POPE PAUL TO DIPLOMATIC CORPS

On January 12th, the Holy Father received in solemn audience the Members of the Diplomatic Corps accredited to the Holy See. The Doyen of the Corps, H. E. Luis Amado-Blanco, Ambassador of Cuba, speaking on behalf of his colleagues, conveyed to the Holy Father their good wishes for the new year.
In reply the Holy Father spoke as follows

Excellencies, Gentlemen:

To all of you We offer Our cordial and respectful greetings, Our lively gratitude, and Our fervent good wishes for the year 1970. We are particularly grateful to your Dean who has kindly interpreted the thoughts and the sentiments of the Diplomatic Corps accredited to the Holy See, expressing them in such noble and respectful words to Our humble person.

Your very presence, which is renewed every year on this occasion and is particularly pleasing to Us, constitutes in its own way a highly qualified recognition of the mission of the Church in the world. As representatives of so many and divers nations, you are like a synthesis of the world, and you testify that the Church and the Apostolic See are not strangers to the multiple and grave problems concerning the world. For Us, this is a precious testimony which comforts Us in the fulfilment of our responsibilities; a testimony which invites Us to reflect with you on a question often discussed today: Is it right for the Holy See to make use of this form of activity called diplomacy? It not diplomacy totally foreign to the nature and the purpose of the Church? Does it not run the risk of becoming assimiliated to institutes and organisms of a temporal order with which it cannot nor should be confused?

When it is a question of States, such a question does not arise because—despite the new forms with which international relations are invested today—diplomatic activity remains for them a privileged instrument, sanctioned by centuries-old historical experience. But for the Church, whose essential role is a religious one, is recourse to diplomacy truly justified?

You, Gentlemen and Ambassadors, with full knowledge of the facts, can answer this question. You can say that there are valid motives for the Holy See to receive you and to negotiate with you, to send its own representatives to perform similar functions with your Governments.

Universality of Church

In fact, the diplomatic activity of the Holy See responds, in a very appropriate manner, to the present developments of international life and to the present needs of the mission which the Church must fulfil in the contemporary world. The Vatican Council II has spoken of this mission by solemnly affirming that the Church is called upon to give—and she intends to do so with all her strength—a determinative aid to society, by fortifying and solidifying the unity of the human family. As the Constitution *Gaudium et spes* says in no. 42: " In virtue of her mission and nature, the Church is bound to no particular form of human culture, nor to any political, economic, or social system. Hence the Church by her very universality can be a very close bond between diverse human communities and nations, provided these trust her and truly acknowledge her right to true freedom in fulfilling her mission ". Such is the activity the Holy See intends to exercise: help to render closer the bonds between nations by mutual dialogue, careful to recognize the rights and the duties of each. The Roman Pontiffs, particularly in the modern and contemporary period, became more and more keenly aware of this responsibility which flows directly from their mission. And they replied to this imperative inherent in their office: that of becoming interested also in civil society, not to interfere unduly in a domain outside their scope, but to foster respect for the basic principles of civil and international life, justice towards all, mutual concord, collaboration among peoples; briefly, to co-operate in the peaceful search for this common good, of which the temporal authority should be the guarantee in order to serve and to defend peace. Let us hearken again to the Constitution *Gaudium et spes,* no. 78: " Peace is not merely the absence of war. Nor can it be reduced solely to the maintenance of a balance of power between enemies. Nor is it brought about by dictatorship. Instead, it is rightly and appropriately called ' an enterprise of justice ' (*Is.* 43, 7). Peace results from that harmony built into human society by its divine Founder, and actualized by men as they thirst after ever greater justice ... That earthly peace which arises from love of neighbour symbolizes and results from the peace of Christ who comes forth from God the Father ".

Could the Pope be truly uninterested in such a task, one which emanates from the very heart of God? Could he forget that peace, announced in the manger of Jesus Christ on the holy night of Christmas, should be on earth the reflection of the peace of God?

At the service of Peace

If one wishes to approach the problems in a really objective way, it is clear that the activity of the Church in the world is at the service of peace.

1) First of all, peace within the various national communities, by helping them " to triumph over egoism, pride and rivalries, to overcome ambitions and injustice, to open to everyone the paths of a more human life where each one is loved and helped as a neighbour, as a brother " (*Populorum progressio*, 82).

To this daily activity of Christians, guided by the responsible pastors, the representatives of the Holy See contribute, in the exercise of their mission, very effective assistance, while at the same time they help the local churches to strengthen their bonds with Us.

In this way, a precious contribution can be provided for human progress under its various aspects: spiritual, moral, cultural, social. Thus, the development of the country is promoted. This is how the society of tomorrow is constructed, in the dynamic balance of groups that compose it. In his own proper domain and with evangelical unselfishness, the representative of the Holy See supports the initiatives which lead to the education of communities, families and persons. To this mission corresponds also, Gentlemen and Ambassadors, your own activity which remains

17

very different, as We have said, from the diplomatic activity in every other State, and which also seeks to establish peace by maintaining continually with the Holy See close contacts which, you may be sure, are highly appreciated.

2) This activity in the service of peace extends also to international *external peace* whose aim is to eliminate differences of all sorts among peoples. On this point, the activity of the Holy See would like to contribute all that it possibly can. It permits the Pope not to limit himself to declarations of principles, to launch out with solemn and purely theoretical statements, but to intervene on the concrete plane of action for peace, and even between parties in disagreement. This is what Our Predecessor Pius XII did during the tragic world war which upset the world; and the documents about to be published are its most convincing proof. This is what John XXIII of beloved memory did during the moments of grave international tension, by offering his very noble mediation. This is what We are modestly striving to do in the wars which, alas, continue to work havoc. All this was possible and is possible, thanks to the means offered by diplomatic activity. Here again, what a precious help the Pope finds, Gentlemen and Ambassadors, in your collaboration which, at times, is the irreplaceable way to achieve such noble and such urgent aims!

Diplomatic activity, therefore, permits the Holy See to intervene on the international level, by helping the efforts made for the happy consolidation of the community of divers nations, by contributing to assure to such efforts this ethical and spiritual content without which they would be doomed to failure, by remaining equally distant from all partiality, from all excess.

To fulfill her mission, the Church also uses means which are invested with new expressions today, particularly in relations with international Organisms. And always pursuing her proper aim, the spiritual salvation of men, she also works to promote the dignity of the person and the progress of nations in justice and in peace. Her qualified contacts in the international domain permit the Holy See to make its voice better heard, to give greater value to its own suggestions, and to negotiate with those who control the fate of nations, in a spirit of mutual respect.

The complete unselfishness of such activity for everything which could have a distinct temporal and territorial end and the Holy

See's total dedication to problems of human life are enhanced, even visibly, by the nature and the universal, Catholic and supernatural physiognomy of the Church and of the Apostolic See. In this domain, We would like to manifest ever more clearly this evangelical poverty which for us is a law of our divine Master. And We would also wish that you, Excellencies and Ambassadors, should understand this well: that when the Apostolic See acts in behalf of ends which We have indicated it is actuated not by calculated and hidden considerations for personal advantage and powers, but for the service of justice, peace and the international community.

And even when the Holy See has a loyal dialogue with States in order to have the rights and the freedom of the Church recognized, it aspires in no way whatever to privileges or to selfish interests. Rather, it acts for the service and for the good of man, the common subject of civil society and of the Church, and for the moral advantage of States, in which the religious community founded by Christ the Lord is at work.

As an expert in human nature, knowing well, therefore, what lies in the human heart, promoting an authentic humanism and one open to transcendence, the Church establishes appropriate and fruitful contacts with your diplomacy in order to help the modern world solve its contradictions and effect a dynamic and constructive peace, centered on the recognition and the promotion of human, personal and social values.

At the close of this interview, allow Us to tell you how much We appreciate your noble work, as well as the intelligent and generous collaboration which you give to your activity, for the benefit, first of all, of your respective Nations, and also on behalf of world peace. Such common efforts that are so profitable certainly make this meeting, which inaugurates the new year, a highly significant symbol. We gladly reap its wholesome value: it is an encouragement for Us and a happy omen for you. With these sentiments, We invoke upon you, your families and the noble Nations you represent, the continuous help of Almighty God who never fails to assist us.

And now, allow Us to add a further word to all We have just said on this special occasion. The painful events of recent days, which have taken place in those African lands so dear to

19

Us, compel all men of good will to do everything possible to ensure that the Nigerian conflict—which seems to be moving toward an end—should not become a frightening tragedy and end with an epilogue even more cruel than the horror that every war entails.

We Ourself, during Our recent trip to Africa, as on every other occasion, have done all in Our power to save human lives and to bring about a peaceful settlement. We have never failed to assist and to help the needy and the hungry with all the means at Our disposal. You can understand with how much emotion We direct this appeal to you, Excellencies and Ambassadors, and through you to all your governments, so that the swift action of all men of good will may succeed in preventing further bloodshed, and in saving innocent lives, in respect for international law.

We know that the Nigerian Authorities have again expressed their intention to safeguard the human and civil rights of all, including their opponents, as they had already requested for some time past the presence of certain Observers from various nations and international Organizations. This represents already a good omen and a happy promise. May history in the future be able to testify to the magnanimity of all those engaged in these decisive events. On its part, the Holy See is ready to do all it can to render human this painful situation, and to that end it is ready to make use of all the means available to it. May this armed conflict cease, and may the voices of solidarity and charity be loudly heard. May the efforts of generous Nations and Our prayer to the God of peace bring these precious gifts to the land of Africa.

FOLLOW THE COUNCIL TO
HALT PRESENT TROUBLES

Beloved Sons and Daughters!

No one in this moment of our history can avoid the bewilderment of uncertainty. We know this. Very many things are changing around us; the feeling of change passes from things into minds. The need to stick to reality is throwing doubt upon our acquired ideas, our inner attitudes, our habits. This is because exterior reality is in continual alteration, the world is being progressively transformed.

We are attracted by experience of new things, of things in movement, of original ideas. That experience often becomes our criterion for judging truth. We believe we are free because we liberate ourselves from what we have learned, because we get away from obedience and rules, because we entrust ourselves to the new and to the unknown. But we often fail to notice that we are becoming followers of others' ideas, imitators of fashion imposed by others, attached to whoever most daringly detaches himself most from common sense.

Those who describe this widespread attitude from a theoretical point of view speak of relativism. That is to say, we become relative to what surrounds us on the outside and conditions us. They talk of historicism which means to say that we should surrender to the transitoriness of time and have no more taste for the things that are still with us and keep their reason for being. They speak of existentialism: that is, they find in what exists or in what is in the process of becoming a higher criterion of value without looking for its measures of truth and integrity. And so on.

But when we speak in the simple language of common sense we have to acknowledge that all are involved in a phenomenon of weakness. Interior inquietude has become habitual and is

21

taking away our security, our satisfaction with what we are and with what we are doing. We are putting our hope in transformation, in revolution, in radical metamorphosis of the inheritance with which tradition and progress itself have provided us.

It is true that we have many good reasons nowadays for striving towards some innovation. More than in the past, we are aware of the many imperfect and unjust things which exist, hold out and sometimes grow worse around us. We make it our duty to find remedies and invent better things.

The Virtue of Fortitude

But people lose their bearings in this very disturbance. They no longer know what is the best thing to think and to. We ought to be grateful to those who are studying, thinking, seeing, teaching and guiding with a true sense of humanity. Reason is being rehabilitated before our eyes: man's good cannot but be reasonable (cf. S. Th. II-III, 123, 1). And there is being restored the magisterium of those who, with responsibility and wisdom, teach others the value of things and the order of finalities. We may add, authority is being rehabilitated; that is to say, the function of those who rightfully provide others with the service of guidance and order. But We would say again: we owe esteem and support to whoever remains strong personally or in the exercise of their duties.

Fortitude is a virtue that does not get sufficient honour today. It presupposes principles, it presupposes logic, it presupposes personal freedom, it often presupposes unpopularity and sacrifice; it presupposes fidelity to an irreversible commitment, to an irrevocable choice, to an unquestionable law.

The Results of the Post-Conciliar Period

Dearly beloved children, at this moment We do not wish to make an anlysis or a criticism of our times. We will barely refer to the confusion which pervades so many areas of modern thought and contemporary action, and We do so only to recall how a certain confusion is unhappily also entering religious life and the very effort which the Church has been making, since the Council, to find herself, to improve herself.

The examination of conscience which the Council set in motion seems to Us to be having excellent results. We may say that everything is being submitted to reflection and many things are being reviewed. You know this; you can see it for yourselves. The Church has a twofold basic purpose: to be what Christ wills her to be, and to make herself better and better fitted to infuse the energies of faith and grace into the modern world, by the means of her traditional institutions and her spiritual experience. If the Holy Spirit helps her in this, her face will appear youthful and calm today also, with that look which sees everything: past history, the present drama, hope, and the beauty of holiness and of conformity to her divine propotype, the Son of God made Son of man (cf. *Rom.* 8, 29).

This is the basis: the Council. Our duty is to remain loyal to that great word which the Church spoke for this hour in history, in the fullness of her authority, in invocation of and in obedience to the charism of the Holy Spirit, who assists her and liberates her, in her vision of the world in which she lives and for which she lives. In the Council there was clarity: in the post-conciliar period may there be fortitude.

Because, you know and you see it, the reawakening which the Council not only authorized but also promoted, is tending to grow weary in many Christians and in many forms of Christian life. Indolence is getting the better of us; laziness seems to be avoiding or reducing every question. Or the reawakening is turning into a spirit of corrosive and destructive criticism. It is impugning obedience and leaving it to individual judgment to fashion a convenient concept of the Church just as it pleases, with more conformity to the spirit and morals of the world than to the demands of the Church's supernatural genius and her apostolic mission.

The Undoubted Voice of Christ

This is why We say to you: hold fast to the Council. It ought to relieve us of that feeling of insecurity which is troubling mankind so much today. We are pilgrims in time. We have a lamp to light our road. For Our part, We would like to give you that comfort that comes from the security of knowing that one is no the right road. We say this to you, Priests, who are being assailed by so many doubts about your being in the Church and in the world. Do not fear. Re-read those passages in the Council which concern you and go forward with confidence and courage. We say this to you, Religious. You too are being attacked by criticisms of the magnanimous choice which is the mark of your lives. You have chosen the " better part ". If you are loyal and strong in your singular vocation, " it shall not be taken away from you " (cf. *Lk*. 10, 42). Fear not.

To you, young people, militant in contestation. The causes of justice and liberty which make you yearn for a new, truer and more fraternal social life, will not be disappointed or ineffective. Only, do bring your many energies into the hive of genuine ecclesial life. Some of the most spirited among you often, perhaps unconsciously, waste them outside, and against Christ's name. Do not fear that the Church will not be able to welcome and understand you and that the firmness of her principles will benumb your lively spirits. Her principles are hinges, not blocks. Have no fear!

All you fervent and thoughtful members of God's People: learn how to belong firmly to the Church, whose living and holy members you are. Do not be afraid. Listen, and above the surrounding uproar, hear the voice of Christ, certain, and, because it is divine, ineffable: " Take courage: I have overcome the world " (*Jn*. 16, 33).

With Our Apostolic Blessing.

THE LAW OF THE GOSPEL IS LOVE

On Monday, January 19th, the Holy Father gave audience to participants in the International Congress on Canon Law, being held under the auspices of the State University of Rome. The delegates were led by Professor Agostino D'Avack, Rector of the University and President of the Congress, who delivered an address to the Pope. His Holiness replied as follows.

Professor D'Avack,
Rector Magnificus of the University of Rome,

We thank you for the elevated, frank and amiable words which you have just uttered. Among them We heard a number of things which We Ourself would like to bring to the attention of the illustrious visitors whom you have led here on this exceptional occasion.

At the same time We thank these visitors for their presence. Their qualifications and their number bear witness to the import-ance, the success and the spirit of this International Congress on Canon Law, now being held in Rome, which, more than any other place, is the home of Law, both civil and ecclesiastical. We greet them all, and in all We honour a subject greatly valued by Us, that juridical science dealing with the Church's life as a society, which we call Canon Law.

We must first of all express Our pleasure that such a Congress as this is being held and that it is being held in the secular University of Rome. This fact alone is acknowledgment of an aspect of the Church which, though exterior and historical, is of undeniable importance for the spiritual life and civil progress of humanity. For Us it is a matter for satisfaction; for you, for the University of Rome and for so many other scientific institutes here represented it is a sign of noble culture and open intelligence.

Our delight in your meeting is increased by the theme which gives it its character and by the historical moment with which it is concerned: " The Church after the Council ". As everyone can see, the Church and the Council absorb Our attention, Our interest and Our passion. Can Our commitment to Our apostolic office and the critical hour through which we are passing allow Us to think of anything else but the Church and the Council held so recently? We are edified and consoled by seeing scholars of great renown such as you coming together in a Congress to study, with special qualifications intensity of thought and mutual intercourse, and (We can have no doubt) free and honest scientific probity. It makes Us feel obliged to inform Ourself of the results of your studies. We gladly respond to this obligation; We consider Ourself fortunate that the many, too many cares of Our ministry, will leave Us the time needed for that task.

Vast and varied programme

The theme of your vast and varied programme calls Us to it. We are impressed by the authority of your names. The few yet significant reports which the press has so far provided about the papers and discussions at your Congress have been enough to tell Us how serious and valuable they are. We will therefore refrain from entering during this talk into the merits of the matters dealt with. We will not even comment upon them. Perhaps some comment might be called for from Us, some further investigations, some reservations. We will only note the happy way in which the themes have been formulated. Those themes derive from the great work of rethinking which the Catholic Church assembled in Council carried through about itself. They are mainly concerned with: Tradition and Innovation in Canon Law (learnedly discussed by Professor Orio Giacchi), Divine Law and Human Law in the Church, Canon Law according to the Council Principles: the Power of the Church (lucidly expounded by Professor Mario Pentroncelli), and so on.

We will restrict Ourself to the evidence which your Congress has thus produced in connection with a twofold order of Principles: those concerned with fundamental truths related to the Church's nature and constitution and those related to the renewal of Canon Law in the Church in accordance with the Council's teaching and desires.

The first Christian Communities

We have just heard the testimony which you offer from the authoritative lips of Professor Peter Augustine D'Avack himself, above all in regard to the rightfulness adn the necessity of the existence of Canon Law in the Church. You have recognized that the Church founded by Christ is a visible society. The idea that the Church may be invisible is revealed as being utopian, not to say simply self-contradictory. That was asserted by scholars and movements which in other times adopted a purely spiritualist and liberal interpretation of Christianity. Likewise the tendency spread to some degree today among persons and Christian groups, to claim a charismatic voice of their own, a free and authoritative one, however one may like to call it, in order to emancipate one's own and others' conscience and one's own and others' conduct from the Church's normative power. This tendency reveals itself as being alien to the genuine community and hierarchical conception of the Church itself. It reminds us of the energetic arguments of St. Paul. He was indeed the dispenser of the mysteries of God (*1 Cor.* 4, 1), but at the same time he was an organizer of the first Christian communities, as quite distinct nuclei, governed by apostolic authority and belonging to one and the same social body, the mystical Body of Christ. At one point he writes almost polemically: " What, was it from you that the word of God went forth? Or was it to you only that it reached? If anyone thinks he is a prophet, or spiritual, let him recognize that the things I am writing to you are the Lord's commandment " (*1 Cor.* 14, 36-37). The Church is a People constituted as an organic social body, by virtue of a divine plan and action and through the ministry of pastoral service, which promotes, directs, instructs, educates and sanctifies in Christ those who adhere to him in faith and charity (cf. DE LUBAC, *Méd. sur l'Eglise*, p. 203).

That is what came from the Council. It deepened doctrine on the Church; it highlighted the mystical aspect proper to it, and therefore obliged the Canonist to seek more deeply in Holy Scripture and theology the reasons of his own teaching. This fact has shaken him up, for he had been largely accustomed to basing his teaching on centuries-old, unquestioned tradition. He reinforced that teaching with the support of Roman Law first of all ("quod ratio scripta est merito nuncupatum", canonists rightly used to say). He compared his teaching with the laws of peoples to whom the Church brought her message of the Gospel, and she will continue to do this in her thought and history, for reasons that are more than sufficiently clear. Yet she will be faithful in this period after the Council to the doctrinal and disciplinary impulse which that great Synod gave; she will seek in herself and in her deep and mysterious constitution the why and the wherefore of her ancient but at the same time renewed canonical discipline (cf. Decr. *Optatam totius*, 16).

The Need for a "Lex Fundamentalis"

To Us this seems to be the new element in the study and formulation of Canon Law. From it derives the current revision of the Code. But, unlike almost all the great juridical compilations in the history of Law, it has not been undertaken mainly for a practical purpose: "*ad communem et maxime studentium utilitatem*" (cf. *Decretum Gregorii IX*), nor, as Dante made Justinian say "to remove excess and futility from the law" (*Par.* 6, 12), but rather to derive canon law from the very essence of the Church of God. The new and original law for the Church of God, the law of the Gospel, is love: *gratia Spiritus Sancti, quae datur per fidem Christi* (S. Th. I-II, 106; 1; & 108, 1). If this is the interior principle guiding the Church's life, it must be manifested more and more in her visible, exterior and social discipline, with consequences which it is easier to hint at than describe.

From this mystico-ethical introspection of the Church there arises the need for the Church to define herself in a *Lex fundamentalis*. Theology is going into this even more deeply than Law. If it were formulated in explicit canons, it would resolve many grave questions concerning Catholic life in our time—and it would perhaps raise others.

The Authority of Tradition

This closer relationship between Theology and Canon Law will infuse into the latter new characteristics. Your Congress has undoubtedly already looked into this and has recognized that

Canon Law is not so much a dominating law and an expression of autocentric power, a despotic and arbitrary *iussum*, but a norm tending for the most part to interpret a twofold law. This twofold law is the superior, divine law, and the interior, moral law of conscience. It is therefore a fostering and protecting law, a law providing balance in the best way possible to our human condition between rights and corresponding duties, between liberty and responsibility, between the dignity of the person and the sovereign demands of the common good. It provides a balance between those things and that which is proper to the Church: her immutable unitary and communitarian constitution and her versatile adaptability to the contingent activities of language and customs ... the particular requirements of various cultures and the particular historical needs of the human family. As always, Tradition will have its supremely authoritative and welcome say in Canon Law, but now with renewed prestige, a title of wisdom and authenticity. It will encourage the ecclesial community to steep itself in the perennial but never wholly attained perfection of the Christian calling.

How many, how many things could be suggested to the mind by even a simple discourse such as this by a matter of such extent and importance!

But We will bring this talk to an end by expressing Our approval and exhorting you to continue your studies in Canon Law and ecclesiastical law. They are more than ever worthy of your devotion because the Council showed their new fruitfulness, the new relevance which they have to the Church's life and, in no small part, to the life of modern society.

The Church and Civil Society

Allow Us to invite you to look at the Church, at its exterior, temporal and juridical aspect, at what it really is and what it is really destined for. We have been appointed by Providence, much to Our own confusion but with immense (We should like to be able to say: incomparable!, cf. *Jn.* 21, 15) love, to be the visible head of the Church, of which Christ is the sole and supreme and eternal Head and generator. The Council helps you, almost obliges you to have this new vision, which is deeper and more realistic.

If churchmen are to be no longer guilty of legalism and formalism, even when they have to lay down the law and govern, you can see that these accusations also apply to canonical studies which hold to old positions of juridical positivism or juridical historicism. You too should penetrate the Church's outward appearance and see in her the *societas spiritus* (*Phil.* 2, 1; St. Augustine, *Serm.* 71, *PL* 38, 462). Do not think that when the Church comes into contact with civil society, she separates herself from it or opposes it (cf. *Gaudium et spes*), or infuses her spirit into it in order to dominate it (cf. *Ep. ad Diognetum* V-VI); or that, by reaching an accord with it, the Church still wishes to grant or claim privileges. Now that she is without temporal power, she is not ambitious to recover its burdens and its advantages. She does not desire anything except the free exercise of her spiritual and moral mission, by means of equitable, trustworthy and lasting demarcations of respective fields of competence.

Do not fear her; rather love her, you too. We would say with St. Augustine: *Amate hanc Ecclesiam, estote in tali Ecclesia, estote talis Ecclesia!* (*Serm.* 138, *PL* 38, 769). And may you too perceive the unique, personal and vital relevance which this mysterious institution has for each of us, as the obligatory means of resolving the central and unavoidable question of our destiny, the religious question. We may indeed call the Church the sacrament of salvation (cf. *Lumen gentium*, n. 48), because Cyprian's words are still true and urgent: " To have God as our Father, we must first have the Church as our mother " (*De cath. unitate*, c. 6, *PL* 4, 503).

May Our Apostolic Blessing help you in this, Gentlemen and Sons.

NO WATERED DOWN,
CAMOUFLAGED CATHOLICISM

Beloved Sons and Daughters:

The Church everywhere in the world is celebrating the Week
of Prayer for Unity, that is, re-integration of all Christians
into the one Church willed by Christ. Those who are distinguished
by the honour and responsibility of bearing the name of Christians are still subdivided and separated among themselves and from
communion with the Church.

The Christian's fundamental duty to preserve unity is becoming clearer. "The unity", St. Paul said, "of the Spirit in the
bond of peace. There is one body, and one Spirit, even as you
are called in one hope of your calling; one Lord, one faith, one
baptism, one God and Father of all" (*Eph.* 4, 3-6). And as it
becomes clearer there is also increased awareness, desire, and
need to restore that which the Church essentially is: communion
(cf. HAMER, *L'Eglise est une communion*, ed. Cerf 1962).

There is an increasing uneasiness and pain at the intolerable
fragmentation of the Christian name; there is increasing impa-
tience to see the results of ecumenism and enjoy its effects. But
at the same time there is an awareness of the difficulties in the
way of reaching sincere and effective reconciliation among Christians. Centuries have passed, and have crystallized this abnormal
historical situation. Debates and polemics have gone on endlessly
on all sides. Personalities of great intellectual, moral and
spiritual eminence have arisen, and have stated and defended their
various positions. Practical compromises were arranged, based
on a politico-religious compromise which was clearly contrary to
Christian unity and the Church's autonomy. An example was the
decision taken at one time to give differing geographical territories
to the differing religious denominations and to allow secular

princes to have dominance in the religious field. This is what happened at the disputed Peace of Westphalia, concluded at Münster in 1648. It established the absurd principle of *cuius regio eius religio*.

A tradition, a mentality and good faith developed in the various separated Churches and the diverse Christian confessions. Volumes upon volumes have been written in defence of their theological systems, each one differing from the other. Each one's own Church has been clothed in a mantle of untouchable orthodoxy, or, on the other hand, free rein was given to the principle of private judgement. Every personal and arbitrary interpretation of the Bible was authorized; the authority of the Catholic magisterium was denied, and innumerable teachers, in dispute among themselves, were acecpted ... Where, where is unity of faith, of charity, of ecclesial communion?

Wrong Attempts

The difficulties seem to be insurmountable! Ecumenism seems to be wearing itself out in an illusory effort! One reason for this lies in the generous attempts which modern non-Catholic ecumenism is making. It has to acknowledge the particular belief of each Christian denomination; it does indeed arouse and stimulate the problem of unity, yet it cannot solve that problem without the authority and the charism of unity which we hold to be Peter's divine prerogative.

But, some say, could not Peter drop his numerous demands? Could not Catholics and dissidents celebrate together the highest and most definitive act of the Christian religion, the Eucharist? Could they not then proclaim that the yearned for unity had at last been attained? Unfortunately, no. Unity cannot be achieved by a *fait accompli*, by intercommunion, as they say. How could there be unity without the same faith, without the same valid priesthood? Just a few days ago the Secretariat for the Union of Christians issued a clear and authoritative notification, giving a reminder of the prohibition against intercommunion (except for special, stated cases). It warns Catholics not to have recourse to it. It is not a good way: it is a deviation.

Not an Insoluble Problem

You will therefore ask Us whether we are not faced with an insoluble problem, so numerous and grave are the difficulties, so vain, indeed harmful, are the unauthorized and conformist attempts to obtain a false unity.

No, dearly beloved Children, we ought not despair of a happy outcome to the ecumenism which the recent Vatican Council fostered, even though the way is hard, slow and gradual. We would remind you first of all that the cause of ecumenism has already achieved much, very much. If it has done nothing else, it has shown that Christianity is one single thing. Unity is willed by Christ. It should be expressed by a single Church. The cause of religion has need of it. If this be the duty of Christians and in their interest, then unity will have to be re-established.

We have already passed out of a centrifugal historical and spiritual movement and have taken a centripetal bearing. Remarkable steps have been taken and are still being taken to see that such a change of direction shall become a movement towards ecclesial and universal communion. The ecumenical movement is becoming more popular; it is spreading and winning to its cause upright and believing people. God's People is thinking, praying, working, waiting and suffering for full and authentic unity.

What Can We Do?

At Rome this year, Our Cardinal Vicar has encouraged more intense and general celebration of this Week for the Unity of all Christians. Studies, meetings and discussions are going on at official and representative levels, with proposals for solving the delicate and manifold problems connected with the divisions which still hold up reconciliation and re-integration in the one and only Church. There is much talk of charity among still separated Christians: no longer scorn, distrust, indifference. Fraternal and sincere collaboration is now taking place between Catholics and non-Catholics through common efforts in the cultural, social and charitable fields. Attempts to get to know each other better are being made on all sides, to respect each other, to help each other.

January 21st, 1970

There are signs of a prospect that what is good, true and beautiful in the differing expressions of Christianity will be saved and integrated in the fullness of one and the same confession of faith, charity and ecclesial communion. It is a sincere possibility. There is need of great souls, pastors, teachers, artists, saints to achieve this miracle.

More could be said to our common comfort and in proof of the existence of positive and progressive ecumenism. But We repeat, the road is long and difficult, and we Catholics have to ask ourselves the question: What can we do to shorten the way, to make it easier? Let everyone ask himself: What can I do to help the Gospel cause of the one fold and the one Shepherd, appointed to represent the one, supreme and invisible Shepherd, Christ the Lord? (cf. *Jn.* 10, 16).

An Examination of Conscience

We must all examine our own consciences. One response is general and valid for all. Let us try to be true Catholics. Convinced Catholics. Firm Catholics. Good Catholics. There cannot be a watered down, approximate and camouflaged Catholicism, still less if it implies denying by our behaviour what will bring ourselves and our separated Brethren mutually closer.

A religious and moral aping of easier and questionable forms of the Christian life will not help our witness or apostleship, nor will it gain anything by way of esteem, example and trust. It will serve only to depreciate the cause of Christ and his Church.

The Council's teaching is relevant here, precisely with reference to ecumenism. That the attraction towards unity of the Church may be effective, " all Catholics ought to strive for Christian perfection " (*Unit. redint.*, 4). We might conclude at this point with a list of the virtues which, on our side, could smooth the way for the meeting with our Christian Brethren still separated from us. The first is unity among us Catholics. All divisions, quarrels, separatisms, all egoism within our Catholic communion, harm the cause of ecumenism and hold back and halt the march towards that happy encounter: they belie the Church, whose members are marked by mutual love, as the Lord taught (cf. *Jn.* 13, 35).

34

Some other virtues: firmness and simplicity of faith, nourished by God's Word and the Eucharistic Bread; humility, because of the gift of the full and true faith; open and generous kindness to all; the spirit of service and sacrifice: love for Christ, for Christ crucified and risen again.

Finally, of course, as always, prayer is necessary. As We have said, the undertaking is so far beyond our strength that we cannot do without the Lord's strength. We should invoke it, piously, humbly and confidently. All of us, and always.

May Our Apostolic Blessing come down upon these thoughts, these proposals.

MARIA SOLEDAD TORRES ACOSTA ENROLLED IN CALENDAR OF SAINTS

On Sunday, January 25th, the Holy Father presided in St. Peter's at the rite of canonization of Maria Soledad Torres Acosta. He delivered the following homily.

Venerable Brothers and beloved Children!

In this hour of tribulation for the Church and sadness for Us, behold a moment of great consolation! Maria Soledad Torres Acosta is acknowledged and proclaimed as a saint. She is inscribed on the roll of saints, and presented to the whole Church on earth as belonging to the Church in heaven. She is declared to be worthy of the cult of veneration, because she is totaly and forever united with the risen Christ and shares in his glory. This is the meaning of the extraordinary and solemn act which We have just carried out. We have canonized this blessed daughter of the Church, and We feel the light, the charm and the mystery of holiness upon Us, upon this exultant assembly, upon Spain the land that gave birth to the new saint, upon the religious family which she founded: the Servants of Mary who minister to the sick, upon the entire Church, upon the world. Let us listen to the voice descending from the heights of heaven, and echo it with our own: " Alleluia! for the Lord God omnipotent reigns. Let us be glad and rejoice, and give honour to him; for the marriage of the Lamb has come, and his spouse has made herself ready. And to her was granted that she should be arrayed in fine linen, pure and bright; for the fine linen is the good deeds of the saints " (*Apoc.* 19, 6-8). This is the voice of the Apocalypse, the final revelation, which unveils the ultimate meaning of things and the outcome of our final salvation. It it a mysterious voice, yet clear; it tells us the secret and the value of sanctity.

Sanctity

Holiness reveals itself in the last analysis as fullness of life, boundless happiness, immersion in the light of Christ and God, incomparable and ideal beauty, exaltation of the personality, immortal transfiguration of our mortal existence, fountain of wonder and joy, solid comfort of our strenuous pilgrimage in time, an inebriating foretaste of the " communion of the saints ", that is, of the living Church which is the Lord's, both in time and in eternity (cf. *Rom.* 14, 8-9).

A phenomenon of this vision astonishes us at this moment especially, for it represents the two aspects of holiness: the one it acquires in paradise, and the one it presents to this world. They are two aspects of a single moral reality, of works of holiness, as we are informed by the sacred text which We just quoted. Works accomplished in this life keep their value in the other: *Opera enim illorum sequuntur illos*, the Apocalypse says of those who have died in the Lord (*Apoc.* 14, 13). But those works affect those who perform them in a very different manner here below than in heaven. In heaven they are splendour and joy. But on earth, how do they appear, what are they like? The perennial Gospel of the Beatitudes tells us in its dramatic way: here below sanctity is poverty, humility, suffering, sacrifice, that is, imitation of Christ, the Word of God made man; imitation of him in his *kenosis*, his twofold humiliation in the Incarnation and in the Redemption.

This confrontation between the two aspects of holiness arouses very lively interest in us. It is interest in first getting to know, then imitating the temporal life of the person who now enjoys everlasting life through the merits of that sanctity. This interest gives rise to hagiography, the study of the lives of the saints. We would all do well to take up this study once again, with greater passion and with the modern methods of historical criticism, psychological analysis, mystical and ascetical analysis, knowledge of the art of narrative and of the Church's judgments. We still have great need of all this today, and we can derive instruction and comfort from it.

A simple, silent Life

The question naturally arises: what was the life of Maria Soledad like? What was her story? How did she become a saint? Of course it is impossible for us to answer this question here and deliver her panegyric. You will be able to satisfy this rightful and praiseworthy curiosity in books describing her life. It was a simple, silent life. It can be summed up with two great words: humility, charity. It was a life wholly devoted to intense interior life, to the work of founding a new religious family, to imitating Christ, to devotion to Our Lady, to service to the sick, to loyalty to the Church.

Maria Soledad's life story does not contain singular, often adventurous and wonderful events, abundance of words and writings such as distinguish other saints. Yet her meek and pure character contains certain features which We feel We ought to mention.

Maria Soledad was a Foundress. She founded a religious family that is now very numerous and widespread. It is an excellent, provident family. She therefore belongs to that band of holy and fearless women who gave rise to rivers of holiness and good works in the Church in the last century. They are an endless procession of virgins consecrated to the sole, supreme love of Christ, and all engaged in intelligent, unwearied and disinterested service of their fellow humans. You know them; you meet them everywhere. There is no need for Us to describe their magnificent expansion.

Nineteenth-Century Saints

The Church's vitality, fecundity, audacity, beauty, poetry, sanctity, are all splendidly displayed in that striking flowering of religious Families, of women especially, which has woven, we might say, the history of Catholic life in recent times. That of the Servants of Mary of Saint Maria Soledad belongs to those elect and hardworking Families. So much does it belong to them that we might regard it as the type of that immense and many-sided manifestation of religious life, which seems to follow a common model, in spite of the special peculiarities of every single Institute.

That model was a formula which was substantially the same in all new foundations in the nineteenth century. The question arises whether the pattern, of which we are admiring an outstanding example, is still valid for our time, in the fervour and excitement of renewal of religious life and occasionally too critical and somewhat over imaginative seeking after new forms of consecration to the following of Christ.

We are happy to give an affirmative answer, in view of St. Maria Soledad's personality and the legion of her daughters. We do not deny that the call to perfect and total following of the Master, Jesus, may be interpreted as admitting fresh manifestations worthy of blossoming in the Church's garden and of adapting themselves to the needs and forms of our times, together with those historical and classical forms which preceded the form of religious life such as we have before us today. However, We confirm Our approval of the pattern of religious life which came into being chiefly during the last century and the present century. The peculiar characteristics which give this form its specific quality justify and glorify this type of seeking after Christian perfection. Those characteristics are: practical and ascetical detachment from ordinary secular life (but many give preference to this life today); common life, organized according to the evangelical counsels of poverty, chastity and obedience; the primacy of interior life, of prayer, of divine worship, of love of God; in a word, unbounded dedication to some work of charity without selfish interest; finally, profound and organic attachment to Holy Church.

These basic characteristics constitute a state of life the principle feature of which is striving towards Christian perfection. They truly accord with the Gospel's requirements, and they are still suited for defining and enriching religious life in our time. The Congregation of the Servants of the Sick, in the name and example of their Holy Foundress, deserves this acknowledgment from Us.

A new sphere for Charity

It merits a further recognition, namely, of that which specifically defines it as a religious Institute dedicated to the care of the sick. That was the choice which expresses, engages and lights up the charity of St. Maria Soledad and her spiritual progeny.

It might be said that it was not a new choice, nor was her aim original. Many other religious institutions have cared for physical suffering, and its almost natural concomitant, spiritual poverty. They have deserved immense praise for their loving and generous practice of the " works of mercy ". This is true. We will therefore class the Servants of the Sick with the heroic army of women religious who are consecrated to bodily and spiritual charity; yet We must ntot overlook a feature which was a specific characteristic of Maria Soledad's Christian genius and a characteristic form of her charity. We refer to the care of the sick in their own homes. We believe that no one had done this in a systematic manner before; no one before her had thought is possible to entrust that task to women religious belonging to canonically organized Institutes.

The formula indeed had existed ever since the Gospel message. And what an idea it was! It was simple, and worthy of the lips of the Divine Master: *Infirmus, et visitatis me.* I, Christ said, mystically personified in sick humanity, was sick, and you visited me (*Mt.* 25, 36). Here was a new field for charity. Here was a programme for souls entirely devoted to visiting their suffering neighbours. In this case the suffering neighbour does not have to go looking for someone to assist and cure him; he does not have to be taken off to places and institutions, where the unfortunate is received and surrounded by medical attention which has been wisely and scientifically planned.

Angel comes to the home

On the contrary, an angel of charity, a voluntary Servant comes in search of the patient in his own home, the centre of his affections and habits, where the malady has not deprived him of his last remaining boon, his individuality, his freedom. This is not a mere refinement of charity. It is a method showing acute penetration of the true nature of charity, which seeks the good of others, and of the nature of the human heart, which is jealous of its own sensibility and its own personality, even when it receives from another. Here we have a ray of social wisdom. It preceded the technical and scientific forms which modern medical assistance has assumed. It once more demonstrates the incomparable originality of evangelical charity, because it was imparted freely and to anyone, for the only requirement was to be in need and in pain.

A Forerunner and a Model

Maria Soledad became a forerunner and a model of the most consummate social and medical assistance known to our social humanism. We ought all be grateful to her; we ought all bless the providential service which she began and which has been followed by more than a few similar entreprises.

The Holy Father then continued in Spanish:

We should now like to point out another feature of the story of this Saint's life which has come to be a common inheritance of her religious Family. It is obvious, yet it is not easy to describe. It is the spiritual treasure which derives from her Spanish up-bringing. Her glorious and blessed motherland infused something of the " humus " of Catholic Spain into this Saint, and into her daughters, through an unnoticed yet vital channel.

We have not now in mind the wealth of talent and feeling in the Castilian spirit which is described for us in history and literature, that knightly honour, that sense of greatness, that extra-ordinary passion for the tragic and for the humorous.

We are thinking rather of the nature of a strong people and its adventurous history, and its religious, Christian, Catholic feeling. We are thinking of its capacity for mystical ascents to absolute expressions of " all and nothing ". We are thinking of its tendency to moral extremism, that is to heroism, to religious heroism, which is sanctity. We are thinking of its deep and lyric humanity, which disdains every sort of pettiness, and battles for fullness of moral personality, prompt to fight, to love, to sacrifice.

We think We are not mistaken in finding marks of that native nobility in Maria Soledad, of that vivid magnanimity which puts a stamp of something extraordinarily beautiful and universal upon this Saint's personality, and consequently upon that of her religious Institute. In her, Spain and the Church find mutual understanding, common glory, their respective vocations to love Our Lord Jesus Christ.

On this day such at least are Our keenest desires.

OBEDIENCE AND LIBERTY IN THE CHURCH

Beloved Sons and Daughters!

I n these years since the Council we have been in search of the style of our moral life, the new art of our actions in relation to our faith, the way of giving practical expression to our Christian faith. To begin, we all know that the Church and theology about the Church ought to exert a predominant influence upon our religious ideas, that a large part of our conduct and religious life ought to depend on the Church's doctrine and the idea we have of the Church. The Church must give a new stamp to our attachment to Christianity. What the Council taught us about the Church influences the form of our morality.

Secondly, We are aware that the Council developed the Church's teaching about several aspects of human life, whereby the person is extolled, increased, emancipated, and in a certain sense placed in the centre of the Christian religion's doctrinal and practical system. The Council talks about vocation, conscience, liberty, responsibility, perfection of man. Anthropology is extolled and enobled, certainly not to the disadvantage of theology and christology. On the contrary, it derives its light and its consistency from these latter doctrines. But it is certain that man came like a giant out of the Council, capable of victoriously pitting his stature and his effectiveness with the stature and effectiveness which contemporary profane humanism attributes to its idolized type of man, thinking, working, trafficking, enjoying and suffering in the modern world.

If the Council's moral teaching looks like this in the extremely simplified yet exact synthesis which We have just given, then We dare offer you a formula to think about. The formula is: The Church is an obedience, a liberating obedience. This is a paradoxical statement and at first sight has little to attract. But just look at it a bit and consider: A liberating obedience.

A Bridge between God and Man

It is clear that the Church is an obedience in the general sense of that word. We know that the Church is a society, a communion, a people organized and governed in a pastoral manner, and all this entails a certain kind of acceptance, an obedience. This is on the horizontal plane, as they say. Something more has to be said about the vertical plane. The Church is a sign; it is a sacrament, the bridge between God and mankind. It lies between God shedding his light of revelation over humanity, and humanity entering by faith into that sphere of light, becoming alive again to grace, obtaining a new principle of life, and called and helped to live in a supernatural form. This is to say, the Church is in a well-defined relation to God, through Christ. God's will, his new will in regard to man, charity, becomes a quite demanding relationship. The divine *fiat* initiating the economy of salvation needs the response of the human *fiat*, of man agreeing to enter that sublime and exalting economy. Mary gives us a lesson in her " Be it done unto me according to thy word " (the word of the angel of the annunciation: *Lk.* 1, 38). Jesus teaches us: " Not everyone who says to me, Lord, Lord, shall enter into the kingdom of heaven, but the person who does the will of my Father in heaven " (*Mt.* 7, 21). The condition, the norm, is to do the Father's will: obedience is the fundamental moral virtue which is the basis of our relations with Christ and with God: the Church establishes those relations and opens our lips to repeat the evangelical prayer: *fiat voluntas Tua*.

The Rule of Faith

Innumerable texts provide documentation, and demonstrate that obedience is the Church's constituent law, to be found in every catechism and every book of Catholic spirituality and social life, even when obedience is considered as a particular virtue, that is, as submission on the part of some to others who exercise authority. For authority exists, as in every society; authority is indispensable. It has two characteristics in this case: authority in the Church does not come from below, nor, *per se*, from numbers, but derives from the original, immutable institution of Christ, as everyone knows. Secondly, authority in the Church has for its object not only the exterior actions of those who accept her guidance, but also to some extent, certain not insignificant interior acts, for example, the rule of the faith: free assent to the faith, but the norm of faith itself then becomes binding, and the Church guarantees and safeguards that norm.

St. Paul says: " The weapons of our warfare ...have divine power ... We destroy false arguments ... and take every thought captive to obey Christ, being ready to punish every disobedience when your obedience is complete " (*2 Cor.* 10, 5-6). Thus spoke the Apostle of liberty, the " liberty ", he declares, " wherewith Christ has made us free " (*Gal.* 4, 31), because, as he keeps on saying to the first Christians, " you have been called to liberty " (*ib.*, 5, 13).

Man and his Power

But the question arises: how do you explain this paradox? what do these words mean: obedience and liberty? What is their practical value? Here we would require a lecture in exegesis to clarify the scriptural terms with which we are concerned, especially these two terms, law and liberty, which have varying meanings in the biblical texts.

For the present, however, We will merely note that what We have just said: the Church is a liberating obedience, does not contain a contradiction. Being associated with a certain order constitutes being liberated from a different order, or rather from a disorder, in the case of man; and what a grave and fatal disorder it is. Thus, belonging to the Church's order demands indeed the acceptance of a conscientious and manly uniformity; but at the same time it frees us from heavier chains: those of ignorance about God and our destiny, sin, solitude, human frailty and death. This liberation sets man's faculties working intensely, freely and responsibly: his faculties of intelligence, will and all the wealth of his soul, his capacity for self-development, and also his ability to express himself in the fields of the good, of justice, of love and of art.

January 28th, 1970

Never tire of the truth

It is all a matter of understanding what the Church is, what kind of formation she gives us, how fortunate we are to be her children, what is required in order to be loyal to her.

Our generation's great temptation is to grow weary of the truth we have received as a gift. Many who recognize the importance and usefulness of changes occurring in the scientific, technical and social fields, lose faith in speculative thought, in tradition, in the Church's magisterium. They distrust Catholic doctrine; they think of emancipating themselves from its dogmatic character. They no longer want definitions binding on all for ever. They deceive themselves into thinking that they have found another liberty, and they no longer value the freedom they already possess. They alter the terms of doctrine sanctioned by the Church, or give it a new, arbitrary interpretation, with a display of erudition and even greater psychological intolerance. Perhaps they dream of shaping a new kind of Church corresponding to their own ideas, which are sometimes noble and lofty. But it would not be the authentic Church, as Christ willed it, and as it developed and matured in the course of history.

So it happens that obedience grows lax; with it liberty—which is characteristic of the faithful believing and working in, with and for the Church—likewise decreases. It is replaced by an unnoticed submission to other obediences, which can become burdensome and contrary to the true freedom of a child of the Church.

Newman, the great Newman, tells us at the end of his famous *Apologia pro vita sua* of his peace in belonging to the Catholic Church. He is an example not to be forgotten.

May Our Apostolic Blessing strengthen you all in your fidelity.

LIBERTY AND AUTHORITY
GO HAND IN HAND

On Thursday, January 29th, the Pope gave audience to the Judges and Officials of the Court of the Sacred Roman Rota at the beginning of the law-term. He addressed them as follows.

We are happy to reply with all Our heart to the words which the venerated Dean of the Sacred Roman Rota, Monsignor Boleslaus Filipiak, has just addressed to Us. He has well expressed your feelings and your state of mind on this particular occasion, beloved and venerated Auditors and Officials of that Court. His words vividly brought to Our mind the image of the Judge in the Church of today, his conscience, and the gifts which are needed to help him carry out his functions, with humility, with a sense of the duty and responsibility incumbent upon him, with discretion, and with clemency joined with dutiful strictness, so as always to be a calm and impartial interpreter of the law when applying it in concrete cases which we meet in life.

Hence the importance of your mission. The service which you give the Church is of such fundamental importance that We cannot but have words of sincere praise, lively gratitude and paternal encouragement for it. We take pleasure in repeating today (cf. *Discourse to the International Congress of Canonists*: *AAS* 60, 1968), to give you comfort in your delicate task, those terse but meaningful words of an outstanding jurist of the past to describe the work of a teacher and jurisconsult of canon law, for his own and for future times: " Quicumque ergo ecclesiasticus doctor ecclesiasticas regulas ita interpretatur aut moderatur, ut ad regnum caritatis cuncta quae docuerit vel exposuerit, referat, nec peccat, nec errat; cum salutis proximorum consulens, ad finem sacris institutionibus debitum pervenire intendat ": " Every ecclesiastical teacher who interprets or moderates the Church's laws in such a way that everything he teaches or expounds is directed towards the reign of charity, neither sins nor errs; since, in his concern for the salvation of his fellow men, he aims at the proper end of sacred legislation " (IVO OF CHARTRES, *Prol. in Decretum*: *PL* 161, 47-48).

By correctly aplying the norm to concrete cases, you complete the legislator's work and contribute to the vital development of Church order.   But what shines out most brightly in your mission is *caritas christiana*.   It gives greater nobility and fruitfulness to that *aequitas* of judgment which was so much to the honour of Roman law.   That *aequitas* has become for you through the Gospel spirit, " priestly moderation ", to use the beautiful expression of St. Gregory the Great.

While We express Our appreciation for the moral sensibility which you show, We should also like to offer you Our encouragement for your ever consistent and generous exercise of your practical functions.

Moral Sensitivity and Equity

1. We praise your moral sensitivity, the lofty and indispensable prerogative of a judge.   We think We are here grasping the essential feature, the one that ought to distinguish you; We are deeply pleased to see that you are profoundly imbued with it. As everyone knows, the judge is the interpreter of objective *ius*, that is, of the law; he interprets it through his own subjective *ius*, that is, *potestas et libertas*, which he should posses in the highest degree.   It follows that he ought to have great objectivity of judgment, and great equity at the same time, so as to evaluate all the elements which he has patiently and tenaciously sifted out, and thus judge with imperturbable impartiality.

In this regard it would be very useful to go more deeply into the concept of *aequitas* just mentioned, in the development of Roman law and in the body of canon law.   It entails a strict evaluation of the matter subjected to judgment.   That explains why in modern trials, both canonical and civil, account is taken of the psychology of the parties to the suit and other subjective elements, as well as environmental, family and social circumstances, etc.   Of course, when applying such objectivity and *aequitas*, the judge will never depart from the fundamental criteria of natural law, that is, human, just law, nor from observance of the laws in force, the *ius scriptum*, which is supposed to be the expression of reason and the demands of the common good.

But a judge requires complete moral uprightness to take account of all these elements. It would be useless to try to establish them in him if he were without them in the first place. We are comforted to know that this requirement and all its urgency and seriousness are well known to this noble circle of servants of the Church.

Liberty instead of Authority

2. We therefore exhort you, beloved sons, to exercise your practical functions as judges with uprightness and fervour. What virtues are needed —and how many! You well know, for you live in daily contact with the realities and difficulties of your work. As We said, there is need of impartiality, and that presupposes profound and unshakable integrity. There is need of disinterestedness, lest interests alien to good judgment: venality, politics, favouritism, should press upon the Court. There is need for solicitude, which takes the cause of justice to heart, in the awareness that justice is high service to Him who is just and merciful: *misericors et misereator et iustus* (*Ps.* 111, 4), *iustus iudex* (*2 Tim.* 4, 8), *fidelis et iustus* (*1 Jn.* 1, 9).

Always do honour to your office by performing your lofty mission in this way. In this manner it will be sublimated and brought into line with God's own justice, of which it becomes a reflection and a faithful instrument.

3. But now We must halt to examine a basic question. The considerations We have just uttered, Our apologia for the judge, as it were, seems to imply a need to defend the judge's function. Exercise of judicial power is criticized nowadays, especially in the Church, almost as if it were a " structure " superimposed upon the spirituality and freedom of the Gospel message. No one is unaware that there is an acute tendency to devaluate authority in the name of liberty. The council stressed this in its very significant document on religious liberty. It observed that " there seem to be

not a few who, under the pretext of liberty, reject all dependence and give little value to due obedience " (*Dignitatis humanae*, 8).

This is the so-called charismatic tendency, which becomes anti-hierarchical, for it stresses exclusively the function of the spirit, which is hard to define, at the expense of authority. This generates a state of mind which presents disobedience as something rightful and justified, as a safeguard of the liberty which the children of God ought to enjoy.

The reasons for this attitude would provide the occasion for a long enquiry, because it is a very big theme. However, since We are unfortunately restricted by the limited time at Our disposal, We can reduce the basic objections involved in it to three.

The necessity of a Juridical order

a) First of all, there is an appeal to *liberty* against *law*, against any law. And there is an appeal to the Gospel in support of this. Indeed, the Gospel is a call in favour of the pre-eminent freedom of the spirit. We cannot forget the severe condemnations which Jesus uttered against pharisaical legalism, in favour of the love and the freedom of the children of God: *Audistis quia dictum est ... Ego autem dico vobis*: You have heard how it was said, but I say to you ... (cf. *Matt.* 5, 21, sqq.). All his preaching was directed towards interior spirituality, to the charity which frees from the yoke of constraint. That is what Jesus' words and example were aimed at. As the Council emphasized in the Decree just mentioned, " Christ ... our Master and Lord, meek and humble of heart, invited and attracted his disciples patiently ... He wrought miracles to shed light on his teaching and to establish its truth, but his intention was to arouse faith in his hearers, and to confirm them in faith, not to exert coercion upon them ... Noting that cockle had been sown amid the wheat, he gave orders that both should be allowed to grow until the harvest time, which will come at the end of the world. He refused to be a political Messiah, ruling by force. He preferred to call himself the Son of Man, who came ' to serve and give his life as a ransom for many ' (*Mk.* 10, 45); ... He completed on the cross the work of redemption whereby he achieved salvation and true freedom for men " (*Dignitatis humanae*, 11).

Hence the lapidary expressions used by St. Paul in his letters to the Romans and Galatians and his polemical teaching about liberty. Opposing the legalism of the Judaizers, he wrote: *Si spiritu ducimini non estis sub lege*: If you are led by the spirit you are not under the law. He set down that code of love which is a stranger to all impositions: *Omnis lex in uno sermone impletur: dilige proximum sicut teipsum*: For all the law is fulfilled in one word: Thou shalt love thy neighbour as thyself (*Gal*. 5, 18, 14).

Liberty, Authority enrich each other

All this is very true. But it is also true that evangelical and apostolic doctrine does not stop at this point. The same Jesus who preached love and proclaimed the primacy of the inward life and liberty, laid down moral and practical prescriptions which oblige his disciples to loyal observance. He willed, as We shall repeat, an authority provided with specified powers, in the service of man.

Therefore those who appeal to the Gospel to defend liberty against law need to be reminded of the many-sided meaning of the term " law ". The Mosaic law has been repealed; the natural law remains with all its innate vigour, and it is supported by the New Testament. It does not deprive man of his freedom, but is an intrinsically just guide for it. Likewise, positive law is always supported or suggested by natural law, and safeguards human good. It disposes and promotes the common good; it provides a guarantee for that inviolable and responsible autonomy of the individual by virtue of which every human being can give fruitful expression to his personality, and it provides this guarantee against all possible interferences or abuses. Liberty and authority are not opposing terms, but values which complement each other. Their mutual cooperation fosters growth of the community and of the capacities for initiative and enrichment of individual members.

Insistence on the principle of authority and the necessity of a juridical order does not detract from the value of liberty and the esteem in which it ought to be held. On the contrary, emphasis is laid on the demands of a secure and effective safeguard of common goods, amongst which is that fundamental good of the exercise of that very liberty which only a well-ordered social life can adequately guarantee. What would liberty be worth to an individual if he were not protected by wise and suitable laws? The great son of Arpino was right when he said, " Legum ministri magistratus, legum interpretes iudices, legum denique idcirco omnes servi sumus ut liberi esse possumus ": The rulers administer the laws: the judges interpret them: all of us are therefore their servants, that we may be free (CICERO, *Pro Cluentio*, 146).

The Church's hierarchical Structure

The law of the Gospel, finally, is reduced to love of God and of one's neighbour. But it has ramifications in three directions: in the conscience, which becomes more developed and operative in liberty bound by truth; in the many precepts and virtues, which do not coerce but extol personal liberty, in respect for God, for oneself, for one's neighbour; and in the charisms of the Holy Spirit, in docile fidelity to the pastoral power and its service for building up the whole body in charity (cf. *Eph.* 4, 16).

b) A second objection, aimed at justifying the current anti-hierarchical attitute, appeals to liberty against *authority*. There is an appeal to the Gospel here too. But the Gospel not only does not abolishes authority, but it institutes and establishes it. It places it at the service of the good of others, not as though it were derived from the community as its servant, but because it is given from above to govern and to judge, originating as it does from a positive intervention of the Lord's will. The fact is that Jesus did not wish his teaching to be subjected to the individual's free interpretation, but that it should be entrusted to a qualified power (cf. *Mt.* 28, 16-20; *Mk.* 16,15; *Lk.* 24, 45-48; *Jn.* 20, 21-23). He willed that his community should be structured and knit together in unity, constituted by hierarchical organs; he willed that it should be a social, spiritual and visible organism, a single complex reality arising from a twofold element, human and divine (cf. *Lumen gentium*, 8). And, since it is also a social fact, the Church requires and demands external structures and norms having the characteristic feature of law: *ubi societas, ibi ius.*

Consequently, though the primacy belongs to the spirit and the inner life, organic membership of the ecclesial body and submission to authority are still an indispensable element, willed by the Founder of the Church himself. The Council reminded us of this: " After his resurrection our Saviour handed over the Church to Peter to be shepherded (*Jn.* 21, 17), commissioning him and the other apostles to propagate and govern her (cf. *Mt.* 28, 18 ff.). Her he erected for all ages as ' the pillar and mainstay of the truth ' (*1 Tim.* 3, 15). This Church, constituted and organized in the world as a society, subsists in the Catholic Church, which is governed by the successor of Peter and by the bishops in union with that successor ... " (*Lumen gentium,* 8). Canon Law does indeed consecrate the primacy of the spirit as its own *suprema lex,* but at the same time it responds to the necessity which is inherent in the Church as an organized community.

Canon Law and Salvation of man

Canon Law is concerned with the spiritual values; it scrupulously protects and safeguards the administration of the sacraments, which are at the centre of its norms. It prohibits administration of baptism to an adult who is not *sciens et volens*: knowing and willing (can. 752). It does not wish anyone to enlist among the sacred ministers, or to remain such, if he has not freely chosen the priestly state (canons 214, par. 1, 1994, par. 2). It does not consider valid the sacrament of matrimony if it is contracted without free consent (can. 1087, par. 1). But at the same time it does not tolerate altering the deposit of revelation (canons 1322-1323); nor that the Church's powers should be allowed to fall into confusion, without distinction of orders and ministerial functions (canons 108, pars, 1-3; 938); nor that free initiative on the part of individuals should upset the order established by Christ. Moreover, it does not permit that the rules of *the communion of faith, sacraments and discipline* should be the oject of human bargaining, promoted by the sole initiative of groups bereft of title or authority (can. 109, 218, 329).

Canon Law obeys a basic precept, which comes from God and was entrusted to the Apostles through Jesus Christ. As St. Clement says in his first Letter to the Corinthians: the Apostles " then established the rule of succession, in such a way that on

their death other approved men should take up their ministry "
(*1 Cor.* 42-44, 2). The organic and hierarchical structure therefore
marks the canonical order as a constitutional law of the Church,
willed by Christ for the good and salvation of men, who, *liberati a
peccato, servi autem facti Deo* (*Rom.* 6, 22), are called to live to
the full the life of the spirit.

Legitimacy of the Juridical power

c) A third objection also appeals to liberty against certain
antiquated or too arbitrary or too severe forms of the *exercise
of judical power*. Discussion of this is open, in connection with
revision of the Code of Canon Law. Everything, for example
concerned with warnings, condemnation and excommunications
arouses a modern touchy sensitiveness to think in terms of rejection, as if confronted by the vestiges of an absolutist power which
has now had its day. Yet it must not be forgotten that the coercive
power is based on the experience of the early Church. St. Paul
made use of it in the Christian community of Corinth (*1 Cor.* 5).
We have only to look at this passage to understand the pastoral
significance of such a severe measure, which was taken solely with
a view to the spiritual and moral integrity of the whole Church
and the good of the guilty one himself: *that his spirit may be
saved in the day of the Lord Jesus* (*ib.* 5, 5).

Such an exercise of authority in due form and measure, is
therefore at the service of the rights of the person, as well as of
community order. Consequently it enters the sphere of charity,
and ought to be considered and presented in this light, whenever
grave and relevant circumstances demand it for the common good;
but it ought to be exercised with the greatest delicacy and understanding for those who have gone astray. Its practical application
is being studied, so as to perfect it more and more, to adapt it
to demands for respect of the human person which have lately
become more pressing and attentive, and in this way bring it more
harmoniously into line with modern sociological reality.

No one will wish to challenge the necessity, the expediency and
the efficacy of the exercise of such power. It is inherent in the
very essence of judicial power, because, as We have said, it too

is an expression of that charity, which is the Church's supreme law. Just as it derives from charity for safeguarding the ecclesial community, so charity makes it understood by those who are subjected to it, and leads them to accept with profitable humility the painful remedial consequences.

Lovers of liberty

We would therefore repeat the call which the Council made in the above mentioned Decree on religious liberty. We would repeat it not only to you, oustanding lovers of the Law and wise interpreters of its rules, but to all Our children. The Council called upon us " to strive to form human beings who, in full acknowledgment of the moral order, will know how to obey rightful authority and be lovers of genuine liberty " (*Dignitatis humanae, 8*). We are very glad that this meeting with you today has enabled Us to talk to you, even though only in a fragmentary way, about such an important and deeply felt problem.

With lively pleasure We repeat to you a paternal exhortation which rises from Our heart on this solemn occasion which is so pleasing to Us: discharge your high office with a lofty Christian conscience. Do honour to the Church by responding with absolute dedication to the trust which she puts in you. Serve souls with humilty, with love and with disinterestedness. May the Lord's grace always accompany you and be your daily light; may it give you the strength you need and grant you profound peace.

This is our wish that We utter with all Our heart on the occasion of the inauguration of the judical year. We accompany it with Our Apostolic Blessing.

THE COUNCIL CAN EDUCATE TO GOOD " SPIRIT "

Beloved Sons and Daughters!

W e are still meditating on the Council's teachings, for We are convinced that they constitute a *Summa* for our time, a very rich, authoritative compendium of doctrine and guidance for its needs. The Council marks a meaningful and decisive moment in the flow of Catholic tradition, by reason of the treasures of truth which it preserves from the past and those others which it opens up for us along the road to the future.

We get a very fruitful and instructive impression of optimism from even a brief moment of general reflection about the moral guidelines which come to us from the Council. What do we mean by optimism? It seems to Us that the first thing it can mean is a sense of goodness, of serenity, of trust, of hope, of good spirits, such as the Council generally arouses in those who recognize its pastoral inspiration, its consoling intentions, and the truthful openness of which its acts and documents are full. The Council is a great lesson to us, a beneficial infusion of good will. Anyone who accepts it, studies it and follows it feels himself stimulated to believe, to hope, to love. He feels a power of good will, an impulse towards renewal and progress; he feels moved to action. We may add that he also feels a charism of Christian vivacity.

The Council's Methods

Why all this? Because the Council considers the positive side, the good in everything it deals with and expounds. It is not blind to the negative aspects of things, yet sees them in the grand framework of human destinies as the darkness of the divine depths, the misfortune that sin has inflicted upon human life, Satan's permanent ambush within the play of our social and personal vicissitudes, and so forth. It also considers them within the context of the Church's history and in reference to the frailty of her members and some of her institutions. Finally, it considers them in the interior of the human heart, where mistake and malice can cause so much ruin.

The teaching of Councils used to end regularly by stating an error, then deploring it, finally condemning it, with the classic phrase *anathema sit*. But the methods of the II Vatican Council are intended to throw light upon what ought to be praised, appreciated, done, and hoped for.

We said that the Council was turned towards the good. It is turned towards that which exists, to acknowledge, to enjoy it in God, to praise it, we might say, like St. Francis, like the Gospel. And it is turned towards that which does not exist: to desire it, to recover it if lost, to foster it where possible. The positive values are always present to its penetrating gaze, are always being expounded by its wise words. The Council can see some real or possible reflection of the divine goodness in everything, in every event. It educates and urges its pupils to discover that reflection too, and graft their good will to it.

A Good " Spirit "

We really should study here the term " good will ". Such study would lead us to look for good will above ourselves, that is, in God's good will, which has mysteriously chosen us as the object of his love (cf. *Lk.* 2, 14; *Rom.* 8, 28), and infuses the supernatural virtue of charity into us. This is a new capacity to love, to move towards the Good (cf. ST. FRANCIS OF SALES, *Theotimus*, II, IX).

But even when we limit our thought to man's natural psychology, we shall have much to think about in regard to good will, because it depends on moral uprightness, on the art of pedagogy, on political eloquence. We shall see that is also depends on rationality, on the idea we form of the good, and that it is therefore always of prime importance to known what really deserves this sovereign name of good, in general, in particular, in itself, and as regards ourselves.

This gives us a line to follow in order to advance our diagnosis of contemporary phenomena of will, which so much impress public opinion—and rightly so. The notion of good which moves the will leads the process, and this becomes habit, fashion or a movement. We need to make this notion clear and attractive, above all, to make it true and authentic, so as to give the will that attitude which confers on it the description of " good ".

We think that the body of teaching which the Council offers is enough to educate us in good will. It does this through the values, that is the goods, which it depicts for us, such as salvation in Christ, man, the world, progress, freedom, justice, peace etc. It does it in another way through the attitude which causes us to aim at these values and love them: an attitude of hope, of vivacity, of serenity, in a word, a good " Spirit ".

Is not inflated

This good " Spirit " is that core of healthy optimism, as it comes through to us in the Council's moral style. This optimism above all sees all things in a calm light (the light of the divine economy for human destinies). Therefore, healty optimism is not distrustful, touchy, irritable, bitter; it does not take pleasure in chewing over defects which can easily be uncovered in every man—the higher a man is the more he shows them. It does not take a special interest in purely satirical and destructive criticism. It does not raise questions in order to show off bravura by de-nouncing and aggravating them and turning them into annoying and injurious agitation. It does not use its " liberty as a cloak for maliciousness " (as we find written in St. Peter's First Letter, 2, 16). It does not derive its strength from hatred and desperation erected into a system.

No. Good optimism knows how to judge evil frankly (evil frequently grows with the progress of modern development). It does not let itself be overcome by evil, but tries to overcome it with the good (*Rom.* 12, 21). It does not take special delight in making problems insoluble in order to find pretexts for violent stands or revolution. But it tries to solve problems. It does not puff up desires until they are impossible, but knows how to be " content with a little " (Manzoni), with healthy and social realism. It does not disdain humble, gradual and constant effort towards

57

the good, which it seeks in little things as well as big. In a word, it always tries to construct, not to demolish. In all situations it looks for traces of Providence, hoping and praying.

In regard to the moral and spiritual instruction which the Council gives us, we might say with St. Paul, " Brethren, whatsoever things are true, whatsoever things are honest, whatsoever things are just, whatsoever things are pure, whatsoever things are lovely, whatsoever things are of good report; if there be any virtue, and if there be any praise, think on these things " (*Phil.* 4, 8-9).

This quotation seems to Us to apply to the Council, for it is a magnificent piece of praise for the moral and Christian renewal which we are in search of; it is a sage piece of advice for bringing up youth in the modern world. It is a fruitful criterion for defining the relationship of distinction and compenetration existing between the Christian concept of the world and the secular view; it is an ability to enjoy the present life, its beauty, its richness and its progressive evolution, without losing sight of that profound secret of " good will " which is in the Cross of Christ. May it be so for you, with Our Apostolic Blessing.

POPE PAUL TO PARISH PRIESTS
AND LENTEN PREACHERS OF ROME

On Monday morning, February 9th, the Holy Father received the parish priests and Lenten preachers of Rome in the Sistine Chapel, and spoke to them as follows.

Sons and Brothers in Jesus Christ, dearly beloved!

T his yearly meeting seems to Us to be assuming extraordinary importance, because it is our only meeting. Therefore it is charged with all desires, all problems and all experiences. They seek to be expressed here and to obtain judgment, comfort, guidance. Each one of you will notice that a change of perspective is imposed on this discourse by a spontaneous demand connected with the present moment in the Church life.

We will not turn Our attention to the many and far from out of date themes of Lenten preaching and preparation for Easter, which custom calls for and which are the origin and reason for this discourse. Instead, We feel obliged to reflect about the persons here present, about you, about the problem of your ministry. In this way the discourse can be a conversation: trust can give it that character, and affection can give it spirit. In other words, We feel gripped by this audience, as by something of major interest to us. Questions concerning Our clergy are at present taking precedence over those concerning the field in which they exercise their priestly and pastoral functions.

Last year We addressed Our attention to the same topic, if We remember correctly when on this occasion We spoke about the controversial sociological position of the priest in the contemporary world. And this year too, dearest Brothers and Sons, We shall only speak about what affects you directly. We certainly do not yield to this inner prompting in order to simplify what We have to say with these simple words and so lighten the burden of Our ministry. Rather We do it in order to be closer to Our responsibility and to give you proof of the place you have in Our mind and in Our charity.

We will choose among the many themes which crowd into Our mind, and speak to you about only one thing: the spirit of community. Community spirit in this community of ours which is the diocese of Rome. There is talk of increasing it. We very willingly acknoweledge that it already exists. It ought to be developed, it ought to be deepened, it ought to be the mark of our spirituality, it ought to be expressed in our pastoral work, it ought to become trust, collaboration and friendship.

Outward community relationships already exist: living in the same place, belonging officially to the Church of Rome, membership of its organic, ministerial and hierarchical structure. The ecclesial community exists. But is it always at the level of perfect communion of minds, purposes and work?

Are we not sometimes solitary men in the great crowd, whereas we ought to be brothers and form a family? Do we not sometimes prefer to be isolated, to be ourselves, distinct, different, also separated, perhaps a bit dissociated, and even unfriendly, in the midst of our ecclesiastical structure? Do we really feel ourselves to be ministers united in the same ministry of Christ? Is fraternal affection always alive amongst us; does it make us concerned for and glad at our fellow priests' welfare; does it make us humbly and holily proud of our calling to be in the ranks of the Roman clergy?

Fraternal Unity

The current revision was inspired by the Council. It raises certain problems, which are made all the more pressing by the fact that many members of different kinds come to join our diocesan community. They vary very much among themselves, by reason of differences in origin, in training, in function, and spiritual and cultural characteristics. There is need to fuse these ranks of priests, religious and Prelates, if we wish really to be a " church ", that is, a congregation, a family, Christ's body, a multitude inspired with the same faith, and the same charity, as that multitude of the first believers was " one heart and one mind " (*Ac.* 4, 32).

There is no doubt that this is how Christ thought. *Unum sint* was his greatest desire (*Jn.* 17). Before he extended this messianic (cf. *Jn.* 11, 52) and divine (cf. *1 Tim.* 2, 4) desire to the whole of humanity he espressed it directly to his disciples (*Jn.* 13, 34). Before he asks for ecumenical unity *of* the Church, the Lord asks us to have fraternal, community unity in the Church. It seems to Us that one of the clearest bearings given by the recent Council is exactly that in which it brings out the communitarian nature of all mankind, especially manifested in the intentions of the supernatural divine plan (cf. *Gaudium et spes*, 23-24). By virtue of the Holy Spirit, the Catholic Church already accomplishes this constitutional design of its Founder, but we still have a duty to work at putting it into practice more and more.

Hierarchical Communion

It seems to Us that two factors come to our aid in the effort to perfect unity and charity, that is, to achieve perfect community in priestly life. The first is the emphasis which the Council's Decree on " the ministry and the life of priests " places on the subordinate participation of the priestly Order in the mission of the episcopal Order. This is a well-known truth, but the Council threw light upon it, in such a way that " from now on anyone who wishes to know what the priest is, cannot but refer to the episcopal priesthood, in which the priest participates and shares, and to the exercise of which he is called to make a contribution " (*Presbyterium Ordinis*, 2, 6, 7; Cardinal GARRONE, *Le Concile*, p. 78).

Communion in the Church is hierarchical. This characteristic constitutes a stricter and more vital principle of cohesion. The second factor is a renewed and clarified notion of the solidarity which unites the priestly and the episcopal orders. That solidarity has been given back its name, *presbyterium*, and together with that name goes a structure and a function. The Council tells us that " priests, prudent cooperators with the episcopal order, as well as its aids and instruments, are called to serve the People of God. They constitute one priesthood with their bishop, although that priesthood is composed of different functions " (*Lumen gentium*, 28).

Some would like to see a more open and active spiritual presence arise under the form of association and the juridical form which the ecclesiastical order thus takes on. Such a spirit does not make ecclesiastical authority rise democratically from the base to the summit, nor does it try to impose arguments based on numbers, in other words, impose plurality of opinions, so paralyzing the charismatic and responsible exercise of that authority. It aims rather at making communion and cooperation between the Bishop and his priests more vital, conscientious and harmonious, and to do the same for the union of priests among themselves.

Common Pastorate

It seems to Us that the right moment has come for giving the ecclesial community spirit better awareness, greater effectiveness, especially among priests and even more so among those, whether diocesan clergy or religious, who are engaged in a pastoral ministry.

Priests have recently been elected to the Presbyteral Council here in Rome. We see importance, significance and effectiveness in this new organism. We think that Our venerated and zealous Cardinal Vicar takes the same view. This group of priests should not become separated from their fellow priests; even less should it become the representative of a current of opinion that will break up the Clergy into mutually antagonist factions. May it rather be a sign and means of concord and collaboration, solidarity and friendship amongst Our priests. May it feed that spirit of community, of unity and of charity of which We speak. We Ourself shall be delighted to foster such fusion of minds and works to the extent that We are made aware of and approve your common aims, and give aid for your common needs.

Such spiritual and practical concord should result in a programme of combined and harmonious pastoral action (" joint pastoral work ", as they say today). There will be greater saving and use of personnel, undertakings and means, and with more effective results.

Vocations to the Church

A number of matters connected with simultaneous and con-certed pastoral work at once spring to Our mind. Very first in line is the question of vocations to the Church!

We do not resign Ourself to the thought that our field of pastoral labour is barren of youthful and adult souls capable of understanding the call to the heroic service of the kingdom of God. We think that the scarcity of vocations in big cities does indeed depend to a large degree on family and social conditions, which make the consciences of new generations unresponsive to the urging of Christ's voice; but We also trust that a priest will have the virtue, rather the grace in him to light in other souls the flame which burns in his own, the fire of love for Christ the Lord, and that he will be able to do this if he be a true priest, neither sanctimonious, nor worldly, but a priest living his priesthood with intense wisdom and sacrifice in contact with the community, especially the young.

We believe that greater attraction to embrace the ecclesiastical state will be exercised by presenting the priestly life through living it in full dedication, together with the sacred celibacy which it entails, to the sole and total love of Jesus the Master and Lord, the High Priest and sole Redeeming Lamb, together with the complete and exclusive following of him in pastoral service to God's People. All this will have greater effect than a more natural and apparently easier formula, from the human point of view, in which dedication to Christ and self-sacrifice are no longer perfectly and sublimely linked together.

It is all a matter of understanding. This is the charism which conditions the life. Shall we doubt that the Holy Spirit will grant it to the more generous spirits in the new generation? Moral fortitude, gift of self, sacred and superhuman love for Christ, most true, most vital and most sweet love (cf. *Mt.* 19, 29), in a word the cross, accepted for one's own and others' salvation, have greater and more effective influence upon the human heart than has an invitation to take on a priesthood which has been eased by combining natural with supernatural love.

Even though there is a pressing need for vocations to the Church, We believe that transfigured and transfiguring celibacy is a better incentive to qualitative and quantitative recruitment than an easing of the canon law which prescribes celibacy firm and entire, and sets it as a seal on the loyalty and love for the kingdom of God, on the historical experience and ascetic and mystic struggle of our Latin Church. You know this, and with Us you also wish it, Sons and Brothers. May you be blessed.

The Seminary

Together with the problem of vocations we must take up the problem of the Seminary, study it and solve it. The Seminary too should be more than ever before a centre of agreement for our ecclesial community, through the affection, the trust and the support which each and everyone gives it. A tradition which must not die out has made our seminary a family circle for very many most worthy ecclesiastics who were students and teachers there —so much so that that it is more a pedagogical arena than a school of knowledge.

The seminary has been and continues to be the home of our incomparable Mother, our Church, a home of affections that never die, of memories that are always green, of resolutions that have directed whole lives. So it is still and so it should ever be, through your collective, cordial loyalty. You, religious, will also derive merit and benefit from it.

The Vicariate of Rome

And then, how many problems are waiting to be dealt with in the spirit of community, through more systematic and more organic thought about modern and broader solutions: problems of the clergy's finances, common life for priests, renewal of preaching, religious instruction of youth and adults, Catholic Action, new churches, assistance to poor districts, Catholic newspapers, methodical application of liturgical reform, religious chant, sacred art, spiritual exercises, and so on. The moment has come for united and vigorous relaunching of every form of apostolate, every way of exercising the ministry, every kind of pastoral care. All must set to work. All must set to work together. There are many differing instruments in the orchestra, and everyone plays his own, but the music is only one, and it must be harmony, the sum of all efforts pitched together. Our Vicariate is unfortunately seen by some as only a bureaucratic and disciplinary institution, but you can see how it can become the centre of fervour, concord, zeal and diocesan charity.

Personal Spirituality

Before ending this exhortation for an increase of community spirit, We would remind you that, as you already know, there is an intrinsic relationship between community spirit and personal spirituality, that one presupposes and fosters the other.

If increase of community spirit is not linked with intense, deep and punctual interior religiousness, we shall fall into externalism, purely sociological calculation, and legalism.

Some Comfort in Love

The apostolate would lose its interior roots and its best and original forms, together with its highest ends, if the apostle were not a man of prayer and meditation. The texture of the people educated in participation in the liturgy would lack true spiritual cohesion and true fruits from communion with the divine mysteries being celebrated, if the minister and the individual faithful themselves did not acquire a religious fervour of their own from the rite and put some of their own into it. The Church would no longer be the Church, if divine charity were not put before the practice of fraternal charity and also infused into it. This requires the soul to have a silent colloquy, listening and contemplating within itself, speaking its childlike, superlative words, stammering them, mournful, imploring, exultant and singing words, but its own words, secret words, perhaps comprehensible only by God, words uttered in an indescribable manner alone with the Spirit and perhaps by the Spirit himself in us: *gemitibus inenarrabilibus* (*Rom.* 8, 26). There are no substitutes for the spiritual life. For us especially who are the Lord's ministers, it cannot, it must not be lacking.

Let us end with the following " liturgy of the word ", St. Paul's words to the Philippians (2, 1-5). Sons and Brothers: " If there be therefore any consolation in Christ, if any comfort of love, if any fellowship of the spirit, if any feeling of mercy, fill up my joy by thinking alike, having the same charity, with one soul and one mind. Do nothing out of contentiousness or out of vainglory, but in humility let each regard others as better than himself, each one looking not to his own interests, but to those of others. Let this mind be in you which was also in Jesus Christ ".

So may it be, with Our Apostolic Blessing.

GREATER SPIRITUAL INTENSITY
SHOULD MARK LENTEN SEASON

Beloved Sons and Daughters!

We are in Lent. That is, we are in the period of preparation for Easter. Our preparation for Easter may be described under two headings: asceticism and mysticism, in other words penance and prayer.

Our penance consists first of all in abstinence: it is not only abstinence from food, fasting, in accordance with the discipline which has been so much mitigated today that it has almost been abolished. It is above all abstinence from everything that separates us from God, abstinence from sin and its tempting ways. Sin makes us less masters of ourselves, makes us less free, less persons and less Christians.

The second element means greater spiritual intensity, nourishment by God's word, reflection and prayer. The Church still maintains, with the Gospel in her hand, that these paths lead to Christ, that through this means we are prepared to celebrate the Easter mystery well in this year of grace also, and that Christians are formed through these moral and spiritual exercises. The Church's school is an austere and fervent one. It aims to form men in whom religious and moral life are closely linked and work together, people who watch themselves and watch the quality of their exterior impressions, people capable of imposing certain renunciations and rules upon themselves in regard to certain things which at first sight seem to be very interesting and part of full modern existence, people who are at the same time ready to assert themselves, by means of tacit but strong command of their wills, in free, practical commitment to those virtues which Christ taught us by his words and example.

Liberated Liberty

Could you describe the human type which comes out of this school? If you try you will have a valuable and ideal experience. You will find that it is not a uniform and impersonal sort of human being. You will find that there are as many features as there are persons in this school of the Gospel. Of course, they all have the main characteristics which mark Christ's followers, but at the same time each has his own particular features. These are unique in a certain sense. The typical products of this school are the saints, that is, true and perfect Christians. Two indispensable factors prevail in them. One, grace, is efficacious; the other, the will, co-operates with it. This second factor, the will, is better known to our experience than is the former, grace, and we are therefore very much inclined to define the perfect, the saints, by the use they made of their wills. That is to say, we define them almost by describing their virtues, which we like to find in a higher, even heroic, degree in them.

From this outline of anthropology, that is, the gauge by which we measure man's stature, we can see that we, pupils and teachers in the Church, like to define a good man in terms of his moral fortitude. The Church does not wish to bring up petty, mediocre human beings. She tries to make them strong through her education. She wants to see virile virtues in them (take St. Catherine of Siena as an example). As St. Augustine said, she wants them to have " liberated liberty " (*Retractationes* 1, 15; *PL* 1, 609) liberty which has been freed from lower and external impulses and impressions.

The question now arises: Is this ideal of the Christian as a strong man still suitable for our time? Does it not belong to other times? This doubt becomes more pressing when we appeal to the Council, for did not the Council relieve the Christian life of many burdens which had been superimposed on it by the medieval ascetic and monastic concept of Christianity? Did not the Council tell us that " by this holiness a more human way of life is promoted even in this earthly society " (*Lumen gentium*, 40)? Did not the Council defend the person and his liberty?

Incredulous and Perverse Generation

Here is a most interesting problem, and we put it before you to think about. The maturity of modern man and the pedagogy of the Church herself not only acknowledge, but also recommend, the use of personal liberty in forming and asserting the human person. Does this use of personal liberty do away with the ancient discipline of penance, abstinence, asceticism, in a word, of moral struggle, so as to grant to our generation a spontaneity of action which frees it from all binding rules that are not strictly necessary for ordinary social living? Does it authorize man to enjoy to the full every vital instinct and, at least for the sake of experience and knowledge, allow him to enjoy what was formerly forbidden and judged to be sinful?

Apply this question by way of example to two expressions of modern autonomy; disobedience and eroticism. The former is rejection of authority, whatever its nature, and the higher the authority the greater the challenge to it. The latter is the acceptance of, indeed the seeking after, a hundred forms of exhibitionist sensuality, which is described as naturalness, youthfulness, art, beauty, and liberation. You will see that these paths lead far from the Christian concept of life, and that the Cross is not the pole by which their course is set.

The result of this enquiry, simple as it is, is discouraging. We, children of our age, are not on the right road in following this order or disorder in thought. We are always looking for what is useful to us, what is convenient and what is pleasing. We have many pretences and many indulgences in this regard in our religious and ecclesial sphere also. We wish to remove from our programme of life renunciation, effort and the Cross. We desire to know everything, and unfortunately we often wish to try everything.

The world, which we ought so much to pity and to love under its human aspect, does not frighten us when it presents itself to us under its no less real aspect of amorality or a theoretical and practical rule for enjoying life. We no longer hear Christ's indignant voice, exorcizing this pleasure-loving world which is so ready for moral vileness: " Oh, unbelieving and perverse generation, how long shall I be with you? How long shall I bear you? " (*Mt.* 17, 16; 11, 16; etc.).

Repentance of the Spirit

However, dearly beloved children, we must not end this rapid account of the moral orientations of our time without noting certain positive tendencies. Whether they intend to or not, they endorse the Church's ancient ascetical wisdom, and we find them coming from many directions. Did not St. Paul make use of the fighting spirit of the soldier (cf. *Eph.* 6, 11-13), or the athlete (cf. *1 Cor.* 9, 24-27), to instruct new Christians in the energetic and ascetical exercise of the will, now stimulated and strengthened by grace (cf. *Rom.* 12, 2; 1 *Pet.* 5, 10)? Do not some forms and some profound motives of current contestation conceal perhaps a rejection of conventional hedonism, bourgeois mediocrity, and spineless conformity? Do they not perhaps express a yearning for a simpler and harder life, and a more personal way of leading one's own life? Are not our consciences touched by some austere demands of youth, demands for sincerity in speech and in life, for poverty, for liberation from the nightmare of the worship of economics and for a courageous attempt to imitate Christ?

Even the decadent customs of our century have some positive phenomena in them, and the Council texts contain optimum programmes for Christian perfection (cf. *Lumen gentium*, 40). Many superficial and short-sighted people, or lazy and lax people, have sought to interpret them as an indulgent amnesty for hedonistic and naturalistic concepts of modern behaviour. Today we need valiant Christians. The Church, though at present very moderate in her practical and ascetical demands, has need of courageous children educated in the school of the Gospel. This is why her call to mortification of the flesh and penitence of the spirit is more than ever relevant today. May the Lord help you to meditate on this and comply with it. With Our Apostolic Blessing.

CHRISTIAN PERFECTION DEMANDS
AN INQUIRY INTO FUNDAMENTALS

Beloved Sons and Daughters,

W e are in Lent. We can widen our perspective, saying: we are also in the post-conciliar period. This suggests to us a revision of our way of life, which raises many difficult questions for our consciences. The reform promoted by the Church in this age of ours, the so-called " aggiornamento ", does not concern only the " structures ", the exterior methods of ecclesial organization, as people are wont to think. It concerns our personal life, it concerns the ideal line we must impress on our conduct, it concerns the principles directing our moral sense.

How are we to live? Taking life as it comes, without thinking about it? Are we to conform passively to the environment, customs, fashions, laws, necessities that happen to surround us, or are we to react somehow, that is, act with a criterion of our own, with a certain freedom, at least of judgment and, where possible, of choice? Are we to be content to be impersonal and mediocre, and perhaps, also full of shortcomings, dishonest and bad, or are we to impose a rule, a law on ourselves? Are we to demand of ourselves a style of life, a moral discipline, perfection, or can we live without scruples, in the easiest, most pleasant way? And if love is the essential qualification of moral life, how are we to understand it, as an affirmation of selfishness, or as a profession of altruism?

Moral discipline

So many questions, which we must all ask ourselves ... But even if they conceal delicate, speculative and difficult problems, the answer is not difficult to find, especially for us who have a Master of life, such as Christ is. In his Gospel Christ teaches us by word and example how we must live. And with the inner help of his Spirit, grace, and the exterior assistance of his community, the Church, he makes it possible for us to carry out his bidding.

Let no one delude himself. Christ is demanding. Christ's life is the narrow way (cf. *Mt.* 7, 14). To be worthy of him, we must take up our cross (cf. *Mt.* 10, 38). It is not enough to be religious, it is necessary to carry out the divine will in actual fact (*Mt.* 7, 21). And the Council will say that, if we are aware of what baptism operates in our regenerated human being, we must feel obliged to live as sons of God, according to the requirement of perfection and holiness, which derives precisely from our elevation to the supernatural order (*Lumen gentium*, 40).

Natural law

But let no one take fright. For the perfection to which we are called by our Christian election does not complicate and aggravate life, even if it requires us to observe many practical norms, calculated rather to help our faithfulness than to make it more difficult. Christian perfection demands from us above all an inquiry into the fundamental principles of our human being. Our duty seeks to equate itself with our being. We should be what we are. This is the principle of natural law, about which there is so much discussion today, but which mere reason vindicates in its fundamental demands. These demands are derived from life itself, and they are interpreted by common sense, ordinary reason (cf. *Gaudium et spes*, 36). It is the law we bear in ourselves, as men: " a law not written, but innate " (CICERO); the law that St. Paul recognizes also in peoples to whom the Mosaic law was not announced (cf. *Rom.* 2, 14), and which the Gospel has absorbed, confirmed and perfected (cf. B. SCHÜLLER, *La théologie morale, etc.*, " Nouv. Revue Théol. ", mai 1966, p. 449 ff.).

We have all, moreover, sufficient knowledge of this law, the most important precepts of which we find enunciated in the Ten Commandments. And obedience to this law makes us men and Christians. It defends us from the accusation with which literature often charges devout persons, that is, of being scrupulous in the observance of pious, detailed rules, and less so in uncompromising fidelity to the fundamental norms of human honesty, such as sincerity, respect for life or for one's pledged word, administrative honesty, consistency of morals with the profession of Christianity, and so on. It is this integrity that confers dignity on man in his inner self and in society. It is this consistency between the believer and the non-Christian. It is this profession of rational justice which upholds the legislative system of civil society, and offers social justice a reason for progress. Even the rebel contestations of our days appeal, after all, to the necessity of a normative rationality that is more advanced and more in conformity with the new needs of a society in evolution. In the present-day confusion of the notion of good and evil, licit and illicit, just and unjust, and in the demoralizing spread of crime and immorality, we will do well to preserve and deepen this sense of natural law, that is, of justice, of integrity and of the good, that upright reason inspires continually within our consciences.

A new life

But we cannot stop here. We must enter the realistic vision of faith, which shows us the inevitable inability of man to be good and just, when left to himself and unaided. It is not only our catechism that tells us so. A large part of modern literature and of films and plays today provide despairing documentary evidence on this point. The pessimism that prevails in art steeped in modern psychology tells us even more eloquently than the religious teacher how sick man is in the innermost recesses of his existence, how he dreams and struggles in vain to reach happiness and the fullness of his being, how inexorably he betrays his moral insufficiency and his inner corruption, and how he feels, condemned to scepticism, despair, nothingness.

For us it is clear. We need to be saved. We need Christ. We need One to take upon himself all our sin and expiate it for us. We need a Saviour who will give his life for us and rise again immediately for our justification (cf. *Rom.* 4, 25), that is, to enable us to lead a new life, the supernatural life, the paschal life.

It is for this redeemed life that the Church was instituted. This year, too, she calls us, gathers us and prepares us for the announcement that is hers: that of the resurrection of Christ and our own.

Prepare yourselves, all of you, with our Apostolic Blessing.

RENUNCIATION AND SACRIFICE:
HALLMARK OF CHRISTIAN LIFE

Beloved Sons and Daughters,

One of the least understood, and we could say least popular, aspects of Christian life for us moderns, is renunciation. We are so stimulated by the variety and the quantity of all the things available today for a comfortable life, rich in experiences, full and happy, that it seems to us absurd to renounce anything, particularly if the renunciation concerns the training, education, culture and welfare of man. We often measure our place in time and in the world by our capacity of feeling, knowing and possessing what time and the world offer us.

To this exterior display there corresponds an inner greediness to see and have everything, to experience and enjoy everything. The progress that surrounds us finds man prepared to take advantage of it, because he is mature, because he is free, because he is convinced that life is like this. His perfection, his ideal is the amplitude of the relationship between the goods of civilization and the human spirit. Even if this relationship is reduced in practice within the limits of the concrete possibilities, be they economic or social, each person is inclined to conceive his own existence in terms of success, wealth, comfort, pleasure. Everyone wants to enjoy life, even if he sets himself a programme of dignity and honesty; to enjoy it, at least as far as possibility and decency permit, but to the utmost. To limit it—never!

This, it seems to us, is the humanistic and hedonistic mentality widespread today. It penetrates, and often with genuine keys, even into the Christian conception of contemporary life. Is not Christianity, it is said, the best form of our existence? Does it not aim at solving all the problems that make its conditions unjust and unhappy? Does it not wish to console all suffering and soothe all distress? And does it not educate us today to look with sympathy on the things of this earth, which science and technology and civil organization have made so fruitful, so prodigal of useful, beautiful, interesting gifts? The Christian, too, sits back with pleasure on the soft cushion of comforts that civilization supplies.

Blameworthy outlook

We will not stop here to make an analytical criticism of this mentality, blameworthy when it becomes dominant and exclusive. We all know, we think, how such an outlook can diminish man, instead of ennobling him. It confines his horizon rather to the external world, to the realm of the senses, to instinct, to the bourgeois or pleasure-seeking ideal, to narrow, selfish emotions. Not to mention that it does not make man happy, but rather insatiable and inclined either towards illusion or towards pessimism. It is the thinkers, the writers, the artists who tell us so today. We knew it, without having thought about it too much, perhaps. Jesus had warned us: " A man's life does not consist in the abundance of his possessions " (*Lk.* 12, 15).

The problem of choice

One cannot have and enjoy everything. A choice is necessary. " The kingdom of heaven, our Lord says again, is like a merchant in search of fine pearls. When he finds a single pearl of great price, he goes and sells all that he has and buys it " (*Mt.* 13, 45-46). This concept of choice, which includes that of renunciation, recurs in other places in the Gospel: " No man can serve two masters ... " (*Mt.* 6, 24); " enter by the narrow gate. For wide is the gate and broad is the way that leads to destruction ... " (*Mt.* 7, 13). This problem of choice dominates the direction of Christian life, right from the beginning, that is, from baptism. Before it is conferred, certain supreme renunciations are required, as a condition. Do you remember? Do you renounce Satan? Do you renounce his works and promps? etc.

For it must be remembered that not everything is good. This

is simple and clear, but then in the course of life the distinction between what is good and what is evil is a very difficult thing. This is particularly so when people refuse to admit a secure ethical criterion, a superior teaching authority which God has endowed with knowledge of man and of his destiny, and when they set up moral indifference as a pedagogical principle. Yes, the pupil—and we are all pupils in the school of life—must have a picture of the possibilities offered by the time and the environment in which he lives; but at the same time he must be able to judge, and he must be able to choose.

St. Paul tells us: " Omnia ... probate; quod bonum est tenete ", " test everything, hold fast what is good " (*1 Thess.* 5, 21). This is what we do in matters concerning physical health, choosing wholesome food, medicines that do us good, fresh air, etc. And this is what the soldier and the athlete does: he judges and chooses what is best to preserve his strength; the sportsman sets us an example. Again St. Paul teaches us: " And everyone in a contest abstains from all things " (*1 Cor.* 9, 25). We must impose renunciation on ourselves, accept a discipline, choose a norm in order to be strong, to be faithful, to be Christians. The cross marks our life. We must understand that though Christian abnegation deprives us of many things, limits our experience of dangerous, harmful things, imposes an austere vigilance of thought and of morality, it makes us really free and living persons, and transforms our weakness into virtue (cf. *2 Cor.* 6, 9; 12, 10).

Christian renunciation is not the arbitrary, burdensome, ascetic and monastic discipline of the past. It is an authentic way of Christian life. Firstly, because it implies a hierarchical classification of its goods; secondly, because it stimulates us to choose the " better part " (*Lk.* 10, 42); thirdly, because it gives man practice in self-control; and lastly, because it establishes that mysterious economy of expiation, which makes us particpants in Christ's redemption. A word which in everyday language now refers to renunciation, reminds us of this: the word " sacrifice ". In itself it takes us back to a mysterious and supreme act of religion, but which now, in the sign of that cross, bringing death and life at the same time, indicates a generous and courageous act, a joyful and voluntary renunciation, carried out with a higher intention of good and of love. Sacrifice: a strong word, which derives from the first " little sacrifices " of the child, who really wants to be good, and spreads over all ages and in various mesaures, to detach us from the many " useless and harmful desires " (*1 Tim.* 6, 9), and to qualify us to give our earthly existence the significance and the value of " a sacrifice, living, holy, pleasing to God " (*Rom.* 12, 1).

May our Apostolic Blessing strengthen you.

POPE SHOWS ROLE OF NATURAL LAW
IN CHRISTIAN CONCEPT OF LIFE

Beloved Sons and Daughters!

We are thinking about the moral concept of man which the Council suggests to us. Our reflection leads Us to make two observations. Both of them are very well known already, yet they are in need of being revised, and clarified, more than at any time before. One observation concerns the existence of the natural law; the other is about the existence of an original Christian moral law. It is clear that the law of action, the moral law, derives from the human being.

Obligation derives from man's nature

Well, who is man? What is a Christian? In order to know how a man ought to behave, we need to have at least an instinctive, intuitive notion of man's nature. We need to have at least some general concept of the Christian man in order to know how he ought to behave as a Christian.

All this is elementary. But is it connected with very difficult complicated problems, which we certainly cannot solve adequately and with due measure here today. We refer to them to indicate that the moral questions raised by the Council, and still more, by the tumult of modern opinion and experience, require a fresh examination and a clear and strong conscience on the part of those who wish to be truly human and Christian.

A Higher Law

Let Us just ask a few questions. Does a natural law really exist? This seems an ingenuous question, for the answer is so obvious and certain. But it is not really ingenuous, when we think of the objections raised on many sides today against the existence of a natural law. To a certain extent we can understand why. When the concept of man becomes confused and altered, then the concept of his life, his behaviour and his morality, is also confused and altered. But We think that We can give an answer, through reflection, enlightened, you might say, by some beam of Christian wisdom. We can respond to the ancient maxim: " Know thyself ". For us the immanent sense of conscience, and the light of reason even more, tell us that we are subiect to a law, combining both rights and obligations, which arises from our being, from our nature. It is not a written law, but one that is lived: *non scripta sed nata lex,* said Cicero. It is the law which Saint Paul recognized in the Gentiles without the light of divine revelation. He said that they are a law unto themselves: *ipsi sibi sunt lex* (*Rom.* 2, 14).

In any case, no one in this time of reform and " contestation " is more continually aware than we are, that the hidden strength of moral unrest not infrequently arises from an appeal to a higher law (in challenge to the law in force), to a more human law which has not yet been drafted, but which is powerful and rises from the discovery of an interior law which demands to be expressed and affirmed, the natural law.

We are still responsive to the formidable, classic conflict which in Greek tragedy is reflected in the frail but very human heart of Antigone, who rose up against the unjust and tyrannical power of Creon. We are more than ever champions of the human personality and human dignity. Why is this? Because in man we recognize a being subject to obligation by virtue of an exacting principle, which we call the natural law.

The Law of Grace

A second question: It this natural law enough to guide man's social life? First of all, it is not enough, if it is not in some way made explicit, codified and social. It needs to be formulated, to be known, to be acknowledged, to be sanctioned by rightful authority. This is why there are lawmakers. They have to interpret true or presumed natural law, and they translate it into public civil norms.

But we have been instructed by divine teaching about man's supernatural destiny, about the sad consequences which he has inherited through original sin, about the regeneration which Christ obtained for us and conferred upon us, for the integration and fullness of our life in his. The natural law is not enough for us: we need the law of grace, and it has its own economy, its own " realm ", into which the Church normally introduces us and in which it educates us. Christ is necessary. Living according to his Word and his Spirit is our salvation.

Tension in the young today

And now another question arises: What is the relationship between the two laws, the law of nature and the law of grace? Have they no knowledge of each other? Are they in conflict; or do they fulfil each other? There would be too much to say about all this. For the present We think it enough to give a preliminary answer, and it is one that derives from many pages of the Council's documents. The answer is this: The Christian concept of life acknowledges as valid and binding the natural laws, and also the civil laws based on the former, and therefore said to be just.

Let one quotation from the Council suffice: " Many of our contemporaries seem to fear that a closer bond between human activity and religion will work against the independence of men, of societies, or of the sciences. If by the autonomy of earthly affairs we mean that created things and societies themselves enjoy their own laws and values which must be gradually deciphered, put to use and regulated by men, then it is entirely right to demand that autonomy. Such is not merely required by modern man, but also harmonizes with the will of the Creator. For by the very circumstance of their having been created, all things are endowed with their own stability, truth, goodness, proper laws and order. Man must respect these as he isolates them by the appropriate methods of the individual sciences and arts " (*Gaudium et spes*, 36).

From this comes a second answer. The law proper to man, that is, the natural law, and the law proper to the Christian, that is, the life of faith and charity, the life of grace, can and ought to be integrated in practice and in the growth of the Christian virtues, to lead man to perfection (cf. SCHÜLLER, *La théologie morale, peut-elle se passer du droit naturel?* " Nouv. Rev. Théol. ", mai 1966; FUCHS, *Teologia e vita morale alla luce del Vaticano II,* 1968).

From this two further questions arise. Should not a Christian distinguish himself in living the fundamental natural virtues, for example, sincerity and justice? Or course he should! More, we should hope that Christian upbringing will always be more and more marked by the awareness and observance of these natural virtues, such as respect for the truth in word and deed, and devotion to justice especially in social relations (cf. *Gaudium et spes,* 30).

The same may be said of the other natural virtues which tradition classifies as cardinal (cf. ST. AMBROSE, *De officiis,* 1, 27). We are delighted to find that modern youth makes a strong and proud appeal to those fundamental moral principles which give to life its authentic and upright human stature. And We should also note that this effort to build up the true man can find a powerful stimulus, a superhuman vocation in the Gospel's requirements, especially in those referring to personal austerity and human relationships. This is one of the finest things about the new generation, one of the hopes a better future.

The Dynamism of the Moral Law

Another question—the last for the present. It is concerned with the dynamism of the moral law, both natural and Christian, in other words, its potential continual progress. Yes, moral progress is always possible, indeed it is always a duty, but the fundamental principles and norms always remain unchanged. It is always possible to have a more perfect application of the moral law. Man is always " in a state of becoming "—*in fieri*. He is becoming man in the sense of corresponding more to the definition of man, or in the sense of becoming perfect according to the Gospel definition, that is becoming holy. Man's true history is the history of his education, his emancipation, as Tommaseo says, of his liberation, as the world of today often ambiguously says.

It is all a matter of seeing what kind of liberation gives to man his fullness. What is said of the individual person may also be said of human society and its civilization. It must always be developing morally, that is, in a human and Christian sense, and therefore culturally, socially, economically, and so on. In the last analysis, this means that the real driving force of our existence is duty. For us Christians duty has an even stronger and deeper name: love. Jesus said, " Thou shalt love God with thy whole heart, and thou shalt love thy neighbour as thyself: this is the whole law ... " (*Mt.* 22, 37-40).

POPE DETAILS ROLE OF LAITY
IN THE CHURCH

On the morning of March 20th, the Holy Father
gave audience to the members of the Council
of the Laity led by Cardinal Roy, Archbishop
of Québec and President of the Council and
the Pontifical Commission " Justice and Peace ".
Present at the audience were the Vice-President,
Bishop Alberto Castelli, the Secretary, Bishop
Marcello Uylenbroeck, and the under-Secreta-
ries, Doctor Mieczyslaw and Miss Rosemary
Goldie.
Cardinal Roy and Bishop Derek Worlock of
Portmouth paid homage to the Holy Father.
Mrs. Branca de Melo Franco-Alves of Brazil and
Mr. Rienze Rupasinghe of Ceylon gave a short
report on the activities of the Council.
The Holy Father delivered the following ad-
dress.

We are happy to welcome you at the conclusion of your work, dear sons and friends, Members of the Council of the Laity. Through your voice We are happy to hear the echo of the magnificent apostolate of the People of God throughout the world. You are, as it were, Our " experts ", Our advisers in this domain, and this is the reason why We have agreed most willingly that several among you speak to Us during this audience. Also, We wish to thank in particular Bishop Derek Worlock, Mrs. Branca Alves, and Mr. Rienzie Rupasinghe who have just been your spokesmen.

They have very well expressed your pride and joy in the great task entrusted to you by the Church, nor have they concealed the difficulties encountered: these " tensions " which are not excluded from the field of the apostolate, tension between the Church and the world, between faith and life, between the clergy and the laity, and so forth. But through your threefold testimony, We seem to notice a determined will to dominate these tensions by transforming them into dialogue and making them serve the common good. We commend your determination to carry on unceasingly the work undertaken, to develop and study it thoroughly. We are glad to give you the assurance that your precious work in the service of the Church will not lack the encouragements and the blessings you have requested from Us.

Now We would like to take advantage of your presence here to consider together with you what the laity are in the Church. What is a layman? What is a Catholic layman? What does the Church expect from your Council to help promote the apostolate of the laity in our times? Here you have matter for instruction, and upon which you especially should meditate in order to assure its implementation within the People of God, according to three essential dimensions.

Threefold dimension of the laity

1. First of all, the *human* person. Every person (must it be recalled) is created to the image of God, is superior to the entire visible universe, and has an eternal destiny.

But this human person, under the specific character of laity as We are considering it, is called to fulfil his destiny in the heart of the secular world, to share the suffering and joys of the human community, to bring about within this community social and cultural solidarities which create his rights and duties, and which also give him the possibilitiy to exercise multiform activities for the organization and progress of the world.

This reveals the eminent role and dignity of the human person, and the obligation of every society to respect the human person as an individual being and as a social and family being.

2. Secondly, the *Christian* person. This is a further title added to the grandeur of the human person, one which opens for him the door to baptism. It is the entrance into a new world, into infinite horizons: the world of faith, the world of grace.

Constant confrontation with the Gospel

Here the layman appears in his superior dignity as a member of the People of God, elevated to a supernatural level, potentially a citizen of heaven, and rich already here below with new rights and new duties which natural man could neither claim nor attain by his own strength.

3. Finally, the *Catholic* layman, member of the Church, the mystical body of Christ, and more particularly, as all of you are, dear friends, the layman who has become aware of his place, his role in this mystical body—so united and divergent at the same time —the layman considered as a subject no longer passive, as was too often the case in the past, but as an active subject in the Church, according to the formal teaching of the Ecumenical Council Vatican II.

Certainly, you in particular do not need to be reminded of the Constitution *Lumen gentium* which, after having spoken about the duty of obedience and prayer on the part of the faithful, requests pastors " to recognize and promote the dignity as well as the responsibility of the layman in the Church. Let them willingly make use of his prudent advice. Let them confidently assign duties to him in the service of the Church, allowing him freedom and room for action. Further, let them encourage the layman so that he may undertake tasks on his own initiative. Furthermore, let pastors respectfully acknowledge that just freedom which belongs to everyone in this earthly city " (no. 37).

Who does not see the vast field of activity thus opened to the Council of the Laity in the trail of conciliar teaching? In what direction will your Council work so that the great perspectives of the apostolate outlined in the various Decrees or Constitutions of Vatican II may be realized? It seems to Us that its role will have a twofold axis: it will be exercised in relation to the laity and in relation to the Hierarchy.

In relation to the laity, your Council must maintain an attitude of attention and dialogue, susceptible of discerning the needs and the possibilities of salvation in your milieus of life. In this way, your Council will strive to stimulate, in liaison with the episcopates in the various parts of the world, those forms of apostolate which respect the spirit and the character of each culture, but which all become united in the community of the Church by the clear affirmation of their Catholic identity. This will be your role: to recall and bear witness that zeal and devotedness are not sufficient. To these must be added reflection, meditation, constant confrontation with the Gospel and the Magisterium of the Church.

Within such a perspective, the trustful exchange of views between priests and laity is imperative. In this mutual exchange of views on the same situations, on the same events, on the same needs of the world, the priests and the laity will stimulate each other to realize their respective vocation and mission.

This is what appears to Us, dear Sons, as the first responsibility of the Council of the Laity. The second one is no less important: it concerns the coordination of the laity with that of the Hierarchy, two forces which the constitution itself of the Church does not permit to imagine as divergent. Here again, your own testimony must be exemplary.

Attentive to the voices of the world, you can consider yourselves as the qualified interpreters of the countless sons whom the common Father would like to hear, but, as We already requested of you last year, We count on you also to be the faithful spokesmen to them of Our pastoral preoccupations on their behalf. Moreover, the position the Council of the Laity is called upon to occupy henceforth in the central organizations of the Church authorizes it to seek the best means to unite and harmonize its role with the role of the various departments, secretariats or commissions of the Roman Curia, respecting the competency of each one. Acquiring thus a comprehensive view of the whole, you will discover therein both your function with its limitations, and your responsibility in its entire range and specification. In this manner, you will also develop more and more a sense of the hierachical Church where everything must be treated in terms of confidence, service, and unity.

The world needs the glad tidings

For the task which We have just broadly outlined, We know that We can count on your fidelity to the See of Peter and on your mature reflections. Both are more than ever indispensable in this turbulent period for the Church and the world.

However different your origins, your formations and your engagements may be, your sole concern must be to preach Jesus Christ, to proclaim joyfully the Glad Tidings of salvation. The world needs these glad tidings, as it needs food. One of your spokesmen has very well expressed this a moment ago. We can even say that the urgent necessity to Christianize the world, this growing and worried world, capable of exploring the cosmos and destroying itself, has rarely appeared in history as clearly as today. More than ever before, this is the hour of the Gospel, the hour of the penetration of the Christian leaven into the whole of society. In the specific and important place you hold, that of the Council of the Laity, be the good artisans of this immense work, dear Sons. May Our blessing encourage you and accompany you in the accomplishment of this work.

ANSWERS TO TODAY'S PROBLEMS LIE
IN THE PERSON, THE WORDS OF JESUS

*To the youth in particular, who were present
in large numbers on Palm Sunday, March 22nd,
Pope Paul addressed his homily after the
blessing of the palms.*

The Liturgy for today, Palm Sunday, shows us two scenes
from the Gospel. One is that of Jesus' spectacular entry into
Jerusalem; the other is that of his passion. They were written
by the evangelist Mark, who probably saw them happen or to
whom they were related by the Apostle Peter, in connection with
the first catechesis given in the early Christian community, perhaps here at Rome. The former of the two scenes, the one which
gives the tone to this Sunday, is known as the Gospel of the
Palms. We will briefly meditate upon it.

You heard it being read out just a while ago. Think about
that scene. It is a singular one in the Gospel story because it is a
public and a festive scene, and one with a purpose. In our reading of the Gospel we have found Jesus surrounded on other
occasions by crowds attracted by his words, his miracles and his
person. But we have also always noticed that Jesus did not wish
to have people acclaiming him for his own sake. Indeed he avoided
arousing popularity for his own person. Yet this time he did
desire to be acknowledged and acclaimed—so much so that when
some Pharisees in the crowd hypocritically expressed concern for
public order, but were really annoyed to see the whole people
running after him (*Jn.* 12, 19), they said, " Master, rebuke thy
disciples ". He replied, " I tell you, if these should be quiet, the
very stones would cry out! " (*Lk.* 19, 39-40).

Jesus suffers freely

Why this new attitude? Jesus wished to enter Jerusalem
which at that time was crowded with people who had come to
celebrate the Jewish Passover. He wished to enter in a new

form—we would say, he wanted to make an official entry. He knew what was waiting for him, and he told his disciples: " Behold, we go up to Jerusalem; and the Son of man shall be betrayed to the chief priests and to the scribes, and they shall condemn him to death, and shall deliver him to the Gentiles to mock, to scourge and to crucify him ... " (*Mt.* 20, 18-19). So he began his sufferings. He desired to bring out the fact that he accepted them freely and voluntarily (cf. *Is.* 53, 7; *He.* 9, 14; *Eph.* 5, 2), but he also wished to show their messianic character. Before fulfilling his sacrifice—that is what his death was—before he immolated himself, he wanted to make it finally and unmistakably clear who he was, and what his mission was. He is the Messiah, and the desired to be freely and openly acknowledged as such by his people.

At this point we should take care to find out what the full meaning of that word " Messiah " is. It means the Christ, the Anointed, the Chosen and Consecrated One. For centuries Israel's worldly and prophetic expectations had been concentrated on him, all the hopes of that privileged nation which through the Messiah was to be the hinge of the world's destinies. The Messiah was regarded as the Son of David, the King of history as it is guided by God's designs, the wonderful Saviour, who would do away with all man's miseries (cf. *Mt.* 11, 3 sqq.).

Jesus was to give deeper, more dramatic and supernatural meaning to that marvellous title of Messiah. He was to claim it, he was to give it to himself, he was to will that it should be openly recognized. And today we are commemorating that fateful moment in which Jesus was acclaimed as the Messiah, as the Christ. It was his moment. The remainder of his temporal life was to be lived by him with this title of Messiah on him.

Mystery of Divine Sonship

The episode of the entry into Jerusalem assumed the importance of an event which solved the problems which had gathered about his mysterious personality. Who was Jesus? Was he a carpenter's son? (*Mt.* 13, 55). Was he that singular figure, " the Son of Man ", as Jesus himself described himself? Was he a prophet? (*Mt.* 16, 14; 21, 11 etc.). Was he really the Messiah? (*Jn.* 1, 41)? Was he actually He who would come (*Mt.* 11, 3, 5)? Was he the Son of David

(*Mt.* 20, 30-31)? Was he to be proclaimed king (*Jn.* 6, 15)? Or was he someone even greater and mysterious, God's own son (*Mt.* 16, 16; *Jn.* 1, 49; 8 passim). Doubts and questions increased as Jesus made himself known by revealing the mystery of his divine sonship, and they went to the point of the challenging question put to him on the last night during the trial in the Sanhedrin: " Art thou the Christ, the Son of the Blessed One? " (*Mk.* 14, 61).

The question of who Jesus really was runs through the whole of the Gospel, and makes it dramatic and tragic at the end.

Jesus described himself in many different ways, and they are the object and the delight of our faith. It is good to recall them. He said, " I am the bread of life " (*Jn.* 6, 48); " I am the good shepherd " (*Jn.* 10, 11); " I am the light of the world " (*Jn.* 12, 46), and so on. And at the last supper, you remember, he said, " I am the way, the truth and the life " (*Jn.* 14, 6).

But in the scene we are meditating now he described himself, with an act, not with words, as the Messiah. It was not an act of triumphalism, but rather a humble, though public and planned, presentation of himself. We will not consider that act's greatness under its modest and popular aspect, but will rather think of the explosion of joy in the crowd, the certainty which the people now had and of the profession of belief and delight which was made especially by the young on discovering the unmistakable messianic character of Jesus. It is He, it is He, who has been awaited for centuries, who has been awaited by this generation, He, the key of all past and future history! Jesus had so far been surrounded by curiosity, doubt, hesitation, fascination, and admiration. These things now all burst out in undoubting and enthusiastic acclamations: It is He, it is He, the son of David, the Christ, the Lord!

An unavoidable choice

Now, pay attention. This meeting is repeated in the liturgy which we are celebrating. The Church recalls to our minds that scene, that decisive hour. Jesus appears before us, humble yet formidable, revealing himself. He speaks, about himself almost, and, a surprising thing in the midst of so much festivity, he weeps. He weeps as he looks at the city close by. Almost speaking to himself, he says, " If thou hadst known, in this thy day, the things that are for thy peace! But now they are hid from thine eyes ... ". He was looking into the future, even though that was a day of glory. He predicted the coming ruin of the holy but unfaithful city, and he added, " because thou didst not know when thou wast visited " (*Lk.* 19, 42-44).

The meaning of this Gospel of the Palms which we have just read arouses an unavoidable question. It offers a choice regarding our life's destiny's. Yes or No, do we acknowledge Jesus for what he is, the Christ, the Messiah, he who has been sent by God, who came down into the world in order to bring mankind salvation? Do we recognize him as the one who came to be a " sign of contradiction " (*Lk.* 2, 34), a compass needle turning between two fatal courses, one leading to salvation, the other to perdition, the one leading to life, the other to death? Have we the happy intuition, the freshness of mind, the joy, the boldness to proclaim even today that Jesus is the One, our choice, that he is our redeemer, necessary and sufficient Redeemer, He who came for each of us; He the Master, the Friend, the Resurrection and the Life? (*Jn.* 11, 25). Yes, He is the life, the truth, the life of our individual existences and of the whole community of those who believe in him. Do they trust themselves to him, do they feel loved by him and do they offer him their poor yet great love?

Jesus the Christ stands by the roads of mankind today, everywhere and at all times. He puts himself forward as the great question, as the supreme and decisive choice which every human being and every people is called upon to make. Jesus is the great responsibility in the story of every human existence; he is the highest degree of tension in the liberty of conscious life. Jesus is the last and also the first junction at which our fates take shape. Jesus is the deepest and most personal invitation offered to our clear and active consciousnesses.

This sermon is for all. It is an elementary, basic one in which the *kerygma*, the announcement, the proclamation of the Gospel is summed up. But it is addressed to you, young people, in a special way. We invited you to this paschal rite, and you represent the present young generation. We dare speak to you directly because, like the children in the Gospel story of Palm Sunday, you are leaders in Jesus, the Christ of the centuries' dramatic meeting with humanity. Many people speak about the young today, but we think that not many speak to them. Perhaps they do not known how to; perhaps they do not trust them. We are speaking to you, because an inescapable duty makes Us. We speak as someone who loves you well, like your parents and your teachers. And We dare say that We speak in even greater and deeper words than theirs, because the words We speack are not really Ours, but Christ's and We do nothing but echo him humbly and faithfully.

Listen to yourselves

We wish to make ourselves clear. Will you listen? If you will, then listen to yourselves first. What voices do you hear rising up from within your own minds? Try and allow yourselves a few moments of interior silence. What do you hear? We believe that you hear many confused voices, some of them even like shouts. What voices? The voices of the world about you are what you hear echoing in you; voices from conversations at home, the voices of your companions, voices beginning to overcome other voices; they are the voices of our time, of our world; big and difficult words, pleasing and frivolous musical voices, human cries, which are beginning to have their effect on you and which generate other voices in you, the voices of your first judgments, the voices of your first experiences, even disturbing and inviting voices, of curiosity, of fantasies, of temptations, as we call them. They are beginning to rouse voices in you which will become imperious, the voices of desires, the voices which seek to give life—take care!— its meaning, its value, its destiny. These are personal voices.

Have you ever heard them? What do they say to you? Something ideal, something very fine and very difficult that you sometimes become impatient and sometimes disappointed and sometimes sad. They are voices crying: liberty, truth, love. Or, greatness, heroism, happiness. They are the very voices of life. Are they sincere or are they lying voices? Can we fill them with reality, or do they remain empty and take away our trust in life? Do they make us good or bad? Do they give us joy in action and hope for something that does not die; or do they make us rebellious and wanting to protest and destroy? Do they alienate us from ourselves and our society, or do they give us a forestate, even a real taste to some degree, of the trueness of our achievements and the trueness of just relationship with others?

We will not go on any further with this introspection, this moral and social psychoanalysis. We will simply say with all the faith and love We are capable of, that there is a supreme answer to all these marvellous and tempestuous questionings. There is One who is the answer itself. There is a Word who is a Person. There is a Person whose name is light: " I am the light of the world ", he said (*Jn.* 8, 12). He is a Person who puts himself forward as a leader: " He who follows me does not walk in the dark " (*Jn.* 6, 48). A Person who says of himself, " I am the bread of life " (*Jn.* 6, 48). We could go on like this, but you know what We mean. That Word, that Person, is Jesus, is the Christ, " who made himself wisdom, justice, holiness and redemption for us " (*1 Cor.* 1, 30). It is he who gives our existence its true love, its untouchable dignity, its responsible liberty, its authentic value, its full love. He is our Saviour; he is the Head of our immense Body which is growing up: believing and redeemed mankind, the Church. It is he who pardons us and enables us to do things greater than ourselves. He is the defender of the poor, he is the consoler of the suffering, in a word, he is our Messiah, he is the Christ-Jesus the Christ!

Do you know him? Do you acknowledge him? Do you too acclaim him today with a responsive hymn of your faith and your ideals?

So, blessed are you, if you have understood this and do it (cf. *Jn.* 13, 17).

THE CROSS: " ONLY HOPE "
FOR A SINFUL WORLD

Beloved Sons and Daughters!

Wednesday in Holy Week! We think it is possible to speak of nothing on this eve of the Easter drama but our own position in regard to the mystery which that drama contains, signifies and renews, the mystery of our salvation. It is a divine mystery and it is a human mystery; it is a deep mystery, reaching down to the fathomless motives of divine justice and goodness.

It is the mystery of Christ: " for (God) has made him who knew no sin to be sin for us, that we might be made the justice of God in him " (*2 Cor.* 5, 21). It is a mystery in which sorrow is transformed into the precious value of our redemption, though it seems to be merely a useless enemy of our existence. It is the mystery of victorious death conquered in the triumph of a new and higher form of life. This mystery contains the knot which binds and looses every problem of human destinies, whether we know it or not, whether we believe it or not. All of us are involved in it.

All have Need of Salvation

But now a fundamental statement must be made. It is this: We are all in need of salvation (cf. *Lumen gentium*, 53; *1 Tim.* 2, 4). Our birth is shipwreck in this inescapable adventure. If we forget this we are blind; if we refuse to accept it, we are lost. We must save ourselves.

Another logical conclusion is that we need to be aware of this need. That is, we need to have consciousness of evil, of the evil in us, of the evil in the world. This is not despairing pessimism; it is realism. For us believers in the salvation which comes from Christ the Saviour, it is a sincere and saving diagnosis, preceding the cure of salvation. We shall do well to get some clear ideas about this aspect of human reality, for there are signs of a twofold kind of confusion.

One kind of confusion is that which arises from ingenuous and " a priori " optimism, such as modern naturalism has taught us to be accustomed to. The other is anxiety-ridden pessimism, which we are taught by a sad master of a certain sort of existentialism. This has pitilessly unveiled the radical unhappiness of human living, but has not been able to offer any comfort but that of resigned fatalism, or drugged hedonism.

What then shall we do in order to get into the light of Christian salvation? We shall accept the light. The light sends its rays from the divine countenance out over us, and shows up our multiform ruins. It gives us a warning and saving awareness of evil, as We said. Our good begins from our awareness of our evil. And our evil is—alas!— like on ocean flooding in. " A wave has broken over my head; I said, I am lost ". This is the voice of Jeremiah, and we shall hear it again in the Lamentations, which arouse incomparable emotions during the office of Holy Week. It is a good thing that their desolate tones return to echo in our souls once more in these days. But now let us sum up our knowledge of evil under two headings, for that knowledge should prepare us to make us willing to take part in the mystery of the paschal salvation.

Original Sin

The first section concerns us all personally. It is that dealing with the supreme evil, sin. It too has a great story, and that story drags us all into the unhappy inheritance of that famous original sin which was the cause of death in the first place, then of the psycho-ethical imbalances which disturb our moral life (cf. *Rom.* 5). Baptism redeemed us from that cursed fate, yet it has not entirely cured us of its consequences. Those consequences give rise to those other evils of which we ourselves are the foolish authors. Those other evils are our mortal sins and our actual sins, all deadly enemies of our true life, which is union with God, the sole, the prime source of life. This is a hard saying, but it cannot be avoided.

We moderns are losing a sense of sin. Our venerated predecessor Pius XII said on one occasion that " perhaps the greatest sin in the world today is the fact that men are beginning to lose their sense of sin " (*Discorsi*, VIII, p. 288). And we can see why. Once we have lost a sense of God and our relationship with him, our sense of sin goes. That relationship with God is a continually pressing one (the moral law) in the field of our action and consequently of our responsible behaviour in regard to him. Man thinks he has got rid of a sense of sin, but in reality he has only cast away the compass guiding his own conscious and vital development. He remains alone, without absolute principles with which to distinguish the good from the evil and to give duty its transcendent vigor.

If there be no God, then everything becomes licit (cf. Dostoyevski). But a dark and indistinguishable feeling of unworthiness and incapacity then enters into the spirit of anyone who acts without reference to God. This should be enough to make us not disdain but rather greet the encounter with Christ with indescribable joy, for such joy gives us consciousness of sin and at the same time an awareness of its merciful and victorious reparation.

In this we are in the midst of full and authentic Christianity. And we are now at the first stage of our celebration of Easter, the stage of penitence, repentance, painful, sorrowful but also beneficial sincerity with ourselves and with God, in sacramental confession. We are together with the Prodigal Son on the threshold of the Father's house. " Father, I have sinned against heaven and against thee; I am not worthy to be called thy son! " (*Lk.* 25, 19-21).

Here is knowledge of consciousness of evil, opening the door to regaining the good! How much could be said about it all! We are sure you already know.

Awareness, Regret, Reparation

The second heading under which this painful knowledge falls is Awareness. And with awareness comes regret, which is followed as far as possible by reparation of the evils which are in the world. Who could ever make a list of them? Who could measure their extent? Who can claim to be innocent? " We know ", the

Apostle John wrote, " that the whole world is in wicedness " (*1 Jn.* 5, 19). We must not be ignorant of this evil which has a thousand faces. We cannot go along with those who fiercely denounce the thousand evils which are outside themselves and their own field of responsibilities, but forget their own duty to say *Mea Culpa* for their own sins and for their own share of responsibility. This attitude of mind is quite common today.

In the same way, we cannot approve those who restrict the field of moral sensitivity to their personal consciences, and will not interest themselves in the evils, sorrows and needs from which society suffers, even though those negative elements belong to the temporal sphere rather than the strictly religious one.

Easter obliges us to look at that part of the human scene. Those evils which annihilated Christ's earthly life; impiety, hypocrisy, injustice, criminality, cruelty, baseness, human weakness, and so on, are still there. But, as the Suffering of the Crucified Christ brings out, they can and need to receive a flood of repentance, of redemption, of rebirth in the paschal mystery.

Even one look at the disorders and the sufferings which fill the historical and social panorama of this hour of modern life, fills Us with immense sorrow. Yet We must look, and what we see can become immense love for Our fellow men and immense confidence in the redeeming charism of the death and resurrection of the Lord Jesus.

The Cross: " Spes Unica "

How can we remain indifferent to what is happening in the world today? There are so many reasons for grief that We will not even try to give a complete and orderly list of them. We will only say that We are especially affected by the armed conflicts which are going on in the Middle East and in the Far East: instead of tending towards peace those conflicts are growing fiercer and longer, increasing armaments strike Us as irrational phenomena and disconsoling portents for the future. In some cases they are a considerable part of trade between big industrial countries and weaker nations which have need of quite different supplies.

Racial intransigence and iniquitous ethnical and social discriminations seem to Us to be ignoble remnants of the past. But

We do not believe that ideals of liberty and justice are enough to justify violence, reprisals, acts of terrorism and guerrilla warfare, often directed against legitimate governments or inflicted upon unarmed populations. We cannot but deplore those cases of police torture which are alleged to occur in Nations dear to Us and of which so much has been said. We hope, for the very honour of those same nations, that the facts will disprove the existence of such cases. We ourselves have made several interventions, in accordance with Our duty, not without positive hopes.

We are caused acute suffering by the intolerable and clandestine traffic in drugs, which is so well, but disastrously, organized. The drugs are poison both to physical, psychical and moral health, yet are even spread among the young, indeed among the young, indeed among the young most of all. It seems to us that it is degrading for civilized society when persons are kidnapped in order to be made the means of acquiring venal and vindicative ends through threats. Our heart is continually weighed down by the economic and civic want of developing peoples and not a few social classes. We are always grieved by negation of religious liberty—but we have to bear that grief silently—when religious liberty fails to be granted sufficient civil rights in some places, in spite of declamations of so many principles. Sometimes there is not even means of civil and private expression of peaceful profession of the Christian faith.

These disorders are all the more out of keeping with the Easter mystery because a factor of will makes them criminal and deplorable. But this painful " review of the situation " must also take in that immense area of suffering which a great part of mankind bears but has not willed. We wish to send that comfort which the Cross offers for human sorrow to the sick, to the poor, to the imprisoned, to the orphaned, to the widowed ... to all who suffer and weep, for the Cross offers redeeming fruit and creative motivations.

But let Us cease here. With our minds full of consciousness of our moral, physical and material ills, let us go on towards the " spes unica ", our only hope, the Cross of Christ, no longer the trophy of death but the trophy of re-arisen life. May your Easter be like that, with Our Apostolic Blessing.

CHARITY BRINGS THE CHURCH TOGETHER

On Holy Thursday, 26 March, Pope Paul went to his Cathedral Church, the Lateran Basilica, and celebrated the Mass in Coena Domini. *After the Gospel he washed the feet of 12 young men and preached the following homily.*

Venerated Brethren and all beloved Children!

We should dearly like to listen in inward silence to the grand voices which rise from the sublime liturgy that we are celebrating in this holy place, which is a *magnum stratum*—a wide place—which is grand and ornate, the cenacle par excellence of the Roman Catholic Church, and at this moment tense with religious and human emotions and thoughts.

But Our ministry requires us to speak, and so We will offer some elementary suggestions to your benevolent attention. May they serve to vivify our thought about evident and fundamental aspects of this rite and raise our minds into a symphony, a common spiritual chorus.

The first thing We wish to mention concerns ecclesial communion. It gathers us here, and here it acquires singular fullness and a meaning all of its own. This is a particular moment of communion amongst us, among those who have accepted our invitation and brought us the gift of their presence. If ever a happy occasion is offered to us in which to know the reality of the Lord's words: " Where two or three are gathered together in my name, there am I in the midst of them " (*Mt.* 18, 20), this is it. His name, and his name alone is the pole of our presence here. It comes through as if he were already here in person, just as he shortly will be in the sacramental way. From this moment on he is filling our souls with himself, is making them fellows in the faith, in concord, in peace, in joy of knowing and feeling ourselves to be " church ", that is, union, the one fold, his mystical body.

Now all distances disappear from among us, all diffidence, all indifference, all estrangement disappear; all resentments, all rivalries go, and may each of us succeed in experiencing " how good and pleasant it is for brethren to dwell together in unity " (*Ps.* 132, 1). May everyone be aware in himself that the good fortune of being " one heart and one mind " (*Ac.* 4, 32), as the first Christian community was, means making a reality of our exacting title of Catholic Christians. The first requirement demanded of us in order to sit at the meal of Holy Thursday (cf. *Lk.* 22, 24) is charity, *inside* the Church, the charity which brings the Church together and composes it, the charity which gives it its specific quality of being " mystical body " and makes brethren of all those who accept its organized sociality (*Mt.* 23, 8; *Lk.* 10, 16), and that humble charity which means friendship and solidarity among us faithful followers and ministers of Christ.

He is here

So let us live this fleeting hour with more togetherness than ever. But what is the purpose, what is the intention in it? Why have we gathered here? This raises the second suggestion which We desire to put to you. It too is very evident. We are here for a commemoration. This is a memorial service. It is still a Mass, as always, but we desire to bring out its commemorative character particularly today. We are celebrating the commemoration of the Lord. We are obeying what we may describe as his last will, expressed in the words, " Do this in memory of me " (*Lk.* 22, 19; *1 Cor.* 11, 25). Our whole mind is being filled with memory of him, of Jesus. We should like to be able to recall him in our imagination, just as he was, his appearance, his face, the sound of his voice, the light of his eyes, the movements of his hands ... No outward picture of him has come down to us. But we can think with wonder of that profoundly touching image that is on the Sacred Shroud; we can think, as our own minds suggest to us, of pious pictures of him painted by our favourite great artists and of descriptions given by learned and holy people. But we will do so always with that dissatisfaction which is peculiar to us moderns, who have too much of the civilization of the image. The reason is that his image is not revealed to our gaze; it is presented solely to our eschatological yearnings: " Come, Lord Jesus! " (*Apoc.* 22, 20).

Our memory must be content with another form of his being present—his words! Then the whole of the Gospel passes before our eyes; but our minds halt at the words which Christ uttered at that last nocturnal supper and which he asked us to remember particularly. What words? Oh, we know them well: " Take and eat: this is my body; take and drink: this is the cup of my blood ".

That ritual meal was the passover meal (cf. *Lk.* 22, 7 sqq.). It was to be the object of undying memory, but under a new aspect, no longer that of the slaying and eating of the lamb, the sign and pledge of the old alliance; it was now to be under the aspect of bread and wine, transmuted into the body and blood of Jesus. At this point the agape becomes mystery. The Lord's presence becomes a live, real one. The sense appearances remain what they were, those of bread and wine; but their substance, their reality is inwardly changed. The appearances remain only in order to signify that which Jesus' divine, therefore omnipotent, words said they were: his body and blood. We are astounded. One of the reasons for our astonishment is that this marvel is exactly what the Lord told us to remember, and indeed to renew.

A matter of confidence

" Do this ", he said to the Apostles, that is, he transmitted to them the power of repeating his act of consecration, not just to think about it again, but to do it again. On that unique evening the sacrament of holy orders was instituted together with the sacrament of the Eucharist, as its custodian, as its source. We are astonished, and are at once tempted. Is it true? Is it really true? How can those sacrosanct syllables uttered by Christ be explained: " This is my body, this is my blood "? Can we find some way of interpreting them that shall not do violence to our elementary way of thinking, to our habits of metaphysical thought? We even find ourselves uttering the repulsive comments of Jesus' audience at Capharnaum: " This is a hard saying; who wants to listen to it? " (*Jn.* 6, 61). But the Lord does not allow doubtings, nor does he permit elusive exegesis of the authentic reality of his words as given in the texts. He made it a matter of confidence: he would let his dearly beloved group of disciples split up rather than exempt them from assenting to his paradoxical but true words. He put this to them in equally hard terms: " Do you want to leave? ".

Love consummated in Death

So this is a decisive hour, the hour of faith, the hour in which Jesus' words are wholly accepted, even though they be incomprehensible. It is the hour in which we celebrate the " mystery of faith ", the hour in which, with blind yet wise abandon, we repeat Simon Peter's reply, " Lord, to whom shall we go? Thou hast the words of eternal life. And we believe and are sure that thou art that Christ, the Son of the living God " (*Jn.* 6, 69-70).

Yes, brethren, this is the hour of faith. Faith absorbs and consumes the immense, dark cloud of objections which our ignorance on the one hand and the refined dialectics of profane thought on the other, pile up on our minds. But our minds humbly and blessedly let themselves be struck by the Master's light-filled words. Tremulous as the suppliant in the Gospel, they say " Lord, I believe; Lord, help thou my unbelief! " (*Mk.* 9, 24).

Yet faith asks questions. What is the meaning of this way of commemorating the Lord? What is the meaning and the value of this memorial, this sacrament of presence, of this mystery of faith? What is the Lord's main aim, the one he desired to impress upon his followers' memory at that last meeting and supper?

There are some who do not ask this question, almost so as not to discover a new astounding truth. But We cannot halt now without taking up the last treasure in Jesus' last testament. Everything obliges us to do so, because everything was extremely purposeful and dramatic on the last evening of his temporal life. If we only observed this aspect of the last supper it would be enough to give us endless ecstatic meditation. The spiritual tension in it all almost takes our breath away. The Master's appearance, words, gestures and discourses are flooded with the awareness and profundity of someone close to death. He feels death, he sees it. He expresses it.

Two notes rise above the rest in this atmosphere of awe, bathed in silence by the Master's acts and predictions. They are the notes of love and death. The washing of the feet was an impressive example of humble love, the commandment, the last and newest commandment: Love one another as I have loved you. Then that anguish at the approaching betrayal, that sadness which comes through in the Master's words and attitudes; that mystical, enchanting air of the last discourses: they are almost soliloquies, overflowing from a heart opening up to make its last confidences. Everything is concentrated in the sacramental action which has just been recorded: body and blood! Yes, love and death are represented there, and one word alone is enough to express them. It is: sacrifice. Death is represented there, bloody death, the death which would separate Christ's blood from his body: an immolation, a victim.

And the victim was a willing one, a conscious one, a victim for love's sake, given for us, to be remembered as announcing the death of Jesus, his everlasting sacrifice, until he should return at the end of the world (*1 Cor.* 11, 26). Christ sealed his offering of himself by means of a rite, which his disciples could renew, once they were made apostles and priests. It was the offering of himself as a victim to the Father, for our salvation, for our love. It is the Mass. It is the example and the source of the love which gives itself, even going so far as death.

This is Holy Thursday which we are recalling and celebrating. It is the heart and sum of Christian life. It is the mandate, the memorial, the passion, the charity of Christ being transfused into his Church, into us, so that we may live from him and for him (*Jn.* 6, 57), offer ourselves up in sacrifice also for the salvation of the world (cf. *Jn.* 12, 24 sqq.), and, one day, rise with him again (cf. *Jn.* 6, 54, 58).

ALL MUST BE MESSENGERS
OF PEACE!

*On Easter Sunday, March 29th, the Holy Father
celebrated Mass at an altar erected in front of
St. Peter's, after which the Pope went to the
central balcony over the main entrance to the
Basilica and there delivered his Easter message.
He concluded by imparting his Apostolic Blessing "Urbi et orbi". The following is the
English translation of his address as supplied
to the press.*

Men and Brothers!

What other greeting can we extend to you on this happy
Easter day, if not that very one which the Risen Christ
expressed to the community of his disciples while they were still
oppressed by uncertainty and fear: " Peace be with you! " (*Jn.*
20, 19)?

Yes, we dare to make our own these tranquil and strong tidings, with our voice faithfully echoing his. In the name of Jesus
alive again in our historical reality and already existing in a new
blessed and eternal reality which is beyond history, we repeat:
Peace be with you!

To you that are united in this forum of peoples and experiencing to some extent his hidden presence promised everywhere that
there is a gathering in his name; to you dearly beloved of Rome,
to you pilgrims and visitors to the City where every citizen of the
world can feel at home; to you that are ministers with us of this
Apostolic See; to you the illustrious representatives of peoples,
bearers here of a message and fellow-builders with us of that
friendship which we hope to make rule over the earth, we extend
our sincere good wish: Peace be with you!

For common progress

And raising the voice that originates in our heart we extend this serene paschal wish to the vaster audience which we wish to hear us: to Italy the nation closest to us; to each and every nation of the world and to all mankind. That in justice and in liberty, concord and collaboration for common progress may be reestablished, we desire that our wish of peace penetrate and be effective in those places where local wars still rage and where negotiations are under way and finding obstacles in overcoming and resolving these conflicts: Peace, peace be with you!

To you, the youth of this generation who find fault with the malfunctions of an advanced society and are looking for future developments in truer human achievements; to you, workers, still in need of greater social equity, not found in destruction but in the balance of the common good; to you, builders of the scientific and technical world; to you, qualified exponents of culture; to you, statesmen, promoters and arbiters of the public good; to you all, workers in the modern world, go our greetings of peace.

To families, to schools, workshops, barracks, hospitals, and prisons, to every place: Peace!

Perhaps many of those who listen to us will ask by what title we make ourselves the bearers of this greeting of peace. At once we answer: all of us must be the messengers of peace because this is the gospel which must become common to all. For our part, we have said it before: this cry did not come originally from us; as we have heard it from Christ, so as his spokesman we repeat it to you. It is his peace, and we proclaim it to all.

Certainty and sureness

And if someone asks us what is the special meaning that our greeting of peace has in this circumstance, we can answer with simplicity that our Easter peace means a great certainty and a great sureness. Do you not see, Men and Brothers, that all of us today have need especially of certainty in thought and sureness in action. This is what happens: the more man seeks, studies, thinks, discovers and builds his giant tower of modern culture, the less sure is he of the validity of his reasoning, of objective truth, of the existential usefulness of knowledge, the less sure he becomes of his own immortality. Doubt assails him, clouds his mind, shakes him, humiliates him. He takes refuge in the evidence of his wonderful achievements, he sustains himself with the sincerity of his experiences, he relies upon high-sounding words, in vogue at the moment. The reality is that fear casts him into reeling doubt as to the value of everything he has done.

On our part, with this Easter wish, we are able to offer man a secure foundation, shipwrecked as he is on the sea of his own humanism. To be sure, it is not a base which we have made ourselves, in competition with all the others that the modern world offers to human uncertainty, for we, small weak men that we are, do not presume to rely on any power of our own. Yet it is true that we possess a sure foundation upon which life may be built; the life of religion—in that incomparable certainty of which for twenty centuries this tribune has given the witness of Peter: Christ is risen (cf. *Ac.* 2, 24). This is the event, new, wonderful, trũe and undeniable, on which everything is based; this is, now and forever, " the stone which was rejected by the builders ... And there is salvation in no one else " (*Ac.* 4, 11-12). But even the life of this world can sense the advantages of such a vital firmness. In the words of the Council:

" Appointed Lord by his resurrection ... Christ is now at work in the hearts of men through the power of his Spirit, arousing not only a desire for the age to come, but by that very fact animating, purifying and strengthening those noble longings too by which the human family makes its life more human and strives to render the whole earth submissive to this goal " (*Gaudium et spes*, 38).

We have this conviction, and with peace we offer it to you. We offer it as a humble fraternal reminder:

An inner dominion

If you, men of our time, do not wish to be deceived by your very wisdom, nor wish to turn your very progress into a weapon of destruction, remember the prior claim of that kingdom of God which Christ proclaimed as the supreme justice of the world.

If you wish freedom to be fully operative, personally and

socially, so that it should not result in the inner dominion of the lower man over the higher one and so that this freedom should not cause smaller and weaker powers to be overwhelmed by those richer and more heavily armed, remember the great champion of conscience responsible before the unchangeable law of evangelical Love, remember the defender of the poor, the little, the weak, the suffering, remember Christ.

If you really want to bring the world to its organic unity, remember the principles from which that unity draws its logic and its possibility—the brotherhood which Christ has taught us and made an easy duty for us.

If you wish to give the modern world its full adult emancipation, do not forget the root from which our civilization takes its inspiration and draws the sap which brings it maturity—the idea of man redeemed.

And in hope we transmit to you and to the world: certainty, the certainty of faith, security, the security of love, the certainty and security which come to us from the Easter message. Indeed, in terms of confidence and hope may our peace be with you, the dawn of an ever new and serene day in the history of the world.

Peace and blessing!

CHRIST'S PLAN OF REDEMPTION
REQUIRES PERSONAL INITIATIVE

We who have gathered here today are still imbued with the memory, the emotion and the grace—may it please God—of the celebration of the Easter mystery.

The paschal mystery. This is a happy modern theological term which the Council often used. It used it to sum up the work of redemption which the Lord accomplished through his sacrifice and his resurrection, through his extension of it to mankind, in other words through the work of grace and the application of it to individual souls by means of the sacraments. The liturgical celebration of the liturgy recalls and renews the wonder of this redemptive economy, especially in the Holy Mass (cf. *Sacr. Conc.*, 5). The expression " paschal Mystery " is full of meaning. It ought to nourish in our minds the synthetic concept of the events, the teachings, the graces and the duties which are linked with the story of our salvation and the permanent relevance which that history has for each one of us.

We shall do well to give as much thought as we can to what refers to Christ in the Easter mystery. This is the central, biblical, theological and spiritual theme of our faith. We have been meditating on it during Holy Week in the absorbing vision of the divine and human person of Jesus. By doing so we have imitated St. Paul, who did not think of knowing anything but Christ and him crucified (cf. *1 Cor.* 2, 2); or like St. Ignatius of Antioch, who said, " He it is whom I seek, he who died for us; it is he whom I desire, he who was raised up again for us " (*Rom.* 6, 1). Finally, like St. Francis at La Verna, and like the faithful people at the Way of the Cross and in the Liturgy of the Easter Vigil. It is always a matter of zeal and devotion, with attention fastened upon him, Jesus Christ.

The Plan of Redemption

But the paschal mystery demands that we give even fuller thought to it. We cannot look at Jesus's personal drama as if it concerned no one but himself and had nothing to do with mankind and with us in particular. The Easter mystery was not an isolated event. It was linked with our own destiny, with our salvation. This broad view, which sees the work of our redemption in Christ's death and resurrection, obliges us to search for the plan, for the operative design in it all, especially in the way it is applied to every single human being. This thought provides the pattern of our spiritual meditations after the feast of Easter. Easter is the feast of Christ risen from the dead. Is it also a feast for us mortal men? Is it his feast only—or is it ours too? When we think about it more deeply, we get a better understanding of the plan of redemption, and we can see that the feast is more joyous if we can really extend it from his passion and death to his glorious resurrection.

St. Paul himself tells us that the resurrection is the necessary complement of the Passover mystery. One striking phrase sums up his many teachings about it: " He was delivered up for our offences, and was raised again for our justification " (*Rom.* 4, 25). A renowned commentator has this to say: " Jesus' resurrection was not a supernatural luxury provided for the elect to admire; it was not a mere reward for his merits; it was not only a means of sustaining our faith and a pledge of our hope; it was an essential consummation and an integral part of the redemption itself " (PRAT, *La Théol. de St. Paul*, II, 256).

Our Christian Life

So, when we fully reconstruct the Lord's paschal mystery we find that a great theological principle enters at this point into the picture of our faith. It is a principle to which we ought to devote our most attentive admiration and appreciation. It is the principle of communion, of solidarity, of extension. It is the principle which properly speaking constitutes redemption, that is, the principle that recognizes the representation, the recapitulation of all mankind in Christ, in the sense that what was accomplished in him may be shared by us. His fate can be ours too. His passion can be ours. His resurrection can be ours.

In this plan for the salvation of the human race everything depends on the living relationship which we can establish between Christ and ourselves. Does this relationship come about all by itself? Does it come *en masse* or in individual cases? God can give his mercy such beadth that it can transcend the very plan of salvation which he himself has established. But this plan tells us that the saving relationship with Christ demands some personal initiative on our part, however slight. In other words, it requires response from our liberty, from our faith, from our love. It lays down conditions which make the flow of Christ's saving causality possible. This aspect of the Easter mystery shows us that our salvation comes about in a number of successive stages, which make up the story of our personal redemption; they make up our Christian life.

As we know, the Christian life begins with baptism, the sacrament of initiation, of rebirth, the sacrament which reproduces the Lord's death and resurrection in every believer (personal faith, the faith of the Church presented to the neophyte, precedes baptism). " Know you not ", says St. Paul, " that all of us who have been baptized into Jesus Christ were baptized into his death? Therefore we are buried with him by baptism into death, that, just as Christ was raised up from the dead by the glory of the Father, so we also should walk in newness of life " (*Rom.* 6, 3, 4; cf. *Col.* 2, 12).

Thinking and feeling with Christ

Now comes the second stage in our Christian regeneration, in which our time in this worldly existence is involved. It is the stage of new life, the life of grace, that is, of the Holy Spirit poured out by Christ into us (cf. *Jn.* 14, 26; 15, 26; 16, 7), a good and holy Christian life. Can we say, *our* life? Do we live *per ipsum, et cum ipso et in ipso*, as the Canon of the Mass says— Through him, and with him and in him? Are we aware of the newness of Christian life? The demands which its mystical and moral genuineness make? Do we really know that " making our

Easters duty ", that is, taking part in the paschal mystery, requires us to have fidelity, consistency and perfection in our way of thinking, feeling and living?

Do we live our baptism? Do we live the communion with Christ which we have received in the Eucharist at Easter? Do we live, shall we live our Easter? We have so often watered down and emptied our specific title of Christian that we have deprived it of its vitality and lustre.

The question of our practical participation in the paschal mystery is basically the most serious and comprehensive problem in our present existence. It is coextensive with the problems, the events, the experiences of our natural existence, and after Easter it gives us feelings of hope and joy.

This sentiment is a gift, a charism, one the Christian ought never be without (cf. *Rom.* 8, 24; *2 Cor.* 7, 4). It is the prelude to the final stage of the paschal mystery, which is: fullness of salvation, complete immersion of our humble life in the infinite life of God, in the other world.

It is not a dream. It is not a myth, it is not spiritual idealism. It is the truth, it is the reality of the paschal mystery. Remember that, with Our Apostolic Blessing.

111

WHAT YOUTH EXPECTS
OF THE " MASS MEDIA "

The following is the text of the Holy Father's message for the " World Day of Social Communications " issued on 6th April.

The theme of World Communications Day this year touches what I am sure is one of your chief interests: " Social Communications and youth ". Undoubtedly, it is clear to everyone that there is an immense responsibility on the part of all, before history and God Himself, to put to good account the extraordinary opportunities offered by the communications media to help young people to inform and form themselves, to bring out the real problems of the world, to seek the authentic values of life and to live up to their calling as individual persons and Christians.

It is indeed a burning issue for all men of good will, for private organizations both national and international, for the Church no less; all are to ask themselves: what are the young people of tomorrow going to be like as they grow up in the world being constructed today? And you young people, what kind of society will you yourselves construct when the destiny of the world will have passed into your own hands?

Dear sons and daughters, in the full consciousness of Our pastoral responsibility, we wish to say to you all: tomorrow will be precisely what we shall have made it with the grace of God.

Need We call to mind once again, now that the phenomenon is assuming ever larger proportions, that the press, motion pictures, radio and television are tending to hide, perhaps even supplant, what the traditional vehicles of culture, that is, contacts at home, at school and in the parish, as well as the teaching of educators, used to allow past generations to hand down to their heirs. These days it is the media of social communications that provide new sources of knowledge and culture, with their considerable power of moving men's feelings and minds, together with the train of

112

ideas and stirrings of the imagination carried by the sounds and sights they transmit.

Truly they are wonderful means for broadening one's outlook, establishing contacts, communicating and sharing. Obviously however, only as long as they remain in actual fact means to an end, the one end worthy of the name: the service of the whole of mankind and of the whole man (cf. *Populorum progressio*, 14). Unfortunately, all too often, the contrary is the case. We witness young people and children, used as easily-secured consumers by an industry that makes itself its own end, being dragged into the pit-falls of eroticism and violence or led along the perilous paths of incertitude, anxiety and anguish. It is not asking too much that all right-thinking persons should unite at last to sound a cry of alarm and to put an end to enterprises that deserve to be called corrupting.

Who is unaware of the urgency of putting to good account the means of social communication with their stirring mode of address through sound, image, color and movement, to make of them real modern instruments for communing among men, that measure up to the expectations of young people? What excellent fare they can provide, so long as it is wholesome and the organism prepared to receive it and assimilate it without being intoxicated! Undoubtedly, they have a great deal to offer to youth: choice of recreation, a wealth of information, for some the beginnings of an education before they can even read or write. We wish to stress this during this " World Year of Education " promoted by the United Nations at the opening of the second decade of development. The communications media are capable of providing youth with access to a culture of quality as well as a taste for the authentic values of brotherhood, peace, justice and general welfare.

This is an enormous task, a truly glorious enterprise, for all who set in motion these exceptionally powerful instruments for the service of youth. All this however, will not take us far, unless parents and educators play their part in helping young people to choose, to judge and to assimilate what is presented to them, so that they too can become complete human persons and Christians. Not much can be achieved if the young people themselves remain passive as though under the spell of these powerful attractions, held captive by desire and incapable of self-control.

Finally, we ask ourselves: who is it that can bring to youth this message of true life, the sincere and courageous word that they consciously or unconsciously seek? Millions of men have shared the same thrill before the images brought to them of man's first steps on the moon. Who is it that can bring them to experience together the same deep emotion before the God of love Who came down to walk on our earth as a man, " to call us all to participate as sons in the life of the Living God, Father of all men "? (cf. *Populorum progressio*, 21).

We lend our words of warm encouragement to the numerous pastors of souls, priests, religious and lay people who with true zeal endeavour to seek through the communications media a new language, and find it they must, to announce to the young the Good News, that always remains astounding. No one will doubt that the young people of today really await this announcement. They yearn for this witness. They too know how to recognize with profound joy Him Who is the answer to their most radical and disquieting questionings, Who " for us has become wisdom, justice, sanctification and redemption " (*1 Cor.* 1, 30).

" Young people, seek Christ, in order to remain young " (St. Augustine, *Ad fratres in eremo*, Sermon 44): this is our hope, this is our prayer.

With the earnest wish that parents, educators and all communicators through the media will make the best of the opportunity offered by the Word Day specially dedicated to them, for beneficial reflection and fruitful resolutions for the greater advantage of youth, We address to all Our affectionate and confident Apostolic Blessing.

From the Vatican, April 6, 1970.

On the Feast of the Annunciation of Our Lord.

PAULUS PP. VI

FAITH—PRINCIPLE OF UNITY AND CHARITY

Once more, the Church is the subject of our spiritual thinking today. The Church is the theme of our time. It is the Council's theme. It rises most readily of all in the minds of those who enter this basilica. It is such a vast and complex theme that it seems to be beyond our powers of thought. Yet it becomes comparatively simple if we meditate upon its various aspects, fixing our minds upon one among the many.

We are once more mindful of the Easter ceremonies. They brought us conviction of a mysterious but quite clear truth: the Church is born out of the paschal mystery. This means to say that the Church is the result of Redemption, and she is always in a process of being perfected. Everyone knows how this concept was symbolized by the blood and water which flowed from Christ's side, pierced by a lance after his death on the cross (*Jn.* 19, 34). " De ipso sanguine et aqua significatur nata Ecclesia ", St. Augustine said: The Church is shown to have been born from that blood and the water (*Sermo V*, 3; *PL* 38, 55), because " sacramenta Ecclesiae profluxerunt "; the Church's sacraments flowed out (in *Jn.* 15, 4, 8; *PL* 35, 1513).

We know that the Church emanates from Christ. He is its founder; He is its Head (cf. *Col.* 1, 22; cf. JOURNET, *L'Eglise*, III, 590-594). That is clear. But now we want to ask a particular question: When does a Christian arise? How are we born into the Church and incorporated into it, that is, into Christ?

But this, too, is well known to all: we are born into the Church and become Christians (the two things coincide, they are inseparable) with baptism. But baptism requires a condition. It is a very important one and forms part of the definition of a Christian. That condition is faith.

The Christian is someone who is faithful; he is a believer. The liturgy of baptism brings out this indispensable condition, this

115

vital principle of the Christian's new supernatural existence. Indeed the liturgy of baptism begins with a dialogue in which a question is put to the catechumen or the child brought to baptism in someone's arms. In the latter case it is put through the godparent, who on the one hand represents the child itself, and on the other hand represents the ecclesial community. The question is " What do you ask of the Church of God? ". The answer is: " Faith ".

A vital Principle

Faith is the entrance key. It is the threshold. It is the first step. It is the first act required of a person desiring to belong to God's kingdom, which leads on from this beginning to everlasting life. The early Church took care to affirm the primary demand of faith in decisive terms: " He who believes in the Son (of God, that is, in Jesus Christ) has eternal life; but he who does not believe in the Son (of God) shall not see life " (*Jn.* 3, 36).

St. Paul had many things to say in testimony of this, and here is one of them which condenses his teaching, " If you will confess with your mouth the Lord Jesus, and will believe in your heart that God has raised him from the dead, you shall be saved " (*Rom.* 10, 9).

Proclamation of the Word

Let us look into this. The true cause of salvation is Christ himself; indeed, it is the Holy Spirit, whom Jesus, the Words of God and man, assumed into the glory of the Father, sends to mankind and to his Church (cf. *Jn.* 16, 17). The Holy Spirit is the principle of our new life, of the life of grace. He is the inspirer of faith itself. But the divine plan of salvation provides for conditions. Two of these are most important. One is interior: free assent to the faith. The other is exterior: apostolic proclamation of the Word of God, of the divine truth in which to believe, the Church's authentic teaching.

We will not here recall the many problems which weigh upon modern man in regard to faith. What a formidable tangle! We all know something about them. Today the faith seems to have become difficult, and even impossible! Some feel that the old clash between faith and reason is coming up again, and in an insoluble form.

Modern psychology raises a series of other difficulties, which makes the way to faith, pedagogy of belief, a rather complicated one. Today fashionable ideas, speculative, practical and social, are making such a noise that they are even replacing faith's enlightening and confirmatory function in the minds of many, at least in certain milieus and at certain moments in life.

Ideologies carry people away. Public opinion dominates. Moreover, there is no lack of those who mistake some spiritual experience of their own for faith. In their conversations with themselves, interiorly, they think they have a sufficient faith of their own; they are content with this conscience they have worked out, even though it remains silent about the supreme questions of human destinies and the world's mysteries. They try to resign themselves with stoic, long-suffering magnanimity.

Then there are others who do not wish to break away from the Christian religion entirely. They apply a selective criterion to their faith. They say they believe in some dogmas, but disregard others which seem to them to be unacceptable, incomprehensible, or just too much. They content themselves with a faith to the measure of their own intelligence. They may even push this criterion of independent judgment of the truths of the faith to the length of that free examination of conscience which allows everyone to think in his own way; it deprives faith itself of its objective consistency and takes away its regal prerogative of being the principle of unity and charity.

Fortunately there is a whole body of writing, from which those interested can gain information and instruction with which to follow in the paths of the faith. These are open to the people of our time, perhaps more than they have ever been. This is not the moment to explore this forest of problems. We will only recall the importance of the relationship between Church and faith. As everyone knows, faith is a free response and a full response to God speaking, God revealing. " To God who reveals ", the Council says, " is due the obedience of faith " (cf. *Rom.* 16, 26; 1, 5; *2 Cor.* 10, 5-6); " with that faith man entirely abandons himself to God ... " (*Dei Verbum*, 5). This will seem an illogical and difficult act, but in reality, when we are desirous of the truth alone, the Spirit infuses an unutterable testimony into the heart (cf. *Jn.* 15, 26). It is therefore an act full of light and comfort, desirous of nothing but to be full and authentic, an immediate yearning for effusion of spirit and communion.

That is how the Church is born. The Church is the school of Christ's pupils (cf. *Jn.* 6, 45). The Church is the society of those who believe. The Church is the community, indeed the communion of the true faithful. Faith is the vital presupposition for membership of Christ's mystical Body, which is the Church. It is whole and perfect faith in revealed doctrine and a blessed and discriminating guarantee of belonging to the one true Church of Christ.

We have the supreme good fortune of having the faith, the faith of the Lord, the faith of the Apostles, the faith of the Church, our " mother and teacher ".

The fact that we are here is a sign that the Lord has offered us his prime and incomparable gift. Let us become aware at this moment of its inestimable and delicate value. Let us ask him to enable us to keep it, like St. Paul, who said *fidem servavi* (*2 Tim.* 4, 7). Like St. Peter, let us be always *fortes in fide* (*1 Pet.* 5, 9). With Our Apostolic Benediction.

HAVE CONFIDENCE
IN THE CHURCH!

On Saturday, April 11th, the Holy Father gave audience to the participants in the VI General Assembly of the Italian Episcopal Conference. The Chairman, Cardinal Poma, Archbishop of Bologna, delivered an address, and the Pope replied as follows.

We welcome the sixth General Assembly of the Italian Episcopal Conference. We welcome you as Bishop of Rome and consequently as a rightful member of the Conference itself. That is to say, We welcome you with feelings of fraternity, solidarity and communion. We welcome you as the Successor of St. Peter. We take note at the same time of the relationship of collegiality and pastoral function which unites Us to one and all of you " as the visible source and foundation of the unity of the bishops and the multitude of the faithful ", as the Council said (*Lumen gentium*, 23). That collegiality expresses in unbounded solicitude for you (cf. *2 Cor.* 11, 28; *Rom.* 12, 8) that unbounded love which we owe to Christ as prompted by his love for us (*Lk* 22, 32).

We might feel tempted to devote a moment, a long moment of analysis, of reflection and contemplation to this dutiful and affectionate pastoral interest of Ours. Your presence brings before Us a vast and all-embracing picture of the life of the Church in Italy. It is a view of history and tradition unlike all others. At the same time it is fresh and new, and is shaped by modern structures which have never existed before and which are already promising rejuvenated and organic vitality. How many aspects of it would have to be admired, examined, and commented upon! What inspiring criteria for the new ecclesial structure would need to be indicated and given encouragement: union, organization, collaboration, renewal, evangelical and social style, and so forth!

What well-deserving names We should have to mention in connection with this process of development, for Our own remembrance and gratitude! We will mention one only: that of Cardinal Giovanni Urbani, Patriarch of Venice and Chairman of the Episcopal Conference, who departed unexpectedly a few months ago " in the sign of faith and ... in the sleep of peace ". And then the questions, the problems, the events, and all the comments and suggestions which We should well have in Our heart for you in view of the picture which this Assembly presents to Us?

But We will not give way to the desire to make a discourse befitting the themes which you present to Us—for discretion's sake; and also because you have already dealt amply and wisely with these matters. We take note of this, and We many return to the subject later in detail when the occasion arises.

For the moment it will suffice to pay sincere tribute to the *Relators* of this Assembly and to express lively thanks for the seriousness with which they have conducted their business. We wish to recommend to your attention Cardinal Poma's wide-ranging and profound address, because of the synthesis of the problems which it provides and the guidelines it indicates for solving our problems.

Let one word alone from Us mark this meeting. It is a word We take from Jesus' exhortation to Peter: " Confirm thy brethren " (*Lk.* 22, 32): and that word is confidence.

Signs of happy renewal

Yes, confidence. It does not disregard the difficulties of the present time nor the disappointments which might depress our optimism. Let us not forget the Apostle's own warning: *In timore incolatus vestri tempore conversamini*: Pass the time of your pilgrimage here in fear (*1 Pt.* 1, 17). We sometimes presume to compare Our own case to St. Paul's autobiographical remark of desolation: *foris pugnae, intus timore*: fighting without and fear within (*2 Cor.* 7, 5). But were we to forget the confidence we owe to Providence, which guides the world's destinies, and, certainly in a particularly merciful way, those of the Italian Church, we would be disregarding or wrongly interpreting so many " signs of the times ".

We would be ignoring the generous and noble leaven of the present generation, if we failed to identify in the tumult of present day restlessness and agitations certain aspirations and promises which appear to Us as omens and elements of a happy renewal. We would not be faithful followers of the Master if we did not battle on with confidence, *contra spem in spem*, hoping against hope (*Rom.* 4, 18) in every situation, so as not to deserve his reproach of being men of little faith (*Mt.* 8, 26).

Confidence, then. And so We pass from things to persons. We deliberately refrain from speaking in detail of the Assembly's themes, and We shall pass rapidly and simply into the " pneumatic " or spiritual sphere which transcends it.

The laity's secular autonomy

The first category of persons present to whom We direct Our call to have confidence is that of the Laity. Our fellow Bishops will allow Us to give them this precedence. We see them officially represented on this occasion also in the General Assembly of this Episcopal Conference. This is something new which gives Us reason for confidence. If the Catholic laity wishes to respond to the vocation proper to the whole People of God, as the hierarchical Church has expected for more than a hundred years and as the Council teaches and exhorts, then it will find that it is modelling itself on the early Christian tradition and on the theological requirements of its constitution. It will see the authenticity of Christian prayer and Christian morals becoming evident and exemplary. It will find its own structure being strengthened in fraternal concord and practical charity. It will see its effect on the world radiating more widely and more beneficially. For that vocation acknowledges the dignity and function of the common baptismal priesthood, it unites the laity organically with the ecclesial body, it destines it to Christian perfection, it authoritatively summons it to the spreading of Christ's kingdom and to the active exercise of the apostolate, it commits it to obedience and collaboration with the Pastors responsible for guiding the faithful.

We have confidence in the Catholic laity. The humble personal testimony of our priestly life affirms that confidence, and the exercise of Our pastoral Magisterium confirms it. We desire that you Catholic lay people should have confidence in the Church. You owe the Church this twofold, generous and heartfelt gift: trust and fidelity. Trust and loyalty do not impose passive assent; they are not docile sloth, as some perhaps may believe. When supported by trust, fidelity is cohesion, coherence, defence and collaboration. It is also relative participation and corresponsibility. It is moreover a stimulus to initiative, both direct and disciplined, entailing the liberty which is proper to the adult and mature Christian who has educated his conscience in the light of the Church's authentic doctrine, especially in the field of temporal activity. In this respect it may be said that the Council has on the one hand given honour to the " ecclesial " character of the Catholic laity, and on the other, has acknowledged it as having a " secular " autonomy, which in its own sphere distinguishes its responsibility from that of the Church. This ought to inspire the laity with the confidence of which We are speaking.

There is certainly no need to believe that the Church's power, both in doctrine and in action, comes to the Pastors from the ecclesial community acting in a democratic way. That would be a false opinion. But when it is borne in mind that in the Church the Pastors—by the will of Christ and by sacramental investiture— are established as teachers and dispensers of the divine mysteries for the service of the whole community and also for the good of those who are outside it, when moreover it is also borne in mind that that entails an original ecclesial order, not modelled on the conventional patterns of temporal society, then it will be easy and a good idea to establish new organic relationships between the Hierarchy and the Catholic laity which will give the latter the dignity and activity assigned to it by the Council. So you must have confidence!

Likewise, We say to you, Priests, to you who are here and to those fellow priests whom you morally represent: Have confidence!

Confidence in whom? In what? And why? The answer to that is more complicated.

But let Us say at once: confidence in Christ. Yes, in him, immense trust, personal and total trust. We must trust greatly in Christ. He desires it (cf. *Jn.* 14, 1; 16, 33; *Mk.* 6, 50). He has called you (*Mk.* 3, 13). He has conformed you to himself, he has loved you to the extreme, divinely. Your spirituality ought to be based on this confidence, on this theology. From it comes that predominant divine causality which is shown in his calling you to be his disciples, his chosen ones, his friends, his witnesses, his ministers, his apostles. You know this indescribable history, which goes down into the depths of your psychology and expresses itself in the exterior events of your life in the humility of your often extenuating and heroic service. Reread that autobiographical part of St. Paul and make his supreme confidence your own also: *Scio cui credidi* (*2 Tim.* 1, 8-12): I know whom I have believed.

An artificial crisis

Therefore: have confidence in yourselves, confidence We would say in the canonical definition of your ecclesial and social identity. We too know the many and grave causes of present day ecclesial unrest. We ponder before the Lord about their validity. We approach with a fresh look and dwell with loving intensity of spirit on the so called " crisis " which is nowadays tormenting so many levels of the Catholic priesthood and which so much engages the attention of public opinion. But public opinion often dramatizes events and dreams up fantasies, exaggerating and distorting the facts. We too suffer as We observe this situation in the ranks of the Clergy, and We suffer all the more because it seems to Us to be sometimes artificially heightened. But We wonder whether weighty problems are not being created which might be avoided if there were a little more reverence for tradition, from which we have inherited all and from which we have received that impalpable treasure of the famous *depositum*. It is not a weight to drag around, but it is a reserve of certainties and energies for the Church living in history.

What distresses Us in this regard is the supposition, more or less current in certain quarters, that it is possible to prescind from the Church as it is, from its doctrine, from its constitution, from the graphical background of which it is the outcome, and that it is possible to invent and create a new one, according to ideological and sociological patterns, which are themselves changeable and not supported by intrinsic ecclesial requirements.

123

Thus we sometimes find that it is not so much the Church's enemies without who jolt and weaken her as some of her own children within, some of whom claim to be her uninhibited champions. And what shall We say of those cases, fortunately very rare, yet much publicized, of priests and religious who proudly parade the open and sacriligious violation of their solemn pledges to Christ and to the Church? *Necesse est ut veniant scandala; verumtamen vae homini illi, per quem scandalum venit* (*Mt.* 18, 7). It must needs be that scandals come; but woe to the man by whom scandal comes.

What courage, what new love we have need of to overcome with fortitude and charity such painful blows!

We would hope that you would not be influenced by such a questionable attitude. To you, priests, and to you, religious, We say, *Sobrii estote, et vigilate* ... together with what follows (*1 Pt.* 5, 8).

Love of Christ and the Church

Have confidence. The essential definition of your character as ministers of the Catholic Church must not be called in question. Be strong and be happy to be what you are. Like Christ, you have been *given* to the Church, and as such you have been assumed into that superlative fusion of twofold love of Christ and of the Church. This confers incomparable interior fullness of charity and happiness upon your personality. It makes your life of sacrifice in the midst of the community of the brethren and in the midst of the secular world such an ardent sign of the kingdom of God as only celibacy together with freely chosen priesthood can achieve.

Have confidence in your vocation. The life of the priest demands many other sacrifices besides this. You know them. His life is a life apart. All this concerns the priest's position in contemporary society: it distinguishes you from it, and it engrafts you into it, as the salt of the earth. You are not inhibited by any knowledge of culture and life. It withdraws you from many experiences which are useless, or harmful to your ministry. It frees you from many cares which, as rights and duties, would claim the greater part of your heart and your time, and thus deprive the pastoral service of them.

But We repeat: Have confidence in the Church. It is passing through a time of tension and search. But it has the Council to guide it. That great event shall not be buried in the past, but shall yield its fruits for the future. You, priests, will experience its new demands and new benefits. The prospects favour the recognition of your personality, to assist your every legitimate need, to promote your closer collaboration and adequate corresponsibility in the Bishop's pastoral care to foster renewal of structures that might be outdated and methods which have become too old and empirical, all for the purpose of greater efficiency in your ministry.

Be strong and be happy in what you are

And now, venerated Brothers, a word of confidence for you. We note every day, as We exercise Our apostolic office, how grave and difficult the bishop's ministry has become. The episcopal function is truly no longer a title of temporal honour, but a duty of pastoral service. The whole bulk of the cares of the Church falls upon the bishop. He may say with St. Paul: *Quis infirmatur, et ego non infirmior? quis scandalizatur et ego non uror?* (*2 Cor.* 11, 29). Who is weak and I am not weak. Who is offended and I burn not? This essential aspect of the sacerdotal ministry, highlighted by the Council (cf. *Lumen gentium*, 24, 32, etc.), and demanded by the Church's historical vicissitude, purifies the episcopal dignity from every possible intrusion of external vanity and earthly power. It marks the figure of the Pastor in a spiritual and practical way as the divine Master desired him to be, in conformity with his example. It assigns him his indispensable great and true function in the ecclesial community, and multiplies his strength even to complete dedication. *Servi enim sumus Ecclesiae,* we shall say to ourselves with St. Augustine (*De opere monachorum*, XXIX; *PL* 40, 577). And we shall be grateful to Cardinal Pellegrino for the Augustinian anthology which he offers us in his fine little work entitled *Verus Sacerdos* (Fossano, 1965). We are therefore not astonished when We often notice, in the exercise of Our Apostolic office, that bishops in office, and not always those who are infirm or aged, and candidates called to the episcopate, try to decline the office. Today, not only because of its intrinsic

125

demands but also because of extrinsic difficulties the office seems to have become insupportable.

This tells Us how you also, Brothers, *socii in passione*, have need of comfort, and of exhortation to confidence.

Vocation and Sacrifices

We could find reasons for confidence in the establishment and increasing efficiency of this Episcopal Conference. It imposes many new duties on the Bishops, but, with marvellous progress, it is also offering them many new helps. We gladly praise and encourage those to whom this is due. But We rather think that some mention must be made of the two chief difficulties which the episcopal ministry is now facing.

The Increasing Efficiency of the IEC

The first difficulty is that of exercising the magisterium. We will not waste words explaining something which all are experiencing with apprehension and sorrow. The firmness and the purity of the faith are being threatened today, not only through the implacable opposition of the thought and morals of the world, but also through a certain " weariness of Catholic truth " and a certain excessive and often incautious pluralism which is spreading inside the Church also. We shall do well to observe these phenomena naturally with respect and caution. They are weakening the orthodoxy of the doctrine of the faith in its substantial content. We should also look at them with responsible and courageous wisdom, which is proper to our office as witnesses, guardians and teachers. The ecclesiastical magisterium is today sometimes attacked by the very ones who ought to defend it, for no other reason, perhaps, than to bolster up their own. But we must not fear. The first to enjoy the charisms of the Spirit are those to whom they have been chiefly promised. The first to have the right and duty to teach the truths of the Christian revelation are the Apostles, and consequently their successors also: *euntes docete* (*Mt.* 28, 19; *Lk* 10, 16; *Mt.* 10, 27 etc.).

April 11th, 1970

Ecclesiastical studies and Renewal of Catechesis

And We can also take comfort for the exercise of our magisterium from some recent concrete facts. The institution of the Pontifical Theological Commission of itself demostrates that the teaching Church values and promotes theological studies, and accepts from their established conclusions a deeper understanding of revealed truth, much greater than that of human speculation. The Church wishes to avail herself of their knowledge to use the most suitable form of expression for spreading her teaching. We look forward to a new and flourishing period in ecclesiastical studies, and trust that the faith may derive therefrom a new splendour.

Another fact, for which the Episcopal conference deserves praise, is the publication of your pastoral document on renewal of catechesis. It marks an historical and decisive moment for the Catholic faith of the Italian people. It reflects the topicality of doctrinal teaching as it emerges from the dogmatic formulation of the recent Council. It is inspired by the charity of pedagogical dialogue, that is to say, it reveals concern for and knowledge of the art of speaking in appropriate, authoritative and plain language to modern man. We shall do well to give it great importance and make it the basis of great, harmonious and tireless renewal of the catechesis of the present generation. It vindicates the function of the Church's magisterium, and it deserves honour and confidence.

The second difficulty is the exercise of authority. The obedience due to authority is lacking on many grounds. On the contrary, it is being contested in a way that is both irreverent and tiresome. It is not easy to be a bishop today! But on this important point We repeat: Confidence! Confidence in the unchallengeable power of our mandate (We speak to teachers, and will say no more). Confidence in the goodness of the very great majority of the Christian People towards the hierarchy. Confidence in the demands of authority, which are implicit in the needs of the community of believers. Finally, confidence in wise and patient renewal, which we ourselves, Pastors of the People of God, shall imprint upon your art of exercising the authority which pertains to us bishops in holy Church.

It is under this last head that we hear repeated and monotonous protests. It is not authority, they say, which is rejected (though there are also some who radically impugn it!), it is the manner of exercising it that must be changed. This objection may be taken into consideration, provided it does not imply that the Superior is to be merely the docile executor of what the subjects desire and decide! Certainly not.

Ecclesial Style in Dialogue

Let us humbly revise our manner of exercising authority. In simple language, there are two ways of exercising authority. The first is to pull rank and, usually by fear (cf. *1 Cor.* 4, 21), to restrict the liberty and action of others. The other is to assist them to express themselves in a good, free and responsible manner (cf. *2 Cor.* 1, 24). *De potestate nostra, quam dedit nobis Dominus in aedificationem, et non in destructionem vestram, non erubescam* (*2 Cor.* 10, 8). I shall not be put to shame for the authority, which the Lord gave for building you up and not for destroying you. We choose this second way (cf. *1 Pet.* 5, 1-3). It is more in accordance with the nature and purpose of authority in the Church. Both systems have their inconveniences. The second reveals them to a greater extent and puts up with them. But the former, even though it may conceal them, increases them.

This is the age of " dialogue ", a term too often bandied about, and sometimes even abused. Yet in itself is seems to Us to offer a good means of expressing pastoral authority, if used when and as it ought to be used. You all know the difficulties and the resources inherent in it; you all know how to find that ecclesial style and that evangelical spirit which the Church and the world now expect from men of the Church.

There is the Presbyteral Council, which is becoming a friendly training ground for this new style of episcopal authority. There is the Statute of Catholic Action which wisely harmonizes the need for coordinating the militant laity with the guidance proper to the bishop, and the maturity of the laity themselves, who aim at acting with practical autonomy and offering freely the contribution of their collaboration.

We could go on. But let these simple remarks suffice to strength-en what hope for in you: a serene and apostolic confidence.

We should have many things to say to you: *Adhuc multa habeo vobis dicere!* (cf. *Jn.* 16. 12). About all the matters which were the object of your discussions: the new diocesan boundaries, the family, the press, the workers' movement, missionary works, vocations, liturgical reform, and so on. It is enough for Us that you should have all these matters in mind. And may it be enough for you that We also have them in mind, and are united with you in prayer, in patience and in charity.

MAGISTERIUM IS THE RULE OF FAITH

A t the last General Audience We took up the matter of the Church. This is a topical question, a local one and a spiritual one, here in this basilica and at this time. And it is more spontaneous and imperative than any other. We asked ourselves how the Church comes into being. We answered: from faith. That is the first inward principle, the prime subjective condition. Without it, baptism, which is true individual and ecclesial sacramental birth in the Holy Spirit, cannot produce its regenerating effect. And this effect, amongst other things, makes faith itself a supernatural virtue of the Christian.

Teaching power

But now we have to ask: How does one come by the faith? We are not speaking of some religious feeling and vague knowledge of God and the Gospel, but of the assent of the mind and heart to God's Word, to the truth revealed by Christ and taught by the Church. The question is as easy as it is important. The first to raise it was St. Paul, and he answered it at once. In his letter to the Romans he wrote: " How then shall they call on him? And how shall they believe in one, of whom they have never heard? And how shall they hear unless he be preached to them? And how shall they preach, except they be sent? " (10, 14-15). He adds: *Fides ex auditu.* Faith depends on preaching, and preaching comes from Christ's word (*ib*. 17). Preaching in its turn requires a mandate, investiture, a mission (cf. CORNELY, *Lagrange, h.l.*).

The concept and importance of evangelization, of pastoral and missionary work, is understandable. These ideas are familiar to our time too. When we consider them in relation to the perennial birth of members to the Church, we can see their greatness and specific functions. The Church is born from the teaching Church, not from itself as such. Or rather, it arises from Christ, who sends his Apostles to save men through his word and his grace. The Apostles were the first and immediate eye witnesses: *Vidimus et testamur*: We have seen, and give evidence (*1 Jn.* 1, 2). Note that the Apostle is the channel of the truths of the faith. He is authoritative because of his personal experience and he has received authorization through his missionary investiture. He will be followed by a series of others, who will spread the same testimony throughout the world and transmit it to history. But the testimony is no longer immediate: it now comes through intermediaries (see ST. AUGUSTINE, *In Ep. Joannis ad Parthos*, 1, 2, 3; *PL* 35, 1979-1980).

From this derive two essential features of this design which derives from Christ and is concerned with announcing his Gospel of salvation. One is jealous textual fidelity to the message. The other is the distinctive and characteristic office conferred upon the apostolic succession to guard the message, propagate it, defend it, and, in a word, teach it.

This shows that the Church possesses within herself an organ which instructs her and guarantees the genuine expression of God's Word. It is the hierarchical magisterium, and it generates the Christian people (the hierarchical magisterium is also part of the people, but it has a function of exercising a providential power, such as the eye exercises for the whole body). St. Paul compared his generating and vivifying teaching function to all the other functions in Christian and profane culture, and he placed it above them. " For you may have ten thousand instructors in regard to Christ, but you have not many fathers: I begot you in Christ Jesus through the gospel " (*1 Cor.* 4, 15). That was to the Corinthians. To the Galatians he wrote: " I make you to be born again, until Christ shall be formed in you " (*Gal.* 4, 19). Almost as if to emphasize the fact that his teaching function was an efficient, though ministerial, cause, he does not call them " brethren " as usual, but " dearly beloved children " and " my little children " (*ib.*). Between Christ and Christians stands a teaching power: the hierarchical magisterium.

This go-between, this power, has been the object of grave and revolutionary challenges in the Church, and it still is. At first sight one might say that those challenges were legitimate.

" The very notion of a power seems to be excluded from the religious field, because religion is the bond that links conscience to its source and to its end ... *A fortiori* when it is a question of Jesus' religion, for he did away with the Law and its observances and he calls every person, even the Samaritan woman, to worship —in Spirit and Truth—which is true worship " (Guitton).

That is what the Protestant reformation did. It excluded the Church's magisterium, and put every follower of Christ into direct contact with " Scripture alone ". It left everyone to interpret it by " private judgment ". But is that how Christ desired his revelation to be communicated to believers? Was there not a danger that Sacred Scripture might lose its unequivocal meaning and crumble in a thousand differing and contradictory interpretations? What has become of the unity of faith that should make Christians brothers, according to the formula: " One God, one faith, one baptism " (*Eph.* 4, 5). The sad story of the division of Christians in to so many sects, still separated, bears witness to it. And how shall the generous ecumenical effort of our time bring back all Christians to the single mystical body of Christ, " that all may come together in unity of faith " (*Eph.* 4, 13), as the Apostle reminds us? We might also ask: If Sacred Scripture were enough to generate Christianity, where does Sacred Scripture come from, if not from an oral apostolic magisterium, which preceded it, which produced it, which guaranteed it, and which preserved it?

The Council's teaching

It is also necessary to note that Christ did not found an abstract religion, a mere school of religious thought. He set up a community of apostles, of teachers with the task of spreading his message and so giving rise to a society of believers: his Church. He promised the Spirit of truth to his Church (cf. *Jn.* 16, 13) and then sent it. He gave it an assurance that no hostile power would be able to prevail over it (cf. *Mt.* 16, 18; SIRI, *La Chiesa*, ed. Studium, p. 54 sqq.).

The Council has left us clear and organic teaching about these basic questions. We shall do well to study its doctrine, in order to re-order our own thought about these matters, especially in regard to the most challenged point of all, that of the ecclesiastical magisterium (cf. Const. *Dei Verbum*, 5-10); BETTI, *Il magistero del Romano Pontefice*, published in this issue, p. 9). There is a great temptation in religious life today, and in Catholic religious life, to undermine the reverence due to the Church's magisterium and dogmatic commitment to the theological doctrine which it entails. There is an effort to change the textual form in which it is expressed and to change the meaning of its terms, so as to attenuate the objective meaning of doctrine, and even sometimes to nullify it. There is consequently a desire to replace it by interpretations, erudite perhaps, but arbitrary and in line with the currents of modern cultural opinion; but they are not always aimed at safeguarding the unequivocal and authentic meaning of revelation, interpreted by the Church and authoritatively taught by her.

Conscience and knowledge

The great argument put forward in favour of such emancipation from the ecclesiastical magisterium is that of the liberty of science. The Church acknowledges this liberty, provided that it really be in the field of science, that is, of truth. Another argument is freedom of conscience. The church acknowledges its rights and also its priority, in formulating a moral judgment about an individual and immediate act to be performed. In this case conscience is defined as the proximate rule for action. This rule may not and ought not prescind from a higher and more general rule, which is called law, just as the eye cannot do without the light which shows it the way (cf. ST. ALPHONSUS, *Theol. moralis*, 1, p. 3).

Conscience on its own is not enough to give knowledge of the reality of things or of the morality of actions. In the field of the faith, that is, the field of revealed truths, conscience alone cannot guide the believer's mind (expect in the case of very special mystical charism). The objective faith is not a personal opinion, but a fixed and delicate doctrine. It is based, as was said, on the strict testimony of a qualified organ, the Church's magisterium, This magisterium is certainly not arbitrary. It scrupulously interprets and transmits the faith. So true is this that St. Augustine (to quote him once again) said, " I would not believe the gospel, were I not moved to do so by the Church's authority " (*Contra Man.*, V; *PL* 42, 176; cf. *Lumen gentium*, 25). A theologian of our day echoes him: " The believer's conscience receives infallible security in the fundamental moral truths from the Church's magisterium, as the most precious of things ".

May God grant that the saving feeling of this security be granted to you during this visit you are making to the tomb of the Apostle Simon, whose name was prophetically changed by Christ to Peter, in whose name We impart to you all the Apostolic Blessing.

IN CONQUEST OF THE UNIVERSE
MAN ENCOUNTERS THE CREATOR

On April 18th the Holy Father received in audience those taking part in the XI Study Week of the Pontifical Academy of Sciences. During the audience he gave the following address.

Excellencies and dear Sirs,

W e thank you heartily for the delicate sentiments just expressed to Us by Reverend Father O'Connel in the name of his illustrious colleagues. As you know, We are always happy to welcome the members of our Pontifical Academy of Sciences, in the presence of the Diplomatic Corps and distinguished personalities. We also experience a certain emotion to see such qualified representatives of the entire world gathered together, a veritable Senate of scholars, at the head of scientific research and of reflection which it stimulates in the human mind. Is not the theme of your work, devoted to the " nuclei of galaxies ", a striking sign of this?

1. Your Plenary Session marks an important moment in the life of the Academy, and We rejoice in this. For this Institute, which has known a certain slackening of activity in the course of these past years, remains highly significant: it can bring to our world appreciable help by the competency and universality of its testimony, and also provide a solid basis upon which believers can reflect for a fruitful dialogue with scientific thought. What roads have been travelled since the foundation of the Academy of " Lincei " in 1603, its revival by Pius IX, its enlargement under Leo XIII, and especially its reconstitution by the enlightened care of our great predecessor Pius XI, with the *Motu Proprio* of October 28, 1936, *In multis solaciis,* under the name of the Pontifical Academy of Sciences, comprised of seventy pon-

tifical Academicians " a Senate of learned men, as it were, or a
scientific Senate to promote the progress of the sciences ", under
the presidency of Father Agostino Gemelli of happy memory (See
AAS, 28, 1936, pp. 423-424).

Unity of the human spirit

Illustrious scholars have never ceased to honour the Academy
by their presence and their work, and We Ourself, yesterday,
had the joy of adding to this select Cenacle twelve new members
who provide a better representation of the ensemble of teachers
who cultivate the scientific disciplines with success throughout
the world. Your studies of mathematical and experimental sciences,
carried on with the liberty that is proper to culture, have certainly contributed to the progress of pure science, and prepared
the progress of applied sciences. But should not such a development be extended to other domains today? While continuing your
specialized researches whose importance does not cease to grow
—experiences of the flights into space, the most recent of which
We have followed these past days with anguish and, at the end,
with thrilling joy and admiration—would it not be desirable and
opportune to foster, in other Academies, other disciplines that are
also essential to the human spirit, such as arts and letters, philosophy, law, history, economics, sociology, and the human sciences that
characterize so profoundly the men of our times? This morning,
We wish to entrust to you this thought upon which We have
meditated for a long time and which, in Our mind, is more than
a dream: a real desire which it would please Us to realize.

2. The very nature of your work prompts Us to underline two
principles of which you are already convinced, and to which your
own experience (We could say: your personality) bears witness
every day. The fact that reason, however advanced it may be, is
not and cannot be opposed to faith: " Science which is the true
knowledge of things is never contradictory to the truths of Christian faith " (Motu proprio, *In multis solaciis, ib.*, p. 421).

Moreover, both faith and reason can be integrated in the unity
of knowledge, while keeping their respective autonomy, as the
first Vatican Council teaches: " Faith and reason ... are a mutual

help to each other " (H. DENZINGER - A. SCHÖNMETZER, *Enchiridion symbolorum, definitionum et declarationum de rebus fidei et morum;* 34th ed. Fribourg in Brisgau, 1967, no. 3019, 1799).

Church encourages discovery of universe

Understand Us well. According to the pastoral Constitution *Gaudium et spes* which " recalls the teaching of the first Vatican Council ", the Church " affirms the legitimate autonomy of human culture and especially of the sciences ", with " their own principles and their proper method, each in its own domain " (*Gaudium et spes*, 59, par. 3). But these sciences which can so well " elevate the human family to a more sublime understanding of truth, goodness and beauty, and to the formation of judgments which embody universal values " (*ib.*, 57, par. 3), can also prepare man to discover and accept the whole truth, provided these sciences do not incorrectly consider " the methods of investigation which these sciences can use as the supreme rule for discovering the whole truth " (*ib.*, par. 5). It is the same God who has created the world with its laws which you scrutinize—" all things in heaven and on earth, everything visible and everything invisible " (*Col.* 1, 16)—and who reveals Himself to men and brings them salvation in Jesus Christ. The same human spirit is capable of scrutinizing the secrets of creation and " of conquering the earth " (See *Gn.* 1, 28), and at the same time, of discovering and accepting " under the impulse of grace " the gift God makes of Himself to man, " The Word of God who, before he became flesh in order to save all things and to sum them up in Himself, ' He was in the world ' already as ' the true light that enlightens every man ' " (*Jn.* 1, 9-10; see *Gaudium et spes*, 57, par. 4). How could the Church not encourage the investigation, the discovery, and the conquest of this universe which, with its marvellous and admirable riches, lead us, from the infinitely small to the infinitely great, towards the invisible which is the source of the visible? (See *Rom.* 1, 20).

3. But the theme you have just taken up, " the nuclei of galaxies ", deserves special attention. Our imagination becomes baffled and leaves us filled with amazement, as though overwhelmed,

almost crushed by the immensity of the perspectives unfolded, " this silence of infinite spaces " so dear to Pascal. We follow with profound respect and great interest your patient work of observation, the coordination of experiments, and the formation of scientific hypotheses on the origin or evolution of astral worlds.

Does this mean that human thought exhausts all its possibilities at the level of these investigations?

" Nuclei of galaxies "

In the background of these investigations, there is the problem of the very being of this cosmos, of this universe: the question of its existence. You remain, in fact, in scientific experimental observation, of a mathematical and cosmological order. But what prevents the mind, on philosophical grounds, from the possibility of ascending to the transcendent principle, to the Creator, " causa subsistendi et ratio intelligendi et ordo vivendi " (St. Augustine, *De Civ. Dei*, I, VII, c. IV). Too often today, we doubt this power. " The more science, while perfecting its methods, subjugates the world to man, the more man, on the other hand, who does not let himself be subjugated, evades ... then comes the temptation to agnosticism " (H. De Lubac, *Sur les chemins de Dieu*, Paris, Aubier 1956, p. 84). But we cannot maintain such an attitude. " The intelligence absolutely cannot abdicate; it cannot renounce its formal law, which is to judge, that is, always affirm " (*ib.*). For the human mind, it is like " an irrepressible need to possess, at every moment of its temporal experiment and in each state of its knowledge, an explanatory idea of the ensemble of things " (P. H. Simon, *Questions aux savant*, Paris, Seuil 1969, p. 41).

We often speak of the " death of God ". But should we not rather speak of the death of man and of his thinking in its superior form? Without this recourse to God, the source of Being, man's thinking seems to become engulfed in the darkness and incomprehensibility of things, in the ignorance of a unity which presides over them, and of the finality of a mysterious order which is inseparable from them, leading to an absurdity which exists only in its own making. Perhaps you are better spared than others from what must be called a true sickness of the mind, you who scrutinize objectively the sciences of nature, of astrophysics, of physics? (See C. TRESMONTANT, *Commen se pose aujourd'hui le problème de l'existence de Dieu*, Paris, Seuil 1969, p. 349). For the intelligence, by its very activity, (if it does not remain in the external appearance of reality), rises to the level of its transcendental cause, the real Absolute, who gives consistency not only to all creation but especially to the human spirit, without ever becoming identical with them. As it has been happily said, the intelligence is " necessarily a power of assimilation as well as a power of ascent ... It understands in all realities that by which realities are, that is, realities open towards the illumination of the act. And thus, it can be rightly said that the intelligence is the sense of the divine, the avid and skillful faculty of recognizing the traces of God " (See Ch. DE MORÉ-PONTIGIBAUD, *Du fini à l'infini*, Introduction à l'étude de la connaissance de Dieu, Paris, Aubier 1957, p. 65).

A springboard to God

Here you have, it must be repeated, a natural development of thought, in its fundamental logic, and not an undue leap as claimed by an anti-metaphysical mentality improperly qualified as scientific. True science, far from arresting the élan of thought, constitutes a springboard which enables it to rise, in this very élan, towards the One who generously provides it with food. For, " the spirit itself is a road that travels ... We cannot get along without God " (H. DE LUBAC, *op. cit.*, p. 78).

We are amazed, as We said before, in the presence of your studies on the nuclei of galaxies. The solar system already appeared so vast and so mysterious to our predecessors! But for all that, we are not disconcerted, knowing that " God prefers rather to create beings in their seed in order to lead them subsequently to their blossoming " (Card. JOURNET, *L'Eglise du Verbe incarné*, t. 3, Essai de théologie de l'histoire du salut, Paris, Desclée de Brouwer, 1969, p. 114). Time and space, matter and form, can develop in a limitless way, indefinitely, as it were.

Mysterious beauty of creation

While listening to your teaching, We find assurance in our faith. And to our mind, to us who are in the school of faith, come the words of Holy Scripture: " God created the heavens and the earth ... And God saw that it was good ... God saw all he had made, and indeed it was very good " (*Gn.* 1, 21-31). This joy God experienced in the presence of his creatures, why should we not have this same joy towards our Creator?

In our turn, we contemplate this mysterious beauty and good-ness of creation. All these beings cry out to us, as they did to St. Augustine: we are not God, but it is God who made us. " Ecce caelum et terra clamant quod facta sint " (*Confessions*, I, XI, c. 4, no. 6; *PL* 32, 811 - Cf. *In Joannem tract.* 106, c. 17, no. 4; *PL* 35, 1910, - Cf. *Sagesse*, 13, I and 9). And him we adore! The meeting with God is wrought before the quasi-limitless grandeur of his works (is it not a grace to be initiated in this grandeur?), in joy, in admiration, in prayer, in the adoration of the One who " in bestowing thousands of graces ... hurried through these forests, and while beholding them ... left them clothed with his beauty " (ST. JOHN OF THE CROSS, *Spiritual Canticle*, verse 5).

Space exploration

At the conclusion of this contemplation of the supreme real-ities of the cosmos in their meeting with the supreme truths of the human mind, We cannot silence our emotions, our admira-tion, our satisfaction which are those of the entire world for the happy ending—yes, happy, very happy, even if the main aim of the adventurous flight of Apollo 13 was not achieved. All of you have certainly followed, with apprehension and then with joy, the un-folding of this extraordinary undertaking. And you will un-doubtedly make it a point to congratulate warmly with Us the valiant astronauts who have escaped the dangers of this grandiose flight, and to render homage to all those who, by their studies, their activity and their authority, have once again brought be-fore the eyes of the world the limitless power of sciences and mod-ern technique. You will also raise with Us an ardent hymn of gratitude to God, Creator of the universe and Father of men, who, by these paths also, wishes to be sought after and found by man, adored and loved by him.

Such are the thoughts, Excellencies and dear Sirs, suggested to Us by this very pleasant meeting. With all Our heart, We encourage you to pursue your scholarly work, to pool it together in an unselfish manner, beyond frontiers, and to help all your brothers answer the questions which science or rather its applications will never cease to ask. You can and should do this, in the light of the faith you bear within you. This is Our dearest wish. We accompany it for your intention with a generous Apostolic Blessing.

PERSONAL PRAYER IS DIMINISHING

Anyone who enters this basilica feels its fascination—especially if he is entering for the first time. Everything about it draws one's gaze, everything moves one: its vast size (which is even marked on the pavement, with comparisons with the other great churches of the world), its monumental character, the sumptuousness of every single part. Everywhere he sees the results of an effort at grandeur and art: the depths of its space, the triumph of height and beauty which is the cupola. The soul sinks in it, is distracted. Impressions of all kinds enchant one: historical memories, esthetic stimuli, effects of architectonic contrasts, strange and wonderful things, a sense of a perfect, giant construction. The soul becomes lost, almost. Is this a museum, one wonders, a marvellous structure which is hard to understand but not for living in? Are we in some incomprehensible temple? In some world of dreams, which is all the more ethereal by being expressed in magnificent solidity?

This is our first, overpowering impression. Then the soul comes back to itself. I am here, it says to itself, to pray, but where shall I pray? How can I possibly pray in this splendid space, which does not suggest recollection, nor repose, nor silence for the mind? Where is mystery in it? How can I establish harmony between the notes of this triumphant symphony and the timid voices in my own heart? How can I express my humble desires, my pains, my doubts, my groans, my ingenuous aspirations and ejaculations? Once more the soul is perplexed and feels lost. The visitor goes to look for some corner in the complex geography of the Basilica, some refuge where he may get his breath back and find his voice, so as to murmur a prayer.

April 22nd, 1970

Centre of unity and charity

And his search meets with success at once. Wherever he turns, there are calls to prayer, which immediately become intense and soaring in the ideal planes of the Basilica. Here is St. Peter, the witness of the faith and the centre of unity and charity. Here is the Church, the catholic Church, the universal Church, that is, the Church of all, my Church, the Church for me, for my world. Here is Christ, present and invisible, but speaking of his kingdom, of his life through the centuries, of his heaven.

It is an ordinary itinerary. Anyone who enters with a pious mind this mausoleum which guards the tomb and the relics of St. Peter, walks through it at once, with joyful effort, with satisfied awe, with renewed desire to go further. Then comes the query which we put to ourselves: the Church, what does the Church *do?* What is it for? What is its characteristic feature? What is its essential motivation? What does its full activity consist in, the activity which justifies its existence and marks it out from other existences?

A society of prayer

The answer flows over from the very walls of this Basilica. Prayer, is the answer. The Church is a prayer association. The Church is a *societas spiritus* (cf. *Phil.* 2, 1; ST. AUGUSTINE, *Sermo* 71, 19; *PL* 38, 462). The Church is mankind which has found the authentic way of praying, through Christ the sole high priest, that is, the way of speaking to God, of talking with God, of speaking of God. The Church is the family of worshippers of the Father " in spirit and truth " (*Jn.* 4, 23).

It would be interesting at this point to look once more into the reasons why the word " church ", the word used to describe the building erected for prayer, is also applied to the assembly of believers, who are the " church ", whether they be inside the house of prayer or not. We might then note amongst other things how the material building, meant to gather the faithful in prayer, can and to a certain degree (here it is a majestic degree) must not only be a place for prayer, a *domus orationis*, but also a sign of prayer, a spiritual edifice and prayer at the same time, an expression of worship, art for the spirit. Hence the practical necessity of giving the Christian people the opportunity to gather and pray together. Hence also the merit due to those who make it their business to build those ' new churches ' which are needed for new communities which have no indispensable *domus orationis* —house of prayer—of their own, and where they can be educated in making their community prayer together.

Prayer is essential

In other words, in this place and at this moment, We desire to remind you of that term which so well describes Catholicism: *Ecclesia orans*: the praying Church. This eminently religious characteristic of the Church is essential and providential for her. The Council teaches this in its first Constitution on the Sacred Liturgy. We ought to remember this characteristic, together with the need for it and its priority. What would the Church be without its prayer? What would Christianity be if it failed to teach men how they can and ought to communicate with God? Would it be some kind of philanthropical humanism, or some sort of purely temporal sociological organization?

The tendency to secularize everything today is well known. It is also well known how this tendency influences Christians, even the clergy and religious. We have spoken about this on other occasions, but it will be well to speak about it again, because prayer is on the decline today. Let Us at once make clear what We mean. Community and liturgical prayer are once more spreading, and experiencing participation and understanding which are certainly a blessing for our people and for our time. Indeed we must continue with the prescriptions of the current liturgical reform. They were willed by the Council; they have been studied and worked out with wise and patient care by the Church's liturgists, and they have been suggested by outstanding experts in pastoral needs. Once it has been properly ordered and well absorbed into the consciences and minds of the Christian people, liturgical life will keep the religious sentiment vigilant and active in our time, which is so secular and so greatly desacralized. It will give the Church a new springtime of religious and Christian life.

Personal prayer is diminishing

Yet at the same time We note with regret that personal prayer is diminishing. This is threatening the liturgy itself with inner impoverishment, with exterior ritualism and purely formal practice of religion. Religious feeling can wither through lack of two characteristics which are indispensable for prayer: interiority and individuality. Everyone needs to learn to pray inside himself and by himself. The Christian needs to have his personal prayer. Every soul is a temple. " Do you not know ", says St. Paul, " that you are the temple of God and the Spirit of God lives within you? ".

When do we enter this temple of our consciences to adore God present there- Shall we be empty souls, even though Christian souls, souls which are not present to themselves and have forgotten that mysterious and indescribable appointment which God, the One and Threefold God, deigns to make with us, for filial and overflowing conversation inside our very selves? Do we not remember the last words of Our Lord at the Last Supper: " If a man love me, he will keep my words; and my Father will love him, and we will come to him and make our abode with him " (*Jn.* 14, 23). This is charity praying (St. Augustine): Are our hearts inspired with charity, enabling us to conduct this inward personal prayer?

The *Ecclesia orans* is a choir of single, vivid, conscious and loving voices. It is an interior spiritual undertaking, personal devotion, meditation worked out in one's own heart, a certain degree of thinking and worshipping, sighing and rejoicing contemplation. It is the Church's petition, and the Church is renewing itself and wishes us to be witnesses and apostles.

Let us listen to this hymn to Christ, to God, rising from this Basilica. Let us try to add our own humble voices, here and now, everywhere and at all times. With Our Apostolic Benediction.

ENLIGHTENED RENEWAL
OF OUR VENERATION FOR MARY

An April 24th the Holy Father celebrated Mass in the Square fronting the Church of Our Lady of Bonaria. After the Gospel he preached the following to the vast throng.

We have now reached the precious moment of the double meeting for which we have come from Rome to your Shrine of Our Lady of Bonaria. The first meeting is between our humble person, the Pope, and the people of Sardinia. The second is our meeting and yours with the Mother of Christ, Blessed Mary, venerated for six centuries in this historic and sacred place as the special Patroness of the City of Cagliari and of the Island of Sardinia.

So we are celebrating at this point the first meeting, our meeting with you, beloved people of Sardinia. We greet you in the Lord. We owe our cordial and respectful greeting first of all to your archbishop, Cardinal Sebastiano Baggio, who gave us the irresistible invitation for this special pilgrimage we are making. We owe it also to our other brother-bishops here present, to the civil and military authorities of every rank whose assistance at this ceremony brings us so much pleasure, to the other personages and to the various special groups of the Church community of the Island, to the clergy, the religious, the seminary students, the Catholic laity, the friends and faithful of the Church of Cagliari and of all Sardinia. But we ask all these categories of persons to allow us to reserve for them another moment of conversation, one especially for them, and to give first place and choice on this occasion to the people, the people here present, offering us in their multitudinous array a stupendous picture, a genuine view representing all the Sardinians. It is to you, dear sons and daughters of Sardinia, that our first affectionate greeting is directed: to you who are the people of this island where the most ancient and varied ethnic and historical lines converge from all points of the Mediterranean, lines of which you, however, constitute a synthesis supremely characteristic and relatively uniform. We are pleased to meet you and to imagine you still marked with your ancestral traits as a simple, industrious, austere, quiet, unspoiled and sad people, but with humane and pious customs; a people used to privation and toil; a people isolated from the world as your land is; a people of proud and tenacious passions, but, at the same time, of natural and gentle sentiments, capable of finding expression in fantasies of legend and in songs that are grave and calm like enchanted echoes, still carrying the voice of distant ages. It may be that we do not know you sufficiently well; but what we do know of you is enough to fill our mind with affection, liking, and esteem. We are very glad to be among you. People of Sardinia, we greet you all with a full heart. Are you also glad that the Pope has come to see you?

Greeting to the shepherds

We have come for everyone. But it gives us pleasure to direct our thoughts in a particular way to you, the shepherds of Sardinia. You seem still to be the typical representatives of the island's rural population. We, like everyone else, know what a hard and rugged life is yours, poor, primitive and solitary in the way it is carried out, and always linked, as was the life of the patriarchs of the Bible, with the fortunes of your flocks. We have been told that some of you wished to come to this meeting, bringing your sheep with you. You would have been a living representation of the Gospel scene of the Good Shepherd, reminding us of what is the first of our obligations, our pastoral duty. That, dear shepherds of Sardinia, shows the community of feeling with which we greet you, and the understanding we have for the humble, unbroken, silent suffering which characterizes your existence. We would like to bring it consolation and improvement. And so we too are grateful to all who devote their care to you, to alleviate your poor material, economic and social conditions. We find comfort in knowing that malaria, which was till now a wound that refused to heal, has at last been vanquished, and that the beautiful wild scenery of your mountains and plains has at last received the gift of wholesomeness. That is a first great conquest, which will doubtless be followed by others, for the improvement of your housing, your education and your work. It is therefore our wish and hope that sheep-raising will continue to be an honoured, renewed and flourishing occupation of the people of Sardinia, preserving the simplicity, and also the unspoiled character of their traditional way of life.

To the miners

Next we wish to greet the miners of Sardinia. Your work too represents an age-old tradition of the Sardinian people. The island's soil, rough and ungenerous on the surface, conceals treasures in its depths. From the beginning of its history, Sardinia has been known as an island of mines. It was due to these hidden riches that Pope Saint Pontian, the only Pope to set foot on Sardinia before us, was deported here. It was at the time of the Roman Emperors, Alexander Severus and Maximinus, over seventeen centuries ago (in 235) that he was condemned, perhaps to your own arduous toil which was then even more difficult. It is certain that he died a martyr here, " adflictus, maceratus fustibus ", oppressed and tormented with floggings (Lib. Pont.) till he died from them, a martyr of Christ and of the Roman Church.

So you miners have a fellow- worker, the miner Pope, who died a victim for the Christian faith because of the harshness of your toil and the cruelty of his persecutors. How could we fail to look on you with particular compassion and affection? Certainly work in the mines today is no longer as inhuman as it once was. But it sill is a heavy and risky work. We look on you, miners, with admiration and with profound regret that we are so much lower than you on the scale of suffering. As followers and heralds of the Cross, we too are meant to suffer. For us you are a reminder and an example and we welcome you therefore with particular honour and with particular love. In the name of Christ, we are grateful to those who seek to improve your conditions, to those who assist you, and to those who remind you that you too are God's children and that being bound more than others to such arduous toil, indispensable for society, you are more than others worthy of general esteem and Christian charity. Miners, to you go our heartfelt greetings.

To the fishermen

And next we greet the fishermen. Here we have another occupation that the Lord wished to use as an example for our
apostolic office. The Lord's first disciples were fishermen. Simon
was a fisherman, he whom the Lord later called Peter, without
however changing the symbol of the activity to which the mission
of Peter and his brother Andrew was to be dedicated. And today
this mission is still ours: " Follow me, and I will make you fishers
of men " (*Mt.* 4, 19). Accordingly, to you fishermen goes also
our sympathy while owe extend to you the invitation for today's
spiritual meeting. And we would like to say the same to those
who work in Sardinia's famous salt deposits nearby. The Gospel
speaks also of salt. " You ", said the Lord to his apostles as he
gave them a special charism, an office, a responsibility, " you are
the salt of the earth " (*Mt.* 5, 13). We have in this symbol of
our hierarchical function an added reason for thinking of you
too as our friends.

To the emigrants

There is still another class of persons which we want to greet
expressly. They are the emigrants from Sardinia, who are represented here today, and especially the immigrants to Sardinia,
which is becoming a land open to all kinds of activity by workers
and industrialists coming from the mainland. May you all find
in Sardinia the friendly country to which you will give and
from which you will receive not only temporal benefits but also
spiritual ones, those of the heart and of the faith.

Seafarers and " Apostolate of the Sea "

And lastly we greet the seafaring people gathered here today.
Where do you come from, seamen who are present here before this
Shrine? And why is it that you come? What boundless horizons
you open before our thoughts! The horizons of the sea, the
horizons of harbours and coastal towns, the horizons of mankind entrusting to the waves its own destiny, to sail, work, trade,

explore and weave a network of relationships of all kinds between the inhabitants of the earth. The sea has the appearance of an impassible element, separating men from each other; yet you make it a highway of communication, indeed the highway that is travelled most often and most restlessly. You make a ship your home, the sea your field of work, the world your homeland. Temporary separation from your families, in continual recurrence is your lot. Loneliness of heart, having strangers for companions, longing for home, frequent dangers and severity of discipline are the normal conditions of your lives. When you are launched on the sea towards distant foreign lands, who is it that thinks of you? Who gives you aid? Who helps you to rest, to think, to pray? Oh! in the Church there are people who have affection for you as seamen, as human beings, as Christians: The " Apostolate of the Sea ", with its network of centres now spread over so many ports of the earth, does not leave you in loneliness, but waits for you and aids you, as you know well. Your presence here says so, for this ceremony is meant also for you. We are happy to meet you on this occasion, in order to offer also to you seamen the comfort of feeling that you are in communion with the great family to which believers all belongs—the Church—and of knowing that you are entrusted to a lofty, reassuring protection, that of Our Lady.

Reasons for our veneration of Mary

And now, here we are, dearest brothers and sons all, gathered before Mary for the second, the main meeting which has today called us to this Shrine of Our Lady of Bonaria. We must not only re-affirm the devotion which for six centuries has made this Shrine for the Sardinian people and for seafarers a point—indeed a bridge—of spiritual contact with her who is blessed among all created beings, Blessed Mary, Mother of Christ according to the flesh and our spiritual Mother (cf. SAINT AUGUSTINE, *De S. Virg.* 2; *PL* 40, 397). We feel we must above all else seek to understand anew the reasons for our veneration and trust with regard to Our Lady. Do we need this? Yes, we all have need of it. It is a need; it is a duty. For all of us this precious moment must mark a point of enlightened renewal of our veneration for Mary, of that special Catholic veneration for the Mother of Christ which is her due and which constitutes a special protection, a genuine comfort, a unique hope for our religious, moral and Christian lives.

It must be so because of what has been happening today. Among the many spiritual upheavals, devotion to Our Lady does not always find our minds so disposed, inclined and contented with professing it in the depths of our hearts as it once did. Or are we today as devoted to Mary as were the clergy and good Christian people until recently? Or are we today more lukewarm and indifferent? Has it happened that a profane outlook, a critical spirit have made our piety towards Our Lady less spontaneous and convinced.

We do not wish here and now to seek out the reasons for this lessening of devotion, this dangerous hesitancy, if such exists. We wish rather to recall now the reasons which bind us to show devotion to Blessed Mary, reasons which are valid today as yesterday. We are not referring here to the forms of that devotion, but rather to the reasons which justify it and must make us appreciate and practice it more than ever. That is what the recent Ecumenical Council did in this regard, in magnificent terms. Here we must considerably simplify that inquiry and reduce it to two fundamental questions.

The first is: what is the question which absorbs, one can say, all religious thought, all theological study today, and which, whether he knows it or not, torments modern man? It is the question of Christ. Who is he? How did he come among us? What is his mission? his teaching? his divine nature? his human nature? his insertion among mankind? his relationship with and importance for human destinies? Christ dominates thought. He dominates history. He dominates the concept of man. He dominates the supreme question of human salvation. And how did Christ come among us? Did he come of himself? Did he come without any relationship with or any cooperation on the part of mankind? Can he be known, understood and contemplated in abstraction from the real, historical and existential relationships which his appearance in the world necessarily implies? Clearly not. The mystery of Christ is made part of a divine plan of human sharing. He came among us by following the way of human generation. He wished to have a Mother. He wished to take flesh through the vital cooperation of a woman, of her who is blessed among all women. The apostle who outlined the fundamental theological structure of Christianity said: " When the time had fully come, God sent forth his Son, born of woman ... " (*Gal.* 4, 4) And the Council reminds us that Mary was " used by God not merely in a passive way ", but " cooperated in the work of human salvation through free faith and obedience " (*Lumen gentium*, 56). It is then no negligible, secondary chance circumstance, but an essential part, one that is of the greatest importance, beauty and comfort for us human beings, that Christ came to us through Mary. We received him from her. We encounter him as the flower of humanity, opening on the immaculate and virginal stem that is Mary. " Thus it was that this flower budded forth " (cf. DANTE, *Par.* 33, 9). As in the statue of Our Lady of Bonaria, Christ appears to us in the arms of Mary. It is from her that he is ours, in his primary relationship with us. He is a human being like us. He is our brother through the maternal ministry of Mary. If we wish to be followers of Christ, we must be followers of Mary, that is to say, we must recognize the essential, life-giving and providential relationship linking Our Lady with Jesus, and opening up to us the way that leads to him.

Let us look to Mary

It is a twofold way: the way of example and the way of intercession. Do we want to be Christians, that is, imitators of Christ? Let us look to Mary. She is the most perfect example of likeness to Christ. She is the " type ". She is the image which better than any other reflects Christ. She is the " excellent exemplar in faith and in charity " (*Lumen gentium*, 53, and 61, 65 etc.). How sweet, how consoling it is for us who wish to walk in the footsteps of the Lord to have before us Mary, her image, her remembrance, her kindness, her humility and purity, her greatness. How close to us the Gospel is in the power which Mary personifies and radiates with human and superhuman splendour! And any fear we would have is dissipated—fear that in marking our spirituality with devotion to Mary, our religious sense, our vision of life and our moral energy would become soft, weak and almost infantile—when we draw close to her, the poetess and prophetess of Redemption, and hear from her pure lips the strongest and most original hymn ever uttered: the " Magnificat "! She it is who reveals the transforming design of the Christian economy, the historical and social result which still draws its origin and strength from Christianity: God, she sings, " has scattered the proud in the imagination of their hearts, he has put down the mighty from their thrones and exalted them of low degree " (*Lk.* 1, 15-52).

And at this point the second way is opened for us by Our Lady, so that we may reach our salvation in the Lord Christ: it is her protection. She is our ally, our advocate. She is the confidence of the poor, of the lowly, of the suffering. She is even the " refuge of sinners ". She has a mission of pity, goodness and intercession for all. She it is who consoles every grief of ours. She teaches us to be good, to be strong, to be compassionate towars all. She is the the queen of peace. She is the Mother of the Church.

Remember all that, sons of Sardinia and men of the sea. And never forget to look to Our Lady as your " supreme Protectress ".

REFORM ROOTED IN LOVE OF THE CHURCH

During the extraordinary general audience on Saturday, April 25th, Paul VI delivered the following address.

W e will greet you with a cry of the season, the Easter season, which, as you all know, puts on the lips of the Church the exclamation: Alleluia! We will therefore say Alleluia to you, too, dear visitors, inviting you all to repeat it in your hearts with Us. It is a cry of joy, which expresses the feeling, at once simple and full, with which the hearts of the Faithful overflow when celebrating the feast of the resurrection of Christ, at the memory of the real, historical fact that concludes the Gospel narration and at the understanding, exultant and dazzling, of the mystery of redemption and of the new life that extends from Christ to Christians.

Alleluia means: praise the Lord, and expresses the joy and enthusiasm that sustains and accompanies, like a song, our pilgrimage, now safe, towards the fullness of eternal life (cf. St. AUGUSTINE, *Sermo* 255; *PL* 38, 1186).

An occasional intention and a pastoral intention suggest this blessed word to us. We should like you visitors and pilgrims, gathered at this extraordinary general Audience, to feel an inner impression of joy, that particular joy that rises all the more from the bottom of one's heart in that it is due, not so much to the stupendous and impressive spectacle of the historical monuments of the Eternal City and the magnificence of this Basilica, as to the fact of being here: the joy of feeling at home in this immense, sumptuous church, the joy of feeling you are authentic, faithful, sons of holy Church, the joy of having reached the pole of unity and charity, the joy of knowing you are above the tomb of St. Peter, and that you too, therefore, are inserted, as living stones, in the mystical edifice that Christ in mysteriously building (cf. *1 Pet*. 2, 5). Alleluia! We would like all of you to enjoy this moment of spiritual happiness, and to understand its truth, its uniqueness, its depth: to be here, Alleluia! Rare are the moments in which one can be happy without limits, without fears, without remorse! Remember the verses of the psalm: " I was glad when they said to me, ' Let us go to the house of the Lord! ' " (*Ps.* 121), the God of victories. And again: " How lovely is thy dwelling place, O Lord of hosts! My soul longs, yea faints for the courts of the Lord! " (*Ps.* 83). Religion, faith, grace have these moments of inner exultation, these surprises of the Spirit, these sweet, impetuous preludes of God's life in us. Yes, Alleluia, in Christ and in the Church. " Joy, joy, tears of joy " (Pascal).

And if We repeat this cry of exuberant gladness, it is also with a pastoral intention. The joy of a moment of plenitude, both sensible and spiritual, is not sufficient; joy must be perennial, even if of a lower degree of intensity. The believer, he who has succeeded in meeting the risen Christ, even though in the incognito of our earthly pilgrimage (cf. *Lk.* 24, 32), should always have within him the charism of joy. Joy, with peace, is the first fruit of the Spirit (*Gal.* 5, 22). And we know that in the divine plan of salvation there is a relationship (which We will not specify here) between the Spirit and the Church. Let us just repeat St. Augustine's vivid sentence: " quantum quisque amat Ecclesiam, tantum habet Spiritum Sanctum ", to the extent that one loves the Church, one possesses the Holy Spirit (*Jn.* 32, 8; *PL* 35, 1645-1646). To enjoy the joyful charism of the Spirit, it is necessary to love the Church. There has been talk of the " sense of the Church ". We would like to carry this interior phenomenon even further and exhort you to " have pleasure in the Church ". This, unfortunately, seems to be lacking in so many people, even among those who set themselves up as reformers of the Church. They have pleasure in contestation, criticism, emancipation, arbitrary views, and often in her disintegration and demolition. No, they cannot have " pleasure in the Church ", and perhaps not even love. We do not see how these restless sons can really experience within themselves a true understanding of what is, of what must be (cf. St. Augustine, *De moribus Ecclesiae*, 1, 30; *PL* 32, 1336).

We hope, Brothers and Sons, that, thinking of the Church, her history, her glories, her weaknesses, her needs, her real postconciliar rebirth, you will always have on your lips and in your hearts the paschal cry: Alleluia!

Our Apostolic Blessing exhorts and assists you.

THE CHURCH IS SUFFERING

M any questions often reach Our ears, like sighs, even like groans. Today let us listen to one of them. It is: What is the Church *doing?*

The Church is doing many things. It is in a period of great activity. The Council reawakened the consciousness of its vocation, consequently its consciousnes of fresh duties, fresh reforms, fresh work. And We trust that the Council has infused fresh energy and fresh impulses from the Holy Spirit. We must give God praise and recognize that the Church is now at a moment of intense vitality. The Church is studying and rethinking itself, without any triumphalism; the Church is teaching and renewing its catechesis and its theology; the Church is praying and reforming its liturgy; the Church is perfecting and developing its structures; it is closing its ranks, it is increasing its internal activity; it is revising its canon law: it is widening its mission filed: it is opening a colloquy with separated Brethren; it is defining and vivifying its position in the world, which has greater and greater need of the Church today, the more it is secularized and the more it progresses.

But there is an even more evident and sensitive aspect of the Church today: the Church is suffering; the Church is holding out; the Church is bearing up. This is why that question, asked in a tone of fear, is a justified question: What is the Church doing today? But the anxious query already contains the answer: The Church is suffering.

It is suffering, just as civil society is everywhere suffering. For all its progress, civil society is not satisfied, it is not happy. Progress has increased its desires, has revealed its deficiencies, multiplied its strife, unleashed extremism, loosened its social morals to such an extent that it is rarely pleased with itself, rarely trusts the very principles which govern it and the ends it is pursuing. It is poisoned with anxiety, rhetoric, false hopes, and exaggerated radicalism.

This collective malaise may be a fever due to growth, but at any rate it has its effect upon the Church. It engenders anxious desire for transformations and conformity; it is reducing its self-confidence, taking away its pleasure in its interior unity, flooding it with individualist contestation, deluding it with novelties which have been torn away from the root of tradition, and so on.

The special characteristic of this malaise is the fact that the causes of it and their champions are often enough in the Church itself, even though the malaise is a copy of that of sociey outside the Church. Treasures of the Church are being threatened or squandered. Some of its children, teachers and ministers, challenge the Church. Some abandon the posts they have chosen and which were assigned to them. These are isolated cases, fortunately, but they are publicized and are sometimes described as gestures of post-conciliar renewal and liberation. Ecclesiastical tradition does not seem to have any more weight or meaning for some. The indispensable canonical order is the protecting garb of the mysteries of revelation, of the community, and of the charisms of the Spirit, yet it is now described as arbitrary, confining and repressive legalism. Authority is being easily combatted and dissolved, sometimes in excessive pluralism, in which a certain instinctive egoism, and not unifying charity, appears to prevail.

Internal and External Causes

We will say no more. The internal causes of the Church's suffering are known in some way to all by now. We might well also refer to external causes which are still numerous and grave in some regions. In some countries they are very grave indeed, and threaten to stifle and do away with the Church. This is well known.

But today We desire to consider the Church's suffering as it arises from all that, as a fate which, in some respects we might describe as normal, as something belonging naturally to its existence. That is how things are. We are quite sure that the Christian life which the Church promotes is the true formula, the good formula, the happy formula both for the individual believer, for well-ordered communities which adopt it, and for temporal society, which feels its benefits in happy integration on the level of liberty and morality. We therefore find it easy to feel persuaded that there is a possibility of acquiring stable tranquillity by this means and enjoying it.

We well remember that profession of the Christian faith naturally entails a drama (because it is different from the world and againts its corrupting seductions and " pomps ", as the rite of baptism used to say, until yesterday). It entails a disadvantage, a risk, an effort, a " martyrdom " that is, a hard act of testimony and a sacrifice. The Lord told his followers: " If they persecuted me, they will persecute you ... " (*Jn.* 15, 20); " ... the world will rejoice; you will be sorrowful, but your sorrow will turn into joy " (*Jn.* 16, 20). I came, he said, not to bring cowardly peace at any price, but the sword of moral courage (cf. *Mt.* 10, 34). He is a " target for contradiction " (*Lk.* 2, 34). Anyone who wishes to follow him will have to carry his own cross (*Mt.* 10, 38).

The crosses with which the Church is afflicted from within her own communion and which offend and rend that communion, are no less cruel and disastrous than those which are imposed from outside. The sharpest pain which a mother's heart can feel is that caused by one of her children.

Communion in Adversity

We could never stop meditating upon the Church's sufferings of yesterday and today. But one beautiful consideration suffices for us today, or rather consoles and edifies us. It is the story written by the silent patience of so many humble brave and loyal souls who accept and share the Church's suffering. A mother's heart can have no sweeter comfort than that strong and delicate comfort which comes from her sincere children.

And how many sincere children there are, comforting holy Church by suffering with her and for her! We know well. We know who they are, and We thank them and encourage them. Communion in adversity is a great thing in the Christian economy. There are so many good Christians who suffer because of legalized difficulties inflicted upon populations in certain regions which are still faithful to the Catholic Church, and are just as saddened by the disturbing internal tribulations wounding her heart and sometimes her honour and peace. These good Christians are generally Catholic priests and laity who have been proved by long and faithful service; or they are young people who wish to reach positive and tangible results at once. They are simple souls who are still firmly attached to the rule of faith and the rule of the Church's law; they are the humble, the poor in spirit, the heirs of that tradition which has brought the announcement and the inauguration of the " kingdom of heaven " through the centuries right down to us. They are the guardians of that *sensus Ecclesiae,* that intuitive Catholic wisdom which germinates holiness such as may miss publicity but is certainly not overlooked by God's eye. " Here is the call for the endurance and faith of the saints " (*Apoc.* 13, 10). This is the existing, enduring and patient Church. This is the Church *sustinens*: the Church bearing up under strain.

Obedient Children

It is in this Church that Christians who *pray* are enrolled. Prayer is the soul of resistance to the Church's afflictions: her internal and external evils. To all those who are conscious of the Church's present difficulties We would recall the Lord's grave and comforting words: " Watch and pray that you may not enter into temptation " (*Mt.* 26, 41). It is in this suffering Church that her obedient children are enrolled. The tendency which some of her children have, to free themselves from her authority, often arises from an instinctive desire to get away from sharing in her firmly borne sufferings. But those who are obedient enter into the state of tension suffered by the Church *patiens;* they themselves feel the charism of fidelity and fortitude which is entailed in it, and they partake of the merit.

In a word, the strong, the faithful, the witnesses who are often also heroes, are children of the pilgrim and suffering Church *sustinens: euntes ibant et flebant* (*Ps.* 125, 6). They go forth weeping. Ought we get away from this fate, which belongs to the Church and is therefore also the fate of anyone who belongs to her and lives her life? Ought we resign ourselves to it? Or ought we accept it with virile joy, remembering that it was Christ's fate: to suffer in order to rejoice, to some extent even now?

Undoubtedly: He that goes forth weeping, bearing the seed for sowing, shall come home with shouts of joy, bringing his sheaves with him (*ib.*).   The end of the suffering Church's painful journey shall be victory and joy.   May this aspiration, which sums up our Christian Catholic life, be given the pledge of Our Apostolic Benediction.

GIVE TO THE WORLD A LOVE MODELLED
ON THAT OF CHRIST

Beloved Sons and Daughters,

H ere are a few words which We hope will give this Audience the significance and value which it ought to have, that is to say, a spiritual one. We utter them in the first place to the chief group for the sake of which this extraordinary audience has been arranged. But all groups present and all Our visitors may listen and take them in, because We think they apply to one and all.

We are very pleased to end this busy morning with this meeting with the numerous group of participants in the National Congress of the Christian Renewal Movement. We greet you and your leaders and the delegations and representatives coming from various countries for the XXV anniversary of its foundation. You have come together in a spirit of Christian fraternity, which is the basis of your common membership of MIAMSI, the Mouvement International d'Apostolat des Milieux Sociaux Indépendants. We are particularly glad to greet members here present of the youth groups of Rinascita Cristiana. They are differentiated by a certain degree of organizational independence, yet at any rate represent your Movement's future. We wish to tell them of the confidence We feel in the apostolate which they are trying to carry out, with clear-mindedness and generosity, in various concrete sectors of life, those which members of the Movement naturally share with their fellow men. We are pleased to be able to spend even these few minutes telling you of all Our appreciation and hopes and to to give you Our best wishes.

Twenty-five Years

1. Appreciation and pleasure above all. You have reached an important stage, and have done so with simplicity and discretion and in silence, also with intelligence, concern and thought for the

new realities of society today, so as to provide a concrete and adequate answer for the problems they present. Without drawing attention to yourselves, as it were, you have been able to spread your ideal like leaven in dough—and with a distinctly evangelical spirit. You have won larger and larger numbers of people to your Movement, and all of them are convinced, conscientious and generous members. You began twenty-five years ago from the ruins of a world which appeared to have collapsed altogether after the war and after its fearful, ideological, spiritual and moral crisis. With the courage of that invincible logic which comes from the Gospel and which needs to be faithfully applied in both individual and social life, you faced up to the demands which bitter experience and the need to live Christianity more intensely and faithfully put before your consciences.

You clearly saw that is was necessary for Christianity to renew itself in a decisive manner and free itself from conditions which sometimes shackle full development of its own personality, so as to be able to renew the world from within and contribute humbly and tenaciously to raising it up. You went ahead in this spirit. Year by year you took inspiration from Our Predecessors and from Ourself. After the Council you made it your task to take your place in the Church's aggiornamento, and did so along the lines of your own specific mission. We thank you profoundly, dearly beloved children, for this fidelity to the Hierarchy's appeals, which calls for respect for Tradition in regard to what is inalienable, and at the same time calls for bold discovery of new ways.

Social Responsibilities

2. This gives Us great reason for hope. The theme of your Congress gives well-founded reason for it too, since it is " For Presence and Commitment in the World of Today ". In the last few days you have been making a thorough examination of the question of the reality of this world of ours as it is today, its contradictions and its condition. No doubt your analysis has been precise and acute.

You have been asking yourselves what queries must be raised, what preoccupations and yearnings people, Christian people, have today. You have been asking these questions in order to be able to answer people, to help them find right solutions. You have been doing this above all in order to help them overcome a dangerous contradiction which Pope John XXIII noted in his *Pacem in terris* and which is evident in institutions belonging to the temporal order in national communities within the Christian tradition. That contradiction is between a high degree of scientific and technical achievement, together with efficiency in attaining specific ends in science and techniques on the one hand, and on the other, poverty of Christian leaven and influence. That Pontiff lucidly stated the cause for the rupture which has occurred in the minds of Christians " between religious belief and activity with a temporal content ". He therefore called for restoration of " interior unity ", so that " the Faith may also be present in temporal activities as a beacon emitting light and as Charity giving out vivifying strength " (cf. *AAS*, 55, 1963, p. 297).

In that patient work of restoring jeopardized interior unity, you undoubtedly take account of the profound and ceaseless action of God's grace, which works all in all. You also know that it needs to be solidly infused into all the values propor to your environment.

Renewing Man

You do not fail to look frankly and with extreme clarity at weaknesses and deficiencies, which can have ever greater consequences in proportion to social responsibilities. To look at reality as God sees it, you should at the same time take note of the riches which you and your fellows hold in trust, and put them more and more at the service of the Church and the human community.

3. Minally, Our good wishes and prayers: Work and commit yourselves in order to renew modern man through contact with Christ. We have seen with real satisfaction how you gave attention in your Congress to the search for the new man, as he is in God's plan and as the ferments of today indicate he will be: the creator of tomorrow, the arbiter of himself and the world, the lord of the cosmos. Never so much as today has man been aware of his own greatness, his power, his daring, for he has launched out to conquer something which only a few decades ago seemed to be closed off with impassable barriers, in all fields. Yet never

so much as today has man been so devastatingly torn by his own crises, his own finiteness, and, as they say, his own incapacity to communicate with others, as well as by his own interior contradictions, which find exterior expression in strident lack of balance, such as a great part of mankind suffer today. The II Vatican Council gave an extraordinarily lively and complete picture of this ambivalence of man of today (*Gaudium et spes*, 4-10). To this mankind that loves and suffers, hopes and dares, extols itself and abases itself, it held up the image of the unique new Man, who is destined to fulfil mankind's expectations, answer its questions and satisfy its aspirations: Christ Jesus, the Saviour of mankind (cf. *Gaudium et spes*, 22).

In the light of this, the new man whom you seek, is he who, in Christ, has been " created according to God, in justice and holiness and truth " (*Eph.* 4, 24). It is he who, regenerated in baptism and open to the influences of the Spirit, strives to be the witness of eschatological realities to the world. This does not make him any less committed to bringing earthly realities up to the proper level of justice, of honesty, of equilibrium, and to infusing them with that love which has its origin and model in Christ alone. Never grow tired of working for this very lofty end. It demands rich spiritual life, sincere search for Christian authenticity, severe commitment to giving, tireless, never downhearted will to practise the apostolate.

Communion of Grace

To Us " Rinascita Cristiana " means all this. The world will not be able to be renewed unless the Church's conscientious children are the first to be reborn every day to newness of life, in communion of grace and of the liturgy, in intimate contact with God, in charity for the brotherhood, and in openness to the breath of the Holy Spirit, as the Saviour himself said, " Except a man be born of water and of the Spirit, he cannot enter into the kingdom of God. That which is born of the flesh is flesh; and that which is born of the Spirit is spirit ... The wind blows where it will; you hear the sound of it but you cannot tell whence it comes and where it is going. So is everyone who is born of the Spirit " (*Jn.* 3, 5-8).

We give you Our encouragement in this exalting task which is so necessary today. We assure you of Our goodwill and special remembrance in Our prayers, so that the Lord may further your work, as he has done so far, and in you find qualified workers for the Church for the salvation of the world. With Our Apostolic Benediction.

THE FAMILY,
A SCHOOL OF HOLINESS

On the 4th of May, the Holy Father received in audience some 2,000 married couples from various countries who are members of the "Equipes Notre-Dame" and met in Rome for a pilgrimage of several days.
During the audience, the Holy Father delivered the following address.

Dear sons and daughters,

1.   First of all, We thank you heartily for your words of faith, for your nightly prayer for Our intentions, and also for your dedication in the service of vocations. We wish to tell you how happy We are to welcome you this morning, and to speak to you, and beyond you, to the 20,000 homes of the " Equipes Notre-Dame ". You were telling Us a moment ago about its influence all over the world, and your preoccupation to live with Christ and to weave with Him the daily thread of your conjugal love. Among Christian couples, you constitute small teams of mutual spiritual help sustained in their efforts by a priestly presence. How could We not rejoice over this? Dear sons and daughters, the Pope heartily encourages you and invokes the blessings of God upon your work.   Too often the Church has appeared, and wrongly so, to question human love.   Today, We wish to tell you this clearly: no, God is not an enemy to the great human realities, and the Church in no way whatsoever under-estimates the values lived every day in millions of homes. On the contrary, the Good News brought by Christ the Saviour, is also good news for human love, excellent in its origins—" God saw all he had made, and indeed it was very good " (*Gn.* 1, 31)—corrupted by sin, but redeemed to the point of becoming a means to holiness, with the help of grace.

2. As all baptized persons, you are called to holiness, according to the teaching of the Church solemnly reaffirmed by the

Council (See *Lumen gentium*, 11). But you are expected to pursue your own proper path to holiness, in and by your family life. It is the Church which teaches us that: " With the help of grace, spouses can lead a holy life " (*Gaudium et spes*, 49), and make their family " the domestic sanctuary of the Church " (*Apostolicam actuositatem*, 11). These thoughts, the forgetting of which is so tragic for our times, are certainly familiar to you. We wish to meditate on these thoughts with you for a few moments in order to strengthen once again, if need be, your will to live generously your Christian and human vocation in marriage (See *Gaudium et spes*, 1, 47-52), and collaborate together in the great design of God's love for the world, which is to form a people " whom God has taken for his own to make his glory praised " (*Eph.* 1, 14).

Earthly reality of matrimony

3. As Holy Scripture teaches you, marriage, before it becomes a sacrament, is a great earthly reality: " God created man in the image of himself, in the image of God he created him, male and female he created them " (*Gn.* 1, 27). We must always return to this first page of the Bible if we wish to understand what a human couple, a family, is and should be. Psychological analyses, psychoanalytic studies, sociological surveys, philosophical reflections will certainly be able to bring their enlightment to sexuality and human love; they would blind us were they to neglect this fundamental teaching given to us from the very beginning: the duality of sexes was willed by God so that man and woman together might be the image of God and, like Him, a source of life: " Be fruitful, multiply, fill the earth and conquer it " (*Gn.* 1, 28).

Moreover, an attentive reading of the Prophets, the Sapiential Books, and the New Testament, shows us the significance of this fundamental reality, and teaches us not to reduce it to physical desire and genital activity, but to discover therein the complementariness of the values of man and woman, the nobility and the weaknesses of conjugal love, its creativity, and openness to the mysterious design of God's love.

4. This teaching retains its full value today, and cautions us against the temptations of a ravaging eroticism. This phenomenon

of the abnormal should at least warn us against the danger of a materialistic civilization that forces itself imperceptibly in this domain, the last refuge of a sacred value. Shall we rescue it from the enslavement of sensuality? Confronted with an encroachment cynically pursued by greedy industries, let us at least suppress its baneful effects on young people. Without barrier or inhibition, we must foster an education that helps the child and the adolescent to become gradually conscious of the power of the impulses that arise within them, to integrate these impulses in the building up of their personality, to control their mounting forces so as to realize a full affective and sexual maturity and, in this way, prepare them for the gift of self by a love that will give it its true dimension, in a exclusive and definitive manner.

Irrevocable indissolubility

5. The union of man and woman does differ radically from every other human association, and constitutes a singular reality, namely, a married couple's based on the mutual gift of each other " and they become one body " (*Gn.* 2, 24). A unity whose irrevocable indissolubility is the seal affixed to the free and mutual engagement of two free persons who " are no longer, two, therefore, but one body " (*Mt.* 19, 6). One body, one couple (we could almost say one being), whose unity will take social and legal form in marriage, and will manifest itself in a community life whose carnal gift is the creative expression. This means that, when they marry, spouses express a desire to belong to each other for life, and for this purpose contract an objective bond whose laws and requirements, far from becoming an enslavement, are a guarantee and a protection, a real support, as you yourselves experience in your daily life.

Exclusive and creative love

6. As a matter of fact, the gift is not a fusion. Each personality remains distinct, and far from dissolving in the mutual gift of each other, affirms and refines itself, continues to grow throughout conjugal life, according to this great law of love: the mutual giv-

ing of each other in order to give together. In fact, love is the cement that gives its solidity to this community life, and the *élan* which draws it towards an ever more perfect fullness. The entire being participates, in the depths of its personal mystery, and of its affective, sensitive, carnal and spiritual constituent parts, thus constituting a more perfect image of God which the married couple has the mission to incarnate day after day, by weaving it with its joys and sorrows, so true is it that love is more than love. There is no conjugal love which, in its exultation, is not an *élan* towards the infinite, and in this *élan*, does not wish to be total, faithful, exclusive and creative (See *Humanae vitae*, 9). The conjugal act, as a means of expression, knowledge and communion, maintains and strengthens love, and its creativity leads the married couple to its full flowering: it becomes a source of life, in the image of God.

The Christian knows that human love is good because of its origin, and if it is wounded and deformed by sin, as everything in man is, then it finds its salvation and redemption in Christ. Moreover, is not this the lesson of twenty centuries of Christian history? So many married couples have found the path to holiness in their conjugal love, in this community life which is the only one based on a sacrament!

Sacrament of the New Covenant

7. The work of the Holy Spirit (See *Tit.* 3, 5), the baptismal regeneration makes us new creatures (See *Gal.* 6, 15), that " we too might live a new life " (*Rom.* 6, 4). In this grandiose undertaking of the renewal of all things in Christ, marriage, also purified and renewed, becomes a new reality, a sacrament of the New Covenant. And behold at the threshold of the New Testament, as at the entrance of the Old, a married couple stands. But whereas Adam and Eve were the source of evil unleashed on the world, Joseph and Mary are the summit whence holiness spreads all over the earth. The Saviour began the work of salvation by this virginal and holy union wherein is manifested His all-powerful will to purify and sanctify the family, this sanctuary of love and this cradle of life.

Cell of ecclesial organism

8. Henceforth, everything is transformed. Two Christians wish to marry; St. Paul forewarns them: " You are not your own property " (*1 Cor.* 6, 19). Both of them members of Christ " in the Lord ", their union is also made " in the Lord ", like that of the Church, and that is why it is a " mystery " (*Eph.* 5, 32), a sign which not only represents the mystery of the union of Christ with the Church, but also contains and radiates it by the grace of the Holy Spirit which is its vivifying soul. For the very love that is proper to God is the love which God communicates to us so that we might love Him and love one another with this divine love: " Love one another just as I have loved you " (*Jn.* 13, 34). The very manifestations of the tenderness of Christian spouses are permeated with this love which they draw from the heart of God. And should the human source happen to dry up, the divine source is as inexaustible as the fathomless depths of the tenderness of God. This reveals to what an intimate, strong and rich communion conjugal love tends. As an interior and spiritual reality, it transforms the community life of the spouses into what we could call, according to the authorized teaching of the Council: " the domestic Church " (*Lumen gentium*, 11), a veritable " cell of the Church ", as John XXIII expressed to you on May 3, 1959 (*Addresses of Pope John XXIII*, I, Typ. Pol. Vat. p. 298), a basic cell, a germinal cell, the smallest one no doubt, but also the most fundamental of the ecclesial organism.

9. Such is the mystery in which conjugal love takes root, and which enlightens all its manifestations. It is the Mystery of the Incarnation that ennobles our human virtualities, by penetrating them from within. Far from scorning them, Christian love brings them to their fullness with patience, generosity, strength and sweetness, as St. Francis de Sales liked to underline when praising the conjugal life of St. Louis (*Introduction to the Devout Life*, III, ch. 38, Advice to Married Peoples, Oeuvres, Bibliothèque de la Pléiade, Paris, Nrf, Gallimard 1969, p. 237). Also, aware of carrying their treasures in earthenware jars (See *2 Cor.* 4, 7), Christian spouses strive, with humble fervour, to translate in their conjugal life the recommendations of the Apostle St. Paul: " your bodies are members making up the body of Christ ... your body

is the temple of the Holy Spirit ... use your body for the glory of God " (*1 Cor.* 6, 13-20). " Married in the Lord ", spouses henceforth cannot be united except in the name of Christ to whom they belong and for whom they must work as His active members. Therefore, they cannot dispose of their body, especially in so far as it is a principle of generation, as well as in the spirit, but for the work of Christ, since they are members of Christ.

10. " Free and responsible collaborators with the Creator " (*Humanae vitae*, 1), Christian spouses see their carnal creativeness acquire a new nobility. The drive which prompts them to unite themselves is a bearer of life, and permits God to give himself children. Having become father and mother, the spouses discover, with wonder at the baptismal fonts, that their child is henceforth a child of God " born through water and the Spirit " (*Jn.* 3, 5), and that he is entrusted to them so that they might watch over his physical and moral growth, yes, but also over the budding and flowering in him of the " new self " (*Eph.* 4, 24). This child is no longer just what they see, but especially what they believe " an infinity of mystery and love which would dazzle us were we to see it face to face " (*Emmanuel Mounier to his wife Paulette*, March 20, 1940, *Œuvres*, t. IV, Paris, Seuil 1963, p. 662). Also, education becomes a real service to Christ according to His very words: " in so far as you did this to one of the least of these brothers of mine, you did to me " (*Mt.* 25, 40). And if it should happen that the adolescent refuses the education of his parents, then these parents participate sorrowfully, even in their flesh, in the passion of Christ in the face of the refusals of man.

Spouses collaborate with the Creator

11. Dear parents, God has not entrusted you with so important a task (See *Gravissimum Educationis*) without giving you a prodigious gift, His fatherly love. Through the love of parents for their child in whom Christ lives, the love of the Father overflows in His well-beloved Son (See *Jn.* 4, 7-11). Through the authority of parents, it is His authority that is exercised. Through the devotedness of parents, we see His providence as " Father, from whom every family, whether spiritual or natural,

takes its name " (*Eph.* 3, 15). Moreover, the baptized child, through the love of his parents, discovers the paternal love of God and, as the Council tells us: " gains his first experience of the Church " (*Grav. Educationis*, 3). The child will become aware of this as he grows older, but divine love already now, through the tenderness of his parents, blossoms out and develops in him his being as a son of God. This reveals the splendour of your vocation, which St. Thomas correctly compares to the priestly ministry: " For some propagate and conserve the spiritual life in a spiritual ministry only, and this belongs to the sacrament of orders; and some belong to the bodily and spiritual life simultaneously, which takes place in the sacrament of matrimony where a man and a woman come together to beget offspring and to rear them in divine worship " (*Contra Gentiles* IV, 58, trad. Dr. Charles J. O'Neil, Image Book, Garden City, N. Y. 1957, p. 250, no. 6).

12. Homes that experience the severe trial of not having children are also called to cooperate in the growth of the people of God in numerous ways. This morning, We simply wish to draw your attention to hospitality, an eminent form of the home.

Is not St. Paul's recommendation to the Romans: " You should make hospitality your special care " (12, 13), addressed to homes first of all, and in formulating it, did he not have in mind the hospitality of Aquila and Priscilla where he had been the first beneficiary, and which home was subsequently to welcome the Christian community? (See *Ac.* 18, 2-3; *Rom.* 16, 3-4; *1 Cor.* 16, 19). In our days, so hard on many people, what a blessing it is to be welcomed " in this little Church ", according to the expression of St. John Chrysostom (*Homily* 20 on Ephesians 5, 22-24, N. 6; *PG* 62, 135-140) to enter into its warmth, to discover its maternity, to experience its mercy, so true is it that a Christian home is " the smiling and gentle face of the Church " (Description of a home of the Equipes Notre-Dame quoted by H. Caffarel in *L'Anneau d'Or*. n. 111-112; *Le mariage, ce grand sacrement*, Paris, Feau nouveau 1963, p. 282). This is an irreplaceable apostolate which you are expected to fulfil generously, an apostolate of the home for which the formation of the betrothed, assistance to newlyweds, help to homes in distress constitute privileged domains. Supporting one another, of what tasks are you not capable in the Church and in the world? With great confidence and with great hope, We invite you to this task: " The Christian family loudly proclaims both the present virtues of the kingdom of God and the hope of a blessed life to come. Thus by its example and its witness it accuses the world of sin and enlightens those who seek the truth " (*Lumen gentium*, 35).

Overcome temptations, trials and difficulties

13. Dear sons and daughters, you are firmly convinced of this: it is by living the graces of the sacrament of marriage that you advance with " unwearying and generous love " (*ib.* no. 41) towards that sanctity to which we are all called by grace (See *Mt.* 5, 48; *1 Th.* 4, 3; *Eph.* 1, 4), and not by arbitrary demands, but out of love for a Father who wishes the full blossoming and complete happiness of His children. Furthermore, to achieve this, you are not left alone, since Christ and the Holy Spirit, " these two hands of God ", according to the expression of St. Irenaeus, are unceasingly working for us (See *Adversus Haereses* IV, 28, 4; *PG* 7, 1, 200). Therefore, do not allow yourselves to be led astray by temptations, trials, and difficulties which arise along the way; and when necessary, do not fear to go against the current of what is said and thought in a world of paganized behaviour. St. Paul warns us about this: " Do not model yourselves on the behaviour of the world around you, but let your behaviour change, modelled by your new mind " (*Rom.* 12, 2). Nor should you become discouraged in times of failures; our God is a Father full of tenderness and goodness, filled with solicitude and overflowing with love for His children who struggle along their way. And the Church is a mother who wishes to help you live to the full this ideal of Christian marriage, of which she recalls to you all its requirements and its beauty.

Priestly assistance

14. Dear sons, chaplains of the Equipes Notre-Dame, by a long and rich experience you know this: your consecrated celibacy renders you particularly available to be, on behalf of families in their advance towards holiness, the active witnesses of the Lord's

love in the Church. Day after day, you help them to " live our lives in the light " (*1 Jn.* 1, 7), to think correctly, that is to say, to appreciate their conduct in truth; to wish correctly, that is to say, to orient as responsible men their will towards the good; to act correctly, that is to say, to conform progressively their life in unison with the ideal of Christian marriage, which they pursue generously. It is only little by little that the human being is able to order and integrate his multiple tendencies, to the point of arranging them harmoniously in this virtue of conjugal chastity, wherein the spouses find their full human and Christian development. This work of liberation, for that is what it is, is the fruit of the true liberty of the children of God. Their conscience demands to be respected, educated and formed in an atmosphere of confidence and not of anguish. The moral laws, far from being inhumanly cold in an abstract objectivity, are there to guide the spouses in their progress. When the spouses do strive to live in truth the profound demands of a holy love, patiently and humbly without becoming discouraged by failures, then the moral laws, present there as a reminder, are no longer rejected as a hindrance, but recognized as a powerful help.

15. The progress of the spouses, like all human life, has many stages. The difficult and sorrowful phases—you experience them year after year—also have their place. But this must be emphasized: never should anguish or fear be found in men of good will, for finally, is not the Gospel good news also for families, and a message which, if it is demanding, is no less profoundly liberating? To realize that you have not yet conquered your interior liberty, that you are still subjected to the impulses of your tendencies, that you find yourself almost incapable of respecting for the moment, the moral law in such a fundamental domain—all this naturally gives rise to a distressing reaction. But this is the decisive moment when the Christian, in his confusion, instead of giving way to a fruitless and destructive revolt, humbly accedes to the staggering discovery of man in the presence of God, a sinner in the presence of the love of Christ, the Saviour.

Way to holiness

16. From this radical insight the entire progress of the moral life begins. The spouses find themselves thoroughly " evangelized ", discovering " in fear and trembling " (*Phil.* 2, 12), but also with marvellous joy, that in their marriage, as in the union of Christ with the Church, the pascal mystery of death and resurrection is being accomplished. Within the great Church, this little church then recognizes what it really is: a weak community, at times sinful and penitent but forgiven, making progress in holiness " in that peace of God which is so much greater than we can understand " (*Phil.* 4, 7). Far from being secure from all failings, " the man who thinks he is safe must be careful that he does not fall " (*1 Cor.* 10, 12), nor dispensed from a persevering effort, at times in cruel conditions which can be borne only with the thought of participating in the passion of Christ (see *Col.* 1, 24), the spouses at least know that the demands of the conjugal life, of which the Church reminds them, are neither intolerable nor impractical laws, but a gift of God to help them come, through and beyond their weaknesses, to the riches of a love fully human and Christian. Henceforth, far from harbouring the distressing sentiment of being driven to an impasse and, as the cases may be, to sink perhaps into sensuality while abandoning all sacramental practice, even revolting against a Church considered as inhuman, or to be unyielding in an impossible effort at the price of harmony and balance or even of the survival of the home, the spouses will open up to hope, with the assurance that all the resources of grace in the Church are there to help them advance towards the perfection of their love.

Faithful homes, hope of the world

17. Such are the perspectives in which the Christian families, in the midst of the world, live the good news of salvation in Christ, and make progress in holiness in and by their marriage, with the light, the strength and the joy of the Saviour. Such are also the major orientations of the apostolate of the *Equipes Notre-Dame*, beginning with the testimony of their own life, whose

persuasive force is so great. Worried and restless, our world wavers between fear and hope. Many young people stagger along the road that opens up to them. Let this be for you a stimulus and an appeal. With the strength of Christ you can and should accomplish great things. Meditate on His word, receive His grace in prayer and in the sacraments of penance and the Eucharist, comfort one another by giving testimony of your joy, simply and discreetly. A man and a woman who love each other, the smile of a child, peace in the home: a sermon without words, but so wonderfully convincing, where every man can already glimpse, as through a transparency, the reflection of another love and its infinite call.

18. Dear sons, the Church, whose living and active cells you are, gives through your homes a sort of experimental proof of the power of saving love, and brings forth its fruits of holiness. Homes that are tried, happy homes, faithful homes, you are preparing for the Church and for the world a new springtime whose first buds already make Us thrill with joy. While beholding you, and united in spirit with the millions of Christian homes spread all over the world, We are filled with irrepressible hope, and in the name of the Lord We say to you with confidence: " your light must shine in the sight of men, so that, seeing your good works, they may give praise to your Father in heaven " (*Mt.* 5, 16). In His name, We invoke upon you and your well-beloved children, upon all the homes of the *Equipes Notre-Dame* and their chaplains, especially dear Father Caffarel, an abundance of divine graces, as a pledge for which We heartily impart to you Our Apostolic Blessing.

Before giving you this blessing, We would like to say a prayer with you, an Our Father which we shall recite together for all the intentions of your Movement:

— for all the homes of the *Equipes Notre-Dame*, as well as the widows and widowers who equally belong to it;

— for all their children, that God may protect them and stimulate vocations among them;

— for all the homes that suffer or are being severely tried;

— finally, that an ever greater number of husbands and wives discover the riches of a Christian marriage.

Our Father ...

THE VOICE OF THE CHURCH
REVEALS MAN TO HIMSELF

Once more let us think about the Church. The Council obliges us to keep going into this endless theme. Let us make one more attempt to understand what the Church is and what it is doing in the world. At this particular moment the question is so simple and at the same so wide, that we can give some attention to begin with to the etymological significance of the word itself.

What does " Church " mean? Church means a summons. A summons from whom? From God. To whom is the summons addressed? To mankind.

The word at once represents a great and mysterious phenomenon. Is there a story behind the phenomenon? There is. First of all, that of the Old Testament. Then there is that of the New Testament, which is our own story, and is marked by the coming Christ the Word of God made man, " to gather together the children of God who had been scattered " (*Jn.* 11, 52), and by the extension of the summons to the whole of mankind. This word " Church " condenses in a focal point, as it were, all the wealth, the originality and the truth of religion and human destinies.

If the call comes from God, then the initiative is his; the plan involved in it is his, and the love that is immediately revealed in it is his. We ought to reread St. Paul's letter to the Ephesians, especially the first and second chapters; we ought to read the dogmatic constitution *Lumen gentium*, especially its first chapters also. They will give us an idea of the Church as a call from God, of a religion which does not start from man, but from God, which does not remain one-sided, incomplete and all

177

too often an ineffective and erroneous religion, like human attempts at religion; but constitutes a sure relationship, true dialogue, finally a communion, consequently salvation and blessedness.

The pastoral and missionary call

The Church is mankind which has been called and has responded. It is the assembly of people called by God in Christ. It is the kingdom of God, it is the People of God, it is the congregation of believers (cf. St. Jerome, *In Eph.; PL* 26, 534). It is a family which has come into being through a call, the vocation of the Word and the Grace of God. Consequently, to use the word " Church " and to think of that supernatural mystery of divine goodness should be the same thing for us. This is our first consideration.

Two other considerations immediately derive from it. The word " Church " may be understood in two senses, one passive, the other active. The Church as " calling " may also be understood as " congregation ", that is to say, the effect of a summoning and gathering together, in other words, an assembly, a meeting. *Ecclesia est idem quod congregatio*: Church, St. Thomas says, means, community. It may be understood as *congregans*, as a voice calling, an invitation, a convocation (cf. De Lubac, *Méditations sur l'Eglise*, p. 78 sqq.).

This last aspect of the Church ought to attract our attention, because it has very great interest for all of us. When we ask, What does the Church do? we can reply: It calls. It is the repetition of the God's Word; it is the continuation of Christ's mission, for he said to each Apostle singly, " Come ". To all men of this world who are in need of comfort and salvation he says " come to me, all of you ... ". Therefore the Church is said to be *Lumen gentium*, like Christ, who is the light of the peoples. It is " the sacrament of Christ ": it not only represents Christ the Lord, it also spreads his light and his grace, his Spirit. It is an invitation (cf. Denz. Sch., 3014); it is a living and permanent invitation, a call, a love which is seeking, a responsibility which admonishes, a choice to be made, a fortune to be acquired. It is an apologetic call, a pastoral call, a missionary call.

A road sign in human history

The Church is an offering of truth, placating and saving. It is the road sign in the history of mankind, it is the outstretched hand of redemption and happiness. The Church calls: we are all called to make its voice our own. But, as you know, the qualified and authorized organ of this voice is the Apostle, whom Christ has made preacher, teacher, pastor, vehicle of the Spirit: the Church's Hierarchy.

And here is one more aspect of the calling Church: the echo which the Church's voice should have in every hearer's consciousness. The situation becomes an interior one, a psychological and personal one, a moral one. Does this voice reach modern minds today? Is it a voice that can be taken in, understood, accepted and followed? How much is said today about this aspect of the Christian life! How many efforts are made to make the voice of the faith intelligible! They are excellent efforts, provident and necessary ones, if they go the way of wisdom and love and try to make the voice of the Christian message, the call of the Church, more simple, more acceptable, more comprehensible, more convincing, more penetrating. Our world is distrustful of philosophic language; it is wholly concerned with the language of history; it is even more concerned with the language of sense expression. So what studies anyone must make who wishes to communicate the voice of the faith and be listened to!

This is where we see the need for a renewal of catechesis, of preaching, of religious symbolism, of social communications! But there is a condition. It is that in this process of reform of the language of religion, the divine and immutable content of the message entrusted by Christ to the Church shall not be altered, shall not be lost; it is guarded by his providential magisterium which is responsible for the Church's perennial fidelity to the received word.

Listen without prejudices

We will add: if people perhaps listened to the Church's voice with more attention, without preconceptions, and without an ambition to interpret it as they pleased, that voice would be now quite comprehensible to them. More, it would be radiating with joyful truth, even though clothed in the garment which is the language of the Fathers, of the Councils, of the Pontiffs, of the theologians of other ages.

But in any case, we see that the Church is an interior call. The voice does not deafen, does not frighten; it is not distracting, it is not offensive; it does not reproach. It awakens, arouses and refills the soul with truth, certainty and energy. It calls on the mind to think, on the will to will, and on the feelings to burst into song. It is the voice of life, the voice of poetry, the voice of prayer. It widens, liberates and reveals. Sometimes it reveals man to himself, makes him understand his right, his duty, his destiny; and, let us say, his call.

This is what still constitutes the Church: the call.

Let us listen to her voice. May you do so, may all do so. With Our Apostolic Benediction.

HOLINESS THROUGH SUFFERING
AND THE CROSS

*On Sunday May 10th the Holy Father presided
at the ceremony in St. Peter's Basilica of the
canonization of Marie Victoire Thérèse Couderc.
He delivered the following allocution.*

Let Us first address a word of welcome in their own language
to Our dear Children from France, who have come in large
numbers to witness the glorification of their humble and glorious
fellow country-woman.

We have the pleasure of greeting Monsieur Marcellin, Minister
for the Interior and other members of the special mission sent
by the French Government for this occasion. We greet Cardinal
Renard, Archbishop of Lyons and the Bishops of France who are
with him, particularly Mons. Jean Hermil, Bishop of Viviers, the
diocese in which the new Saint was born.

Is there any need to say that it is with very special satisfaction
that We greet the numerous Daughters of St. Thérèse Couderc and
their Superior General?

Finally, We have the honour and joy of having an exceptional
guest with us today, the supreme " Catholicos " of all the Armenians, Vasken I, who has come from the holy city of Etchmiad-
zin to bring to the Church of Rome the greetings of the glorious
Armenian Church, which is so rich in saints and martyrs. We
thank Providence for having enabled a canonization ceremony to
take place during this historic visit, so enabling Our Armenian
guests and their most worthy spiritual Head to share in the joy
of the whole Church.

The solemnity being celebrated here and now calls for a long
discourse in praise of God, " who comforts us in all our tribulations, that we may comfort them who are in trouble " (*2 Cor.* 1, 4),

and who does so through the appearance of saints along our earthly pilgrimage. It calls for praise of the new saint, Marie Victoire Thérèse Couderc and for words of appreciation and congratulation to the Congregation of Our Lady of the Cenacle, which she founded. It calls for exhortation to the Church, which finds help and protection in this chosen daughter of hers; it calls for a comparison with our own century, which has inherited her experience and work. It calls, finally for praise and good wishes to France, which produced this Saint and provided her field of action.

But We must limit Ourself to a few words only, just enough to do homage to the Saint who has now been canonized, and to indicate the main lines for wider thought about her life and the institution which she founded. Even these few words take the form of queries rather than information about this new heavenly Daughter of the earthly Church. The questions are: what was St. Thérèse Couderc's personality? What was her work? We should be glad to be answered by those Religious present who are her daughters and followers. They are certainly very well informed about her, as their duty and their privilege, but at this moment they will be curious to know what We think about her. What was your Saint's personality like? We do not intend to trace the history of her life. We will speak briefly and be content with just a few indications about her.

The Church has a fine array of holy religious women, holy foundresses, saints who lived in the last century, saints who grew out of the fertile soil of France, which was turned up by the Revolution, then ploughed through, as it were, by the epic of Napoleon. What characteristic features identify and distinguish her whom we are honouring today?

Life of angelic poverty

We can take it for granted that she possesed the general characteristics of a nineteenth century woman religious: the traditional features of a life of ardent love, but a life detached from the ordinary way of living (the honest and worthy life of family love), a life aimed at and borne towards total consecration to

182

the Lord, an angelic life of poverty, a life forming part of a strictly organized and disciplined community, a life marked by one or other work of charity. Such religious life was no longer cloistered, yet, it was still protected within a house apart. The nun was succeeded by the " sister ", a religious who was no longer stationary and contemplative, that is, dedicated solely to prayer, but one who was also active as well as contemplative. Awareness and voluntary effort, freedom of choice and practical abnegation give this form of religious life interior intensity and exterior dedication. It has an ideal of piety, generosity, holiness, which has formed an admirable type of woman dedicated to Christ. It is a type which has been adopted as a model by myriads of strong virginal souls, and, by God's grace, it still flourishes in the Catholic Church. One can understand how it has exerted a powerful attraction.

What attitude, then, did Marie Victoire have towards this kind of life before she became Sister Victoria? We know the various kinds of attitudes adopted by souls which turn towards it. The phenomena of vocation are quite rich and complex; they reflect the most varied interior histories, which are marked by uncertainties, are painful and sometimes dramatic. But the case of Thérèse Couderc was one of the clearest and simplest that could be: it was the case of a vocation which, we might say, was born with her. From her very earliest years she had one single, most precocious desire: a wish for the religious life, though she did not know what particular kind and it was not easy for her to find out. That innate inclination as it were which precedes the experience of life and cultural formation, even though it must delay the attainment of its goal until the age of reason is reached, was nevertheless free of doubts, free of flaws, and unconditional. It was an ingenuous and secure vocation. The family circumstances in which she lived certainly played a big part in all this. They were the circumstances of country and mountain people who were modest and honest, pious and hardworking, rather austere, and rather patriarchal. Rural France of those times attests that strong Christian virtues had remained in the hearts of its people.

This seems to Us to be a distinctive mark of Thérèse Couderc's personality: her vocation. Why should not the same marvel be repeated today by Providence, through the prayers of that simple, elect soul, who did not so much choose her vocation as feel herself chosen by it? It would add support to holy Church, which is now in very different historical and social circumstances, and has so much need of new vocations.

A whole life a vocation

But how did this vocation come about, and how did it develop? Let us look at its outlines. It seems to Us to be marked by two apparently contradictory characteristics: fortitude on the one hand, abnegation on the other. But they are summed up and fused, in conformity with the saying of the Gospel: " I do always the things which please him (my Father) " (*Jn.* 8, 29). This undoubtedly sums up Christ's human personality, the mystery of his holiness. He was obedient unto death (*Phil.* 2, 8). His heroism is conformity to the will of God, and that is how our redemption is accomplished (cf. ADAM, *Christ Our Brother*, p. 4).

So we can say of our Saint: her will was continually extended. Her will was exercised in continual renunciation which was total in itself.

In this respect we ought to remember the influence which Father Terme, the priest from whom it all began, had upon her. He was a man of ardent religious fervour and charity, and an outstanding guide in the paths of spirituality and in practical undertakings. He was more generous and impulsive than reflective and enlightened, and he was all energy and enthusiasm, but he led the way on the royal road of God's will, with that blind dedication which reveals the light of the Spirit. He said of himself, " I only ask to accomplish the work to which God destines me, without even knowing what it is ". And so the new little religious family arose at La Louvesc, where the Saint's mortal remains now lie, and near by is the tomb of a Saint who was another example and master of exceptional energy and apostolic enterprise: St. Francis Régis.

The course of events seemed to be revealing the presence of God's hand, guiding men and things. The nascent institution came under the inspiration and guidance of the Fathers of the

Company of Jesus. It was shaped and developed along the lines of its spirituality and rule. It separated from its original trunk, which was the foundation aimed at the apostolate of country schools, and, still following suggestions of Father Terme, devoted itself to the work of spiritual retreats and exercises. Father Terme soon died, and the institution then derived its spiritual character from Father Fouillot, a distinguished son of St. Ignatius and a good religious. To him it also owed its constitutions and its title of the Congregation of Our Lady of the Cenacle.

But this development was also the Foundress's way of the Cross. It was along this way that Thérèse Couderc mainly showed that she was a saint, if sanctity is truly formed and truly manifests itself through the cross. She bore it for forty-five years. That cross is such that the religious life weighs upon the person who takes it up, sometimes in a particularly heavy and strange manner upon anyone who has the grace of being a founder. A Foundress's mission can become painfully dramatic in certain circumstances, especially when the difficulties come from those in authority in the Church and from those who share the lot of community life; in other words, when the person who causes the suffering is venerated and good, and has a paternal relationship or that of spiritual filiation to the sufferer.

This is a kind of suffering which we would not suppose to be possible at first sight, indeed we would not even imagine it to exist. It occurs in relation with ties established in the field of ecclesial charity, the most demanding and finest of the things the Lord left us. It is for this very reason that every wound inflicted upon such relationships produces the most acute pain.

Love increases sensitivity, and transmits feeling from the exterior to the heart. But we are human beings, which means that we are capable of making our fellowmen suffer, those nearest and dearest to us above all, and even with the best of intentions. If our defects aggravate the wrong in the injury we do and make it offensive, bitterness sinks deeply in, and causes reactions such as only superior virtue can contain.

We might say that this is the story of Thérèse Couderc. It may be that imponderable motivations of a social kind went to suggest humiliating measures which were taken in her regard, for she was of modest peasant origin and had had limited schooling.

The spirit of the humble religious was loaded with vicissitudes, acts of ingratitude, rivalry, reproaches, mortifications. She was practically deposed from her position of Superior, her right to be regarded as Foundress was disputed, she was given posts and tasks below her capacities and deserts (cf. FOLLIET, p. 17). And this is where her greatness came out. She was above all great in humility. She was great in giving herself, in *se livrer*, as she often said. Her conduct consisted in silence, obedience, patience, conscious and constant interior immolation. This was also her defence. It was a tacit apologia of her virtue, and her virtue was not recognized until the sunset of her life. Today it is being glorified. In this regard Thérèse Couderc stands out as an heroic soul, as an extraordinary teacher, as a Saint. This is an aspect which serves to establish that feeling of sympathy, devotion and admiration and trust which we owe to the Saints.

And her work? It was the work of the Cenacle. Everyone knows about it. It was known above all to Our venerated and great Predecessor, Pope Pius XI. When he was working at the Ambrosian Library in Milan, he exercised his wise and hidden priestly ministry for forty years with the Cenacle of Milan. We Ourself have had occasion to go there for some religious occasion, and to the one at Rome also. The Cenacle is a religious institute dedicated to Our Lady, who remained in the midst of the first Christian community, and awaited, invoked and received the outpouring of the Holy Spirit on the day of Pentecost. It is a religious institute which recalls (and imitates by living) two aspects of the presence of the Spirit in Jesus' human life. The interior aspect is one of silence, of prayer, of contemplation and intimate colloquy with God, in exercise of the sublime, most delicate, most delightful and patient art of prayer, to the point of making it one's own nourishment, one's own breath, one's own personal fullness, one's own continual communion with Christ. The exterior aspect consists in *contemplata aliis tradere*, in transmitting the treasures of truth and virtue to others. It makes of the religious apostolate, consequently of the imitation of Christ, the exercise of one's charity. It is a school of Christian life and Christian doctrine. It is a refuge of silence and meditation; it is a clinic for rehabilitating moral and spiritual forces. The Cenacle is a simple and happy religious formula, a synthesis of contemplative life and active life; it is a synthesis of personal, community and social life, of silence and of speech. Ascetic effort and mystical abandon are here harmoniously integrated, as has been said: " Christian perfection supposes constant union of the ascetic and the mystic, on differing levels " (BRÉMOND, *Introd. à la Ph. de la prière*, p. 338).

The Cenacle is a specialized institution for giving a social service of spiritual exercises. It draws inspiration from the great school of St. Ignatius, yet is open to all currents of Catholic spirituality. It seeks to apply an Encyclical which ought not to be forgotten: *Mens Nostra*, which that same Pius XI issued in December 1929 and which deals with the Spiritual Exercises (*AAS*, 1929, p. 689 sqq.). In other words, the Cenacle is organized in such a way as to offer to many kinds of people the possibility of enjoying a few days, perhaps even a few hours of retreat, of recollection, of silence, meditation, prayer and sacramental regeneration. It offers it to the world of women especially, to young women and mature women belonging to every social class.

We are children of the modern world. We are therefore in a position to appreciate the providential character of such an institution and to feel obliged to make our gratitude to Saint Theresa Couderc our best way of expressing the devotion which is due to her. We are caught up by the " assembly line " of the demands and the rhythm of our external activity; we are fascinated by the charm of the tanglible scene, pressing around us relentlessly and taking us away from ourselves into fields of reality, of representations and of interests which do not leave the spirit any possibility for remaining within itself and disposing those things which concern its own destiny. We therefore feel the need, sometimes even the duty to recuperate, in mental reflection and freedom of will, in spontaneous enjoyment, or in pure experience of our personal feelings. That is, we feel the need to live with ourselves (it was said of St. Benedict that he lived with himself —*secum vivebat*), and by these means to rise by an easy ascent as it were to God. So we hear the call to seek Christ our interior master, and to breathe the mysterious air of the Spirit. We may repeat to ourselves St. Peter Damian's words: *Dedimus corpori annum, demus animae dies*: We have given the whole year to our bodies (our temporal lives), let us give a day to our souls (*Serm.* 12; *PL* 52, 186). This need to compensate through religious and personal intensity for a life which has been dissipated in *fascinatio nugacitatis*—the fascination of valueless things (Wisdom 4, 12), or secular interests, applies to modern people who wish to remain Christian and not lose sight of the true and ultimate end of existence.

And it is a very fine thing that this should be possible under the sign of the Cenacle, that is, in surroundings where the primacy of contemplation is observed by pure and consecrated souls; in a place where the fact, or rather the mystery of the Church is recalled in the wholeness and liveliness of Pentecost, for it was at Pentecost that the Mystical Body of Christ was born in the shape of its visible and organic institution, through supernatural infusion of life, in the presence of Christ's Mother. That institution has continued living for centuries in unity and has spread itself, and the Mother of Christ is the spiritual mother of that same Church.

All this is fine and beautiful, consoling, attractive and promising, thanks to this humble Saint, Marie Thérèse Couderc, Foundress of the " Cenacle ".

May 13th, 1970

WE NEED FIRM FAITH AND ACTIVE CHARITY

T he Pilgrim Church. This is an expression which the Council
brought back into use. What does it mean? It occurs often in
the Council's documents. We find it in the Constitution on the
Sacred Liturgy, for example, where the Church is said to be
" present in the world and still a pilgrim " (No. 2). In the Constitution *Lumen gentium* it appears in reference to a beautiful
quotation from St. Augustine: " The Church continues its pilgrimage among the world's persecutions and God's consolations "
(No. 8; *The City of God*, 18, 51, 2; *PL* 41, 614). Again, it says that
" everything good which the People of God may offer to the human
family during the time of its earthly pilgrimage, comes from the
fact that the Church is the universal sacrament of salvation "
(*Gaudium et spes*, 45), etc.

The Pilgrim Church

What is the meaning of this pilgrimage? The image of the pilgrim
is clear and tells us many quite important things, yet they are
not simple or easily understood. Still, it is well to keep them
in mind. The image of a pilgrimage tells us that the Church has a
twofold life. One is in time, that in which we now find ourselves.
The other is beyond time, in eternity, that to which our pilgrimage is headed. Awareness of the fact that the Church exists in
the changeability of time—as does every creature and every single
individual—will make us realize, not only in a speculative way but
also on the practical and moral plane, the unstable and frail
nature of everything that goes to make up our present world.

We know that everything is in flux, that everything passes
away, that we ourselves are ephemeral, mortal. Yet in practice
we think and live as if things and life itself were stable and should
always be the same. Even when we accept the inexorable law

189

of time and try to move towards some goal in the future, we always think that it will be a fixed point, a place of rest. This is one of our habitual illusions, from which the Lord has constantly awakened us. For example, he gave us the warning: " Do not labour for the food that perishes, but for that which endures unto life everlasting " (*Jn.* 6, 27). The Lord left us two fundamental lessons about this puzzling matter of time. He told us how fleeting it is (cf. *Lk.* 12, 20), in the story of the rich man who was wholly concerned with accumulating goods, and was suddenly carried off by unexpected death (cf. *1 Cor.* 7, 31: " the scene of this world passes away ... " etc.). He told us how precious it is (cf. *Jn.* 12, 35: " Walk while there is still light ... "; *Mt.* 20, 6 etc.). But it is precious in relation to an end to be won beyond time. We ought to use time, use it with feverish intensity, not enjoy it with slothful indifference and anxious hedonism (" carpe diem "—pluck every passing day ...).

Now this might call for some hard thought about the nature of time (cf. ST. AUGUSTINE, *Confessions*, XI, 14; *PL* 32, 816) and the general ideas which derive from such thoughts, ideas about evolution, development, progress (cf. GUITTON, *L'Existence temporelle*, Aubier 1949). But for the moment it will be enough for us to remember that God has made creation and human destinies a becoming; he has placed mankind in this stream of continual change together with everything else; he has placed the Church in it; the Church is sailing in time, through history.

Unerring aim

We have just uttered a magic word: history. It is very fashionable today, in theology too, in the study of religion, so much so that the whole of the Christian religion is now being commonly described as the history of salvation. In other words, the relationship between man, or rather mankind and God is now regarded as a series of events occurring in time, over the centuries, as the fulfilment of a mysterious divine plan (cf. *Col.* 1, 26; *Eph.* 1, 10; *Gal.* 4, 4, etc.), and that the divine design became plain at a certain moment, " the fullness of time ", in the coming of Christ. But it is not a completed plan, for it leads to a second, future coming of Christ, which will be the last, the eschatological coming. The Church is living in this second period, the one which runs from the Christ of the Gospel to the Christ of the Apocalypse. It is living in time, like every other human institution; it is living a history of its own, which we call a pilgrimage.

The pilgrim Church means the Church passing through time with these two characteristics which distinguish its history. One is that the Church has certain values which must be safeguarded (St. Paul called them the " depositum ", *2 Tim.* 1, 12; 1, 14). Those values are the faith, grace, Christ living in the mystery of his Mystical Body which is the Church itself. This is to say that the Church is alive and bears the divine guarantee that the adversities of history shall not be able to destroy her (let us recall the Lord's own prophecy: " portae inferi non praevalebunt ": the gates of hell shall not prevail *Mt* 16, 18), and that this adventurous but unconquered pilgrimage shall last " even until the end of the world " (*Mt.* 28, 20).

The other characteristic is certainty that the Church's pilgrimage through the centuries has a fixed goal. That shall be the final, glorious and endless meeting with Jesus Christ living at the Father's right hand, that is to say, in God Himself, with the Holy Spirit, in the indescribable mystery of the Most Holy Trinity. This goal gives the Church the sense that it is near and almost imminent; it inspires the final invocation, " Amen. Come, Lord Jesus! " (cf. St. Augustine in *Ps.* 137; *PL* 37, 1781; *Apoc.* 22, 20; cf. Journet, *L'Eglise*, III, *Essai de Théologie de l'Histoire du Salut*, p. 102).

It is hard to keep balance

This view of the Church is recalled to our attention today by the fact that the title of pilgrim is repeatedly applied to her. It can teach us many things. Their deeper meaning is hard to understand (cf. Mouroux, *Le mystère du temps*, Aubier 1962), but they have become the currency of ordinary discussion. The first thing to understand is the meaning or direction of history, not as a mere succession of human vicissitudes within the blind and inescapable play of natural and cosmic becoming and of human liberty, but rather an evolutionary process which man is under-

191

going and which we believe to be guided by a dominant thought, leading all things towards a possible and free result which is salvation (cf. *Rom.* 8, 28).

We Christians are not afraid of history. We are not afraid of the events and changes of which history consists and which devour and generate men and things. " Non habemus hic manentem civitatem ", we have not here a lasting city, " but we seek that which is to come " (*He.* 13, 14). Consequently we are always ready for newness and progress, and we do not lose confidence and courage, whatever may happen. We are on a journey. But our journey is in history, and we are travelling in the world, not as fugitives and aliens, but as participants in the world's complicated and tumultuous life, happy or sad as it may be (cf. the entire Constitution *Gaudium et spes*). Precisely because we are Christians, we have a mission to perform here in the world; we have responsibility towards it, and a work of charity to carry through.

And this brings up the big problem of relations between us Christians—and, We must add, the Church—and the world. The world is in a maelstrom of unpredictable transformations. Two attitudes suggest themselves. One is immobility, the other is relativism, and the latter has a particularly tempting attraction today. Neither one nor the other ought to be excluded. We must find the line of complementarity. We ought to be firm in maintaining our reason for living and the source of our life and energy, the " deposit ", as We said. This means most loyal and coherent attachment to the tradition from which the Christian life comes to us with its irreplaceable and immutable elements. We ought to be equally expert at shaping the contingent forms of ecclesial life to the needs of our modern way of living and, even more, equally adept at shaping the contingent forms of our mission according to the changes of circumstances, places and times. This is well known, yet in practice it is difficult to strike a balance and achieve a synthesis between the two attitudes. This is the characteristic problem of the present moment: We need firm faith and active charity.

This is the path the pilgrim Church is taking. Let us pray to St. Peter, above whose tomb we are gathered, to ask him to give us the pastoral guidance we need.

Our Apostolic Benediction to you all.

THE COUNCIL, THE PROGRAMME
OF POPE PAUL'S PONTIFICATE

> *On May 15th Paul VI received in audience
> members of the Council of the General Sec-
> retariat of the Synod of Bishops who have
> recently held their first reunion. The Pope
> delivered the following address.*

Dearly beloved and venerable Brothers:

We are very happy indeed to welcome you and to greet you with most cordial affection. Your presence here recalls to our thoughts those days of fraternal communication, of intense activity, of prayer and recollection last October at the Extraordinary Session of the Synod of Bishops. We see again the thoughtful faces of so many " called by the Holy Spirit to rule the Church of God " (*Ac.* 20, 28). Representing the Episcopal Conferences of the whole world, they were our companions in the spiritual atmosphere of the sacred rites celebrated in the Sistine Chapel and in the Liberian basilica, as they were also in the austere surroundings of the Synod Hall. Here they took part in a work that knew no intermission, a work of maximum importance for exploring the depths of the principle of episcopal collegiality, demonstrating also its relationship with the humble successor of St. Peter, guardian of the supreme precept of love and fidelity to Christ, and its relationship with the individual bishops.

We have no intention of reminding you at the moment of what is already well known to you all. But we would like to express our sincere and immense satisfaction at your presence here in Rome which is coming to an end today. We are also very pleased with the concrete answer of the votes of the Fathers, and express our determined intention to fulfil them. In a welcoming speech on October 27 last year we did in fact clearly manifest our purpose to impart greater efficiency to the Synod Secretariat: " Nostrum esse propositum—we said—ut Secretaria Synodi ampliore efficientia donetur " (*AAS*, 61, 1969, p. 728).

That wish has now become a reality: and now you are here, Venerable brethren, Cardinals and bishops from every continent, and you have reached the conclusion of your first working reunion. Once more we see confirmed the immense benefit conferred upon· the government of the Church by this meeting of Bishops. This is in accordance with our clearly expressed intention at the end of the Motu proprio *Apostolica sollicitudo*, September 15, 1965: to draw ever increasing advantages " from the comfort of your experience, the support of your counsel and the weight of your authority ".

Continuity of the Synod

The dynamic effect of the recent Ecumenical Council is thus being developed for the greater good of the Church. As far as we are concerned, it is our firm intention to hold fast to its perspectives and to put them into practice untiringly, day after day, in our pastoral activity and service for the whole Church, nor shall we permit ourself to be influenced by certain unwonted pressures, perhaps motivated by lack of knowledge. In close union with you, my Venerable brothers, who from one Synod to another represent for us the continuity of the Synod, we wish progressively to further the Council teaching in the life of the Church. We are happy to have you near us, you who have been chosen as trust-worthy by our brothers in the episcopate; and—although it is hardly necessary to say so—we have the same confidence in you that they have shown. Thus, far from noisy publicity, in an atmosphere of fraternal dialogue and fruitful collaboration in the service of all the Churches, episcopal collegiality becomes a living thing, as the Council has declared, and finds ever wider applications for the greater good of the Church.

" Conciliar constancy "

For our part, the Council stands, in fact, as the programme of our pontificate. It has been most consoling for us to learn lately that a member of your Council, Cardinal Francis Marty, Archbishop of Paris, recalling our vocation to be *reassembleur du Collège apostolique* (the one who again assembled the Apostolic College), has spoken of our " conciliar constancy " (*Eglise de Paris*, 1ᵉʳ mai, 1970). In effect, we set great store upon the Council as a most precious gift of the Holy Spirit, and we endeavour to show respect for Episcopal Collegiality. This is in sharp contrast to what has recently been said, to our amazement and sorrow, and said in a way which, in our opinion, does not seem suitable either to the fraternal style required by collegiality or to the gravity of the problems, problems which, as everyone is aware, are at present being studied by responsible and competent people.

The Pope bears witness to the faith

These voices, which wish to pass for that of the Council, disturb conciliar agreement, dissent from collegial harmony and are merely spokesmen for a certain theological opinion. A particular theology—we take the opportunity of repeating—is not the Council, even though it may be a legitimate opinion. The Pope is not, and cannot be, either the supporter or the spokesman, still less the prisoner of any given school. He is the Successor of St. Peter by will of Jesus Christ. To him it falls as a primary duty to stand at the head of his brothers, and in close union with them to be a witness to the faith of the Church of which he is the appointed spokesman, authorized to expound the conciliar teaching in accord with its whole tradition. This is our mission: this, with the help of the Holy Spirit, is our service to the Church.

And now we would like to speak to you of the happiness your presence has brought us, of the hopes which we entertain for this enlarged and representative institution which has its origin within the Synod of Bishops. It is a sign of the Synod's vitality; it is a guarantee of order, of research, of co-ordination of the problems which you will deal with by degrees in the sittings which, please God, will take place every two years, as we have already stated. It offers promise of an increasingly harmonious and fruitful development of the work of the Synod so that, in these troubled and extraordinary times, the activity of the bishops will truly respond with ever-increasing fidelity to the Will of Christ for his Church, to the love of Christ for his Church the Church that he willed to be " sancta et immaculata " because " Christus dilexit

Ecclesiam, et seipsum tradidit pro ea, ut illum sanctificaret mundans lavacro aquae in verbo vitae " (*Eph.* 5, 26, 27). It will likewise assist the bishops to come to grips with questions for the good of humanity.

It is our ardent wish that this work which is but the extension upon an ever-widening field of the pastoral solicitude of the bishops for the Church of God, should be based upon two leading principles: unity and charity. This we have already recalled at the opening of the Extraordinary Session of the Synod on October 11, 1969 (*AAS*, 61, 1969, p. 719). We are sincerely grateful for the collaboration you have already shown in this direction; at the same time we have the highest confidence in your experience, in your prestige, in your zeal and in your love for souls.

I assure you that the Synod of Bishops and its Secretariat will ever receive on the part of this See of Peter the most cordial and careful attention, as well as the efficacious support that is due to it. With all our heart we impart to you our special Apostolic Blessing which we extend in one wide embrace to all our brothers in the Episcopate, to beloved priests, the apple of our eye, and to their individual dioceses, the chosen portion of the one, holy, Catholic and apostolic Church.

PAUL VI ORDAINS 278 PRIESTS
IN ST. PETER'S SQUARE

*The Pope's homily during the Mass of ordina-
tion of 278 priests held in St. Peter's Square
on Whit-Sunday 17th May in celebration of
the 50th anniversary of his own ordination to
the priesthood.*

T oday is Pentecost, the commemoration of the fact and the
mystery which gave life to the Church as Christ's Mystical
Body. Christ sent the Church his Spirit, according to his promise
(*Jn.* 15, 26; 16, 7), and that divine Paraclete continues to enliven
the Church. Pentecost thus comes to mind, not only to recall that
event, but also to relive it. It is as if our customary invocation,
" Come, Holy Spirit ", were met by the reality of his response and
his presence, infusing into us some tiny yet living experience of
his beatifying coming. It is as if that indescribable current of
undying history, that is, the history of supernatural life, passes
into our mortal limbs, while the sound of the first sermon delivered
to the newborn Church echoes in our ears. That was Peter's
prophetic sermon: " And it shall come to pass in the last days, says
God, I will pour out my Spirit upon all flesh; and your sons
and daughters shall prophesy, and your young men shall see
visions, and your old men shall dream dreams " (*Ac.* 2, 17; *Joel.*
2, 28).

Pentecost grips us all; it moves us all, makes us think. In our
souls there shines a ray of new brightness, that " light of the
heart " which is full of love and truth. This is the feast of the
Holy Spirit, the feast of the nascent Church which shall never die;
it is the feast of souls set on fire by the divine inward presence.
It is the feast of wisdom, the feast of charity, of consolation,
of joy, of hope, of holiness. It is the feast of the beginning of
Christian culture and civilization. It is Pentecost.

Two circumstances unite to make this celebration a singular
and particularly vivid one. The first is the occurrence of the

fiftieth anniversary of Our own ordination to the priesthood. Fifty years have not cancelled in Us the memory of that beautiful yet in itself simple event in Our humble personal life. We would have preferred to have meditated on it in exterior silence and interior recollection. But the very nature of that priesthood conferred upon Us then imposes also the duty upon Us of enabling those who have the right to demand its ministry to take note of this anniversary and to recall it with signs of their piety and their goodness. That right belongs today to Our most beloved Church of Rome and to equally well beloved entire Catholic Church. This solemn ceremony tells Us all this and fills Us with gratitude and consolation.

The Priesthood and the cross

We feel obliged to thank all, family relations and friends, teachers and fellow workers, those present and those absent, those whom We know and those whom We do not know. We feel moved to sum up Our feelings for them in one single auto-biographical testimony, which is not original, because every priest can make the same act of witness for himself—what a wonderful thing it is to be a priest! Experience gained by the vicissitudes of the years may increase our sense of the intrinsic relationship between our priesthood and the Lord's cross, yet that never exhausts its beauty and its happiness. Every day, every year, every anniversary renews enjoyment of that beauty and happiness, and brings greater and greater knowledge and inner experience of them (cf. *Jn.* 7, 38).

As the priestly consciousness becomes more mature and profound, the Virgin's song rises up from it: *fecit mihi magna qui potens est.*

But We also feel obliged, today as then, to extol the divine mercy! Let Us do so in the following prayer: Thanks be to you, O Father, who regarded not Our littleness but rather seeing in it a reason for the exercise of your power, bestowed on Us a vo-cation, confirmed it by that of a paternal and wise Pastor, strength-ened it through the influence of good and patient teachers, and gladdened it with a desire to dwell in your house.

Thanks be to you, Lord Jesus, who associated Us, an unworthy but not useless instrument, in a living way with your ministry of salvation and communion, and placed Us among brethren whose hearts were turned towards the lowly. You then destined Us to walk with hastening steps by the side of youth and to carry out modest, painstaking work for this your Apostolic See, wholly and entirely for that which was the object of your love, your Church, and with a corresponding love.

Thanks be to you, enlivening Spirit, who have been Our inspirer and comforter in the weighty yet sweet ministry of fifty years, and who still come to Our aid so that We may not betray but rather show forth the image of our Master Jesus, and may always seek to be holy by you, to sanctify in you.

Then, O Lord, you called Us once more, timid and inept, closer to yourself and to your cross, saying: He who impose the burden will give the strength to bear it. Our reply rose up from Our heart: In your name, Lord, be it done according to your word.

" Traditio potestatis "

This, Brothers and Sons, is the testimony We owe you in relation to Our priesthood, the long duration of which you have so kindly wished to commemorate, thereby foretelling its not too distant sunset.

But another, truly Pentecostal event, enhances the reality and splendour of this festive celebration: the priestly ordination of these Deacons.

Greetings, dearly beloved chosen ones!

We have many things which We might say to you. But the time of day does not permit of long discourses. In addition, We do not wish to add new considerations to the many which already fill your minds, which you have certainly already gathered in your minds for this solemn moment. We will try to sum up in a single word everything which can be thought and said concerning the event which is about to occur for you. That word is transmission. Transmission of a divine power, a miraculous power of action, which *per sé* belongs only to Christ.

Traditio potestatis. Through the laying on of Our hands and the meaningful words which confer on the action a sacramental power, Christ sends down his Spirit from on high and pours into you that Spirit, the Holy Spirit, the vivifying and powerful Spirit.

He comes to you not only to dwell in you, as in the other sacraments, but also to enable you to perform certain definite actions which are proper to Christ's priesthood, and to make you his way, he produces in you a certain effect, so that you can not only represent Christ, but you can also act in a certain measure as Christ, through a delegation which imprints upon your souls an indelible character, and makes you like to him, everyone of you an " alter Christus ", another Christ.

An indelible character

Never forget that this marvel happens in you but not for you. It is for others, for the Church, which is to say, for the world to be saved. Your power is one of function, like the power of a special organ which works for the benefit of the whole body. Become instruments, become servants at the service of the brethren.

You can see the relationships which arise from this choice which has been made of you: relationships with God, with Christ, with the Church, with mankind. You understand what duties of prayer, charity and holiness, flow from your priestly ordination. You perceive what kind of conscience you will always need to form in order to be equal to the office with which you are invested. You understand with what spiritual and human mindfulness you will need to look at the world, with what sentiments and what virtues you will need to exercise your ministry, with what dedication and courage you will have to live your lives, in what a spirit of sacrifice united with that of Christ.

You know all this, but you will never cease thinking about it for as long as your earthly pilgrimage lasts—may it be long and serene. Never fear, dearest Sons and Brothers. Never doubt your priesthood. Never isolate it from your bishops and from its function in Holy Church. Never betray it! We will not now say any more to you. But We will repeat the prayer for you, as We have done on other occasion for new priests ordained by Us.

This is how We will pray for you today.

Come, O Holy Spirit, and give these ministers, dispensers of the mysteries of God, a new heart. May it renew in them all the education and training they have received. May it cause them to perceive the sacrament they have received as a surprising revelation. May it cause them to respond always with new freshness, as they do today, to the ceaseless duties of their ministry towards your Eucharistic Body and your Mystical Body. May it be a new heart, always young and gay.

Come, O Holy Spirit, and give these ministers, disciples and apostles of Christ the Lord, a pure heart, trained to love him alone who is God with you and with the Father, to love with the fullness, joy and depth which he alone can infuse, when he is supreme and the total object of the love of man living in your grace. A pure heart, which does not know evil except in order to describe it, define is, combat it and put it to flight. A pure heart, like the heart of a child, capable of enthusiasm and capable of trembling.

Come, O Holy Spirit, and give these ministers of the People of God a big heart, a heart open to your silent and powerful inspiring word, but closed to every mean ambition, a stranger to every kind of miserable human competition, but totally imbued with a sense of and feeling of Holy Church. A big heart, yearning to be like that of the Lord Jesus, wide enough to contain within itself the Church, and the world. A great and strong heart to love all, to serve all, to suffer for all. A great and strong heart to bear all temptations, every trial, every annoyance, every weariness, every disappointment, every offence. A big, strong and constant heart when sacrifice calls, happy only to beat with the heart of Christ, and to carry out humbly, faithfully and manfully the divine will.

This is Our prayer for you today. It embraces in blessing all here present, your companions, your teachers, especially your kinsfolk.

The moment for action has come: it is Pentecost.

GREAT COURAGE DEMANDED
FROM THE MEMBERS OF THE CHURCH

*On Monday morning, May 18th, after the Con-
sistories the Sacred College of Cardinals offered
the Pope their Congratulations on the fiftieth anniversary of his ordination to the priesthood. Cardinal Aloisi Masella, acting as Dean
of the Sacred College, delivered an address, to
which the Holy Father replied as follows.*

Lords Cardinals,

W e have been greatly moved by the affection with which you
surround Us on this happy occasion, through the delicate
expressions of dear and venerated Cardinal Aloisi Masella. We
like to see your concern as a sign of the unanimity of the
Catholic faith, which unites us all in Christ's name, and of that
priestly fervour which has inspired our lives—Ours with the
graces of half a century, yours too with so many years—lives
which have been passed in announcing the good news of Christ
the Saviour and in service to the Holy See.

We have no greater joy than that of sharing Our priestly joy
with you, and through you with all Our Brothers in the episcopate,
and all priests and faithful. We desire to tell all of the satisfaction
We feel because of their affection, of Our gratitude for their
prayers, and Our joy at their generous apostolate in the Church's
service. This is a difficult time in the Church's life, yet it is also
a time which God is blessing, a time rich in grace and full of hope.
Today as yesterday, the Church is carrying out her mission
of salvation throughout the world, and transmits the promises
of redemption and everlasting life. The Church today may be
groaning as St. Paul said of every creature, by reason of the
pains of giving birth, which go before exultation at the appearance of new life; yet the Church also bears the Spirit of God
within herself, the creator Spirit, the Spirit of love and charity.

202

The spirit of division may be at work as usual in the Father's field and is sowing cockle there (cf. *Mt.* 13, 25), but we were fore-warned, and we will not allow ourselves to bed taken in by its deceptions or discouraged by its intruisons. We will go on with Our humble, modest, fervent and disinterested work, watching the signs of the times, in a genuine climate of sincere and loyal dialogue and fraternal conversation, inspired by prayer and nourished by charity.

The Lord's Spirit is also at work in his Church. He is not a spirit of contestation, but a spirit of renewal and peacefulness. He is uninterruptedly stirring up fresh undertakings, those of the apostolate and of holiness. Now that we have celebrated the feast of Pentecost we ought to make ourselves even more attentive to his voice, more docile to his inspirations, more fearless in re-sponding to his urgings. He is launching us out into the deep, that is, towards the needs of the new age. Let us meet these needs with love, serious thought, and, without giving in to the unwise tendencies of the secular world, without fearing the traps set by the Evil One, but being certain, as We are certain, of being in God's hands, of being carried along by his love.

Today we must fervently beg a great grace from the Holy Spirit. The hour now striking on the clock of history demands great courage indeed from all the Church's children. In a very special way it calls for the *courage of truth*, that which the Lord in person recommended to his disciples, when he said, " Let your **yes** be yes, and your no, no " (*Mt.* 5, 37).

Facing the demands of the new age

The flood of contestation, negation and violence is now sub-merging even the most secure dykes. Man is at grips with his destiny, and often resembles a seafarer who has lost his way on the high seas, has lost contact with the shore. Man may also be said to be like a climber who has been surprised by a storm during an ascent and is experiencing the dizziness of the abyss.

How could a Christian not be overcome by this tempest, which seems to be striking against the Church herself? At the very moment when the Church is asking the Holy Spirit for the energies for spiritual and apostolic growth, necessary to surmount a new and difficult stage in her history, we see destructive forces arising in the Church herself. Some would like to see her turn back on her tracks to regain her lost security. But others abandon themselves to the exultation of a dangerous transformism. It appears that they no longer know who Christ really is, what the Church really is, or what is the faith that enables us to serve Christ and the Church.

The Courage of Truth

How often divine Scripture warns us about such things! Let us not listen to those who claim to be bringing us a different Gospel (cf. *Gal.* 1, 8-9). How many gnoses have disappeared during the course of the centuries, even though in their own times they seemed to be much more intelligent things than the mystery of the Cross and the name of Jesus the Saviour (cf. *1 Cor.* 18-25)! Idols are always rising up again. But what would Christianity be if it sought to reduce itself to an ideology, to a naturalistic sociology? What would the Church be if it let itself break up into so many sects? No, Christ came to free man from all idols, above all from those idols which his own mind shapes from century to century: " with the savage energy of the passions and the destructive scepticism of human intelligence in religious matters ... no truth, however sacred, can long resist it " (Cardinal JOHN HENRY NEWMAN, *Apologia pro Vita Sua, A History of my religious Opinions*, London, Longmans 1902, Chap. 5).

The courage of truth is demanded from Christians more and more if they are to remain faithful to their vocation of animating this new world which is being sought. May our faith in Christ never weaken in this age of ours which is distinguished, as was St. Augustine's, by real " poverty and penury of truth " (Serm. 11, 11; *Miscellanea Agostiniana* 1930, 256). May everyone be ready *vitam impendere vero*, to pledge his life to truth (JUVENAL, *Sat.* IV, 91)!

Courage to proclaim the truth is the first and indispensable charity which pastors of souls ought to exercise. Never, not even under the pretext of charity towards one's neighbour, let us permit a minister of the Gospel to utter a purely human word. The salvation of mankind is at stake. Therefore, while the memory of Pentecost is still green, We appeal to all responsible pastors to raise their voices when necessary, with the strength of the Holy Spirit (cf. *Ac.* 1, 8) to cleanse what is dirty, to warm what is lukewarm, to strengthen what is weak, to enlighten what is dark.

More than at any other time this is the hour of clarity for the Church's faith. That faith calls on us to illuminate the darkness of human realities with the lightning of the gospel message, in search of that spiritual peace which arises from possession of the truth and from love of prayer, according to the great and beautiful saying of Our Predecessor upon the Chair of the Church of Milan, St. Ambrose: *Est bona pax et necessaria, ut nemo disputationum turbetur incertis neque passionum corporalium tempestate quatiatur, sed simplicitate fidei et tranquillitate mentis quietus circa Dei cultum perseveret affectus*: Peace is good and necessary, so that no one shall be troubled by uncertainties or shaken by the storm of bodily passions, but that calm attention to worship of God shall continue in simplicity of faith and tranquillity of mind (*De Spiritu Sancto*, I, 12, 126; C.S.E.L. ed. Faller, 79, 9, p. 69).

Bloodshed in Indochina and the Near East

This inward peace ought to be reflected outwardly, in the tranquillity of order. This is indeed the daily concern which assails us in Our tremendous ministry. It is that to which, with God's help, We try to bring the full and total contribution of Our humble powers, so that peace may be established in the world and be strengthened more and more. It is such a precious and such a frail gift that it too, as neverbefore, seems to be in jeopardy in many parts of our tormented world. Your Eminence chose to refer to this matter with delicate words, and We are grateful to you for it.

The fact is that ever since the beginning of Our priesthood an exclamation which is also a call has continually resounded in Our ears: *Quam pulchri pedes evangelizantium pacem, evangeli-*

zantium bonum! (How beautiful are the feet of them that preach the gospel of peace and bring glad tidings of good things!) (*Rom.* 10, 15). And, especially since the Lord called Us to serve his Church as Supreme Pontiff, We have been firmly resolved to dedicate the whole of Our work to the service of peace. Now We can affirm, with a humble but tranquil conscience, that in these years Our mind has never entertained thoughts other than thoughts of peace, and that We have always tried as far as We have been able, to follow up thoughts of peace with action and effort aimed at conserving or re-establishing harmony among mankind and among the nations, in justice and love. We do so incessantly, without being discouraged by lack of success, or, sometimes, even by incomprehension of the purposes which move Us, but certain that We are making the deep yearning of mankind Our own, and above all confident, in the aid of him who is called the God of peace.

Unfortunately, We must acknowledge that the great conflicts which have been shedding blood for years in the regions of Indochina and the Middle East are far from turning towards the hoped for solutions, and have lately become even more difficult and complex. Not only are the fields of warlike operations spreading, but the people directly concerned seem also to count for less and less, though the wars are being conducted in their names. An increase in the military commitment of the great powers is actually making the conflicts more dangerous, because of the threat of unforseeable wider developments. It makes the outcome depend on conditions and the will of people other than those who have for years been suffering the sorrowful consequences of the war.

While We express Our lively and paternal participation in the sufferings of the latter, We desire at the same time to repeat an urgent appeal to those who have power and responsibility in these matters. We wish to do all We can—on one side and the other—and at the cost of sacrifice if need be, to search for a just and equitable negotiated settlement which shall take account of the rights and legitimate interests of all the peoples involved in the conflicts and of the expectations of mankind, which is trembling for its own fate.

Conquer poverty among peoples

Mankind which has the right to peace, has also the right that all should pledge themselves to get rid of the causes which foment conflicts within a nation and between nations. This is a difficult matter, but it is our duty to dedicate ourselves to it with sincere and tenacious wills.

We think of the inequality among peoples, of the poverty which still burdens such a great part of our brethren. We think of the injustices both old and new which are now being perpetrated or are already established, and of the reactions which they provoke. We think of the antagonisms and selfishness of social classes and of the World Powers, of the oppression of the weak and defenceless.

On the other hand We cannot but deplore the fact that there should be adopted as a means of warfare methods of terrorism which the civilized conscience rightly rejects. It is not by new injustices that we shall combat those against which people are in revolt. It is not by the violation of human rights that we can re-establish the order which has been upset by actions however criminal.

For Our part, We will not tire of raising Our voice, of intervening, with action often veiled in discretion, the purpose of which is to ensure that the action shall be as effective as possible and to ensure that no one's honour shall be offended. Our interventions are aimed at seeing that arguments of justice and —We would like to hope—the requirement of human brotherhood may find the hearing due to them and may become the basis of that true and sound peace which We pray for. May Christ hear those prayers, for he " is our peace "!

There, Venerable Brothers and Our Sons, dearly beloved Sons, is what We have desired to say to you on this occasion which is so intimate and dear to Us, and which you have willed to make so solemn through your presence and your solidarity. We thank the Holy Spirit together with you, and We beg him to confirm everyone's good resolutions in this hour of courage and truth, so that—and once more We are using St. Ambrose's word—*magis in bonis operibus et sermonibus et sensibus ambulantes, repleamur voluntate Dei* (*De Spiritu Sancto*, I, 7, 89; *op. cit.*, p. 53).

Amen, Amen.

THE HOUR OF COURAGE
FOR THE TRUTH HAS STRUCK

We want to add to something We said during the Consistory (that is, in the meeting of the Cardinals) held the other day. We think that it is important and topical and may be repeated in a general audience such as this is because it was said for all. We declared: " The hour now striking on the clock of history demands great courage from all the Church's children, and in a very special way the courage of truth, which the Lord himself recommended to his disciples when he said, ' Let your yes be yes and your no, no ' " (*Mt.* 5, 37).

This duty of courageously professing the truth is so important that the Lord himself described it as the purpose of his coming into this world. Standing before Pilate during the trial preceding his condemnation to death on the cross, Jesus uttered these solemn words: " For this I was born, and for this I have come into the world, to bear witness to the truth " (*Jn.* 18, 37). Jesus is the light of the world (*Jn.* 8, 12), he is the truth manifested. In order to fulfil that mission, from which our salvation comes, Jesus was to give up his own life, as a martyr for the truth, which he himself is.

The cornerstone

Hence two questions arise. The first sprang to the lips of Pilate himself. Perhaps he was not ignorant of philosophical discussions in the Greco-Roman world about truth, but perhaps he had a sceptical attitude towards them. He was a magistrate with the task of judging crimes and wrongs, not speculative theories. He was amazed that this Rabbi, who had been brought before him as someone worthy of death for high treason, should declare himself a witness of the truth. He at once interrupted him, per-

haps with some irony in his voice, *Quid est veritas?* what is truth?
(Someone has cleverly worked out a marvellous answer, an
anagram on this Latin phrase: *est vir qui adest*, it is the man who
stands before you). Pilate did not wait for an answer. He
tried to end the interrogation by dismissing the case. Yet the
question remains, for us, for all: What is the truth?

This is a big question, and it involves conscience, facts, history,
science, culture, philosophy, theology, faith. We feel the force
of the last mentioned: the truth of the faith. This is because the
Church's whole structure and that of Christianity are based on
the truth of the faith. Therefore the structure of our salvation
is based on it too, consequently that of human destinies and
civilization, to which they are linked. For this reason the truth of
the faith comes before us more than ever today as the fundamental basis on which we ought to build our lives. It is the
cornerstone (cf. *1 Pet.* 2, 6-7; *Eph.* 2, 20; *Mt.* 21, 42).

And what do we find? We find timidity and fear, uncertainty,
ambiguity, compromise. The situation has been well described as
follows: " Once it was human respect that spoilt everything. That
was what made pastors suffer. The Christian did not dare to
live according to his faith ... But now, are we not beginning to be
afraid of believing? This is an even worse evil, because it attacks
the foundations ... " (Cardinal GARRONE, *Que faut-il croire*, Desclée
1967). We felt obliged to make an explicit profession of faith
at the end of the Year of Faith on St. Peter's Day, 1968, to recite
a Creed, which followed the line of the authoritative teachings
of the Church and authentic Tradition, back to the evidence given
by the Apostles, which testimony is in its turn founded on Jesus
Christ. And he himself is described as the " faithful witness "
(*Apoc.* 1, 5).

" Daring to mistake their own blindness for the death of God "

But today truth is in crisis. Objective truth, which gives us
possession of reality through knowledge, is being replaced by
subjective truth: experience, conscience, free personal opinion,
not to mention criticism of our capacity to know and think
validly.

Philosophic truth is giving way to agnosticism, to scepticism, to the snobbery of systematic doubt. People study and research in order to demolish, not in order to find. They prefer emptiness. The Gospel warned us about this when it said, " Men preferred darkness to the light " (*Jn.* 3, 19). Together with the crisis in philosophic truth (oh, where has our sound rationality gone, our *philosophia perennis?*) religious truth has also collapsed in many minds which have not been able to bear the great and crystal-clear statements of the science of God, of natural theology, much less those of the theology of revelation. Their eyes have been darkened, then blinded. They have dared to think that their own blindness was the death of God.

So Christian truth is undergoing fearful shocks and crises today. They will not accept the teaching of the magisterium which Christ set up as a safeguard and for the logical development of his doctrine,, which is God's own teaching (*Jn.* 7, 12; *Lk.* 10, 16; *Mc.* 16, 16). There are some who try to make the faith easy by emptying it, the whole, the true faith, of those truths which appear to be unacceptable to the modern mind. They follow their own tastes, to choose a truth which is considered to be acceptable (selected faith). Others are looking for a new faith, especially a new belief about the Church. They are trying to bring her into line with the ideas of modern sociology and secular history. In this they are repeating errors of other times, by seeking to model the Church's canonical structures on existing historical structures. Others again would like to put their trust in a purely naturalistic and philantropic belief, a utilitarian belief, even though it might be based on the authentic values of the faith itself, those of charity. They would thus erect it into a cult of man and neglect the prime value, which is love and worship of God. Still others show a certain distrust for the faith's dogmatic demands, and take up the pretext of pluralism, which would enable them to study the inexhaustible wealth of divine truths and express them through a variety of languages and mentalities. Under this pretext they would like to legitimize ambiguous and uncertain expressions of the faith, and content themselves with research into it in order to avoid affirming it. They would like to turn to the opinion of the faithful in order to know what they wish to believe, and attribute the faithful with a questionable charism of competence and experience which puts the truth of the faith at the mercy of the strangest and most easily voiced choices.

All this happens when one does not submit to the Church's Magisterium, which the Lord willed to protect the truths of the faith (cf. *He.* 13, 7.9, 17).

The Magisterium's Guarantee

But, through divine mercy, we have this *scutum fidei*, this shield of the faith (*Eph.* 6, 16), that is, truth which is protected, secure and capable of withstanding the onslaught of the impetuous opinions of the modern world (cf. *Eph.* 4, 14). For us therefore a second question arises, the question of courage. We ought to have, as We said, the courage of the truth. We will not now make any analysis of this moral and psychological virtue which we call courage, and which all know to be a power of the mind, implying human maturity, vigour of mind, boldness of will and capacity for love and sacrifice. We will only note that, once more, Christian education shows itself to be a training ground for spiritual energy, human nobility, self-mastery and consciousness of duty.

We will add that such courage of the truth is chiefly required from him who is a teacher and champion of the truth, but that it also concerns all baptized and confirmed Christians. It is not a pleasant, sporting activity, but a profession of dutiful fidelity to Christ and his Church; and today it is great service to the modern world, which, more than we perhaps think, is looking to us for this beneficial and invigorating testimony. May Our Apostolic Blessing, together with the Lord's, help you in this respect.

HOPE—THE DRIVING
FORCE OF THE CHRISTIAN

For us believers one of the big questions in regard to the modern state of mind is that of man's attitude towards progress. The question is usually raised in the form of an objection. The believer, it is said, is a man with a static psychology; it is fixed, motionless. His dogmatic faith does not allow him to understand new things, to desire them, to develop them. The believer is living in the past, at that moment of history in which the gospel events occurred, two thousand years ago; time has not gone on for him, and his eyes are permanently looking backwards. Consequently his psychology is by its very character alien to the great and onrushing events of our time. He distrusts changes which are occurring in every field of human life: in thought, in science, in technology, in sociology, in behaviour, etc. He cannot be " a man of our time ", he cannot understand the young; he has no desires, no hopes; he is basically apathetic and afraid. And in the Church, he belongs to before the Council ... There is need for a new religious state of mind, a new theology, a new Church.

This description of a certain preconceived idea of the believer could continue indefinitely. The question is a big and important one, and the usually brief and elementary style of Our discourse will only permit Us to put it before you as We just have, and to add a simple query: Is it a true description? Does the believer really avoid the demands of the present, does he flee from the fascination of progress? (cf. DAWSON, *Progress and Religion*).

Faith is promise

Let us agree about one essential feature of the believer, but let us also defend it. It is true that he is a man of tradition, of the tradition in which he lives. He is the man of the Church,

212

that is, he is a child of that living and mystical social body which draws its life from its head, Christ. Christ lived in the history of the Gospel and is now living in the glory of heaven, in the divine fullness, at the right hand of the Father, as we say in the Creed. In other words, the Christian lives by an inheritance, on a memory which comes down from a past historical event which was decisive for the destiny of mankind: the Gospel; he also lives in the present which is communicated to him by the Holy Spirit from a sphere beyond time and natural reality. This is to say that he lives by faith and grace. If this line should break, man's life as a Christian is extinguished. It is a matter of life and death.

But let Us say at once: this link with the past and with the transcendent supernatural does not draw the believer away from the present and from the future, in time and in the other world, but on the contrary draws him more deeply into them. How is this? It is so because the faith to which he assents is a promise by its very nature. Rather, it is assent to truths which have still to be completely revealed to our knowledge and enjoyed by us. How does the letter to the Hebrews describe faith? It uses that celebrated formula: " Faith is the substance of things hoped for, the certainty of things not yet seen " (*He.* 11, 1). Therefore faith has an essential relationship with hope.

Desire for the supreme good

Yes, with hope. Hope is the moving force of human dynamism; more than that, as a theological virtue, it is the force which moves Christian dynamism. This raises the question of making an analysis of hope in the modern mentality, and We will leave you to do that. You will immediately see that modern man lives by hope. That is to say, that his soul is tensed towards the future, towards some good which is to be attained. What he has now does not satisfy him, but urges him on and torments him to get more, to find something else. Study, work, progress, contestation, and even revolution are so many forms of hope in action. This rush forwards, so characteristic of our time, is wholly moved by hope. Those who have least liking for the past and the present give their hearts to the future, that is to say, they hope. St. Thomas well says (S. Th. I-II, 40, 6) that hope abounds in the young. But if they are disappointed in their hope of attaining some kind of better thing in the future, they fall into despair. This often happens in the critical and pessimistic psychology of so many other people who are also children of our time.

But the Christian is the man of hope, and does not know despair. There is a difference between the Christian and the modern secular man in regard to hope. The latter is a *vir desideriorum*, a man of many desires (there is a close relation between desire and hope; hope comes under the instincts of strength, but desire comes rather under the instincts to enjoy; yet both strive towards future goods). The man of desires seeks to shorten the distance between himself and the goods to be attained; he is a man of short-term hopes; he wants to satisfy them soon. Tangible, economic and temporal hopes are more easily satisfied; they are therefore quickly exhausted, become empty, and often leave the heart disappointed. His hopes do not ennoble the mind; they do not give life its full meaning and they turn the course of life along paths of questionable progress.

But the Christian is the man of true hope, that which aims at attaining the supreme good (cf. St. Augustine's, *Fecisti nos ad te, Conf.* 1, 1). He knows that in his efforts to attain his desire he has the help of that same supreme Good which unites with hope the confidence and the grace to fulfil it (cf. S. Th. I-II, 40, 7).

Both hopes, secular and Christian, are motivated by deficiencies in our present conditions, by pain, poverty, remorse, need, dissatisfaction. But they are kept going by another, different force, and Christian hope can absorb all the truly human and honest tension in secular hope. Is not this the leading idea in the great pastoral Constitution *Gaudium et spes* published by the recent Council? " These is nothing truly human which does not find an echo in the hearts " of Christ's disciples (no. 1, cf. Terence's, *Humani nihil a me alienum puto*: nothing human is alien to me).

The gift of salvation

So let us conclude by correcting that false view of the believer as a hidebound reactionary, a professional quietist, a stranger to modern life, a man blind to the signs of the times and bereft of hope. Let us say that he is rather a man who lives by hope, and that his Christian salvation itself, however incipient and incomplete, is a gift to deal with, a goal to reach, because it is as it were something received on credit, for only " in hope are we saved " (*Rom.* 8, 24). Such a man will not allow himself to fall into the devouring relativism of time which passes, and he will not give in to blind fashion for novelties cut off from the coherence of Catholic tradition. But this does not make him an enemy of renewal and progress which have the stamp of the divine design on them. On the contrary, it will make him a ready and intelligent promoter of such renewal and progress, for he is the man of Hope.

Let us think about this a little. With Our Apostolic Blessing.

ONLY JESUS CAN TEACH TRUE
MEANING OF LOVE

*On the evening of the feast of Corpus Christi,
May 28th, the Holy Father celebrated Mass in a
square in the new Roman parish of Our Lady
of Hope, on the Salarian Way, on the north-
eastern outskirts of the City. After the gospel reading he spoke as follows.*

Dearest brethren and children!

We will begin, as is Our custom, with greetings.

Our first, reverent and respectful, greeting is for Cardinal
Angelo Dell'Acqua, Our Vicar General for this most beloved
Diocese of Rome. Through this We mean to greet and bless, in
deep union of faith and charity, all Our Diocese of Rome, present
or represented here.

And next a cordial greeting to your parish priest, Don Carlo
Bressan, a worthy son of Don Bosco, who together with his good
fellow-priests is exercising his pastoral ministry in this new parish
which has the beautiful title of Our Lady of Hope. It is becoming
a numerous, lively and organic parish, with its Salesian clubs, one
for boys, two for girls. Our affection, blessing and greeting go to
one and all of the parishioners, especially to the Christian families. We extend it to the neighbouring parishes, to the whole
quarter, and to all who have come to this celebration in order
to honour Lord Jesus Christ in the sacrament of the Eucharist.
Thank you all for being here; your presence will not lack plentiful
blessings from the Lord.

Some more special greetings. To youth, who We know are
here assisted and inspired by the spirit of St. John Bosco. A big
greeting to you, young people! We have you in Our heart and
We will pray for you in this special Mass today. We have trust
in your faith in Christ, in your sense of social charity for the
good of this whole newly formed and flourishing parish community. And now Our thoughts go to all who need comfort or

aid: the suffering, the poor, strangers, children, the unhappy. For all We implore the Mother of Hope and Christ, the friend of all who are in trouble, for consolation of the heart and the assistance of the charity of the brethren. We hope that it will not let them go unaided.

We give a big greeting to the Salesian University, nearby. Besides its other high merits, it has that of providing a church, until the parish has one of its own. To all the institutions which belong to this new yet already renowned university, especially to its worthy Rector Don Luigi Colonghi and the whole of the illustrious teaching body and students. Our best wishes for prosperity and special assistance from the divine Wisdom.

Finally, a devoted and cordial greeting to Cardinal Charles Wojtyla, Archbishop of Krakow, and Our Venerated Brethren the Polish Bishops who are with him and together with him are leading a numerous and most dear group of Polish priests on pilgrimage to Rome and are here present today. Their presence reminds Us that they are celebrating their anniversary of ordination to the priesthood. We recall the great sufferings which not a few of them experienced as prisoners and deportees during the war, which they bore with unconquered fortitude and Christian patience. It reminds Us of their country, Catholic Poland, most dear to Us. We will pray sincerely today for civil and religious prosperity for it. We are sincerely grateful to have such a large number of representatives of that heroic and Christian country here with us today.

In order to celebrate well this feast of the Body of the Lord, Corpus Christi, we need to have a few moments of reflection.

A lively community

To begin: Who are we? We are the Church, a portion of the Catholic Church, a community of believers united in the same faith, in the same hope, in the same charity, a community which is living by virtue of a life which comes to us from the Lord, from Christ himself, and which is nourished by the Spirit. In this way we are part of his Mystical Body.

Now, inside itself the Church has a secret, a hidden treasure, a mystery. It is like a hidden heart. It possesses Jesus Christ himself, its founder, its teacher, its redeemer. Note well: It possesses him present. Present? Yes. Through the legacy of his Word? Yes, but also through another presence. That of his ministers? Of his Apostles? Of his representatives? Of his priests? Of its ministerial tradition? Yes, but there is more than this.

The Lord gave his priests, these qualified ministers of his, an extraordinary and marvellous power—that of making him really, personally present. Living? Yes. Really he? Yes, really he. But where is he—we cannot see him. This is where the secret lies, this is the mystery: Christ's presence is true and real, but it is sacramental. That is to say, it is hidden, but is identifiable at the same time. It is a presence which is invested with special signs. These do not enable us to see his divine and human person; they only assure us that he, the Jesus of the Gospel and now Jesus living in the glory of heaven, is here, in the Eucharist.

So it is a miracle? Yes, a miracle. He, Jesus Christ, gave his Apostles the power to perform it, to repeat it, to multiply and perpetuate it. He did this when he made them priests and so gave them this power to make all his divine and human being present in this sacrament which we call the Eucharist and which contains the body and the blood, the soul and the divinity of Jesus Christ under the appearances of bread and of wine. This is a mystery, but it is the truth. It is this miraculous truth, possessed by the Catholic Church and guarded with jealous and silent conscientiousness which we are celebrating today. It is this truth which we wish in a certain sense to publish, manifest, make seen, cause to be understood, and extol. The Church, Christ's mystical Body, is today celebrating Christ's real body, present and hidden in the sacrament of the Eucharist.

A miraculous truth

But is it hard to understand? Yes, it is hard, because it is a matter of something real and most unique which is accomplished by the divine power and which surpasses our normal natural capacity to comprehend. We have to believe it, on Christ's word; it is " the mystery of faith " par excellence.

But, let us be careful. In this sacrament the Lord presents himself to us not as he is but as he wishes us to consider him, as he wishes us to approach him. He offers himself to us under the aspect of expressive signs which he himself chose. It is as if he said: Look at me in this way, get to know me like this. The signs of the bread and wine are to tell you what I wish to be for you. He speaks to us by means of these signs, and tells us: This is how I am amongst you now.

Real presence

Therefore, though we cannot enjoy his tangible presence, we can and ought to enjoy his real presence, under these significant forms. What is Jesus' intention in giving himself to us in the Eucharist? Oh! If we think about it well, we shall see that his intention is most patent! It tells us many, many things about Jesus. Above all, it tells us about his love. It tells us that he, Jesus, though he conceals himself in the Eucharist, also reveals himself in it, reveals himself in love. The " mystery of faith " opens up as the " mystery of love ". Think of it: this is the sacramental garb which at the same time hides and reveals Jesus: bread and wine, given for us.

Jesus gives himself; presents himself. This is the centre, the focal point of the whole of the Gospel, of the Incarnation, of the Redemption. *Nobis natus, nobis datus*: born for us, given for us.

For each of us? Yes, for each of us. Jesus has multiplied his real but sacramental presence in time and number, in order to be able to offer each of us—We mean each of us—the good fortune, the joy to approach him, and to be able to say: He is for me, he is mine. " He loved me ", St. Paul says, " and gave himself—for me "! (*Gal.* 2, 20).

And for all, too? Yes, for all. This is another aspect of Jesus' love which is expressed in the Eucharist. You know the words with which Jesus instituted this sacrament and which the priest repeats in the consecration at Mass: " eat, *all* of you; drink, *all* of you ... ". For this same sacrament was instituted during an evening meal, a familiar and ordinary occasion and means of coming together, of being united. The Eucharist is the sacrament which represent and produces the unity of Christians. This aspect of it is very dear to the Church and is highly valued today.

For example, the recent Council used the following extremely meaningful words about it: Christ " instituted in his Church the wonderful sacrament of the Eucharist by which the unity of the Church is both signified and brought about " (*Unit. red.* 2) St. Paul, the first historian and first theologian of the Eucharist, had already said the same thing: " We form one body, all of us who partake of the same bread " (*1 Cor.* 10, 17). We must exclaim with St. Augustine: " O sacrament of goodness, O sign of unity, O bond of charity! " (In *Jo. Tr.* 26, *PL* 35, 1613). So, infinite light, radiant love, flows out from the real presence which is symbolically expressed in the Eucharist. It is radiation of permanent love, of universal love. Neither time nor space put limits to it.

Another question: Why is this symbolism expressed by means of the appearances of food: bread and wine? Our Lord's intention is clear here also. Food enters into him who nourishes himself with it, it enters into communion with him. Jesus wishes to enter into communion with the believer who takes the Eucharist, and this is how we have the custom of using the term ' receiving communion ' to describe this sacrament. Not only does Jesus wish to be close to us, he also wishes to be in communion with us. Could he have loved us more? And why does he do this? Because, as food for the body, he wishes to be the principle of life, of new life. He himself said so: " If any man eat of this bread, he shall live for ever " (cf. *Jn.* 6, 48-58). Where will Christ's love ever end!

Sacrifice and Salvation

Then there is another aspect to be considered. Why two foods, bread and wine? In order to give the Eucharist the significance and the reality of flesh and blood, that is of sacrifice, of being a figure and a renewal of Jesus' death on the cross. Once more the Apostle: " As often as you eat this bread and drink this cup you will renew the announcement of the Lord's death, until he come " (*1 Cor.* 11, 26). Jesus' extreme love! His sacrifice for our redemption is represented in the Eucharist, so that the fruit of salvation may be extended to us.

Christ's love for us: behold the Eucharist! Love which gives itself, love which remains, love which communicates itself, love which multiplies itself, love which sacrifices itself, love which unites us, love which saves us.

Dearest Brothers and Children, let us listen to this great lesson. The sacrament is not only this dense mystery of divine truth about which our catechism tells us. It is a teaching, it is an example, it is a testament, it is a commandment.

On the very same fateful night of the last supper Jesus translated this lesson of love into unforgettable words: " Love one another as I have loved you " (*Jn.* 13, 34). That " as " is tremendous! We ought to love *as* he loved us. Neither the form, nor the degree, nor the strength of Christ's love expressed in the Eucharist will be possible for us! Yet this does not make is commandment, which emanates from the Eucharist, any less binding and demanding, for if we are Christians, we ought to love: " By this all men shall know that you are my disciples, if you have love for one another " (*ib.* 35).

Today we are celebrating Corpus Christi. Consider: we are celebrating the feast of Love. The feast of Christ's love for us. It ought to become a feast of our love for Christ and through Christ for God, for that is the most important and indispensable thing which we ought to do in our life, since our lives are destined for love of God. And then it is the feast of our love of one another, of our love for the brethren—and they are mankind, from the nearest to the most distant, the littlest, the poorest, the neediest, and even those who might be unlikable or enemies.

This is the source of our sociology, this is the Church, the society of love. It is therefore the source of all the religious and human virtues which the love of Christ entails, of the gift of self for others, of goodness, of justice, of peace especially.

There is so much talk of love—alas, of what kind of love?— that we think we already know the meaning and force of this word. But only Jesus, only the Eucharist, can teach us its whole, true and deep meaning. This is why we are here, to celebrate the feast of Corpus Christi, in humility, in recollection and in exultation.

SAINT JOHN OF AVILA—A
MODEL FOR PRIESTS TODAY

On Sunday, May 31st, 1970 the Holy Father presided in St. Peter's at the canonization of St. John of Avila. He addressed the assembly as follows.

Venerated Brothers and dearest Children!

We thank God because through this exaltation of Blessed John of Avila to the splendour of sainthood he sends the universal Church a call to study, to imitate, to be devoted to and to invoke a great example of the priesthood.

The Spanish Episcopate is to be praised for having made the request for his canonization to this Apostolic See. It has not remained content with the title which Our Predecessor of venerated memory, Pius XII, conferred upon the apostle of Andalusia, Blessed John of Avila, when he proclaimed him Special Patron of the Diocesan Clergy of Spain. And its request most deservedly found the Sacred Congregation for the Causes of Saints and Ourself most favourably disposed to such an important celebration.

May God grant that this elevation of Blessed John of Avila to the roll of saints, to the glorious army of the children of the heavenly Church, may serve to obtain a new and powerful intercessor for the Church in pilgrimage on earth, a considerate and wise teacher of the spiritual life, an exemplary renewer of the Church's life and Christian morals.

Post-conciliar times

An historical comparison between our own times and those in which the Saint lived and worked suggests that this prayer of Ours is being heard. The two periods certainly differ greatly,

222

yet they also have certain ressemblances. These lie not so much in the facts as in certain principles guiding human events then and now; and awakening, for example, of vital energies, and a crisis of ideas, such as was a characteristic of the sixteenth century and is a feature of our own twentieth century. That was a time of Council reforms and discussions, and so also is the time in which we are living. It seems moreover providential that the personality of the Master of Avila should be evoked in our days by reason of the characteristics of his priestly life, for these make the Saint very relevant to our own day, thus giving him a quality of topicality which is much prized by our contemporaries.

St. John of Avila was a priest whom we may in many respects regard as modern, particularly because of the many-sided character his life offers for our consideration and limitation. Not without reason has he already been held up to the clergy of Spain as an exemplary model and heavenly protector. We think that he may be honoured as a many-sided example by every priest in our day. It is said that the priesthood itself is now suffering a deep crisis, a " crisis of identity ", as if the nature and mission of the priest have no longer a sufficient reason to justify their presence in such a world as ours, which is deconsecrated and secularized. Every priest who might be in doubt about his vocation can approach this saint and get a reassuring reply. Like any of the learned who are inclined to reduce the priest to the bounds of the patterns of secular and utilitarian sociology, he would have to modify his restrictive and negative judgments about the priest's function in the modern world.

A mere priest

John was a poor and modest man, through his own choice. He did not even have the support which comes from belonging to the work structures ordained by canon law. He was not a parish priest, he was not a religious. He was just a priest, with poor health, and in ill fortune, which followed his early experiences in the ministry, for he underwent the bitterest test that can be imposed on a faithful and fervent apostle, that of a trial.

He was imprisoned on suspicion of heresy, as was the custom then. He did not even have the chance to get over it by devoting himself to a great and adventurous ideal. He wished to go as a missionary to America, to the West " Indies ", just then discovered, but they would not let him.

John did not doubt. He knew his vocation. He had faith in his priestly election. A psychological examination of his life would lead us to see this certainty of his priestly " identity " as the source of his fearless zeal, his apostolic fruitfulness, his wisdom as a clear-minded reformer of Church life and a most delicate director of consciences.

St. John of Avila at least gives this lesson to the clergy of our time: Do not doubt your own being, as a priest of Christ, a minister of the Church, a guide to the brethren. He had profound awareness of something which some priests and many seminarians no longer understand as a duty and a specific title to the ministerial office in the Church. The definition of that something—we may also call it a sociological definition—derives from St. Paul's definition of himself as a servant of Jesus Christ and an apostle: " Set apart for the gospel of God " (*Rom.* 1, 1). This segregation, this specification, is thatof a distinct organ which is indispensable for the good of an entire living body (cf. *1 Cor.* 12, 16 sq.). Today it is the first characteristic of the Catholic priesthood to be called into question and challenged. The motives for this are often noble and acceptable in some respects; but when they tend to do away with this " segregation " and assimilate the ecclesiastical state to the lay and secular state and justify the chosen man in experiencing worldly life under the pretext that he ought not to be less than any other man, such arguments can easily turn the elect away from his path, turn the priest into any man, salt without savour, a man unable to make interior sacrifice, one who has lost the power of judgment, of word and example such as pertains to a strong, a pure and a free follower of Christ. The Lord's incisive and demanding words: " No man, having put his hand to the plough and looking back, is fit for the kingdom of God " (*Lk.* 9, 62) struck deeply into this singular priest. In the wholeness of his gift to Christ he found that is energies were increased a hundredfold.

Preaching that renewed

He was a powerful preacher and his message was renewal. St. John of Avila can still be a master of preaching today. He deserves to be listened to and imitated, with all the more reason because he did not indulge in the oratorical and literary artificialities of his time, and was much more deeply imbued in wisdom derived from the Bible and the Fathers. His personality came to light and distinguished itself in the ministry of preaching.

In apparent contrast with his use of the public and exterior word, St. John of Avila also used the personal and interior word, that belongs to the ministry of the sacrament of penance and spiritual direction.

Perhaps even more in this patient and silent, extremely delicate and prudent ministry, his personality surpassed that of his oratory. The name of John of Avila is linked with his most significant work, his celebrated *Audi, filia*. This is a book of interior magisterium, full of religious feeling, Christian experience, and human goodness. It came before St. Francis de Sales' *Philothea*, which in some ways resembles it, and a whole series of religious books which have given depth and sincerity to Catholic spiritual formation from the period of Trent down to our own day. In this too John of Avila was an exemplary master.

And how many other of his virtues could We not mention for our edification! He was a fruitful writer. This also brings him him wonderfully close to us, and presents us with his conversation, that of a Saint.

And action. His activity was varied and unwearied: correspondence, direction of spiritual groups, especially of priests, conversion of great souls such as Louis of Granada, his disciple and biographer, and like the future St. John of God and Francis Borgia, friendship with the great spirits of his time, such as St. Ignatius and St. Teresa; foundation of colleges for the clergy and for youth. Truly a great person.

A faithful precursor

The Holy Father continued in Spanish:

But Our attention is particularly drawn to that personality of a reformer, or rather an innovator, which we find in Saint John of Avila. The Saint lived in that transition period full of problems, debates and controversies which preceded the Council of Trent. He lived during the course and the aftermath of that great and long Council, so he could not but take a stand in regard to it. Because of his precarious health, he could not take part in it, but he wrote a well-known Memorial entitled, *Reformación del Estado Eclésiastico* (1551), followed by an appendix: *Lo que se debe avisar a los Obispos* (What the Bishops Must Be Told). The Archbishop of Granada, Pedro Guerrero, made it known in the Council of Trent, among general applause. Other writings, such as *Causas y remedios de la herejias* (Second Memorial, 1561), likewise show the intensity and intentions with which John of Avila shared in that historical event. Fidelity, love and hope shine forth from his limpid diagnosis of the gravity of the evils afflicting the Church at that time. And when he addresses the pope and the Church's pastors, what evangelical sincerity and filial devotion, what fidelity to the tradition and confidence in the Church in its original inward constitution, what prime importance is given to the true faith as the cure for the evils and as renovation of the Church itself!

" John of Avila was a forerunner both in reform and other spiritual fields. The Council of Trent adopted decisions which he had outlined long before " (S. Charprenet, p. 56).

But he was no critic and contestator, to use today's term. He was a clear-sighted and ardent spirit. To denunciation of evils and suggestions for canonical remedies he added a schooling of intense spiritually (study of Holy Scripture, practice of mental prayer, imitation of Christ—he made a Spanish translation of the book of the same name—devotion to the Eucharist, devotion to the Most Holy Virgin, defence of sacred celibacy, love for the Church, even when a certain minister of the Church was too hard on him). He was the first to practise the precepts of his school of spirituality.

Once more, he was a great figure. He was a son and a glory of the land of Spain, of Catholic Spain, which is impelled to live its faith dramatically, and from time to time, at the crucial moments of its history, draws the hero, the sage and the saint from out the depths of its moral and spiritual traditions.

We feel joy in raising up this Saint before the Church. May he be a favourable intercessor for her, to obtain the graces which she now seems to need most: firmness in the true faith, authentic love for the Church, sanctity for her clergy, and imitation of Christ such as it ought to be in these latter days. And may his prophetical figure which is now crowned with the halo of sainthood, send forth over the world the truth, the charity and the peace of Christ.

A SENSE OF COMMUNITY

O ne of the salient features of the Christian's spiritual formation as it comes to us from the Council is undoubtedly the
sense of community.

Anyone who seeks to learn the spirit and the norms of the
Council's renewal becomes aware that he is being shaped by a
new kind of training. This causes him to conceive and express
religious, moral and social life in terms of the ecclesial community
to which he belongs.

Everything in the Council speaks of the Church. Now, the
Church is the People of God, it is Christ's Mystical Body, it is
communion. It is no longer possible to forget this existential
reality if we wish to be Christians, if we wish to be " faithful ".
The religious life cannot be lived as an individualistic expression
of the relationship between man and God, between the Christian
and Christ, between the Catholic and the Church. Nor may it be
conceived as a separate expression, as that which finds its own
satisfaction in an autonomous group shut off from the great
ecclesial communion, and avoids interventions from outside, both
those of superiors and those of colleagues or followers who are
strangers to the exclusive mentality of the closed group satisfied with itself. Community spirit is the atmosphere which
the believer needs. The Council called back Christian religious
consciousness and practice to breathe that atmosphere.

But We will immediately make two reservations, or rather
two obious observations. The religious fact, in its essence and
in its profound and inescapable demands, remains a personal fact.
It is therefore free, and proper to him who places it. The relationship between man and God occurs in the individual conscience,
exactly at that moment when man feels himself a person, fully
responsible and inclined by innate tendency towards deciding his

228

own destiny (cf. S. Th. II-III, 81). More, belonging to the Church's community life arouses and demands such a free act; it does not prescind—far from it—from the individual faithful's personal contribution, both in prayer—liturgical prayer—and social relationships, those of justice and charity.

Is not faith given to us through the Church? Has not grace channels that run through it? What should we know of Christ if the Church had not taught it to us? (cf. J. A. Moehler, *Die Einheit in der Kirche*, I, 1, 7; *L'unité dans l'Eglise*, p. 21). " The liturgy itself requires that the soul shall strive towards contemplation; and participation in liturgical life ... is eminent preparation for union with God through contemplation of love " (Maritain, *Liturgie et contemplation*, p. 14). We might go deeper into this matter by observing how the community spirit to which the Church is now being educated is no novelty; it is rather a return to the origins of the spirituality of Christianity. Far from stifling the single faithful's personal feelings, it enlivens them in remembrance and in the practical attitude of that " royal priesthood " which pertains to the baptized and about which so much is being said, now that the Council has reminded us of its existence, its dignity, and of its exercise (*Lumen gentium*, 10-11, ect.).

Similar observations may be made about the legitimate and providential existence of groups which constitute themselves to imitation of Christ and practice of the evangelical counsels in accordance with criterions of their own which are recognized by the Church authorities as conducive to Christian perfection (*Lumen gentium*, 43). But these too live within the Church, in their own way, live of the Church and for the Church. They are not detached from internal and external communion with her; they too have the sense of and taste and zeal for community life. They often have it more than others.

We may say the same about the existence of particular Churches with their own traditions, rites and canonical norms. Their existence is more than acknowledged. But for them too " communion " is the indispensable requirement for belonging to the one true Church of Christ. On this blessed word " communion " turns the whole question of ecumenism, to which the Council likewise drew our attention and in which it desired to educate us.

We can also mention local Churches. They are not detached from the universal Church's unity. They are integrated parts of it; they are her living members, flourishing branches, having their own vitality, emanating from a single principle of faith and grace. In their effort to give fullness to their interior and original communion, they too are expressions of the whole Church communion, evidence of inspired and original harmony, of variety in unity.

But, having said this, the fact remains that the Church, after being renewed and enlightened by the Council, is visibly more communitarian today than in the past. Indeed the more it spreads in the world, the more it shows itself to be " communion ", by intrinsic and constitutional necessity (cf. HAMER, *L'Eglise est une communion*, 1962, and article in *L'Osservatore Romano*, English edition, June 4, 1970). Note the social peak of this description. Mankind may be regarded as a mass, a numerical quantity, or as a simple category of human beings, a shapeless crowd lacking deep, willed, inner links; or as a community held together by particular purposes or interests; as a people, a nation, a society of nations ... Then finally there is a " communion ", and this is the mankind which Christ willed.

You know the requirements, the factors in this superlative expression of humanity. They are faith, the Spirit, hierarchy. That is, the Church. Our Church.

If that is communion. what does it entail? In other words, what it the dynamic of that definition? If the Church is communion, it involves a basis of equality, personal dignity, common brotherhood; it entails progressive solidarity (*Gal.* 6, 2); it entails disciplined obedience and loyal cooperation; it entails having a share of responsibility for promoting the common good. But it does not entail equality of functions. These are very distinct from each other in the ecclesial communion, which is organic, hierarchic, and a body of diverse but and well-defined responsibilities, etc.

The conclusion? It is this We need to increase our community feeling and exercise the corresponding virtues more. That is, we ought to grow in charity. This ought to acquire greater meaning and value and be better practised by us. This is the community spirit in which the Council desired us to be well-formed faithful.

At the very beginning of the Church St. Paul taught us the same thing: " Following the truth in love, let let us grow in charity towards him who is the head, Christ, from whom the whole body ... fulfils its development in the measure of each of its parts, for building up of itself in love " (*Eph.* 4, 15-16).

Genuine community spirit!

With Our Apostolic Benediction.

POPE URGES " COMMUNION "
THROUGH " COMMUNICATION "

On Thursday 5th June, the Holy Father received in private audience in the Throne Room, the President, Members and Consultors of the Pontifical Commission for Social Communications, convening in Rome for a Plenary Assembly. He spoke to them as follows.

Lords Cardinals,
Venerable Brothers, Beloved Sons:

This meeting gives Us much pleasure. You, Members and Consultors of Our Commission for Social Communications, have gathered in the Vatican for your annual plenary meeting. You have come here today to assure Us of your loyalty and collaboration, and We express to you Our gratitude, Our praise and encouragement.

You assist Us in a particularly vast and complex field of Our pastoral responsibility, one full of problems and pressing needs. It is a new, modern sector, with ever increasing demands, such as arise from the powerful dynamism of a special, enormous and irreversible social reality. Your help therefore deserves Our complete gratitude and appreciation, for it strengthens and consoles Us in the difficult task of being engaged in the field of social communication in an active, apostolic way, at the service of Our Brothers in the Episcopate, of the faithful entrusted to their care and Ours, and at the service of men of good will.

We desire to emphasize two circumstances. They are positive features in the present situation of the Pontifical Commission for Social Communications, and they are a good sign. In the first place, the Commission's membership has been renewed, and you who have come here today represent that renewal. It is ready to face a further five years of work. In addition, it is about to complete the Pastoral Instruction on application of the Council's Decree *Inter Mirifica*, on which it has worked long and hard.

You will give approval to this important document in the next few days; it will then be submitted to examination by the Episcopal Conferences of the various countries. This will achieve another, very provident and fruitful form of collaboration, and will give further and wider expression to that episcopal collegiality which is already a fact in Our Commission, because many Bishops already participate in it. This will also be one more way of giving just and due recognition to local fields of competence and local organisms. These have really indispensable functions, also in the sector with which we are concerned.

The Church's activity in the field of social communication is based on structures both central and local that are sufficiently adequate, though obviously capable of further improvement. This activity will soon be regulated by complete and up-to-date norms, thus bringing to maturity one of the many precious fruits of the Second Vatican Council.

The means are ready, and Our Commission in ready. We say this with fatherly satisfaction and feelings of fervent good wishes. Now we must act, we must use the structures and norms which are the means at our command.

What shall We put before you to consider at this demanding and promising moment, to encourage you in your mission with enlightenment and skill?

The risk of alienation

Two thoughts will suffice: two indications by way of setting directions.

First o fall, it seems to Us to be fundamentally important to foster and encourage strict and thorough study from the doctrinal point of view of that reality which we describe by the now classic term of social communication. It is a reality of gigantic dimensions, for it is as big as the means it uses and the communities to which it is directed and the fabric which it penetrates irresistibly. It makes itself part of them. It involves the sciences of man and the sciences of nature. So it is on a world scale, and is enormously influential.

It challenges the whole man, his individuality and his social nature. It sets up dramatic tensions within that vital duality which is " society and person ", because of its ambivalence; whereas it ought to give harmonious encouragement to development of the person both in his deeper and social values, for these derive from the person himself and reach upon him. It involves a grave risk of alienation, conformism, passive, unchecked acceptance of models of thought and behaviour. But at the same time it is capable of fostering equality and fraternity, common and reciprocal enrichment of ideas and behaviour, and simultaneous, convergent interest on the part of all mankind, or large parts of mankind, in problems of life and history. It is a reality which is capable of fostering " communion " through " communication ".

It is differentiated according as it covers the family, the school, the young, or comes before the traditional—but still irreplaceable—means of upbringing and education. It is further differentiated according as it is created by the press, the cinema, radio or television.

A phenomenon

Social communications is therefore a phenomenon which needs to be explored; its components, its mechanisms and its formal laws need to be known.

Then there is the grave problem of content. There is that content which can be brought to light in a positive way through using the methods of sociological surveys; but the results, unfortunately, are often painful. On the other hand there is that content which *ought to be* there, especially when social communications enter into particular environments, such as the family and the school, or are aimed at particular sectors, such as the young. It is always wonderfully surprising to see how man, so frail, so ephemeral, so powerfully affected, indeed almost overwhelmed by the surrounding reality, is nevertheless capable of overcoming that same reality and can judge it and direct it.

The phenomenon of social communications is consequently something for us to think about philosophically and critically. It becomes an object for deontology, which goes beyond what it is as a simple fact at a certain moment and shows and teaches in what way it ought to be in conformity with moral imperatives, from the point of view of correct use of methods and from that of the content and messages of which the methods and instruments are the bearers. This consideration extends towards the boundless horizons of theology, since social communications can and ought to be included under the mystery of salvation.

Influencing public opinion

But just a few indications will do for the present. We wish only to add that the problem of social communications takes on particular characteristics when viewed in connection with the Church. Doctrine here needs to be stricter and deeper, in order to avoid, as is necessary, indiscriminate and fallacious application of concepts which arose in a different field. But humiliating limitations to " social communications " in the Church will not arise from this. In particular, it will be necessary to give further study to the problem of public opinion in the Church. This is a delicate and not an easy matter,—it is full of possible consequences both on the positive and negative side, which will arise according as the question is correctly posed and solved, or not.

But we cannot remain content to encourage doctrinal study of social communications on the scientific and specialized level by carefully following literature on the matter and making or calling forth fresh contributions. It is also necessary to spread, to disseminate this doctrine, to make it accessible in such a way that the mass—particularly the *milieux* and sectors already mentioned— may become aware of the phenomenon and so be able to use it critically and rightly. In a word, there is need to develop a vast movement of public opinion—right opinion—on social communications.

Responsible use

The work to be done in this sector of doctrine calls for commitment from all of you, Members and Consultors of the Pontifical Commission for Social Communications. Your Central Office, which is established permanently here with Us, will have to encourage and coordinate your thought, gather information from you, collect your suggestions, give out information, and set bearings.

National Episcopal Commissions ought to benefit in a special way from the methodical attention you will give to doctrine on social communications and the best way of extending it for formation of consciences. The Pontifical Commission will thus do them useful service. At the same time it can ask them for the collaboration it will need, which will be more than commonly fruitful and valuable because it will be coming from varied and diverse cultural regions. This joint effort will also benefit qualified people such as professional men and women, experts, critics, managers, technicians—all those indeed who have positions of particular responsibility in the field of social communications.

The second thought, the second consideration, is more strictly concerned with the active sector, with the duty and urgency of intensifying efforts to obtain good use of the press, of radio, cinema and other forms of spectacle, of television, in regard to transmission of matter with valid and positive human content and of the message which Christ entrusted to his Church for the salvation of all men.

Direct pastoral commitment

It is a question of means of social communication such as newspapers, broadcasting stations, cinemas. Catholics themselves possess these or ought to possess them. We can never insist enough on the need for having them (especially their own newspapers!). It is a question of Catholic professional people being engaged in all fields of production and distribution. It is a question of the apostolate of the *milieu* and of that more general one which engages all lay apostleship movements. They cannot but give most special attention to the problems of mass media, in view of the consoling and promising re-awakening which they are experiencing today. Such attention can be given through timely, suitable and efficacious coordination of efforts and undertakings.

Again, it is a question of schools and specialized courses, of particular training centres such as cineforums. These and other activities on the diocesan, national and international levels, need support from the Hierarchy, that is, from Our Commission and from the Episcopal National Commissions for social communications media, in collaboration with other organs of the Holy See (such as the Sacred Congregation for Catholic Education and the *Consilium* of the Laity) and local organs of the various Episcopates.

It should also be borne in mind that there is an ever wider and clearer possibility of direct pastoral use of the means of social communications. We would above all wish to see encouragement given to every undertaking likely to add power and effectiveness to presentation of the Church and her constant work in the world, through prompt and accurate distribution of news about her. But we also have to face new problems, and others which have not received enough attention—for example, use of audio-visual means in catechesis, in liturgical training, in evangelization, in Catholic religious education. Study, effort and collaboration need to be increased here also.

We know that your minds are giving these few suggestions a perfect and generous welcome, and you are now accustomed to think and be concerned about the great problem of social communications, in view of the human and divine mission which has been entrusted to us. The field of labour is boundless and difficult, but We trust in your efforts and in the Lord's help above all. In pledge of his aid We give Our Apostolic Blessing to you from Our heart.

MESSAGE OF HIS HOLINESS POPE PAUL VI
FOR MISSION SUNDAY

T o all Our brothers in Christ, this year as in the past, We address Our message for Mission Sunday. We cannot omit it, even though it may say nothing new, for the missionary cause is so vital for the Church and so important for the world that We feel obliged to speak out strangly in its favour on this annual occasion.

Mission Sunday has rightly become an important event in the Church's life. It has a direct bearing on Our apostolic ministry and brings to mind the command of Our Lord Himself, which makes us realize how great and how grave is our duty of preaching the Gospel not only within the Church but also beyond its geograpical and structural confines. We cannot let slip the opportunity to remind the whole Church—Our Brothers in the Episcopate, the clergy, religious, and each individual Catholic—of this missionary vocation.

Missionary by nature

In the post-Conciliar period the duty of spreading the faith imposes itself with even greater urgency on all, though in difforent ways and degrees, for the Council taught, with deep theological insight, that " the pilgrim Church is missionary by her very nature " (*Ad Gentes*, 2); she is the sign and instrument of God's plan of salvation for the whole of mankind (*Lumen gentium*, 9); and those who wish to really live their Christianity should realize its essential dynamism (cf. *Ad Gentes*, 1, 2, 6), its innate urge to spread, its intrinsic duty to communicate the faith to all men (cf. *Ad Gentes*, 28).

This is the Church's mission as such. And it makes Us turn Our mind to those particular institutions which strive to widen the bounds of the Gospel preaching and which are specifically and traditionally known by the blessed name of Catholic Missions (cf. *Ad Gentes*, 6).

We wish to confirm once more the apostolic mandate which belongs to them, and which invests them with the power of the Holy Spirit for the accomplishment of their incomparable task; and We want all who consecrate their lives to the missions, or who pray, work and suffer for them, to know that they have, in a very special way, Our affection and Our gratitude.

Signs of the Times

Why this preference? Because, apart, from the duty and necessity of spreading the word of salvation, there are particular circumstances today which seem to Us to be " signs of the times " for a vigorous renewal of missionary activity. The words of Jesus to his disciples come to Our lips: " I tell you, lift up your eyes, and see how the fields are already white for the harvest " (*Jn.* 4, 35). Today's circumstances favour communication between men: the earth has been explored and opened up; transport is quick and widespread; the arts, commerce and international relations promote contact between different cultures and tend to unite the world ... On what level? On the practical level, yes; on the civil level, yes; but do we not see that this same process of bringing men closer to each other contains within itself deficiencies which can turn into threats of new and graver conflicts; that it does not pay sufficient attention to that affirmation of principles, that outpouring of spiritual energy, that solution of discordant ideologies in a single, fraternal, higher truth, which, even in the temporal order, can come to the world only through Christ? (cf. *Lumen gentium*, 13).

New Approach is needed

A new era has dawned for the missions. New difficulties and new facilities lie on the path of those who, in the name of Christ, " preach the good news " (*Rom.* 10, 15). The present state of the world offers a far wider and more inviting field of endeavour, though certainly not an easier one, to the courage and wisdom of the missionaries. We would like, today more than ever, to repeat Christ's pressing invitation: " Follow me and I will make you fishers of men " (*Mt.* 4, 19). Let us not waste time in corrosive criticism, or let slip this historical moment which seems decisive for the future direction of mankind, and which offers to the talents and generosity of the young an opportunity to be bearers of new and exalting charisms of faith and charity.

Evangelization, development

This means that missionary activity must be conceived in broad and modern terms. A new approach is necessary: in the underlying theological principles; in publicity, recruitment, training; in the methods and organization of the actual works. We know that this renewal is already, in fact, taking place, on a large scale, among those who have experience and competence in the matter, under the guidance of Our worthy Congregation for the Evangelization of Peoples.

In this re-thinking o fthe Church's missionary vocation there is one question that stands out in particular, opposing two different concepts of what the general direction of missionary activity should be—concepts which may be summed up in the two words: evangelization and development. By evangelization is meant strictly religious activity, aimed at the preaching of God's kingdom, of the Gospel as a revelation of the plan of salvation in Christ, through the action of the Holy Spirit—activity that has the ministry of the Church as its instrument, the building-up of the Church itself as its aim, and God's glory as its final end: this is the traditional doctrine and to it the Council has given its authoritative support. By development is meant the human, civil, temporal promotion of those peoples who, by contact with modern civilization and with the help that it provides, are becoming more conscious of themselves and are stepping out on the road to higher levels of culture and prosperity. The missionary cannot excuse himself from taking an interest in this promotion (cf. *Ad Gentes*, 11).

The confrontation between these two concepts is a serious one and entails two dangers: that we may consider them as mutually exclusive, and that we may fail to establish a correct relationship between them.

June 5th, 1970

Complementary terms

We hope that the confrontation will not be looked upon as a dilemma that precludes a synthesis between evangelization and development, in which the one complements the other. For us believers it would be unthinkable that missionary activity should make of earthly reality its only or principal end and lose sight of its essential end: namely, to bring all men to the light of faith, to give them new life in baptism, to incorporate them into the Mystical Body of Christ that is the Church, to teach them to live like Christians, and to hold out the expectation of an existence beyond this earthly one. And likewise it would be inadmissible for the Church's missionary activity to neglect the needs and aspirations of developing peoples and, because of its religious orientation, omit the basic duties of human charity. We cannot forget the solemn teaching of the Gospel on the love of our needy and suffering neighbour (*Mt.* 25, 31-46), reiterated by the apostles (cf. *1 Jn* 4, 20; *Jam.* 2, 14-18), and confirmed by the Church's whole missionary tradition. We Ourself, in Our encyclical " Populorum Progressio ", have stressed the duty of resolutely and intelligently fostering the growth of economic, cultural, social and spiritual well-being among peoples, and especially among those of the so-called Third World, where missionary activity finds its main scope (cf. *Ad Gentes*, 12).

There should be no dilemma. It is a question of priority of ends, of intentions, of duties; and there is no doubt that missionary activity is concerned primarily with evangelization and that it must maintain this priority both in the concept that inspires it and in the way in which is it organized and exercised. Missionary activity would be failing in its *raison d'être* if it turned aside from its religious axis; the kingdom of God before every thing else; the Kingdom of God understood in its vertical, theological, religious sense, freeing man from sin and presenting him with the love of God as the supreme commandment and eternal life as his ultimate destiny. That is to say, the " Kerygma ", the word of Christ, the Gospel, faith, grace, prayer, the Cross, Christian living. We must realize that fidelity to this primary programme of missionary activity may stir up great difficulties, difficulties which at times may prevent it from developing and expanding: our mission is « folly and scandal " (cf. *1 Cor.* 1, 18 sqq.). But that is precisely its strength and its wisdom, today no less than in the beginning. Even today, in fact, what by earthly standards would seem an obstacle to evangelization, namely its spiritual character, can help it by freeing it from the fetters of economics, from suspicion of colonialism, from the inefficiency of naturalism when faced with differing cultures.

The debate between evangelization and development is rather, then, a question of method: which should be attended to first. The answer cannot be the same for all cases, but must depend on particular circumstances, studied in the light of experience with a watchful and patient empiricism which is faithful to the apostolic spirit and to the needs of different situations, always with a view to the efficacy and sanctity of the work (cf. *Ad Gentes*, 6). We may consider three phases. Before, during and after evangelization, which always retains its essential priority, development, with its use of temporal means, may be given pastoral priority. There is first what some refer to as pre-evangelization: that is, making contact with future Christians by living among them, helping them and giving the example of a good Christian life. Then there is service: when the Gospel comes to a place, charity comes with it, bearing witness to the human validity of Christ's message, and taking the form of schools, hospitals, social assistance and technical training. In the third phase, there comes the result of this activity, in a higher standard of living.

Blessing to all missionaries

In conclusion We may observe that if the debate between evangelization and development is considered on the doctrinal level, in terms of end and purpose, then the answer is to be found in the words of the Council decree: " The specific purpose of missionary activity is evangelization and the planting of the Church ... " (*Ad Gentes*, 6; cf. Enc. *Fidei donum, AAS*, 1957, 236).

But, on the practical level, those who are engaged in missionary work must realize that evangelization is helped by activities concerned with the temporal and human development of the peoples being evangelized. Those activities can become one with evangelization when, raised to the level of charity, they become ends, as it were, themselves, and also when, used rather as means, they precede and complete the work of evangelization. This is especially important for the laity, called as they are to " seek the Kingdom of God by engaging in temporal affairs " (*Lumen gentium*, 31), for " even when preoccupied with temporal cares, the laity can and must perform eminently valuable work on behalf of bringing the Gospel to the world " (*ib.*, 35).

Development work, when linked with that of evangelization, itself sheds a Christian light, bringing out the concept of human dignity, of the rights of man of freedom, responsibility, duty, work, social harmony, and the good use of all values, even temporal ones; it lights up the human scene and reveals its beauty, richness and dignity. It also shows up its imperfections, injustices and misfortunes ... which the new man, the Christian, knows now how to judge and how to remedy. And development then draws profit from it for progress and unity, justice and peace (cf. *Ad Gentes*, 12 etc.).

Need We say more, to recommend the missions to your prayers and generosity? When the missions are rightly understood they need no defence. In the name of Christ Our Lord, We recommend them to your human and Christian wisdom and to your charity.

To all of you missionaries and friends of the missions, We send Our apostolic blessing, wide as the world's horizons.

From the Vatican, June 5, 1970.

PAULUS PP. VI

JUSTICE AND LAW, SUPREME PRINCIPLES
FOR THE LIFE OF THE HUMAN COMMUNITY

On June 8th the Holy Father received the Heads of Mission of the Diplomatic Corps accredited to the Holy See, who presented to him their best wishes on the occasion of the 50th anniversary of his ordination. Paul VI delivered the following address.

Excellencies and dear Sirs,

This meeting is a very great joy for Us. We were really touched by your spontaneous step, your desire to join in the celebration of the fiftieth anniversary of Our priestly ordination, and the personal part you wished to take in it.

Such a circumstance makes Us more aware that together We form a family, which shares the joys and sorrows of all. You are not only, in fact, the representatives of the interest of your respective countries, actuated only by the concern to present to the Holy See what directly concerns them, according to the duties of your high diplomatic mission; but you are men of feeling, attentive; to what concerns Our life, even in its most personal aspects.

Allow Us to confide in you this morning that all the Pope's activities, all the obligations inherent in his pastoral charge, his universal, ministry, all that has no *raison d'être* for Us except in the priesthood, which is the heart of Our most intimate and deep life.

And We are particularly sensitive to the fact that, beyond differences of religious attitudes and beliefs, you have realized this, and that you wished to take part in this spiritual event, this joy of the priest that We are.

In connection with this remark, to which our particular meeting this morning has given rise, We would be tempted to repeat the two fundamental principles that justify and characterize the relations We have the honour of maintaining with you, with the countries you represent so worthily at the Holy See, and with international life.

The first of these principles is the conviction, humbly but firmly rooted in Our mind, that We can in the course of Our conversations recall incessantly the supreme principles on which the life of the human community should be based, to be good and always progressing: We mean justice and law, which stem from a certain and sacred ethical conception of the life both of individuals and of peoples. In civil society these principles find their application on the temporal plane, and it is on this plane that Our dialogue with you takes place; but for Us they have their origin and their strength in the religious faith that We bear in Our heart and which it is Our duty—at once grave and sweet—to profess as a believer and as a minister, as a priest, and particularly in the post that has been assigned to Us in the Church.

Secondly, this religious character that is Ours and which, so kindly, you wish to honour today, gives you the assurance that Our relations both diplomatic and human with you and with your countries, have a quite particular aspect. These relations are not established on conflict, nor on interests opposed to your own interests, nor on emulation or prestige; but they are relations of service, and therefore of love for your peoples. In fact, by reaffirming these universal principles of which We have spoken and to which We unceasingly appeal, We seek to collaborate in the welfare of your peoples—in their development, and in their civil, social and moral progress. These relations, in a word, are made up of friendship for peace; peace for each of your countries, and peace for the whole world. Such are the perspectives opened to Us and imposed on Us as a duty by Our priesthood, this priesthood honoured today by your visit which is so agreeable to Us, and for which We are so grateful.

We wish to tell you too how touched We were by the choice you made in this circumstance of a scholarship for a young priest or seminarian, who will thus be able to prepare himself better for the great and grave responsibility that will be his in the world of tomorrow. As a result of your functions at the Holy See, you are in fact better qualified than anyone to know intimately its concerns, its problems, its plans. And you know that at the present moment of her history, the Church is more concerned than ever about her priests, her future priests, their formation, their lives. So We greatly appreciate your delicate attention, this collective gift that manifests your deep human understanding of what is at the heart of the life of the Church, and your desire to take a share in it.

This tells you with what gratitude We accept your gesture, happy to see the human and spiritual ties that unite us thus become closer, beyond the requirements of protocol and the duties of our office. You are, Gentlemen, men of feeling. In this not one of the most eminent qualities of the diplomat, the most necessary, too, perhaps, for the exercise of his high functions in the service of his country, as well as of the common good of men: concord, in mutual respect, of the different groups that constitute the large human family? If We do not always have the opportunity to talk to you about your personal and family life, about what you have set your heart on in the world. We can at least assure you all this morning that, in Our priestly prayer, We take your intentions to God Almighty, from whom come " whatever gifts are worth having, whatever endowments are perfect of their kind " (*Jam.* 1, 17). Recommending to the Most High, with your persons, those who are dear to you, We call down the abundance of divine blessings on all of you.

POPE THANKS CATHOLIC WORLD

W e feel it is Our duty to speak to you who are listening to Us here today so that Our voice may also reach all those who participated spiritually in the commemoration of the fiftieth anniversary of Our ordination to the priesthood, and bring them Our lively thanks. As you perhaps know, We should personally have preferred that the anniversary had passed unnoticed, that it might have been celebrated only by Us, in silence, in prayer, as a fact unknown to others, and surrounded by Our own personal memories and in interior consideration of the sacerdotal character which has marked Our humble person and made Us a " dispenser of the mysteries of God " (cf. *1 Cor.* 4, 1; *2 Cor.* 6, 4; *1 Pet.* 4, 10) and a minister of the Church. But We recognized that it could not be so, for two reasons.

A priest belongs to all

First, because a priest no longer belongs to himself. His very spiritual life is conditioned by the communion of the brethren, to whom our ministry is directed. He is at their disposal, at their service. Whatever helps to edify them is a matter of obligation for a priest. This is more than ever true for Us, for We have been invested with the pastoral office of this Apostolic See; *spectaculum facti sumus*, we are exposed to the view of all (*1 Cor.* 4, 9), and We have a title which is a programme: Servant of the Servants of God.

We therefore had to lend Ourself to the desire for celebration which so many children of the Church, and so many others who are outside its canonical bounds, wished to give Us. We therefore express Our lively thanks to all those who desired to be spiritually near Us on this singular occasion, and at the same time We direct to the Lord that tribute of congratulations and good wishes which was offered to Us. But it was not so much an offering to Us as rather one that ought to be given to him, " Giving thanks always for all things to God the Father in the name of Our Lord Jesus Christ " (*Eph.* 5, 20).

We for Our part, overwhelmed as We are by so many signs of good wishes, ought not only to be grateful, but also glad that they do honour to the priesthood. This not so much because the priesthood has been exercised by Us for fifty years, as because it was instituted by Christ for the salvation of his Church and of mankind. Our joy in the priesthood is all the greater even though today We find—to Our immense sorrow and to the regret of the faithful Church—this mysterious and admirable ministerial priesthood being contested, called in question, depreciated, betrayed and denied. It is a divine institution, which flowed from the heart of Christ at the very hour in which Christ turned himself into sacrificial food to be communicated to each of his followers and to make himself, the Redeemer, the principle of charity and unity for the whole of the mystical Body, the Church, by overcoming the narrow bounds of time and space.

Indeed, Christ's intention was that the Eucharist should be a means of overcoming that solicitude in which every man with a personal life finds himself, whether he be a child or an old man. It is a means of overcoming that distance which history and geography put between the generations and among the various situations in which man is scattered over the earth.

Jubilee

A human instrument was needed for accomplishing that unheard of and wonderful plan; there was need of a delegated power which might renew the sacramental miracle, a ministry to announce and distribute the Word made the bread of life, flesh and blood of the paschal Lamb, the saviour and liberator (as was done in the prophetic and symbolic episode of the multiplication of the loaves). There was need of a qualified minister, there was need of a qualified ministry, of the Priesthood of Christ himself, transfused into men, who would be raised up from being disciples to become apostles and priests.

It will be a great good fortune, and there will be great exultation in the Church and in the world when theology, liturgy, spirituality and, We may add, sociology, bring out afresh those secret and light-filled truths into our day, in the way proper to the divine realities which they contain and the cognoscitive capacities of modern man. The divine Priesthood of Christ, as communicated in the ministerial priesthood, will then be vindicated, in its dignity, and in its mission. For this reason, dearest brethren and children, We have welcomed the simple but sincere honours which have been given to Our priestly Jubilee—not so much to Us, who are frail clay, but to the Priesthood of Christ, to the divine treasure which has been entrusted to Us as to every other priest (cf. *2 Cor.* 4, 7).

The goodness of so many faithful

But there is an explanation, which We must mention, for the commemoration of Our priestly Jubilee. The reason is the goodness of those who promoted it and of those who took part in it.

Oh! We are not unaware of this goodness, your goodness, brethren and children of Holy Church. We know it, We experience it every day. It is something We admire, something We are grateful for, something We have trust in, something for which We pray. Do you think it could possibly be disregarded in Our evaluation of the Church today—the goodness of the Bishops, of the Priests, of men and women Religious, of the Catholic Laity, of so many of our youth, of so many innocent children, so many who are suffering, so many missionaries, so many fellow-workers, so many friends, so many faithful?

Do you perhaps think that the Pope has no eyes, no heart? Of course not: you know that this fidelity, this goodness are always very much in Our mind.

But on this occasion We have experienced so much goodness! We can say that We have had a fresh, tangible proof of it. From you, from the entire Church and from so many other people who are near the Church for one reason or another, We heard a chorus rise up, a great chorus which could not but fill Us with emotion and consolation. How many voices, how many voices rose up in harmony to congratulate Us on Our priesthood in Christ, which was conferred on Us and has been exercised for fifty years.

We have listened, weeping and blessing God, to this great

wave of authoritative and, some of them, weighty, voices, of affectionate and pious voices, of innumerable human voices from near and far. Let Us give this sign of gratitude to all for the goodness, the courtesy, the piety which have been shown in these days, and let Us give Our best wishes to all. Above all, let Us tell you what comfort these voices have brought Us, especially some of them, those of persons consecrated to the Lord, those from Our seminaries and novitiates, of Christian workers, of so many schools and hospitals: clear and innocent voices, faint and suffering voices.

Two meaningful voices

People say to Us: how good the Church is! And how good also is secular society surrounding us! What testimony of Christian virtues and human virtues has come to the poor Successor of Peter, who in the present vicissitudes often cannot hide the pain he feels because of various things which are well known to all and which give rise to apprehension for the faith, for charity, for peace in the Church and the world.

We want to mention two by way of example, two oral testimonies—without excluding any of the others!

First, that of a boy coming from a country from behind the Iron Curtain. It was given during a general audience. He was a lad from the people, timid yet bold, with transparent simplicity and innocence. He had learnt some words of Latin by heart, together with some in his own language, in order to tell Us of his own loyalty and that of his country. He obliged Us to halt for a moment in order to listen to him. How could We not do so, even at such an awkward moment, charmed as We were by his candour and evangelical goodness?

The second case was that of a venerable old man, an old man who trembled a little, but who was sure of the message which he had resolved to give Us after a ceremony in St. Peter's. His message was *Coraggio, Santo Padre, coraggio!* Courage, Holy Father, courage! He was Saverio Roncalli, Pope John's brother. It was like listening to a messenger from Our Predecessor!

So it is! Thank you, thank you all! And Our Apostolic Blessing to all!

ENTIRE CHURCH HAS TASK
OF SERVICE

Our search for the ideas of the Council is continuing. It is a search for those ideas which occur again and again in its teachings and documents and tell us about that ecclesial style with which the whole Council is imbued. As We do this We cannot but fix Our attention on one particular idea—the idea of service.

This is certainly not a new idea in the religious concept of an order established by God, in which every creature—including man, a free creature—is involved and has its place. Fear of God, which is the essence of the natural religious sense, is described as " the beginning of wisdom " (*Ps.* 110, 10; *Eccl.* 1, 16). It is the logical and ontological principle of the Bible's philosophy. At the same time it proclaims the absolute sway of God the creator and man's dependence on him, a dependence which is free, yet morally necessary. The fundamental duty of worship (*latria*) develops into that of service (*diaconia*). In the context of the religion of revelation, this concept of service takes on particular features in the second part of the Book of Isaiah, for it is there that we find that mysterious figure, " the Servant of the Lord ". It is open to various interpretations, but that of the redeeming Messiah is clearly dominant (cf. *Is.* 42, 1 sqq. 4, 3-6; 52, 13-53).

As everyone knows, Jesus chose to take on the nature of a slave, even though he was the Son of God; by making himself like man " he humbled himself and became obedient, even to the death of the cross " (cf. *Phil.* 2, 6-8). The whole of the Gospel story proceeds in a spirit of submission to the Father's will and of service for the sake of others. This spirit fills the whole of Christ's mission, and he openly said of himself that " the Son of man —Jesus the Messiah—did not come to be served, but to serve and

251

give his life for the redemption of many " (*Mt.* 20, 28). We all know that Jesus made his example a law for his disciples, and it is worth while quoting the whole text of that great statement. which gives the Church a lesson in reform and government: " The kings of the Gentiles lord it over them, and they who exercise authority over them are called benefactors. But let it not be so with you. But he who is the greatest among you let him be as the youngest, and let him who governs be as one who serves ... I am in the midst of you as one who serves ... " (*Lk.* 22, 25-28).

Power and ministry

The Council expressly and deliberately made this teaching of Our Lord its own; it related it explicitly and directly to the authority which governs the People of God. In doing this it took a line which runs right through all ecclesiastical tradition: that which identifies power with ministry (cf. CONGAR, *Pour une Eglise servante et pauvre*, p. 15 & no. 2). St. Augustine provides us with more incisive formulations, and so does St. Gregory the Great (cf. CONGAR, *L'Episcopat et l'Eglise universelle*, p. 67 ss., 101-132). And ministry means service, service, for love, for others' good together with sacrifice of self. What the Council had to say about this (cf. *Lumen gentium*, 32) is intended to bring it back to forms of genuine pastoral expression, to reveal that the fundamental title upon which hierarchical power in the Church rests, is love, and, in humility and dedication, to champion both its dignity and the necessity for it.

A touchstone

That statement refers before anything else to the office which has been entrusted to Us in the universal Church. We pray to Christ the Lord and We commend Ourself to the piety of Our brothers and children so that We may be able to perform that office faithfully and in an exemplary way, as behooves him who bears the title of Servant of the Servants of God.

This idea of service as the reason for authority in the Church leads to many considerations. Some may wish to follow the echo of Jesus' masterly words through the pages of the New

Testament; someone else may prefer to go looking for it in patristic and theological text (cf. e. g. S. Th. II-II^{ae}, 88, 12); others again may choose to go through the Church's long history in order to see how the pastoral power was linked with civil authority and how various complications and alterations in the Gospel account of the hierarchical office arose from that. Finally, others may seek for the forms and styles in which the Church ought to exercises its hierarchical authority. This is somethings that is being done today. In all of these cases the idea of service remains the touchstone for testing canonical perfection of the power conferred by Christ upon his Apostles and their successors for guiding the People of God.

The hierarchy's authority

But We will limit Ourself here to a few simple and rapid observations. The fact that Jesus Christ willed that his Church should be governed in a spirit of service does not mean that the Church ought not have hierarchical government exercising power. The keys given to Peter mean something; they mean a great deal, just like the words with which Jesus transmitted his divine authority to the Apostles. He said: " He who hears you, hears me; he who despises you despises me " (*Lk.* 10, 16). In saying this he almost identified with the Apostles and he showed us the power which is conferred on those who represent Christ. It is always pastoral power, and it is intended for the good of the Church, and it is strong and efficacious. But it does not come by election from below or by investment by the community: it comes through apostolic transmission, by means of the sacrament of holy orders. This explains how the Apostle Paul, who was very conscious of being at the service of all—*debitor sum* (*Rom.* 1, 14)—did not fear to threaten to come back among the turbulent Corinthians if need be *in virga*—with a rod to punish them (*1 Cor.* 4, 21). Nor did he fear to threaten to consign to Satan an unhappy person guilty of incest, that is, to excommunicate him.

Another observation: The whole of " the ecclesial order can be understood only when considered as an order for service. In order to get an exact understanding of the ecclesiastical hierarchy's ministerial task it is necessary to link it with the wider problem of the function of service which pertains to all the Church's members ... Ecclesial service is the particular task of all members of the Church " (LÖHRER, *La gerarchia al servizio del popolo cristiano,* in " La Chiesa del Vaticano II ", p. 699).

Two ecclesial tasks

This applies to every single one of the faithful, but it applies to the whole ecclesial body even more. The entire Church is at the service of humanity: this is the central idea of the Pastoral Constitution *Gaudium et spes* (cf. nos. 3, 11, 42, 89 etc.). There can be no doubt that, if the Church is imbued with such awareness of the service of salvation which it owes to the world, it will be more desirous and more zealous to be united, to be holy, to be disinterested, to be missionary, to be open and understanding towards the needs of our time. It will become more careful to be faithful to two tasks which have been assigned to it for this purpose. The first is that of keeping the faith intact, that is, of preserving that inheritance of truth and grace which Christ left it. The second task is to make itself more and more capable of communicating its message and charism of salvation to mankind.

In this way the idea of service is far from weighing upon the Church as an oppressive and paralyzing burden; on the contrary, it enables it to renew its authentic inner vocation and go outwards in ever new, ever inspired, ever generous apostolate. This is the regenerating power possessed by duty; this is the expansive energy of love.

We should still have to explain how this idea of service can be brought into accord with that of liberty (unforgettable teachings about which were also left us by the Council). But We think that everyone will be able to find the harmonious connection between these two ideas of the Council for himself, so long as he understands them rightly. We hope that everyone will. With Our Apostolic Blessing.

POPE PAUL APPEALS
FOR GREATER PEACE EFFORTS

On June the 23rd, the Holy Father received the Sacred College of Cardinals in audience who presented their feastday wishes to the Pope, the day before the feast of St. John the Baptist. After a speech of homage by the Dean of the College, Cardinal Tisserant, the Pope spoke as follows.

After our recent meeting in the Consistory, when on the fiftieth anniversary of our priesthood you showed us your affection, we again have the joy of being with you, Venerable Brothers, members of the Sacred College. We thank you for your presence. We thank your chosen spokesman, Cardinal Eugène Tisserant, for the thoughtful wishes he has conveyed to us and for the prayers which he promised in the name of all.

To be among you brings us always serenity and consolation. We now reciprocate your good wishes and prayers, entrusting their fulfilment to the powerful intercession of the Precursor of Christ. Going beyond the personal reason, pleasing though it be, which has brought you here, we desire to take the occasion to invite you to turn with us your gaze towards the future. Are we not called, like the Precursor, to prepare the way of the Lord? And is it not the Church's mission to proclaim the message of salvation to all generations and, as our predecessor Pope John XXIII put it in the bull of convocation of the Ecumenical Council, " to bring the modern world into contact with the vivifying and perennial energies of the gospel " (*Humanae Salutis*, 25 december [1961]; *AAS*, 54 [1962] p. 6)?

That wish of the Church, to be present in the changing world, was given a splendid manifestation in all the work of the Second Vatican Council, which laid down guiding principles that have been providential for our time. To the man of today, as he actually is, the Church brings the living water of the word of life, ever welling up; she brings him the joyful announcement of salvation, the source of hope and certitude for the new generation which burns with ardour and is filled with dreams for the future, to build tomorrow's world. As we said at the opening of the second session of the Council, a bridge must be built to the world, in order to bring it the leaven of the gospel and to regenerate it in depth, revealing to it the grandeur of its destiny and helping it to bring it to realization by fulfilling the design of the love that creates and redeems.

Total dedication

An event of such greatness and significance demands total dedication on the part of all the Church's children if it is to be brought about effectively. Such an outpouring of graces calls for receptive souls and generous wills in order that the Church's life should expand abundantly in the world and transform it by means of the energy which animates it from within. However, it should be clear to all that the fulfilment of so important a task requires breaks that are at times painful, revisions that are often agonizing, graftings that are always delicate, in order that the tree of faith may take ever deeper root in the soil of our day and spread in rich abundance all its branches (cf. *Mk.* 4, 30-32).

Efforts toward expansion

All the Church's children, each at his post and following out his own vocation, are answerable for this great task. For the Pope this has been the predominant thought of all his pontificate from the first moment, in the innumerable sectors to which the Church's life extends. To ensure the renewal which the Council willed, we have adapted the offices of the Holy See, beginning with the Sacred Congregation for the Doctrine of the Faith, where we have set up a theological commission. We have great expectations of this commission, in view of the promise given by its first work. In the boundless field of theological reflection, problems are posed of such importance and scale that it is necessary to give them replies in which today's Christian will find the certitude of which he has need.

The Christian thinks; he also prays. His prayer also has received an appropriate renewal at the hands of the Council. Much has already been done in this field, in accordance with the directives of the constitution on the liturgy. The Consilium set up for that purpose brought to fulfilment an important and delicate task. For their part too, the episcopal conferences are fulfilling a task of adaptation for which they have competence and mandate. Moreover, the episcopal conferences are as it were the organs for coordination and advancement of the local Churches in communion with the Church of Rome, and this increasingly developed collaboration between the Holy See and them has been one of the richest results of the post-conciliar period. These fraternal links are marked by a living exchange that is ever more intense. They are being consolidated by the Synod of Bishops through its periodic meetings and through its secretariat, made up of representatives chosen by the episcopal conferences and by us. Its first meeting gives ground for great hopes, for it is truly the organization which now ensures the Synod's continuity.

" Ratio Fundamentalis ... "

On the one hand the bishops offer fruitful collaboration with the offices of the Roman Curia, participating in the yearly meetings for laying down general principles and making decisions concerning the activities of the organizations concerned. On the other hand, these offices take care to work in ever closer connection with all the episcopal conferences. This is what was done recently for the preparation of the " Ratio Fundamentalis Institutionis Sacerdotalis " and for the working out of regulations for mixed marriages. In both cases the principal care of the Congregation and of the Commission involved in the work was to decide on a text that was truly the work of all; this was done by means of manifold exchanges and by correspondence, allowing both sides to express their own thinking. In each case general regulations have resulted which can be considered a legal framework in which the essential guiding principles find their definition. It is now for the episcopal conferences to apply them in accordance with the various pastoral needs, The same procedure is already in use for the revision of canon law, the major objectives of which is to bring up to date in accordance with the Council's guidelines the Church's indispensable legislation.

Work continues

The Commission for the Revision of Canon Law is continuing with alacrity its studies for the preparation of draft canons. It is an attentive, patient work of examining, research, consulation and deeper understanding from every point of view of the problems which the new codification must face in the context of the ecclesiology of the Second Vatican Council, of its pastoral effects on the world of today, and of the development and progress of juridical science. The principal guiding lines and the systematic order of the new legislation have been approved, and now some schemes are already in the concluding stage, so that before long examination, above all by the episcopate, will begin. In fact, though the new law of the People of God must be promulgated by the Pope, it is highly fitting that it should receive the valuable contribution of the Church's Pastors, who will in turn be spokesmen for the sentiments of the People of God. The work of consultation and re-examination will undoubtedly take considerable time; but it is time very well spent, not only because through consultation the law will become potentially more effective, but also because a more fruitful acceptance of the new legislation will thus come to maturity, and that legislation must be for those who believe in and love Christ and the Church: a " law of life and knowledge " (*Ecclesiasticus* 45, 6), without which the Spirit would be suppressed (cf. *1 Thessalonians* 5, 19).

Under the guidance of the Spirit

At the same time fraternal relationships have developed with our separated brothers. We ourself have recently had the joy of welcoming Vasken I, the Catholicos of the Armenians. And other meetings have taken place between Catholic and non-Catholic bishops and between the ecclesial communities. Ecumenism, developing on the level of important working commissions of theologians, is thus finding its pastoral dimension. We likewise rejoice that the Jerusalem Ecumenical Institute for the History of Salvation (Tantur) is now on the way to completion.

While contacts are becoming ever more frequent with the representatives of the non-Christians religions, and especially with the Moslems, the Jews and the Buddhists, a difficult, complex and delicate dialogue is being developed with various representatives of modern humanism, according to the desire which we expressed from the time of our first Encyclical *Ecclesiam Suam.* This dialogue is accomplished, day by day, in charity, patience and hope, through the medium of the new Secretariats set up for this purpose, and also through the various bodies established at the wish of episcopal conferences.

Thus the Church is endeavouring to bring her presence properly adapted and diversified, to the world which is slowly and painfully taking shape. As a witness to the catholicity of the Church and as a guarantee of her unity, the Pope, for his part, and with the untiring assistance of the Roman Curia, wishes to favour with all his strength this fruitful work which is going forward on a worldwide scale under the guidance of the Spirit. Many are the echoes that reach us concerning all these achievements and hopes, as also concerning all the troubles and worries of all the Churches when we have the always fresh and real joy of meeting our brothers in the episcopate during their ever more frequent visits *ad limina Apostolorum.*

Problems in today's Church

We have already had the unforgettable joy of opening at Bogotà the assembly of our brothers in Latin America, and of closing at Kampala the first Symposium of the African bishops. In November next, God willing, we shall make direct contact with our brothers in Asia and Oceania. But this contact will be different and much deeper than the previous ones, because it will involve studying, with them and among them, the problems that face the Church in those two continents and the opportunities offered to her there, even though this will mean a certain prolonging of our absence from Rome. New times demand a new style, while our sole preoccupation is to be fatihful to our pastoral mission, which, by divine disposition, is exercised as service (cf. *Mt.* 20, 28; *Mk.* 10, 43-44). In order the better to serve, the Pope seeks to become better acquanted with situations, to immerse himself in them, to listen and to make a certain direct personal contact with the historical reality of the Church. This will be our way of meeting the desires expressed at the recent session of the Synod, in accordance with our vocation as Vicar of Christ the Lord.

How we wish that, with this brotherly visit, the whole Church could reveal herself, in the burning words of the Council, as a truly missionary Church, in all her members! What a call will go out, we hope, from those vast continents, which contain more than a half of the entire human race! These are the most pressing problems of today's post-Conciliar Church: how to proclaim Jesus Christ, how to witness to his gospel, how to initiate dialogue between the Church and those countless millions. Today, the whole Church, through her bishops, her priests and the most generous and responsive of her laity, must live in this missionary condition. Our ministry is firmly orientated in this missionary direction too, as we announced in our first radio message to the world seven years ago, and as we repeated once again a few days ago in our message for Mission Sunday next October. For this purpose, Venerable Brothers, we ever ask for your collaboration, together with that of the whole Church. In doing this, we shall be careful to draw attention to the need not to forget the specific assistance that Christians must bring to a world in the grips of the grave problems of development and peace. We take our inspiration from the vistas opened up by the conciliar Constitution *Gaudium et spes*, developed in our Encyclical *Populorum progressio* and recently made the subject of the missionary message just mentioned.

Justice and brotherly love

If evangelisation must always be the first and basic intention, development remains an essential requirement of justice and brotherly love. Let us face the fact: in spite of generous efforts being made everywhere to solve the most urgent and often dramatic implications of the whole question, which involves the entire world, we have to say that the inequalities between wealthy countries and developing countries have not been removed, and unfortunately in some respects they are continually increasing. There rises from the Third World a cry for help; trusting expectation is turning into terrible denunciation, which could explode in ungovernable rage, whose consequences could be lethal for peace and true progress; we do not wish here to enter into the merits of the case, for the evangelical duty of sincerity towards all men does not exempt us from recognising that this threatening demand can not always be accepted without question. But the fact remains that the imbalance which we have pointed out before seems to be growing in inverse proportion, to the profit of him who has and the loss of him who does not succeed in making good his own lack with the fruits of his labours (*Populorum progressio*, 54-57; *AAS*, 59, 1967, pp. 283-285).

If the indisputable good will of so many worthy international bodies and the efforts they have made have not prevented this painful disproportion occurring, it is a sign that the system adopted has not been correctly applied, and that something is not working properly. We therefore wish to call the attention of the organizations responsible, and especially our own, and to ask them to reflect, to pause. Has the effort hitherto made by all been the right one? Has it been the method best suited to resolve the problem of the unequal distribution of wealth between nations with an abundance of goods and nations prevented from reaching an adequate level of well-being? If the problem is not solved equitably and if the current inequalities are not progressively evened out, then we shall not attain the balance of justice, and peace which is the ultimate aspiration of all men and the visible sign of harmony among brother nations will be increasingly endangered.

Peace threatened

Peace: this too is another urgent problem that calls for the action of the Church in her relations with the world. In various parts of the world peace is still being threatened, violated, or stifled. Innocent peoples are being thrown into confusion by forces greater than themselves; they are made the uncomprehending pawns of a cruel and merciless game, which snatches its victims not only from the ranks of strong men, torn away from their peaceful work, but also and above all among the children, the mothers, the sick, the old and the defenceless. As a result of war, every day there are people dying in the world, through violence which is at the same time blind, wily and insidious, through vengeful and malicious reprisals, and through the resulting terrible lack of security and food. In today's world the young people no longer believe in fine words; they see, with their intuition of reality and their instinctive knowledge of the moral bases of situations, that in spite of so many speeches—for everyone is in agreement in speaking about peace—armed conflicts are increasing frighteningly, like a patch of oil spreading inexorably towards a flame. The Near East, the Middle East and the Far East are the areas that most hold the attention of public opinion, without mentioning the scars that still ooze blood elsewhere.

Also on this theme it is necessary to pause. It is necessary to reflect, and to reflect seriously, to see if what is done in the world, even with good will, is sufficiently effective, or if rather greater courage is needed in the real promotion of peace. For this we turn to all, and in particular to the nations which by their international prestige and their real possibilities are truly able to contribute to the liberation of the world from the scourge of war; we turn to the international organizations which have the responsibility of the defence of peace in the world. Our appeal to them is sad and vibrant. What we seek is that the moral principles of humanity and brotherhood prevail over every other criterion and every other interest for a more valid, concrete and conclusive work of peace. At stake is the credibility of the words spoken and actions performed for that supreme goal.

Conciliar " aggiornamento "

These are some of the very serious problems which today hold the consciousness of the Church and of the world; as we have said in the Encyclical *Ecclesiam Suam*, the Church is not separated from the world, " rather, she lives in it. For this reason her members undergo its influence, breathe its culture, accept its laws, absorb its customs ", but only in order to draw near to these forms of thought and life " in order to purify them, enoble them, vivify them and sanctify them " (*AAS*, 56, 1964, pp. 627-628). All effort at conciliar " aggiornamento " and all the interior renewal of the Church would be in vain if they did not permit her to go to the world with fresh vigour and new youth in order to announce the good news of which she is the bearer. Will we indeed be able to bring the faith to men of the modern world in the unmeasured amplitude of its geographical dimensions as well as in the turmoil of its currents of thought? Will we know how to lead them to discover the countenance, always young and attractive, of Christ the Saviour? Will we know how to undertake " with a candid trust " the formidable dimension of such a mission before the bewildering novelty of modern times (*ibid. AAS,* 56 [1964], p. 649)? Will we know to awaken the laity to a sense of their responsibility? Will we know how to stir up in the young the desire to follow Christ, to consecrate themselves to his service? In the already long history of salvation, it is up to us with the help of God to write a new page. We must bring back to their true source those values which animate and mould the world in its present gigantic effort of spiritual rebirth; we must give them their complete fulfilment.

Far from bringing us to a halt, the difficulties of this undertaking stimulate us to confront it with greater enthusiasm and generosity. The dialogue of salvation which must be conducted on a world-wide scale obliges us to follow the magnetic example of the great traveller Apostle: " I made myself all things to all men " (*1 Cor.* 9, 22). Strong in faith, unshakable in hope and moved by a love without limit, the Church goes out to meet the oldest religions as well as the most recent ideologies and the most difficult human problems to bring to them her secret and her treasure. These are not those of perfected organization or tested technology, but " a seed, a leaven, salt and light " (*Ecclesiam suam; AAS,* 56, 1964, p. 649), and she brings them with very simple words which everyone understands as a promise and a liberation. " She speaks of truth, justice, liberty, progress, concord, peace, civilization " (*ibid.*). To the new man being born in these last decades of the twentieth century, from the regions of old Europe to the immense confines of Asia, the Church brings the light of Christ the Saviour, the strength of his presence, the flame of his love, the certainty of his word. To peoples agonized by the search for peace and struggling with the formidable problems of development, she offers her message of universal brotherhood, " leading them to recognize, across all frontiers, the faces of their brothers, the faces of their friends " (*Populorum progressio,* 75; *AAS,* 56, 1967, p. 295.

June 23rd, 1970

" For the sake of the Church "

That is the Church's future in the world of tomorrow; that is the humble contribution which with boundless hope we wish to make—modestly and firmly—to bring it about. We thank you with all our heart for all your efforts to help us fulfil it, each one of you at the post to which Divine Providence has called you to work. Besides being directed to yourselves, our thought goes also to our brothers in the episcopate and to their fruitful collegial toil, to priests, our co-workers in sacred orders, to religious, whose consecrated life is an appeal and a promise, to Christian couples, who in their married love, live the mystery of the union of Christ and the Church, to lay apostles, who give untiring witness to the good news, to youth, who place their enthusiasm at the service of the gospel, to the suffering, who are fulfilling the precious function of making up all that has still to be undergone by Christ for the sake of the Church (cf. *Col.* 1, 24), to the aged, who are ripening thoughts of heaven in their tested wisdom. To all of them we say what joy is ours in the community of faith which unites us, of hope which urges us on and of love for Christ which inspires us. To all men we address our fraternal greeting: may God our Father and Jesus Christ our Lord grant you grace and peace. It is our wish for you, with our Apostolic Blessing.

THE " POOR IN SPIRIT "
TAKE FIRST PLACE

As we examine the Council's spirit, that spirit which ought to create in us a new and authentic Christian state of mind and find expression in a new style of ecclesial life, we are soon led to the subject of poverty.

Much has been said about poverty. Our venerated Predecessor John XXIII set the matter going with the radio message which he broadcast to Catholics throughout the world one month before the Council. He referred as early as that to the problems which the Church had to face inside and outside its bounds. He declared that " the Church presents herself for what she is and what she desires to be, as the Church for all, particularly as the Church of the Poor " (AAS, 1962, 682).

These words set up an immense echo. They themselves echoed words in the Bible, words coming from afar, from the prophet Isaiah (cf. Is. 58, 6; 61, 1 sqq.), words which Jesus made his own in the synagogue at Nazareth: " He has anointed me to bring the good news to the poor " (cf. Lk. 4, 18). We all know what an important part the theme of poverty has in the gospel, beginning from the Sermon of the Beatitudes. In it the " poor in spirit " take first place—not only there but in the Kingdom of heaven also. Then there are those other passages in which the lowly, the little ones, the suffering, the needy are all extolled as the favourite citizens of that same kingdom of heaven (Mt. 18, 3), as living representatives of Christ himself (Mt. 25, 40). And Christ's example above all is the great argument in favour of evangelical poverty (cf. 2 Cor. 8, 9; St. AUGUSTINE, Sermo 14; PL 38, 115).

We know this. We shall do well to remember it, in homage to that Christian authenticity which we are all looking for, under the Council's auspices and in accord with the spiritual genius of our time.

June 24th, 1970

A theological and moral principle

It is a very big question. We will not try to deal with it all here. We mention it only because of its theological importance. The fact is that evangelical poverty entails a corrective to our religious relationship with God and Christ. The reason is that this relationship creates a prior claim. That claim is for spiritual goods to be first in the list of values worthy of being put in the forefront of our existence, our seeking and our love. That claim is expressed in the command: " Seek you first the kingdom of God " (*Mt.* 6, 33). Then (this is what poverty is!) it puts temporal goods, wealth, present happiness, low down on the list in comparison with the supreme good, which is God and in comparison with the possession of him, which is our everlasting happiness. Humbleness of heart (cf. St. Augustine, *Enarr. in Ps.* 73; *PL* 36, 943), temperance and, often, detachment in regard to possession and use of economic goods, are the two marks of poverty which the divine Master taught us with his doctrine—and even more by his example, as We said. He revealed himself socially through poverty.

We can at once see that this theological principle upon which Christian poverty is based turns into a moral principle, and this moral principle inspires Christian asceticism. According to it, poverty is more than a mere fact for man. It is the willed result of a love preference, a choice of Christ and his realm, together with renunciation (which is a liberation) of covetousness, of riches, Desire for riches entails a whole series of temporal cares and earthly ties which occupy great and overwhelming space in the heart. Let us not forget the gospel story of the rich young man. He was given the chance of following Christ and therefore abandoning his riches. He preferred his wealth to the following of Christ. The Lord " looked upon him and loved him " (*Mk.* 10, 21), but still had to watch him go sadly away.

The Church must be poor

But, even more than to the practice of the personal virtue of poverty, the Council called us back to search after, to practice another kind of poverty—ecclesial poverty, that which the Church ought to practise as the Church, as the assembly gathered together in the name of Christ.

One passage in the Council's documents on this matter is a great passage, and We choose it for quotation from among very many others on the subject to be found in those documents. The passage is as follows: « The spirit of poverty and of charity are the glory and the testimony of the Church of Christ " (*Gaudium et spes*, 88).

These are luminous and vigorous words. They arose from an ecclesial conscience which was becoming fully awake, was hungry for truth and authenticity and desired to free itself from historical habits which had now been clearly revealed as causing deformations in the Church's evangelical genius and apostolic mission. There is imperative need for critical, historical and moral examination of conscience, so as to give the Church her genuine and modern features, in which the present generation desires to be able to recognize those of Christ.

Those who spoke in the Council on this matter dwelled particularly on this function of ecclesial poverty, that is, on its function of illustrating the Church's proper appearance (cf. CONGAR, *Pour une Eglise servante et pauvre*, p. 107). Cardinal Lercaro spoke especially in this way at the close of the Council's First Session (December 6th, 1962). He emphasized a certain " aspect " which the Church of today ought to show people of our time in a particular way, the aspect with which Christ's mystery was revealed. That aspect is the moral one of poverty; it is also the sociological aspect, namely, that the Church rises by preference from among the poor.

Historical experiences

We can all see what a power for reform there is in exalting the principle that the Church ought to be poor. The Church should also be seen to be poor. Perhaps not everyone can see the justifications which can be adduced for various aspects assumed by the Church during the course of her centuries of life and her contacts with particular cultural conditions. There was a time, for example, when the Church had the aspect of a great land-owning power, when she was engaged in re-educating peoples in the work of agriculture. She had the aspect of a civil power, at a time when civil authority had broken down and there was need to exercise power with human authority. There was a time when she adorned her worship with magnificent churches and rich vesture, in order to express her sacred character and her spiritual genius. In order to exercise her ministry she had to ensure food and decent living to her ministers; in order to encourage education and social assistance for the people, she founded schools and opened hospitals. Again, in order to identify herself with the culture of certain historical periods, she expressed herself supremely well in the language of art (See, for example, G. Kurth, *Les origines de la civilisation moderne*).

Economic means and ends

It would be easy to show that the fabulous riches which a certain kind of public opinion attributes to the Church really have very different dimensions. To do this would be to honour the Church's economy of poverty. Her riches are often insufficient for the modest and legitimate requirements of day to day living, the ordinary needs of so many churchmen and religious, so many welfare and pastoral institutions. But We do not wish to embark upon an apologia of this kind at the moment.

We accept rather the earnest entreaty of people of today, especially looking at the Church from the outside. They wish the Church to show herself as what she ought to be: certainly not as an economic power, not as a Church invested with the signs of ease, not as a Church devoted to financial speculations and unresponsive to the needs of people, of classes, of poor nations.

Nor do we wish to go into that immense field of ecclesial manner of life. We will only mention it, just to show you that We have it in mind and are working on gradual but not timid reforms.

We note with watchful attention that, in this period of ours, which is all absorbed in gaining, possessing, enjoying economic goods, a desire is apparent in public opinion both inside and outside the Church, to see evangelical poverty practised. It is almost a need. People want to see it most where the gospel is preached and represented; and We may add: in the official Church, in Our Apostolic See itself.

We are aware of this request which is directed to Our ministry from inside and out. By the grace of God many things have already been done in regard to giving up temporal things and reforming ecclesial style. We will continue along these lines, with the respect that is due to legitimate situations and facts, but also trusting that We are understood and are assisted by the faithful in Our effort to eliminate situations which are not in accordance with the spirit and the good of the authentic Church.

There is need for economic and material means. That entails the necessity to look for means, to ask for them, to administer them. But may those " means " never get the better of the concept of the " ends " which they ought to serve. The means ought to reflect the restraint created by the limits of the ends, the generosity of commitment to them, and the spirituality of their significance.

In the Divine Master's school we shall all remember to love poverty and the poor at the same time. We shall love the former in order to make it an austere norm of Christian life. We shall love the latter in order to devote special interest to them, whether they be persons, classes or nations in need of love and aid. The Council told us about this too. We have listened to its voice, and We shall try to listen again.

But the discussion on the Church of the Poor must go on, for Us and for all of you, with the Lord's grace. With Our Apostolic Benediction.

MEDITATE UPON
LISTEN TO THE SACRED SCRIPTURES
AS VATICAN COUNCIL II DIRECTS

T he Council again! You will have noticed that much has been said about Holy Scripture since the Council. References appear everywhere in the Council's documents, but they are most frequent in the Constitution on the Sacred Liturgy (cf. nos. 24, 33, 35, 51 ...), in the Constitution on the Church (cf. nos. 6, 15, 24 ...), and in the Decree on Ecumenism (no. 21). If we tried to list them all, we should never finish.

A most important document was deliberately devoted to Holy Scripture itself. That document is the Dogmatic Constitution on Divine Revelation, which is called *Dei Verbum*, from the words with which it begins. It is one of the Council's most weighty documents. It may be described as a fundamental one, together with those on the Church (*Lumen gentium*) and on the relationship between the Church and the world (*Gaudium et spes*). It outlines the doctrinal process which has gone on in the Church since the Council of Trent. It indicates the weightiest biblical problems which have arisen in these latter times. It establishes the function of Holy Scripture in respect to Revelation, namely, that it takes God's Word down in writing (cf. *Dei Verbum*, 7), and it defines its relationship with Tradition (nos. 8-9). It states its relation to the Church's Magisterium (no. 10), that is to say, to the rule of faith.

It has been noted that the " the economy of salvation " was accepted for the first time in explicit language in an official Church document in this text. The idea of doctrinal development was accepted along with it (cf. B. D. Dupuy, O.P., *La Rév. div.* 1, 15 sqq.). Likewise, disciplinary innovations have been brought in, so modifying those of the Council of Trent (cf. Denz.-Sch. 1853-1854) and those established by Pope Clement XI after the controversy about

Paschase Quesnel's Jansenist doctrines (cf. DENZ.-SCH. 2479-2485). Among such disciplinary novelties was the hope expressed that it might be possible with the Church's approval to prepare translations and editions of Holy Scripture in collaboration with the separated Brethren (nos. 22 and 25).

The II Vatican Council and the Popes' Encyclicals

The first five chapters of the Constitution deal with many questions concerning doctrine and studies about the Bible. This ranks the Constitution with the great papal documents which have been issued about that matter of such prime importance, especially over the last century (the Encyclical *Providentissimus Deus* [1893], issued by Pope Leo XIII; Pope Benedict XV's *Spiritus Paraclitus* [1920], Pope Pius XII's *Divino afflante Spiritu* [1943]). But We will only refer to chapter six of the Council's Constitution *Dei Verbum*. It speaks of Sacred Scripture in the life of the Church, and is therefore directly concerned with the whole People of God.

What does this chapter tell us? First of all, it tells us how the Church has venerated the Books of Scripture " as the supreme rule of faith " (cf. no. 21), together with sacred Tradition. Perhaps it had some apologetic purpose in doing so. Perhaps it made this statement, with history and sacred literature on its side, to defend the Catholic Church against the accusation of having valued and esteemed Holy Scripture less than Protestants did in the sixteenth century. The Protestants regarded it as the sole rule of faith. " Holy Scripture alone ", they said, and cut it off from the Church and from original Tradition, as well as from interpretations of it which were provided by later Tradition. This enables them in practice to allow every reader to take the meaning he chooses, in accordance with enlightenment from the Holy Spirit, which was also claimed. This was to the detriment of the Bible's content and of the unity of faith. For the Church Holy Scriptures is God's Word, inspired by him; therefore its own authentic meaning has the guarantee of divine inerrancy (*Dei Verbum*, 1).

There are innumerable testimonies to prove the value which

the Church attributes to Holy Scripture. We will quote St. Jerome's famous words: " Ignorance of the Scriptures is ignorance of Christ " (*Comm. in Is.*, Prol.: *PL* 24, 17).

A new field for seekers after God

What does the Church recognize in Holy Scripture? It recognizes the unchangeableness of her doctrine (cf. *Jn.* 10, 35: Jesus said, " Scripture cannot be broken "). The Church recognizes the validity and permanent authenticity of God's Word contained in it; she recognizes its inexhaustible spiritual fruitfulness: she recognizes a prophetic value which can infuse with the breath of the Holy Spirit every human situation, whether it be historical or sociological; she recognizes the source of her preaching and catechesis. She particularly recognizes a spiritual nourishment.

Let us reread at least one paragraph from that enlightened teaching: " Therefore, like the Christian religion itself, all the preaching of the Church must be nourished and ruled by sacred Scripture. For in the sacred books the Father, who is in heaven, meets his children with great love and speaks with them; and the force and power of the word of God is so great that it remains the support and energy of the Church, strength of faith for her sons, the food of the soul, the pure and perennial source of spiritual life. Consequently, these words are perfectly applicable to sacred Scripture: ' For the word of God is living and efficacious ' (*He.* 4, 12) and is ' able to build up and give the inheritance among all the sanctified ' (*Ac.* 20, 32; cf. *1 Th.* 2, 13) "(no. 21).

The idea of nourishment for the soul recurs twice more in *Dei verbum*, and is on both occasions a reference to the celebrated words in *The Imitation of Christ* (1.IV.11) which associate the food of the Word of God with the food of the Eucharist: " The Church has always venerated the divine Scripture as it has venerated the very Body of Christ; it has never failed to nourish itself with the Bread of life (above all in the liturgy) from the table of the Word of God and the table of the Body of Christ, and to offer it to the faithful " (no. 26).

Therefore, if we wish to be attentive and observant pupils of the Council, we must all give new and great importance to Holy Scripture. Above all, we must take care to listen to it, now that liturgical reform has given such a place and such honour to the Word of God. Yet listening is not enough; we must also meditate, that is, assimilate. This is why it is necessary to read Sacred Scripture, it is necessary to study it.

We shall run into many difficulties, but, St. Augustine says *orent ut intelligant*: pray in order to understand (*De Doctrina christ.* 3, 56: *PL* 34, 89). Those who do so and who seek the guidance of good exegetes, who are guided by the Church, will find that the difficulties encourage us to acquire ever better understanding and so come in the end to closer union with the Word of God (cf. *Const. Dogm. sulla Divina Riv.*, P. Martini, pages 417-465, Elle Di Ci - Turin, Leuman).

So here is a new field for seekers after God, for faithful children of the Church of the Council to enter. We exhort you to enter, with Our Apostolic Benediction.

POPE DESCRIBES
PASTORAL FEATURE OF COUNCIL

In preceding audiences we have already considered features of the II Vatican Council which gave it a special character. Now one more: its pastoral character. Pope John XXIII wished it to have such a character, for in his introductory address he expressed his intention that the Council which he had summoned should be of a mainly pastoral nature (*AAS*, 1962, p. 585).

And so it was. We have only to remember that one of the Council's documents, the last and the most widely read, is entitled " Pastoral Constitution on the Church in the Modern World ". It is the now famous *Gaudium et spes*. And the other chief Constitution, the dogmatic one on the Church, entitled *Lumen gentium*, continually reminds us of the notion and duties of the pastoral office (cf. nos. 26-27). So does the Constitution on the Sacred Liturgy (cf. nos. 33-36; 43-46). Needless to say, the contents of the Decree *Christus Dominus* on the office of Bishops, are chiefly concerned with the pastoral character of their functions (especially no. 16). Likewise the Decree on priestly training, *Optatam totius*, 12; 19-20; and the one on the Missions, *Ad Gentes*, 5-6, and so on. The meaning of this word " pastoral " is very clear, from the continual use that is being made of it. Still, it is helpful to recall its origin. It derives from the ancient and classical language. Homer described kings as shepherd of the people. It derives in a special manner from the language of the Bible (cf. *Jer.* 31, 10; *Ez.* 34). But it took on the special meaning it has for us when Jesus uttered it, for he loved to describe himself as a shepherd: " I am the good shepherd " (*Jn.* 10, 11, 14; *Mt.* 15, 24; *Lk.* 15, 4-7; *He.* 13, 20; *1 Pet.* 2, 25). It derives from the pastoral function which the risen Christ conveyed to Peter, in a thrice-repeated statement, as the consequence and the proof of Peter's love for him (*Jn.* 10, 21, 15-17): If you love me, shepherd my flock.

July 8th, 1970

His life for his sheep

So we see that the pastoral office is not only important in the Council's thought; it is important in the Gospel. This coincidence once more shows us how the Council follows in the footsteps of the Gospel.

But what does this concept of shepherding involve? We should have to give a lot of thought to analyzing it, so We will only summarize here. There is no doubt that the pastoral function entails exercise of authority. The Pastor is the head and guide. He is the teacher. We might also say, if what Jesus said is true, that his flock hears and follows the voice of the Good Shepherd which he is (*Jn.* 10, 3-4). His authority is not conferred by the flock. He has a prerogative, a responsibility and a power of initiative which antecede the flock: *ante eas vadit*: he goes before them (*Jn.* 10, 4). He does not let himself be led by the flock, contrary to what is favoured by a certain view of authority today.

We at once observe a second mark which characterizes the Pastor in the Gospel's constitutional design. It coexists with the mark which is authority. It is service. In Christ's thought authority is not for the benefit of him who exercises it, but for the advantage of those over whom it is exercised. It is not from them, but it is for them.

Authority is justified by this conception of it. Let us once more recall the celebrated formula which Manzoni used in connection with his description of that ideal pastor, Cardinal Frederick Borromeo: " There can be no rightful superiority of one man over others, unless it be in their service " (*The Betrothed*, chapter XXII).

We have often spoken about this. Authority is a duty, a burden, a debt, a ministry to others, to lead them to the life of which God has made authority the dispenser (*Tit.* 1, 7; *1 Cor.* 4, 1-2; *1 Pet.* 4, 10; *Lk.* 12, 42), and which God wills that we too should reach. It is a channel, an obligatory, necessary, but saving channel, and it is called " the cure, or care of souls ". This is the pastoral function.

This aspect of it, " cure of souls ", is the aspect in which the concept of shepherding or pastorate is perfected. It also opens up a new outlook to us and shows us a third mark, in addition to

275

authority and service, and going beyond them. This third mark is love: service done for love and with love. And love, if it really be that, immediately leads to its absolute expression: total giving of self, sacrifice. This is what Jesus said of himself, and this is what he did. He offered himself as an example for those in the pastoral office to follow: " The good shepherd gives his life for his sheep " (*Jn.* 10, 11).

The rule of pastors

A twofold sum of pastoral requisites is involved here. The are subjective ones, consisting of the virtues proper to whoever exercises the cure of souls. And how many there are! They include concern (remember St. Paul's *sollicitudo*: 2 *Cor.* 11, 28), disinterestedness, humility, tenderness (cf. St. Paul again, in his moving address to the Christians of Miletus: *Ac.* 20, 19). On the other hand there are the objective requisites for the pastoral art: study of and experience in the business of caring for souls (this has already reached the point where the pastoral function may be classified among the sciences derived from theology); then there is pastoral theology, among the treasures of which is psychology (take, for example the third book of St. Gregory the Great's famous *Regula pastoralis*). And there is sociology, so much in fashion at the moment. These all have a rightful and dignified place in the sum of objective requisites for pastoral office.

We way conclude from all this that the pastorate is not just empiricism and goodfellowship applied to community relationships. Still less is it neglect to have recourse to doctrinal principles which are indispensable for energy and fruitfulness in the pastoral apostolate. On the contrary, it means concrete, existential application of theological truths and spiritual charisms to the apostolate, that apostolate which reaches both individual souls and communities of persons, and which, as We said, is called the cure of souls.

" Operation heart "

You will tell Us that all this is for the hierarchy, the ministerial priesthood, the Pastors, who, in the People of God, are invested with the specific function of imparting the gifts of the word, of grace and community charity to the faithful. This is true. It is our full and direct responsibility. The higher the grade uniting us to the person of Christ and his mission of salvation, the more demanding it becomes.

But remember that the Council held in honour memory and exercise of the common priesthood of the faithful (*Lumen gentium*, 10-11). As St. Peter himself said, this is a royal priesthood (*1 Pet.* 2, 5-9), and the Council aroused every Christian's sense of his responsibility in the great framework of salvation (cf. *Lumen gentium*, 30-34). Every one of the faithful ought to be a missionary (cf. *Ad Gentes*, 36). Indeed the Council acknowledged that certain forms of apostolate cannot be properly exercised except by the laity (*Lumen gentium*, 31 and the entire Constitution *Gaudium et spes*). It devoted an entire Decree to the apostolate of the laity (*Apostolicam actuositatem*). We might say that the Council made its own the Bible's words: " (The Lord) has given everyone commandments in regard to his neighbour " (*Eccli* 17, 12). It wished to create an atmosphere of collective, reciprocal pastoral work. It desired to tighten the active links of charity which unite us all in Christ. It wished to give back to the Church and its modern structures the solidarity, the enthusiasm and the solicitude of the early Christian community (cf. *Ac.* 4, 32 sqq.).

" Operation Heart ", we might call it, using the language of publicity. That is what the Council wished to be when it gave such prominence to its pastoral character. It is our work—let each one of us say. With Our Apostolic Benediction.

HOLY FATHER URGES THREEFOLD FIDELITY:
TO THE COUNCIL, THE CHURCH, TO CHRIST

W e have often spoken about the Council at these General Audiences. We have always done so in simple terms, such as are suitable for our brief familiar encounters here. We know that a great deal still remains to be said. We shall always have the opportunity, God willing, to return to that great school which the Council truly is, in order to learn from it old things and new, and especially to obtain light and guidance for the work of *aggiornamento* (to use the celebrated word which Pope John XXIII used in his opening discourse to the ecumenical Council).

The work of *aggiornamento* means adapting the Church's life and ways of expressing doctrine to the demands of her apostolic mission, according to the events of history and the circumstances of mankind, to which that mission is directed, always however safeguarding the integrity of her essence and her faith.

But we all want to shift our gaze from the Council itself to its aftermath, to the results which came from it, from the consequences that derived from it to the reception which the Church and the world gave to it. As an historical happening the Council already belongs to the past. Our modern temperament urges us to look at the present, or rather, to the future.

The post-Conciliar period is now of great interest. What effects did the Council have? What other effects can it have, or ought it to have? We are all convinced that the five years that have passed since the Council ended are not enough for an accurate and definite judgment on its importance and effectiveness. On the other hand we are all convinced that we cannot say the Council ended with its closure, as happens with so many events which time passes over, buries and leaves to students of past events to keep their memory alive. The Council was an event which is lasting, living on, not only in memory but also in the Church's life; it is destined to last for a long time yet, inside and outside the Church.

Tensions and transformations

This first aspect of the aftermath of the Council deserves a great deal of thought, even if only to discover whether the Council's legacy is merely something static or whether it is also a process of development. In other words, we have to decide which of the teaching it left us ought to be regarded as fixed and stable, and which ought to be developed. The ancient Councils generally established the former kind of teaching: they concluded with dogmatic definitions which are still valid parts of the patrimony of faith. We may suppose that those of the II Vatican Council belong chiefly to the latter kind.

It was described as a pastoral Council more than anything else; that is, it was directed towards action. It is important but difficult to examine all this. We can do it, little by little, only with the assistance of the ecclesiastical magisterium.

Another aspect of the matter, which is attracting everyone's attention today, is the present state of the Church, in comparison with its state before the Council. We may say that the present state of the Church is marked by much agitation, many tensions and novelties, transformations, discussions, and so forth. Opinions are consequently divided. Some sigh for the supposed tranquillity of yesterday; some are enjoying the current changes. Some talk about the Church going to pieces; others talk about a new Church arising. Some find the innovations too many and too sudden, that they are subverting the true Church's tradition and authenticity. Others again make the accusation that reforms already carried through or begun are being handled slowly and slothfully and even in a reactionary spirit. Some would like to reconstruct the Church according to its early form, and challenge the legitimacy of its logical historical development, but others would like to push this development so far along the lines of the secular life of today as to desacralize and laicize the Church, break down its structures for the sake of simple, gratuitous and inconsistent charismatic vitality.

The present time is a time of storm and transition. The Council has so far not given us the desired tranquillity in many sectors. Rather, it has stirred up turmoil and problems certainly not in vain for an increase of the Kingdom of God in the Church and in individual souls. But it is well to remember; this is a moment of trial. Those only who are strong in faith and in charity can enjoy the experience of risk (cf. II$^{a\text{-}ae}$, 123, 8).

We must watch

We will not go any further into that. Reviews and bookshops are flooded with publications dealing with the fruitful and critical stage which the post-Conciliar period has been for the Church. We must be vigilant. Today we must invoke the Spirit of knowledge, of counsel, of understanding and wisdom with special fervour. New ferments are at work around us. Are they good or bad? New temptations and new duties spring up. Let us repeat St. Paul's exhortation: " Rejoice always, pray constantly, give thanks in all circumstances; for this is the will of God in Christ for you. Do not quench the Spirit, do not despise prophesying, but test everything: hold fast what is good, abstain from every form of evil " (*1 Th.* 5, 16-22).

Study the II Vatican Council

We will simply add a recommendation to a threefold kind of fidelity. Fidelity to the Council: Let us try to get to know it better, explore it, go deeper into its magnificent and most rich teachings. Perhaps their very abundance, intensity and authority have discouraged many people from reading and thinking about their deep and demanding doctrine. Many who talk about the Council do not really know its marvellous documents. Some who are more concerned with contestation, with hasty and subversive change, dare to insinuate that the Council is already finished with. They dare to think that it served only to tear down, not to build up. But anyone who is willing to see the Council as the work of the Holy Spirit and the Church's responsible organ, will assiduously and respectfully take up the Council's documents and use them as nourishment and law for his own soul and for his own community. We should remember the theological terms adopted by the very first Council of Jerusalem: *Visum est ... Spiritui Sancto et nobis* (*Ac.* 15, 28). " It has seemed good to the Holy Spirit and to us ".

The second kind of fidelity is fidelity to the Church. We ought to understand her, love her, serve her and develop her both because she is the sign and the means of salvation, and because she is the object of Christ's immolated love. " *Dilexit Ecclesiam et se ipsum tradidit pro ea*: He loved the Church and gave himself up for her " (*Eph.* 5, 25). We are the Church, that Mystical Body of Christ of which we are vital members and in which we ourselves shall have our everlasting reward.

This fidelity to the Church, as you know, is betrayed by many today; it is debated, interpreted according to private views, and minimized. Its deep and authentic meaning is not understood, and the Church is not given that respect and generosity which she deserves, not for our humiliation but rather for the sake of valuable experience and honour.

Finally, fidelity to Christ. Everything is contained in that. We will only repeat to you the words of Simon Peter, whose unworthy yet true successor We are and above whose tomb we are at this moment. He said, " Lord, to whom shall we go? Thou alone hast the words of eternal life " (*Jn.* 6, 69).

Fidelity to Christ. This is what the post-Conciliar period should be, dearest Brothers and Children. With Our Apostolic Benediction.

THE WAY TO GOD—REASON AND FAITH

L et us talk about God for a while. Rather, let us talk about ourselves in regard to the great question of God. We ask you to perform this act which is fundamental for our thought, consequently for our moral life, for the lives we lead. It is a permanent question, existing at all times and applying to all people, but it is more urgent for all today.

Let everyone ask himself, What do I think about God? The answer can be many-sided, and we may classify these aspects according to three kinds of people living today. One group accepts religion; they accept it without discussion, perhaps without thought, and without feeling the giddiness, the inebriation, the happiness which the name of God can cause, without going deeply into that vague, yet always profound feeling which that mysterious and potent name produces or should produce within us. Then there is the kind of person who doubts, those for whom God's name is wrapped in a cloud of uncertainty, doubt, dissatisfaction. They therefore prefer not to think of it, not to believe in it any more. They abandon themselves to practical scepticism, a pseudo-superior and apparently convenient and elegant attitude, particularly in fashion among young people engaging in scientific studies in which rational certainty becomes the sole gauge of truth. Finally, there is the kind of people who deny the name, the idea and the reality of God. They who do this by adopting an attitude of simple but conscious rejection are the atheists; those who do it with an attitude of rebellion are anti-God, God's declared enemies both in theory and practice.

Reason and Faith

If we look for a common denominator in these summarily described categories, perhaps we may find that it is a different and more or less deep-seated lack of confidence: a belief that it is impossible to know God. Some have even gone so far as to say that " God is dead ". Perhaps some say this without bad intentions, because this blasphemous and sacrilegious negation was meant to refer to false, incomplete and unsupportable concepts of God. These are the idols which men have often set up to suit their own religious feeling or ideas, in backward and empirical states of mind, in cultures which we call pagan, in historical periods of superstitions that have passed away and within philosophical systems which are not acceptable.

In others, this devouring temptation to lack of confidence in the possibility of knowing God was felt as an unfortunately agnostic acknowledgment of his being inconceivable, of his absolute, consequently unreachable transcendence, of his incomprehensibility. It was almost as if it were understood as an act of humility before the infinite mystery of the divine Being.

But nowadays non-philosophic, exclusively scientific thought more frequently does not make it easy for man to get beyond the experimental sphere and rise to the sphere of metaphysical rationality. It halts him at knowledge of realities which seem to be the only positive ones, the only useful ones for technical, social and temporal purposes. The human mind resigns itself to, or rather takes pleasure in admitting that it is impossible to acquire real knowledge of God.

Have you ever done any mountain-climbing? Four young men were once sitting around a fire in a mountain village, talking of the great peaks surrounding them. Naturally someone brought up the bold idea of attempting a climb, but a new climb, one never tried before by anyone, a very daring one, therefore a most attractive one.

One said: It must be possible. The second said: Of course it is. The third added: Yes, but certain conditions must be fulfilled. The fourth asked, What conditions? The discussion continued, and they ended by agreeing to try the climb. That is what theology and religion are: conquest of knowledge of God.

We children of the Church declare: It is possible to know God. There are two royal roads to it: Reason and Faith. Is reason alone perhaps good enough for attaining to knowledge of God? Yes, it is valid, but not entirely sufficient. It is good enough, on condition that the constituent requirements be respected—that is to say, you must use it as it ought to be used. This is the first condition. These conditions are not so difficult that they surpass the normal powers of thought. They are not out of accord with those of " common sense " (cf. GARRIGOU-LAGRANGE, *Le sens commun*).

We might also remark in passing that it is not only the science of God, *theodicea*, which has recourse to those same requirements of reason. The experimental positive sciences do so too. They likewise are intelligible and authoritative to the degree that they too make use of the same rational principles, such as reason for being, finality, causality, etc., according to the nature of their work.

We children of the Church are often accused of obscurantism. But we are actually optimistic about human reason's capacity to solve (to a certain extent, of course), its greatest problem, the problem of truth, of the supreme Truth, which is God. If the testimony given by the wisdom of the centuries and of the great thinkers, if the testimony of Holy Scripture, and that of our own conscience and our own experience were not enough, we might at least be grateful to the I Vatican Council for having defended human reason and provided us with teaching in this regard which is certain, and full of clarity, comfort and nobility (cf. DENZ.-SCH. 3016).

The Creator and the Creature

But we have to pay attention to a fundamental distinction in this matter of the knowableness of God. It is one thing to say that God exists and another thing to say who he is. We can know the existence of God with certainty, but his nature is mysterious to us. What we can glimpse of him comes by way of analogy, by way of negation, by way of exaltation of that which we know of things which are not God; their limited being helps us to have some intuition of what may be said of his infinite perfections. The Church's Magisterium warns us that " between the Creator and the creature we note not so much similarity but rather dissimilarity " (DENZ.-SCH., *IV Council of the Lateran*, 806-432).

God remains a mystery. But a positive mystery, which gives rise to ever continuing and never ending investigations and discoveries from our incipient notions about it. Our knowledge of God is a window looking out on the light of heaven, the infinity of heaven. But he is the intrinsic requirement of thought, the absolute principle of being. " I am, who am " (*Ex.* 3, 14), he said of himself.

If we join the evidence of reason to the evidence of faith, then our knowledge of God will become marvellous. " No one ", the Gospel says, " has ever seen God, but the only begotten Son, who is in the bosom of the Father, has manifested him to us " (*Jn.* 1, 18). We shall have the very face of Christ, the Son of God and son of man, as the mirror of God the Father. " Who sees me ", Christ said, " sees the Father also " (*Jn.* 14, 9). Christ is an image even more than a Teacher. St. Paul told us this when he said, " He is the image of the invisible God " (*Col.* 1, 15). So, in order to know God we have a Way to which all other ways—if such there be—lead, by which all are tested, are straightened and are strengthened: He is the Way, the Truth and the Life (*Jn.* 14, 6).

We must overcome that temptation which is so strong nowadays, of thinking that it is impossible to acquire knowledge of God such as shall be adequate for our cultural maturity and respond to our existential needs and spiritual duties. To think so would be sloth, it would be cowardice, it would be blindness. Instead we must seek. Seek in the book of creation (*Rom.* 1, 20); seek in study of God's Word; seek in the school of the Church, the Mother and Teacher; see in the depths of one's own conscience ... Seek God, seek him always. Know that He is near (cf. *Is.* 55, 6).

To you Our encouragement and Blessing.

GOD IS REAL PURPOSE
OF OUR EXISTENCE

As We have said before, Our discourses at these General Audiences are only notes on matters which deserve to be dealt with in a very different way. It seems to Us that in circumstances like these the material itself is more important than the way it is developed. We are thus making an act of trust in you, Our visitors, in your understanding and in your resolve to study and reflect.

Let us speak about God. Everything said about God—just think, about God!—needs such a qualification, for We are the first to recognize that what We say here is absolutely elementary and incomplete.

We are concerned at present with the grossest and most widespread temptations about the name of God. Last time We chose what We consider to be the chief of those temptations: the idea that it is impossible to know God. Now let us talk about another temptation. It seems to be a more commonplace one, but it is really just as deep and dangerous, namely, that it is useless to worry about God.

This temptation can easily be put into practice. That is to say, it becomes practical negation and immediately finds an application, which is abandonment of the search for God, the giving up of the practice of religion, acquirement of an easygoing conscience, both as regards the speculative question of whether our relationship with God is well founded, and as regards the moral consequences deriving therefrom. We are told that it is useless to raise a religious problem, for either it cannot be solved, or no benefit is derived from its having a solution. We have to go on living just the same; there is no need to raise a problem which is so difficult, and in practice unnecessary.

There is no more need of God: for many this is an axiom, which sounds like a discovery, a liberation, a removal of barriers.

The vanity of scientific rationalism

The modern mind is imbued with scientific rationalism and satisfied with results in the field of knowledge, which not only provide the satisfaction of understanding what one is studying, but also of converting one's knowledge into action. In reaping the results of his knowledge and in the enjoyment of the conquests of his study and labour, the modern man asks for nothing else. Indeed, having proclaimed the uselessness of God, he asserts that life is better. Time is saved; attention and effort are concentrated on things whose reality can be measured; those problems which seem to be the only true and interesting ones are solved, especially the economic ones, and then social and political problems, and so on. So many bonds which are now superfluous for adult and progressive man are broken: annoying bonds of convention and superstition. The ancient saying of the Psalmist might be quoted: *non est Deus*, God no longer exists (cf. *Ps.* 13, 1; 52, 1).

A hundred differing ways could be chosen to describe the typical attitudes of very many people in view of this assertion (either in the speculative or empirical sense) about the uselessness of God, and consequently of religion, faith, prayer, and finally of the confrontation of one's own conscience with the ultimate and inexorable demands of the divine law. We find such attitudes everywhere in the world in which we live; we find them described in so much of modern literature: indifferentism, agnosticism, pessimism, irrationalism, anticlericalism, atheism, and so on. These go to make up the psychology of so many people today, and they are often fed from this same source of the alleged impossibility of having a logical and fruitful solution to the problem of God.

Man's highest duty

As you can see, this is not our view. We baptized, we believers, especially we ministers of God's mysteries, not only do we not admit the opinion or even the hypothesis of the uselessness of the name of God in human life, but we affirm the contrary. God is necessary! He exists of necessity! He is the sole necessary being, and he is necessary for us. We must be convinced of this fundamental principle. It is this most real, this most blessed name of God which has the greatest value and the most importance for us.

This is the constitutional law of the universe: " I am the Lord thy God " (*Ex.* 20, 2; 20, 7). The greatest prayer ever runs as follows: " ...hallowed be thy name, thy kingdom come ... ". The supreme lesson of the Gospel which governs our existence always admonishes us to " seek first the kingdom of God ... " (*Mt.* 6, 33).

Someone may perhaps object: duty, not utility. But if we analyse the intrinsic necessity of this moral duty, we shall see that the prime and greatest utility coincides with our first and greatest duty. That moral duty is free, yes, but it flows from the constitutional demand of our being. Even if we sacrificed for this duty everything, even life itself, our choice would not be mistaken. Jesus himself, our teacher, has told us so, and he suffered death for his teaching: " He that loves his life shall lose it; and he that despises his life in this world shall keep it for everlasting life " (*Jn.* 12, 25).

If God is the real purpose of our existence, then by dedicating to him our mind, heart and actions, we will not only gain our essential end, but we will also achieve our fulfilment. St. Ignatius reminds us of this in the first meditation of his Spiritual Exercises: *homo creatus est* ... In the catechism class, which is a school of the highest wisdom, when the child is asked: " Why did God create you? " he replies: " To know, love and serve him in this life, and to enjoy him forever in Heaven ".

Light, the true Good, Love

But the temptation remains: *Cui bono?* What is the use of serving God in this life? All our judgments are measured by immediate and personal profit. We are anthropocentric, which is to say that we are more concerned about ourselves than with the honour and service of God. We are utilitarians, we are egoists. We do not think of being and duty so much as of value, in the sense of usefulness. In the scale of values, of precious things, our own interests, our pleasures tend to outweigh the supreme Good, which is so mysterious to us and so difficult to fit in with our usual experience. That Supreme Good is called God.

Another saying of Christ, grave and dramatic, which obliges us to check how our scales are weighted: " What does it profit a man ", he asked, " if he gain the whole world, and suffer the loss of his own soul? " (*Mt.* 16, 26). And how can a man save his soul? Here the temptation about the uselessness of God reveals its deceit. For how can we solve the great, the supreme question of our salvation if we forget what faith, in God, in Christ, in the Holy Spirit, teaches us about it? This indispensable advantage, this sole true utility can come to us only from God, from him who says, " I am thy salvation " (*Ps.* 34, 3).

And how many further benefits come to us if God's name shines upon our life! Even to give a bare account of them would require too comprehensive and too long a list. Benefits in the field of thought: God is the light. In the field of action: God is the true good, God is Love. How, after all, can you maintain an ethic without God? And a Christianity which is wholly horizontal, to use the modern expression, that is to say, without God and even without Christ-God, directed to others, to men, how can it maintain itself without the vertical flow of the love of God, descending from God and returning to him? Will it not rather wear itself out and become distorted, because it can no longer bear this intimate compelling name of God, and thus cannot really give to others the name of brothers, that is, sons of the same God the Father?

Let us not relegate the name of God to the category of vain and outmoded concepts, which are no longer useful to a free man who is his own master. But the more we are freed from vain thoughts and obsolete myths, the more we shall feel the power, the fullness, the goodness of that blessed name, and celebrate its indescribable reality in faith and love.

May Our Apostolic Blessing strengthen you for that.

MODERN MAN
TEMPTED TO REJECT GOD

C ontemporary man has many grave temptations in regard to God and religion. We will briefly refer to them today, as is Our custom in these brief General Audiences. We do so not so much in order to provide a doctrinal reply to these temptations as to warn you about them here, and help you to defend yourselves against them. This you must do by study, by thought, by purifying your religious outlook, if necessary, and by fortifying your threatened faith by means of prayer and good will, so that you may be able to resist *ut possitis sustinere* (*1 Cor.* 10, 13).

One of these is a formidable temptation, namely, that God and religion are obsolete ideas. They belong to other ages. Ours is an adult age. Modern thought has progressed so much that it can exclude every assertion which transcends scientific reason. God is said to be transcendent. Consequently he is outside the range of modern man's interests. He belongs to the past, not the present, still less to the future. Civilization is moving towards an increasing and total secularization; that is to say, it is moving towards autonomy of temporal values, and liberation from their alleged link with religion. You will certainly have heard of this tendency. It begins by making a distinction between earthly realities and their higher and final relationship with the religious world. It is right to do this (cf. *Gaudium et spes*, 36). But then it goes on to restrict all man's knowledge and all his interests to the scope of these earthly realities, by secularizing, laicizing and desacralizing every form of modern life. There will no longer be any place for religion, nor will it have any reason to exist, unless it be reinterpreted in a purely humanistic way so as to proclaim that for man the supreme being is man (cf. Marx, Nietzsche, etc).

Progress and History

As you can see, this objection tends to subvert our faith. It is very strong and widespread at present, and has even gained entrance into the field of theology, but not always with subversive purpose in the field of Catholic theology.

What is its driving force? It seems to be that movement, that evolution, that change in ideas which arises from progress, from the mutation which modern life is undergoing in respect to life in other times. We usually call that flow of events and social changes history when it is a matter of the life of man. History seem to be the fatal cause of the dissolution of the religious idea. Our understanding of this process going on in things and in mankind tempts us to describe religion as antiquated, as indefensible, as an unjustified survival. It tempts us to regard the very name of God as mythical, that is, imaginary, unreal. A religious man is a reactionary, an old-fashioned simpleton, an unhappy person, who has not yet freed himself from the shackles of an obsolete state of mind.

There is no need for Us to tell you how powerful and persuasive this temptation is today. The facts speak for themselves, and books document it all. Young people above all feel the fascination of this kind of atheism, because of the appearance of modernity which it has, that air of open-mindedness which it fosters and authorizes, and because it seems to be supported by elementary evidence. This kind of atheism is said to be a sign of mental progress, the cause and effect of scientific progress and technical, social and cultural progress. History, that is, evolution, is the secret of this metamorphosis of the modern world. It would be possible to go on talking endlessly about atheism, especially in a speculative way. Catholic literature has produced a wealth of studies and general works on the subject and we shall do well to get to know and value them. But We will limit ourself now to the negation of God and of our relationship with him, as a temptation caused by what is known as " our age ".

291

Fashion of thought

We invite you to examine this expression. It would be an insult to your intelligences to suggest that of itself it would suffice, to provide you with certainty, especially in a matter of such importance. It can at most establish a presumption of truth, that of public opinion, or that of philosophical currents of thought which are considered to be valid.

But the modernity of a doctrine is not enough in itself to endow it with credibility. Those who let themselves be carried along by fashions in thinking and mass opinions are often not aware that their attitude is a servile one. They enthuse about the words and ideas of others, and of convenient opinions. They make no mental effort of their own; they rejoice to feel that they have been freed from the mentality of their surroundings (which is often not without wisdom and experience); they let themselves be carried away by triumphant ideas of others. They think they are free!

But they do not notice another weakness. It is that ideas which triumph in time and with time can change and do change. They therefore expose themselves to disavowals and disappointments which may come tomorrow. Perhaps they will smile at themselves, but perhaps they will weep, for having abandoned the helm of their own personalities into the hands and minds of others, for having become failures as men, and walked in the dark.

Let intelligent people reflect. Let the young reflect. Let workers reflect. We all ought to reflect—above all today, when the idea of human " progress " and self-sufficiency is undergoing a fearful crisis and its fiercest and most desperate challengers are arising from among its most faithful exponents.

The Topicality of the Faith

If the reasons for repugnance to the God of faith were different, we should still have to reflect that serious and patient analysis of these reasons will finally show that they are fallacious. And we shall not see this without having sure aid from God, that very God whom we are calling into question (cf. St. Irenaeus:

" we cannot know God without God ", *Ad. Haer.* IV, 5, 1). We shall find that he is not the phantom which ignorant and emotional people create for themselves. We shall find, as the Council says in a wonderful passage, " that recognition of God is in no way hostile to man's dignity ", and, in accordance with modern man's tendency to look for fullness of life in the future, " eschatological hope does not reduce the importance of earthly commitments, but rather provides fresh motives to support and accomplish them " (*Gaudium et spes*, 21). Father De Lubac writes: " They reject God as the one who limits man, and they do not see that man has ' something infinite " in him through his relation with God. They reject God as the one who places a yoke on man, and they do not see that through his relation with God, man is freed from all servitude, particularly that of history and society ... " (*Sur les chemins de Dieu*, p. 268).

God is not obsolete. Nor is the idea of God, in the fullness of his being, in the mystery of his existence, in the wonder of his revelation. But we need to regenerate it in our minds, which have deformed it, profaned it, reduced it, expelled and forgotten it. We can regenerate that idea in seeking, in Christian faith, in charity going in two directions, towards him and towards the brethren, in order to rediscover its topicality, the greatest of all topical things, the light of the age, the promise of the future.

His name is " Everlasting "

With the Biblical singer let us also say, " I will bless the Lord at all times; his praise shall be always in my mouth " (*Ps.* 33, 2). With Our Apostolic Blessing.

RELIGIOUS RENEWAL—A CONTINUAL PROCESS TOWARDS PERFECTION

R eligion must be renewed. This conviction is shared by all who are still concerned about religion, whether they stand aloof from its concrete expression, namely, a faith, a way of life, a community, or whether they belong to some religious denomination or take part in discussion of religion. It is all a matter of seeing what renewal means. There is need to renew one's own religious awareness. This is rather a question than an objection, but it is a many-sided question, with many meanings. In other words, it presents itself under very diverse aspects, with principles, methods of study and conclusions which are different and easily opposed to each other. Religious renewal may be understood as a continuous process towards perfection, or as a process hastening to dissolution, or yet again as an attempt at a new interpretation according to stated criteria.

This is a topical matter. We all accepted that celebrated word *aggiornamento* as a programme for the Council and for after the Council, as a personal and a community programme. This was a clear sign that it is precisely in the heart of orthodoxy that there should operate, as an active leaven. (cf. *Mt.* 13, 33), the impulse of new life, the vivifying breath of conscience, the moral tension, its present expression which, like love, is always original. Religion is life. Like our biological life it needs to be in continual renewal, the purification and growth, in a subjective way. All the discipline of the spirit tells us this. St. Paul never ceases to repeat it: " The inward man is renewed day by day " (*2 Cor.* 4, 16). " Put off your old nature which is corrupt through deceitful lusts. Be renewed in the spirit of your mind, and put on the new nature " (*Eph.* 4, 22-23). " Let us seek to grow up to him (Christ) in all things " (*Eph.* 4, 15) " increasing in knowledge of God " (*Col.* 1, 10).

Inward renewal

This ceaseless exhortation has many meanings. It gives us a genuine picture of the religious fact. It shows us that it grows up from small beginnings and has to develop (remember the parable of the seed?) (*Lk.* 8, 5, 11 etc.). It tells us that it too is subject to decay and perversion (remember Christ's dispute with the Pharisees? *Mt.* 23, 14 sqq.). It means that religion is often in need of being reformed and is always in need of being perfected, that it will reach its fullness only in the future life. All this is known to disciples of the divine Word, of the school of the liturgy and the Church's life. Hence we gladly accept *aggiornamento*, and try to understand its meaning, and reap its revitalizing harvest —first in souls (*Eph.* 4, 23), and, if need be, in external laws.

But this renewal is not without dangers. The first danger is that of change which is wished for its own sake or for the sake of keeping up with the transformism of the modern world. Such change would be out of harmony with the Church's inalienable tradition. The Church is Christ continued in time. We may not break away from her, just as a bough, wishing to burst into new flower in the springtime, may not separate itself from the tree and the root whence it draws its life. This is one of the capital points of the contemporary history of Christianity. It is a decisive point. It is a question of either belonging faithfully and fruitfully to the Church's authentic and authoritative tradition, or of cutting oneself off from it mortally.

Normal contact with Christ cannot be achieved by one who wishes to follow him according to ways chosen by himself, creating a doctrinal and historical gap between the present Church and the original preaching of the gospel. " The Spirit blows where it wills " (*Jn.* 3, 8). The Lord himself said so, but he also instituted a channel, when he said to his disciples, " Receive the Holy Spirit. Whose sins you shall forgive they are forgiven, whose sins you shall retain they are retained " (*Jn.* 20, 23). Christ is certainly the sole source, the only " true vine ", but the sap of the vine reaches us through the living tendrils which it puts out (cf. *Jn.* 15, 1 sqq.; *Lk.* 10, 16).

Continuous development

The Church is not a wall of division. She does not place a distance, a dogmatic and legal block between Christ and his twentieth-century followers. The Church is a channel, a link, a normal development that unites. She is the guarantee of authenticity, of the immediacy of Christ's presence amongst us. " I am with you until the consummation of the world ", Christ said when bidding farewell to the Eleven and giving them a sight of the times that would succeed.

We may not think up a new kind of Christianity in order to renew Christianity. We must remain tenaciously faithful to it. This stability of existence, with its continuity in movement and development, this existential consistency, proper to every living being, cannot be described as reactionary, obscurantist, archaic, sclerotic, bourgeois, clerical, or by any other disparaging title, as a certain kind of modern literature unfortunately defines it, through hatred of everything of the past or distrust of what the Church's Magisterium makes an object of faith. The truth is such, and so it remains. The divine Reality contained in it may not be fashioned as we like, but imposes itself. This is the mystery. Anyone who has the good fortune to enter it through faith and charity, enjoys it inexpressibly, and has unutterable experience of the outpouring of the Holy Spirit.

Someone will ask: is there not anything requiring renewal? Has immobility become the law? No. The truth remains, but it is demanding. We must know it, we must study it, we must purify its human expressions. What a renewal this implies! The truth remains, but it is a fruitful truth. No one can ever say that he has fully comprehended and defined it in the formulas whose meaning however remains untouchable. It can present aspects still worthy of research. The truth throws light on many fields concerning the progress of our doctrine. The truth remains, but it needs to be made known, translated and formulated, in a way suited to the pupils' capacity for understanding. And those pupils are people of various ages, and of different education and culture. Religion is therefore open to being perfected, increased, deepened. It is a science which is always engaged in a sublime effort, striving towards better understanding or to a better mode of expression.

Pluralism, then? Yes, a pluralism which shall take account of the Council recommendations (*Optatam totius*, 16; *Gravissimum*, 7, 10). On condition that it refers only to the ways in which the truths of the faith are stated, not to their content, as was affirmed with great force and clarity by Our venerated Predecessor Pope John XXIII in his celebrated discourse at the opening of the Council (cf. *AAS*, 54, 1962, pp. 790-792). He was tacitly, but obviously referring to the formula of the *Commonitorium* of St. Vincent of Lérins (d. 450). The truths of the faith may be expressed in different ways, provided that they have " the same meaning " (cf. DENZ.-SCH. 2802). Pluralism must not give rise to doubts, equivocations or contradictions. It must not serve to legitimize subjectivism of opinions in dogmatic matters which would compromise the identity and, therefore, the unity of the faith. Progress, yes, to enrich knowledge and further research, but demolition, no.

The Church's road

We would have much else to say about the question of religious renewal, for example, theological progress, the relation between religious doctrine and the historical and cultural environment (a deeply felt and very delicate problem), the Church's moral teachings and men's changing ways. But let these remarks suffice about the great theme of religious renewal, so that it may also be the object of your serious reflection and help you to appreciate the effort which the Church is making in these years, with suffering, fidelity and pastoral goodness, to safeguard the faith with jealous care and to provide it with a loving openness. And this will also ensure that the teachers of the faith, Bishops, theologians and catechists, will not lack your support, and gratitude.

With Our Apostolic Blessing.

" REJECT TEMPTATIONS AGAINST THE FAITH "

W e want to give you a sign of pastoral love for man of today, as is proper for Our ministry. We mean common man. We consider him in this way, not in order to lower his level, but in order to widen the range of Our interest in him. We wish to draw your attention to a number of conventional temptations about faith in God and religion in general.

The question of God

One of these is the temptation which finds its way into the modern outlook, and says that, after all, we can get on without God, and put other values in his place. More precisely, we can get on without faith in God and the religious practice which such faith calls for. It is not a matter of absolute denial, of radical or rational atheism. It is simply practical lack of interest, an attempt to base life on other foundations than the traditional religious ones. This conclusion is often reached after a rather empirical but complex process of reasoning, which demolished that bit of certainty which early catechism lessons infused into the soul of the child at school. When some doubts arise, with nascent intellectual activity, and when an attractive prospect of liberation from tiresome duties opens up, that certainty seems to vanish. This question of God is difficult, people say. And how easy they find it to get away from its theoretical and practical claims! How convenient! For some the temptation takes the form of Minerva, the goddess of pagan wisdom, who suggests that abandonment of religion is a liberating victory over childish pseudo ideas (like Chanticleer's idea that when he crowed the sun rose because of it, if you remember). We are told that modern man has no

298

need of the religious world, which appears to be imaginary and superstitious. He is content with other ways of thinking: thoughts of his interest, his duties, his loves, his experiences, his daily work, his business that he calls real life.

As in the Parable of the Seed

This is the first form of that temptation to get rid of God which We have mentioned. We may illustrate it by referring to the parable of the seed that fell among thorns, which strangled the growing corn (*Mt.* 13, 7, 22). This means that temporal concerns take up all that room in the soul which ought to be kept for the duties and rights of religion. We call this practical positivism. Failure to rest and pray on Sundays and feast days shows how strong and overpowering the temptation is. Those who give in to it are legion today, just when the importance of individual and collective participation in the liturgy of the Eucharist on holy days and Sundays has become clearer than before. This participation is important because it is the wise way to mark the stages of the passing of time and secular occupations, to give the spirit a breathing space, comfort and consolation its proper place, that is, first place.

Life without religion easily becomes unsatisfying and meaningless. Intelligent man becomes aware that he is walking in the dark; when the light of truth and religious practice are not there, his experience of life loses body and significance, his personality becomes mediocre, and his liberty falls into servitude to passions which are not good and into other peoples's influence. He feels the need of some superior ideal, above him and before him. Current opinions, rhetorical sayings, and fashionable philosophies offer him idols which can easily be put in God's place. We acknowledge that such substitutes are often noble, lofty concepts, put up before modern man in order to provide him with a substitute religious faith. Science, liberty, art, labour, progress, duty, love, are among them. Other concepts are no less high-sounding, but have something ambiguous about them: wealth, power, glory, politics, happiness and so on. These are values, of course, but can they be on that same absolute level which we acknowledge to be that of the godhead, and which does not require to be justified by a higher authority?

And, even if we do content ourselves with them alone, are they capable of filling that place in our spirits which is for God only? Is it not truer to say that by themselves they leave empty the greater and better part of the soul—as we shall do well to remember? If we restrict our capacities to these isolated values, do we not reduce their true extent, and diminish, rather than widen the breadth of the human spirit, which is boundless? Is this not so because those very same values demand to be brought into relation with a source and order of a much higher degree? This is the very well-known warning which St. Augustine gave (cf. *Conf.* 1, 1). It runs through the whole story of human spiritual ity, both before and after him. It is: Man has an irreplaceable need for God.

It is not a question of describing this insatiable need as " metaphysical anguish ". Neither modern materialism nor (on other grounds) immanentist idealism want to hear that even mentioned. It is rather a question of recognizing the existence of a profound need in the human soul. The soul is open to the infinite, and longs to expand to it, to be assimilated in knowledge and love to that God whose mysterious imprint it bears. Substitution of this kind, cases of which we sometimes find in men of great intellectual and moral stature, is unjustified. It does injury to God, who began his biblical message with that jealous first commandment, " I am the Lord thy God; thou shalt not have strange gods before me " (*Ex.* 20, 2-3). It does injury to man, for it eludes him with the dazzle of reflected, artificial lights, and stops him from seeing the prime light, the dazzling mystery of God.

Purely human dimensions

But another way of replacing God, Christ, faith and religion is in fashion today. It is not so much an effort to repudiate the benefits of religion itself and the Christian religion in particular, as of annexing its benefits for modern man, but at the same time distinguishing and separating them from their roots, their relationship with the divine world. People talk about the vertical source having a horizontal beginning and end, no longer in God but in man. An attempt is made to formulate Christianity in terms which may please the secularized, laicist mentality of today, so hostile to the transcendent and mysterious reality of the living God and his Christ, the incarnate Word and our Saviour in the Holy Spirit. This attempt gives rise to an effort to interpret Christianity in terms of purely human dimensions. Many will still remember a celebrated article written by an eminent idealist philosopher immediately after the war. He explained why we must call ourselves Christians. He acutely aknoweledged that Christianity has the undeniable merit of having provided doctrine of the spirit with new and inextinguishable values; but he considered that authentic Christianity has been absorbed and therefore replaced by idealist immanentism.

Nowadays we hear of thinkers who offer a secular reinterpretation of the Christian faith, a Christianity without religion. Christ plays a large part in it, but as a man; but God is not there at all. These thinkers have some fine and deep things to say. They enchant Christians of our time who are doctrinally securalized and consequently deny the religious truth which the Church defends and diffuses.

What they write is often impressive, just as roses draw forth admiration, but are cut off from their roots. They flourish beautifully, and affirm praiseworthy ethical values, but how can they develop when they are cut off from their true root and are reduced to merely human dimensions? How can they last and save man, to whose same level they are fatally reduced? Can they last *l'espace d'un matin?—the length of a morning?* (cf. DE ROSA, *Civiltà Cattolica*, 1970, quaderno 2877 and 2878).

God, Christ, the Church cannot be replaced with impunity. Let us try to get over this temptation, by finding in our Catholic faith once more that certainty, fullness, and salvation which it alone can give.

With Our Apostolic Benediction.

WE MUST SEARCH FOR GOD

L et us speak about God once more, with the simplicity which these talks require. Let us ask ourselves: Isn't it time we set out to discover or rediscover God?

We ought to do so, and the first reason is that we believe in God. Is this basic affirmation, " I believe in God " enough to content our mind and relieve it from worrying about the great key truth of the whole of our thought and all our lives? Is that supreme act of our reason, this initial act of our religion, enough to free us from the consequences which it entails? The first of such consequences sets us off on conscientious and thorough search for that supreme reality which is God, and hence brings us into his presence. " Into his presence " means obtaining some sense of his Infinity, his Totality, his Otherness, his transcendence and his immanence, his mystery, his absolute and necessary Being, his most personal and most blessed life. It means experiencing the tension in which this act of faith and reason places us: not only tension, but also desire and joy to proclaim, celebrate and adore him who is our Beginning and our End. It is a striving, which attracts us because of what He is and for whom he is. At the same time it tends to distract us and draw us away, because of our incalculable inadequacy and our incurable unworthiness (cf. *Lk.* 5, 8; *Gen.* 18, 27). And what shall we do when we know that we have to call God our Father, the Supreme Good, in himself, and as regards us? Shall we ever be able to remain inert and lukewarm? Shall we not rather feel the duty to look for him, to seek him with that commitment which is called love? Love is *studium*, love is search. The Bible is full of this imperative invitation: " Seek the Lord and his power, always seek his face " (*1 Par.* 16, 11).

302

God is not dead

And there is another reason why we ought to look for God: it is that nowadays people are inclined not to seek him any more. They look for everything except God. We notice a resolve to exclude him to cancel his name and memory from all forms of life, thought, science, activity, society. Everything, people think, ought to be laicized, not only in order to give man's knowledge and action their proper scope, but also in order to claim absolute autonomy for man, to make him self-sufficient, content with human limits alone, proud of a freedom which has given up the light of every binding and guiding principle. They look for everything except God. God is dead! they say, don't let's worry about him any more! But God is not dead: he is only lost. So many people of our time have lost him. Is it not worthwhile looking for him again?

They look for so many things: new things, old things, difficult things, useful things, good things, bad things—everything. We might say that modern life may be described as a search. Why not search for God? Is he not a " value " worth being looked for by us? Is he not a Reality, demanding better knowledge than that purely nominal everyday one? Is it not better than the superstitious and fantastic knowledge of certain forms of religion, which we ought to reject because false, or purify because imperfect? Better than that knowledge which claims to be already quite well informed and forgets that God is indescribable, that God is a mystery?

Is not knowledge of God our reason for living and the cause of everlasting life? (cf. *Jn.* 17, 3). Is not God a " problem ", if such is the term we want to use, which concerns us closely? Concerns our thinking, our conscience, and our destiny? And what if a personal meeting with him one day should be inevitable?

Again: if he were hidden, because of a most significant form of game which has decisive results for us, just why is it that we have to look for him? (cf. *Is.* 45, 19). On the contrary—just listen— supposing God himself were in search of us? Is not this the mysterious and sovereign plan of the story of the our salvations *quaerens me sedisti lassus* ... (cf. Const. *Dei Verbum*, 2).

We all ought to set about looking for God.

It is an immense problem. What are we to do? Where can we begin? Fortunately we are not alone in this spiritual undertaking. There is a whole most vast and centuries-old body of literature before us. Read St. Augustine's *Soliloquies*, for example, or St. Bonaventure's *Journey of the Mind of God*. A modern bibliography of works at all levels is at our disposal. You only have to choose. There are works of theology which contain fruit of sound doctrine and modern experience; they are open to people of good will, and they can give valuable help.

But why does not each of you dare to try a few steps on his own? Each of you, for example, can observe the reality of the religious or the anti-religious phenomenon in our world for himself. He can see it in the environment in which he lives, in surrounding society, in the various kinds of activity in which he takes part. He can also ask himself what are the causes of the religious decline of our times: Why is God absent? Why is faith undergoing an eclipse?

We only have to put such questions to see that the reply is generally concerned with the existential circumstances of the persons observed. The cause usually does not touch on faith in itself, but the state of mind, the mentality, environmental conditioning of man's life. It is man who has changed; not the religious relationship and the content of religion: the human eye does not see today, even though the light is the same as before. That is to say, subjective conditions are no longer favourable to thinking about God, about faith, about prayer.

Why is this? Ah, that is a hard question! But We can give a brief answer: Because of the changes going on in modern life. The astonishing thing is that these changes consist generally of what we may call progress, both as regard people's cultural life and the development of society. We are told that adult man has no more need of God, that religion is a childish thing. How is it that this negative result for religion derives from modern man's positive development? We offer the following diagnosis, only as a guide, not as a solution.

Intelligence and will

There are two factors: use of the intelligence and polarization of the will. Intelligence has become passionately involved in scientific knowledge which is subject to rational experimentation. This is all very well, had not this kind of mental education stopped at this degree of knowledge, had it not refused to go higher; from knowledge of phenomena, of the tangible and the calculable side of things, up to knowledge of the essence of things, to that knowledge which we call metaphysical and which is the basis of entry into the religious sphere.

The will for its part has been mainly turned towards practical and economic problems: to the earthly sphere. When man seeks this with overwhelming or exclusive interest, it stops him from entering into the sphere of higher goods, the heavenly sphere. These two atitudes in man have cut him off from his tendency to rise to the religious sphere, which is a natural tendency also.

A sense of God

The problem is not concerned with the reality of man and things; it is not an ontological but a psychological and pedagogical one. How can God be sought in these conditions? It would be rash to give a reply to a problem of such scope and complexity in words so brief and transient as these. Yet We will point out a way; it is not the only way, or the decisive way, but an indication and a beginning. We can start by arousing man's desire for true and complete, full and authentic humanism (this is the apostolate of today). That desire contains a connatural way of getting beyond man's one-dimensional, that is, materialist and positive level; it also stirs in him a wakeful *sense of God*, together with interest and hope.

Then, if the Master comes to meet him, that really becomes a search, but more than a search, for it also becomes an initial divine victory and turns into modern man's existential adventure. It will be very fine. And how can we start if off? With love and with charity. Charity is a method: it is truth's preparatory school. That would take too long to explain, but think and pray about it. With Our Apostolic Benediction.

REASON AND FAITH NEEDED
BY MAN IN SEARCHING FOR GOD

We are going to go on with this theme of search for God. Not in order to avoid the grave and pressing problems of the present historical moment, with which We are in fact continually concerned in another part of Our office. No, We are going on with this matter, because We think that the question of our attitude towards religion is always one of prior importance —not only in itself but also because of the supreme realities to which it refers. Those realities are God and man, but its importance goes further, because of the theoretical and practical consequences which flow from that first question.

The first question is the fulcrum of the whole system of human ideas. Nowadays it is fashionable to give a negative answer to it; there is a habit of neglecting it and (through the fierce secularism of today) there is almost an obligation to ignore it, as if in defence of hard won emancipation. We therefore think that we have a duty to talk about it once more, yet again. We feel obliged to say: We ought to seek God.

It is strange how so many people claim the right to utter opinions about that supreme and mysterious name of God, just as if they knew the real meaning of the words they use—false, empty, doubtful, immense, indispensable, and so on—and without ever having honestly looked for him and conscientiously tried to learn about him. Would we dare speak about some science without having studied it, or without having at least obtained the aid of a competent person?

Personal aspects

The search for God! Our intention in talking about this is an apostolic one. That is to say that We wish to relate what We say to the spiritual condition of the public and its opinions, to people's ordinary ways of thinking today. But method demands that we linger on the personal aspects of the search for God, not in order to give a full account of them, but only to point some of them out, so as to suggest useful lines of thought.

So let us begin by asking, How can we look for God? The question makes the head whirl. But let us make an effort to keep calm and prepare our minds for orderly and efficient use of its faculties, and try them out in this extremely demanding and important matter of seeking for God. God is not obvious to us. If we thought that he were, just through the superficial use of our conoscitive powers, we should be deceiving ourselves. This explains why so very many do not believe in him. The mental habits of modern man are not usually disposed either to undertake conscientious research or to obtain that degree of knowledge of God which is possible for us. Our brain contains too many sense images, too many figurative, imaginative, fantastic and representative elements for it to get past this sphere of easy, pleasurable and muddled experience and go on searching beyond and above itself. When we make this effort to ask ourselves what is the reason, the significance and value of the many-sided experiences of this life which we have, we are at once overcome by a babel of ideas and names.

Philosophic reason is so rich and so confused now, that many are content simply to put the results of human thought in historical order, or at most link them up with a chain of mental processes. The history of thought is taking the place of rational and real evaluation of thought itself. But if we devote our thought to exploration of what we call the real, we halt when we come to scientific rationality, with a justified feeling of success. Science gives us two kinds of mastery: sure knowledge of things and ability to use them practically, technically, economically. This is a great gain, but it is not enough for the insatiable demands of reason, which wants to know more.

307

Reason alone not sufficient

Reason is not content to know how things are, it also wants to know why they are. This brings us to our first conclusion, and We think that no one will object to it. Our conclusion is: If we let reason go its own way, follow its natural movement, obey its own healthy powers and make use of its full and superior function, it will lead us to that reflected knowledge of God of which St. Paul speaks. He said that it is possible to go from things visible to a certain, indeed to certain knowledge of the invisible God (cf. *Rom.* 1, 20). The I Vatican Council confirmed this when it affirmed human reason's capacity to get to know something of God through knowledge of created things (DENZ.-SCH. 3004).

In other words, we ought to make good use of our reason; we need to give it back its truly normal and efficacious logical functions. We ought to restore its confidence. We should not make capricious use of this gift, of this eye, which was made in order to discern the truth. Reason has an irreplaceable function in religion. Indeed it has a place of honour and a high-ranking job. As men we ought to be proud of it; as religious people we should be watchful and humble with it, for reason is a most valuable and delicate tool, a valid and powerful one which is always making progress. Father De Lubac has well said, " Let man, then, have the boldness of his own reason! ... Whatever the meanderings of his thinking let him learn how to get up in the end to that Source, let him reach the focal point! " (*Sur les chemins de Dieu*, p. 15).

Where will our search lead, when guided by purely natural reason? It will indeed reach a very great height, certainly beyond the agnosticism-line. Yet the goal will remain a desire rather than an achievement. It will turn into that well-known expression of the schools: *intellectus quaerens fidem;* the intellect looks for faith, that is for knowledge which will be granted to it by revelation. This brings us into the gratuitous order or the supernatural.

" Unless God teaches us, no one can know God ... It was impossible to learn about God without God; through his Word he teaches men to know God ". This is what St. Irenaeus said

(† 200; *Adv. Haer.* IV, 6, 4; 5, 1; *PG* 7, 988). He was referring to Christ's words: " No man knows the Son but the Father, and him to whom the Father will reveal him " (*Mt.* 11, 27). " No man has seen God at any time; the only begotten Son, who is in the bosom of the Father, has announced him " (*Jn.* 1, 18). St. Thomas begins his *Summa Theologica* by affirming " that a certain doctrine according to a divine revelation going beyond the natural sciences explored by human reason is necessary for human salvation ". Christ is the Teacher, the revealer, the light: " If you remain in my word, then you are indeed my disciples, and you shall know the truth, and the truth shall make you free " (*Jn.* 8, 31-32).

Hence faith, hence further rethinking, an act of reflection by reason upon this new and higher science of God, theology, *fides quaerens intellectum*, to repeat the celebrated expression of St. Anselm of Aosta, Archbishop of Canterbury († 1109). Faith has need of the services of reason; it does not suffocate reason, contrary to what is often said, nor take its place (cf. Denz.-Sch. n. 2751; 2756; 2813). But it joins reason with acceptance of the Word of God, exalts it and involves it in the most arduous and lofty of tasks, that of exploring and expressing revelation, as a lofty, as a logical and dialectical principle of the deepest and most vital rationality: *credo ut intelligam.* The understanding is raised to its supreme test, and is aided in it by the whole man, by his moral virtues, which make it possible for him to pass from the speculative to the vital stage of thought, aimed at making divine truth the principle and beginning of human-divine life.

" *No intratur in veritatem nisi per caritatem* ": We enter into truth only through charity, St. Augustine wrote (*Contra Faustum*, 41, 32, 18; *PL* 42, 507).

So you see, dearly beloved children, how the search for God becomes broad and marvellous; it does not lead our steps astray into vain and abstruse speculation, but interprets, exercises and increases the deepest and most authentic longings of our spirit. No one is shut out from it. The little ones are in the front ranks in this school of God (cf. *Mt.* 11, 25). With Our Apostolic Benediction.

TO SEEK GOD IS ALREADY TO FIND

W e say that it is our duty to seek God. It is a duty which still applies, indeed applies in an outstanding way to us moderns. We are full of so much science, so much culture; we seem to be satiated with them. And this is exactly why we have greater need and a greater obligation to look first of all for the higher and principal reason for all the things we know. For if we do not we are in danger of not grasping their deep meaning, of running aground on doubt and finally falling into despair or condemning our thought to mediocre and conventional electicism. This pressing duty remains with us and calls for special attention, particularly since it is neglected and denied these days. At the same time hunger for God, which we perhaps do not recognize, breaks into the human spirit in spite of resistance from the spirit itself, which is intent on satiating itself with substitutes. These are sometimes noble, but they are often ignoble, and " after the meal, hunger is greater than before " (DANTE, *Inferno*, 1, 99).

Keep on looking all the time. But a question springs to mind: when shall we find God? Can we moderns find him too? How? If we do find him, what will happen then? Shall we be satisfied, or disappointed; happy, or unhappy?

Can we find God?

So we have another question, which belongs to the great religious debate of all times, to our own time just as much as to the others. Can we find God, and if so how? Or is our search to be endless and unsuccessful? Let us pay attention to this matter, for our search has to be endless in this life, which is a pilgrimage, a journey through a strange land towards a goal which is the final, complete and everlasting meeting with God. Then we shall see

310

him " as he is " (*1 Jn.* 3, 2), " face to face " (*1 Cor.* 13, 12). Yet our search will not be without results in this life also, though, in comparison, with knowledge and possession of God, this life is lived in darkness, lived as if it were in the night, as a vigil, yet not without stars, not without the *lumen Christi* of the Easter Vigil. This is to say that we can in some way, to some degree find God even in the present circumstances of our existence. Let us bear this well in mind: we can find God, and in some respects already have found him.

To seek is to find

But has he already been found? This brings us back to the celebrated words of Pascal: " You would not be looking for me if you did not already possess me " (*Le mystère de Jésus*—at the end). To seek is already to find, already to have, if we really cannot know God without him, without his natural or supernatural light (cf. *Rom.* 1, 11), whether it be interior or exterior (cf. St. Th. in *Ep. ad Rom.* 1, 6). God is already present in him and for him who looks for him. If we grasp this, we can already sail upon the ocean of prayer: " Oh God, my God, early do I seek thee, my soul thirsts for thee " (*Ps.* 61, 1).

But that is not enough. We want something more. What does finding mean? It means knowing with certainty, knowing as we know the things of this world, with clear evidence, concretely. Is that how we can find God? Oh, how complex the world of our knowledge is! We ought to be able to understand that it is impossible to find God in the way we find any ordinary thing at all. If it were possible, then that which we sought would not be God—if he were capable of being discovered with the concreteness with which we know things. He would no longer be God, for he would only be a thing. " No name ", St. Thomas says, " can be properly applied to God " in accordance with our way of conceiving existing things (cf. *Contra Gent.* 1, 30). So we ought to take note of the dramatic ambiguity of the names we give to God. On the one hand, we can affirm such names. We can say, for example, that God is good, God is living, God is the Father, by reason of the goodness, life and fatherhood which are his. But at the same time we have to deny that he is good, living, and a father in the same way as beings of which we have ordinary knowledge, and which we qualify with such terms (ib., *De Potentia* 7, 2, and I & II).

This is the hardest yet also the most fruitful part of our journey towards the discovery of God. It could give rise to a long discussion on so-called analogical knowledge, that is, true, but not identical, knowledge which we can have of God (cf. S. TH. I, 13, 1). We could also talk for a long time about our way of affirming the divine reality by denying those limits within which each and every one of our concepts is expressed (God is not finite, God is not corporeal, God is not mortal, and so on; this is the so called *via remotionis*, that is, an affirmation which includes the reality which is conceivable to us, but excludes its boundaries in a way which is inconceivable to us). Then we have the *via excellentiae*, which means attributing to God in a sublime degree those positive realities of which we have knowledge. God, we say, is wise, that is, infinitely wise; God is good, that is, infinitely good, and so forth. Consequently, when we try to find God, we see that he evades us by withdrawing into the profound heaven of his infinite mystery, just when we hoped we were reaching him. He remains absolutely transcendent, indescribable, mysterious. If it were not so, then he whom we hope to find would not be the true God. We can recognize that he exists and we can see what attributes belong to his sovereign existence, yet we cannot adequately know anything of him. So it comes about that our search never comes to rest: it is a course which never ends during this life.

Desire for Miracles

And then? Is our search defeated? Shall we never find him? No. There is still a great deal to be said. There is another degree of search for and attainment of God. It is more than rational knowledge: it is spiritual experience, mystical experience, vital experience. This too has its scale, which begins from those signs of the presence and action of the godhead which we call miracles. It is a strange thing that our incredulous world is never so curious about anything as it is about miracles—but it requires them to be true and real.

If such a miracle should occur, then the crowd runs to it. It was miracles that drew the interest, trust and then faith of the people to Jesus in the Gospel. A desire for miracles exists at the bottom of every soul. Modern critics are on guard, and wish to challenge the truth and reality of miracles, but the fact is that they are afraid of them. And that is a kind of presage, for unreligious people are more hungry for miracles and more curious about them than anyone else. The faithful would like to see a miracle, of course, but they know that such things are exceptional and very rare and the Lord makes use of them to get into contact with us (cf. ZSOLT ARADI, *I miracoli*, Vita e Pensiero, 1961).

The Lord usually wishes to draw us to him by other ways than by means of these marvellous sense experiences. He wants to attract us by spiritual and moral ways, the way of faith, the way of love, the way of the example given by saints, through whom shines the light of a relationship with God, and he wants to draw us also by means of the authorized voice of the Church.

But there is still another form, another step towards mystical contact with God, and it is perhaps less rare than we might think. It is an interior manifestation of Jesus, such as was promised to him who really loves him. He said, " I will show myself to him " (*Jn.* 14, 21). It is that " light of hearts " which makes the faith light and secure. It is inspiration from the Holy Spirit, that guidance which God exerts over faithful souls, especially those which are devoted to interior silence, prayer and contemplation. It is a gift or fruit of the Spirit (cf. *Gal.* 5, 22; *Eph.* 5, 9), a charism which infuses into the heart an unmistakable pull towards the Living and Present Being of God.

The spiritual growth which occurs on this level of mystical encounter with God is rare, but very varied and very rich. Its most beautiful and characteristic flower is knowledge through the means of love. We shall shortly decree the title of Doctor of the Church to two saints, Teresa of Avila and Catherine of Siena. Both reached, suffered and enjoyed such mystical knowledge and left wonderful evidence of it to the Church and mankind. Many other saints have been like them. Take the vision of Stephen, for example (*Ac.* 7, 55), St. Peter's vision at Jaffa (*Ac.* 10, 11), St. Paul being taken up to the third heaven (*2 Cor.* 12, 4), St. John on Patmos (*Apoc.* passim) and St. Augustine at Ostia. The phenomena of the mystical way are rich and numerous, both as regards

313

psychology (cf. Plotinus, 3rd century) and as regards theology (cf. Denis, known as the Areopagite, 5th century). They form a special branch of theology and hagiography.

Yet it all seems to concern a very singular class of privileged religious persons. Yes, so it does. But this will do to show that it is possible to find God. Then we might come along to our own times and go out among men of today, and there we shall find literary testimonies (cf. Bernanos), philosophical ones (Bergson, Maritain) and ones based on experience (cf. MERTON, and A. FROS-SARD, *Dieu existe, je l'hai rencontré*, Fayard, 1969). These all provide confirmation of what We have been saying. But, as for ourselves, if we really wish to find God with our own humble forces, let us remember what Jesus said to the apostle Philip, " Who sees me, sees the Father also " (*Jn.* 14, 9). With Our Apostolic Blessing.

FAITH MADE FOR MEN
OF TODAY

These talks of Ours are about the state of mind of the people of our time in regard to religion, to faith in God and in Christ. Their main idea is concerned with finding out how and why people of today are unreligious or irreligious. The reasonings which seem to justify their negative attitudes may be reduced to two current objections: progress in culture and social transformation. But We are convinced that the Catholic religion could and ought to have a better hearing and be given better expression just because of those reasons. We are convinced, in other words, that our faith is made for man, for what is contemporary to us even more than for what belongs to yesterday. The faith is not an alienation, it is not an artifice which is bound to disappear, it is not an obsolete concept, nor is it a sterile and burdensome science. On the contrary, it is a light, a fullness, a life. The greater the need for it and the greater the enjoyment of it, the more advanced, cultivated, mature, adult and hungry for certainty is the person who has liberating and redeeming experience of it (cf. J. Daniélou, *L'avenir de la religion*, Fayard, Paris 1968).

But now comes the big question: Why is it so difficult to get religion accepted by modern man? Is there not a religious decline going on? Are not the dispositions of human psychology unfavourable to the thought of God, to religion, to accepted and lived faith? The question is too vast for a ready, simple answer to be given. Such an answer would above all demand ample and careful analysis of the conditions in which society and individuals live, so as to be able to say something about this widespread negative predisposition towards religion. We will not speak about that now, but it will be a good thing for everyone to think about it for himself, since there is so much talk of a current " religious

315

crisis ". Everyone can ask himself why people seem to have become almost obdurate against religion? Because of what ideas,
what habits, what teachers, what phenomena, what circumstances?
We put this question to each of you.

Faith and Man

But in this brief meeting, We will take up another aspect of
the problem. It does not concern restive, indifferent man, man
hostile to the religious message, so much as the teacher who
delivers the message. We mean the form, the method, the language, the zeal, the love with which that message is propounded.
A very great deal of attention is being given to this side of the
religious question today. To put it briefly, we have to ask ourselves how we can present the Catholic religion to our own
generation. This is the capital question of the relationship between faith and man, seen above all from the point of view of
instructional method. How are we going to say it? How are we
going to make it comprehensible? Acceptable? Welcome? Effective? Modern?

If the faith fails to find hearers and believers, is this because
it is taught and preached in an old, abstruse way, cut off from life
and contrary to the tendencies and tastes of today? Ought we
not renew the *kerygma*—the announcement of the Christian message—if we want it to find hearers and followers?

If We had time, We should have to dwell on this point, because
the relationship between faith and man just mentioned, is decisive
for one and the other, as everyone can see. What does the Church
do, what does the bishop, the pastor, the teacher, the apologist,
the catechist, the missionary, the writer, the preacher, the theologian do? They are continually trying to bring God's work close to
human life, so that the latter may find salvation in that Word.

We are here overlooking a most important but mysterious side
of the question; it is that saving acceptance of God's Word is a
grace. So we come to the most delicate problem of grace. This
is a gift towards which human liberty has a responsibility but in
regard to which it cannot be efficacious; it cooperates, but does
not operate. Hence Jesus' words remain tremendously true:
There are some who look but do not see, who hear but do not

understand (cf. *Mt.* 13, 13). Saint Augustine says that preaching the truth is useless to man unless there be grace: *Nihil prodest homini omnis praedicatio veritatis* (*De civ. Dei* XV, 6; *PL* 41, 442). So, in the end, the effectivenesse of the religious effort made by each one of us is God's secret.

The Art of Explaining

But let us merely try to bring out the wisdom and the danger entailed in the effort to adapt religious teaching to the learner's receptive abilities, whether the learner be a person or a whole people. Wisdom: here we find the whole of the Church's apostolic genius—the art of spreading, explaining the Lord's doctrine and proportioning it to the mind and mentality of the pupil, that is, of man in need of religious instruction, and causing it to be understood to some degree. Was not this one of the Council's aims? Was not one of the liturgical reform's purposes to make the rites comprehensible? Was not this why the spoken languages were introduced into worship and theological studies? Is it not the constant concern of teaching of religion to present it in accessible and acceptable terms? To adapt it to the age, the nature, the education of those to whom the doctrine is being brought?

So great is this duty to take account of the intellectual and spiritual capacities of those who approach the threshold of the faith, that we can never carry it out fully.

In this continuous effort to transmit religious doctrine in a way that shall not be useless, we find that *caritatem veritatis*—that charity of the truth—(*2 Th.* 2, 10), proper to the Church. But this desire to multiply the means and forms of expression in Catholic religious instruction obeys a fundamental law: The wholeness of doctrine must not be infringed.

Religious truth may be clothed in various languages, contained in brief catechetical forms, spread in theological treatises, interpreted according to one philosophical system or another, on condition of always being in conformity with sound reason (cf. *Gravissimum educationis*, 7, 10, etc.); it must always be authentic and at least virtually complete, even though brought into comparison with the extremely diverse conditions of human life.

A Manifold Temptation

But this effort, so praiseworthy in itself, to have religious doctrine accepted by people of our time conceals, or rather reveals a danger, a many-sided temptation, which we may describe as doctrinal relativism.

It is said that we need a faith for our time. Very well, the Council, especially in the Constitution *Gaudium et spes*, was all intent on drawing the Church and the world into closer contact; it tried to bring out the values of creation, the values of man considered in respect of his natural life and the values of modern progress. It teaches us how our faith is still made for human salvation. But not because it makes people's opinions its measure; rather because it goes on, in accordance with the Council, bearing its paradoxical Cross, a scandal and foolishness to the world yet nevertheless, the power and wisdom of God (cf. *1 Cor.* 1, 20 sqq.). When borne humbly and bravely by believers, that Cross will today still have power to convert people to Christ's salvation. This is what is expected of the Pastors and the Faithful of the People of God. This is what is expected to all of us, in our conviction that all attempts to call others to listen to Christ would be vain and precarious, unless marked by religious truth and fidelity.

REPLACES GENERAL AUDIENCE SPEECH WITH CONFIDANT APPEAL FOR PEACE

We will not deliver Our usual General Audience discourse today. The state of affairs in the Middle East appears to Us to be so grave and so threatening that We cannot speak to you about anything else with a quiet heart. We are very worried about what is happening in that region. We have no other news except what everyone knows, but that which has come in the last few days has been really sad. We think of the thousands of dead and wounded, and the hostages, who still do not know what their fate is to be; We think of the many new ruins, and the unbearable sufferings of the people. But even more We are afflicted by the mark of civil war which has been added to that long and implacable conflict; Our pain is worsened by the increase of bitterness of spirit, the aggravation of the dangers. These can take on enormous proportions and generate incalculable catastrophes.

We do not want to dramatize the situation, but by imposing this halt on Our weekly talk, We hope to move minds more efficaciously to reflection and prayer.

We look with confidence to highly placed Persons and Organizations, who have declared themselves in favour of the truce and are trying to ward off the worst. We too encourage them to work resolutely for peace. We admire those who are making prodigious efforts to bring relief and to reawaken feelings of humanity and wisdom in those countries and in the whole world. As for Us, We will not lose hope of peace, and We will have all the more compassion for every human suffering, We will still believe in the possibility of an understanding among the parties to the conflict. So far as We are able, We will aid every attempt at finding a reasonable solution to the crisis. And above all, together with you and with the Church, We will call down God's mercy and assistance.

" YOU BELONG TO THE WORLD
BY A SPECIAL TITLE ... "

On Saturday, September 26th, the Holy Father received participants in World Congress of Secular Institutes, being held in Rome, and spoke to them as follows.

Beloved Sons and Daughters in the Lord,

Welcome! We receive your visit with particular appreciation, in view of the feature which distinguishes you in the Church of God, the exterior signs of which are not discerned by the world. For you are the Representatives of Secular Institutes, united in congress. We note the intentions which have inspired your visit: you come to us under two aspects. One is the aspect of trust, which is shown by the fact that you are persons whose lives in the world are consecrated to God. The other is one of self-offering, which is a declaration of generous fidelity to the Church, and expresses the principal purpose of every offering of oneself: that of celebrating the mysterious and supernatural union of men with God, the heavenly Father. This union was established by Christ the Master and Saviour, through the pouring out of the Holy Spirit. Self-offering is also aimed at establishing union among men, by serving them in every way, both for their natural well-being and for a higher purpose which is eternal salvation.

This meeting interests Us and deeply moves Us! It makes Us think of the prodigies of grace, the wealth which is hidden in God's Kingdom, the incalculable resources of virtue and holiness which the Church still has at its disposal today. The Church, as you know, is immersed in profane, sometimes profaning humanity, which is exalted by its temporal victories and is adverse to meeting Christ even though it needs to meet him. The Church is being traversed by so many currents, not all of which are positive

320

for her growth in that unity and truth of which Christ desired her children to be always avid and jealous. The Church is an age-old olive tree, with a scarred and twisted trunk. This might seem to be an image of age and suffering, rather than of springtime vitality, but you show that the Church of our times is capable of putting forth vigorous shoots and new promise of unthought of and abundant fruit. You represent a characteristic and most consoling phenomenon in the contemporary Church. We greet and encourage you as such.

Much discussion today on conscience

It would be easy and it would be very pleasing to Us to set out the description of yourselves as the Church sees you and as she has recognized you in recent years. We mean your theological reality as defined by the II Ecumenical Council of the Vatican (*Lumen gentium*, 44; *Perfectae caritatis*, 11), in other words the canonical description of those institutional forms which such grouping of Christians consecrated to the Lord in the world are assuming. We mean the identification of the place and function which they are taking in the structure of the People of God, the distinctive characteristics which qualify them, the dimensions and forms by means of which they testify. But you know all this very well. We have information of the care which the Sacred Congregation of the Roman Curia charged with guiding and assisting you takes on your account. We have knowledge of the careful and deeply considered papers which were presented during your Congress. We do not wish to repeat what has already been said with such competence. Rather than sketch out the canonical picture again, We prefer, if We are to say anything to you on this occasion, to take a look with discretion and sobriety at the psychological and spiritual aspect of your special dedication to following Christ.

Let us look at this phenomenon for a moment; let us look at its interior origin, its personal and spiritual origins; let us look at your vocation, for it has features in common with other vocations in the Church of God, but also has characteristics of its own which distinguish it and merit specific consideration.

We wish above all to note the importance of considered,

reflective action in man's life. They are much prized in Christian life and are very interesting, especially in certain periods of youth, because they have decisive effect. We call them *conscience*—and everyone well knows what conscience means and what it is worth. There is a great deal of discussion of conscience in modern conversation, beginning from a continual evocation of its dawn with Socrates, then its reawakening, principally through the work of Christianity, under the influence of which, a historian said, " the depths of the soul changed " (cf. *Taine*, III, 125). We will here attach Our attention to that particular moment, known to you all, in which psychological consciousness, man's inner perception of himself, becomes moral conscience (cf. S. TH. 1, 79, 13). This occurs in the act by which the psychological consciousness becomes aware of the requirement to act according to a law, which is uttered within man and written in his heart. This is obligatory for one's external life, the life that is seen and has a transcendent responsibility, ultimately in relation with God, so becoming religious conscience. The Council has this to say: " In the depths of conscience man discovers a law, which he has not given himself, but which he ought to obey; its voice is always calling him to love and do good to others and to avoid evil ... Man really has a law written by God within his heart; to give obedience to this law constitutes his dignity, and he will be judged by it (cf. *Rom.* 2, 14-16). Conscience is the most secret kernel and shrine of man, where he is alone with God " (The Council then refers to a marvellous discourse uttered by Pius XII in March 23rd, 1952, *Discourses* ... 14, p. 19 sqq.).

In that first stage of the reflective act which we call conscience, a sense of responsibility and personality arises in man, with an awareness of existential principles and their logical development. This logical development in the Christian, when rethought in terms of the baptismal character, generates the fundamental concepts of theology on man. Man knows and feels himself to be the child of God, a member of Christ incorporated in the Church and adorned with that common priesthood of the faithful the fruitful doctrine of which was recalled by the Council (cf. *Lumen gentium*, 10-11). From that priesthood arises every Christian's commitment to holiness (cf. *ib.* 39-40), to fullness of Christian life, to perfection of charity.

Vocation demands total response

This conscience, this commitment, is enlightened interiorly at a certain moment, not without a dazzling ray of grace, and becomes a vocation. Now vocation demands a total response. It may be a vocation to true and complete expression of the evangelical counsels or a priestly vocation. It may be a vocation to perfection for whoever perceives its inner fascination; vocation to a consecration, through which the soul yields to God, with a supreme act of will; that of abandonment, of gift of self. Conscience rises up as an altar of immolation: *sit ara tua conscientia mea*, Saint Augustine prayed (*En. in Ps.* 49; *PL* 36, 578). It is like the fiat which Our Lady uttered when she heard the Angel's announcement.

We are still in the domain of reflective acts, the domain which we now call interior life. At this point it is already developing as dialogue: the Lord is present: *sedes est (Dei) conscientia piorum* as Saint Augustine, once again, says; The conversation is with the Lord, but it is a search for practical decisions, just as at Damascus Saint Paul asked, " Lord, what do you want me to do? " (*Ac.* 9, 5). Baptismal consecration of grace then becomes conscious, and expresses itself in willed moral consecration, which is extended to the evangelical counsels and strives towards Christian perfection. This is the first, principal decision, the one which will give the whole of life its character.

The second? This is where the novelty comes in. This is where your originality is. What will the second decision be? What way of living this consecration will be chosen? Shall we leave our secular way of living, or shall we be able to keep it? This is the question you asked. The Church replied: you are free to choose; you may remain secular. You did choose, guided by many motives, which you certainly pondered well. And you decided. We will stay secular, that is, we will keep to the way of living which is common to all. By a further choice, in connection with the pluralism which is allowed to Secular Institutes, each has decided for itself what it shall be in accordance with its own preference. Your Institutes are therefore called secular in order to distinguish them from religious institutes.

This does not mean that your choice is easy, in view of the end of Christian perfection which it too sets before itself. It is not easy, because it does not separate you from the world, in which temporal values are preferred and where moral rules are so often exposed to formidable temptations. Your moral discipline will therefore have to be always in a state of vigilance and personal initiative; at every hour of the day it will need to draw on your sense of consecration in order to keep your work upright. The *abstine et sustine* of the moralists shall have to be continually at work in your spirituality. There we have a new, habitual reflective act and consequently a state of personal interiority which goes along with the course of your exterior life.

" Your field is the world "

So you will have your own immense field in which to do your two kinds of work: the work of personal sanctification of your soul, and the work of *consecratio mundi*, to which you have a delicate and attractive commitment. Your field is the world, the human world, just as it is, with its restless, dazzling topicality, its virtues and its passions, its possibilities for good and its gravitation towards evil, its magnificent modern achievements and its secret deficiencies and unfailing sufferings. You are walking along the edge of an inclined plane; it tempts you to take the easy way of descent; it stimulates you to undertake the labour of ascent. It is a difficult path to walk: it calls for mountaineers of the spirit.

Remember three things in your bold programme for life. Your consecration will not be only a commitment, but it will also be a help, a support, a love, a beatitude to which you can always have recourse. It will be a fullness, which will compensate for every renunciation which you make, and will make you capable for that marvellous paradox of charity: to give, give to others, give to one's neighbour in order to obtain in Christ. The second thing to remember is this: You are in the world and not of the world, but you are for the world. The Lord has taught us to find his and our own mission of salvation in this formula, which seems to be just a play on words. Remember that, just because you are members of Secular Institutes, you have a mission of salvation to carry to the people of our time. Today the world has need of you who live in the world, so that you may open the paths of Christian salvation to the world.

And now We will tell you the third thing to remember. It is the Church. The Church also comes in to be part of that reflection which we have mentioned. It becomes the theme of continual habitual meditation, which we may call *sensus Ecclesiae,* such as is in you as an atmosphere of interior breathing. You have already experienced the inebriation of this breathing, its inexhaustible inspiration, into which theology and spirituality pour their bracing airs, especially since the Council. One of the themes of theology and spirituality should always be with you: It is that you belong to the Church by a special title, that of consecrated seculars. You may be sure that the Church has trust in you. The Church follows you, supports you, considers you her own, as children of election, active, conscious members, who on the one hand are firmly attached to her and on the other are skilfully trained for the apostolate, members who are ready to give silent testimony, ready for service, and ready for sacrifice, if necessary.

You are lay people who turn your Christian profession into constructive energy which aims at supporting the Church's mission and structures, dioceses, parishes, Catholic institutions especially, and to inspire their spirituality and charity. You are lay people who can have better knowledge of the needs of the Church on earth, through direct experience. Perhaps you are also in a position to uncover its defects. But do not make them occasions for corrosive and ungenerous criticism. Do not make them a pretext for going apart and standing egoistically and disdainfully aside. Make them a stimulus for more humble and filial help, and greater love. You, Secular Institutes of the Church today! Take our greeting and encouragement to your Brothers and Sisters, and may all of you have Our Apostolic Benediction.

ST. TERESA—AN EXCEPTIONAL WOMAN
AND A RELIGIOUS ...

On Sunday morning, September 27th, the Pope presided in St. Peter's Basilica at the ceremony of proclamation of St. Teresa of Avila as Doctor of the Church. About thirteen thousand clergy and faithful from Spain were present. The Spanish State was represented by Prince Juan Carlos. The Holy Father spoke as follows.

We have now conferred—rather, We have acknowledged Saint Teresa of Jesus' title of Doctor of the Church. The mere act of uttering the name of this most singular and most great Saint in this place and under these circumstances gives rise to many thoughts. Our first thought might be to recall the kind of person she was. We see Teresa appear before us, an exceptional woman and a religious. Veiled with humility, penitence and simplicity, she radiates the flame of her human vitality around her. Then we see her as the reformer and founder of an historical and eminent religious Order, a fertile writer of great genius, a mistress of the spiritual life, an incomparable contemplative who was tirelessly active. How great she is, how unique! How human, how attractive is this personality!

We feel tempted to speak of her before referring to anything else, to speak of this Saint who was very interesting in so many ways. But do not expect Us to talk about the person and work of Teresa of Jesus at this moment. The two biographies collected in the volume published with so much care by Our Sacred Congregation for the Cause of Saints would be enough to discourage anyone from trying to sum the historical and biographical picture of this Saint up in a few words, for she escapes from the descriptive outlines in which we might wish to contain her. In any case it is not strictly upon her that We wish to concentrate Our attention at this instant. We wish rather to consider the act that We have just performed, that fact which We are inserting into the Church's history and which We entrust to the piety and reflection of the People of God. We refer to Our act of conferring the title of Doctor upon Teresa of Avila, Saint Teresa of Jesus, the great Carmelite.

Charism of Wisdom

The meaning of this act is very clear. It is deliberately intended to be enlightening, and might be symbolically represented by means of a lamp lighted before the humble and majestic figure of the Saint. The act is enlightening because of the pencil of rays which the lamp of the title of Doctor projects upon her; it is enlightening also because of the other rays which this same title sends out over us.

The light of the title shows up on Teresa unquestionable values which have already been fully acknowledged to her: the holiness of her life, above all, is a value which was officially proclaimed so early as March 12th, 1622—she had died thirty years before—by Our Predecessor Gregory XV. This was at that celebrated act of canonization in which, together with our Carmelite, Ignatius of Loyola, Francis Xavier, Isidore of Madrid, all glories of Catholic Spain, and Philip Neri, a Florentine who lived in Rome, were all inscribed on the roll of saints. This act also brought out " the eminence of her doctrine ", in second place, yet in a special way (cf. PROSPERO LAMBERTINI, later Pope Benedictine XIV, *De Servorum Dei beatificationis*, IV, 2, c. 11 No. 13).

Saint Teresa of Avila's doctrine shines with charisms of truth, of conformity to the Catholic faith and of usefulness for the instruction of souls. And We might mention another particular point, the charism of wisdom. This makes us think of the most attractive and at the same time most mysterious aspect of Saint Teresa's title of Doctor: the flow of divine inspiration in this prodigious and mystical writer. From where did the wealth of her doctrine come to Teresa? It undoubtedly arose from her intelligence and her cultural and spiritual education, from her letters, from her conversation with great masters of theology and spirituality, from her singular sensibility, from her particularly intense and habitual ascetic discipline, from her contemplative meditation; in a word, from her response to grace, received in a soul that was extraordinarily rich and well prepared for the practice and experience of prayer.

Encounter with Divine Love

But was this the only source of her " eminent doctrine "? Or ought we not recognize in Saint Teresa acts, facts and states which did not come from her but were undergone by her, things both undergone and suffered, mystical, things in the true meaning of the word, things which have to be attributed to extraordinary action on the part of the Holy Spirit? We are undoubtedly before a soul in which extraordinary divine initiative was active, and was perceived and described by Teresa, simply, faithfully, stupendously, in a literary language of her own.

Numerous questions now arise. The originality of mystical action is one of the most delicate and complicated of psychological phenomena. Many factors can play a part in it, and oblige the observer to maintain the severest caution. But the marvels of the human soul are manifested in mystical action in a surprising way. One of these marvels is the most comprehensive of all. It is love, which has its most varied and fullest expressions in the depths of the heart. It is a love which we must finally describe as an espousal, for it is an encounter with a flood of divine love, descending to meet human love, which strives with all its might to ascend. It is the most intimate and the strongest union with God which is given to a soul living on this earth to experience. It turns into light, it turns into wisdom: wisdom in divine things, wisdom in human things.

Teresa's doctrine speaks of these secrets, which are the secrets of prayer. This is what her doctrine is. She had the privilege and the merit to get to know these secrets through experience. And that experience was lived in the holiness of a life consecrated to contemplation and committed to action at the same time. It was experience which was suffering, and at the same time was enjoyment of a pouring out of extraordinary spiritual charisms. Teresa possessed the art of expounding these same secrets, to such a degree as to place her among the great masters of the spiritual life. It is not in vain that the statue of the Saint in this Basilica, here because she was a Foundress, bears an inscription that describes her very well: *Mater Spiritualium.*

Message of Prayer

Saint Teresa's prerogative of being a mother, a teacher of spiritual persons, had already been acknowledged, we might say by unanimous accord. She was a mother who was full of entrancing simplicity, a teacher who was full of marvellous depths.

The tribute of the tradition of the Saints, of thelogians, of the faithful, of the learned, was already assured to her. Now We have confirmed it. We have taken care to see that, having been adorned with this title of Master, she may have a more authoritative mission to perform in her religious Family, in the praying Church and in the world, through her perennial, ever present message—the message of prayer.

This is the light which is today rendered more lively and penetrating and is reflected over us by the title of Doctor just now conferred on Saint Teresa—the message of prayer! It comes to us children of the Church at a time marked by a great effort at the reform and renewal of liturgical prayer. It comes to us just when we are tempted by the great noise and the great business of the world outside to yield to the frenzy of modern life and to lose the real treasures of our souls in the effort to win the seductive treasures of the earth. It comes to us children of our own times just when we are losing not only the habit of conversing with God, but also the sense of the need and the duty to worship and call on him. The message of prayer comes to us as song and music of the spirit which is imbued with grace and open to the conversation of faith, hope and charity. At the same time psychoanalytical exploration is disintegrating man, that frail and complicated instrument, no longer in order to hear the voice of sorrowing and redeemed humanity, but rather to listen to the troubled mutterings of his animal subconscious, the cries of his disordered passions and his desperate anguish.

Sublime mission of Woman

The sublime and simple message of prayer of the wise Teresa exhorts us to understand " the great good which God does to a soul when he disposes it to practice mental prayer with desire ... because in my opinion mental prayer in nothing else but a friendly way of dealing, in which we often find ourselves talking, just two alone, with Him who we know loves us " (*Life*, 8, 4-5).

This sums up the message to us from Saint Teresa of Jesus. Doctor of the Church. Let us listen to it and make it our own.

We must add two observations, which seem to Us to be important.

The first is that Saint Teresa is the first woman upon whom the Church has conferred this title of Doctor. This has not been done without mindfulness of Saint Paul's severe words: *Mulieres in Ecclesiis taceant* (*1 Cor*. 14, 34). This still signifies today that woman is not meant to have hierarchical functions of teaching and ministering in the Church. Has the Apostle's precept been violated, then?

We can give a clear answer: No. It is really not a title entailing hierarchical functions of teaching, yet we must point out at the same time that this does not in the least signify less appreciation of the sublime mission which woman has in the People of God.

On the contrary, having come in to be part of the Church through baptism, woman partakes of the common priesthood of the faithful. This enables and obliges her « to profess before men the faith received from God through the Church " (*Lumen gentium*, 2, 11). So many women have reached the highest peaks in such profession of faith, to the point that their words and writings have given light and guidance to their brethren. That light was fed every day by intimate contact with God, even in the noblest forms of mystical prayer, and Saint Francis of Sales did not hesitate to say that women have a special capacity for it. That light is turned into life in a sublime manner for the good and service of mankind.

The Council therefore wished to acknowledge the lofty collaboration with divine grace which women are called upon to give, in order to begin God's Kingdom on earth. In extolling the greatness of their mission the Council had no hesitation in calling on them likewise to cooperate " in order that mankind may not decline ", in order to " reconcile men with life ", and " to save peace in the world " (*Message to Women*).

Glory of Spain

In the second place, We do not wish to overlook the fact that Saint Teresa was Spanish, and Spain rightly regards her as one of its greatest glories. In her personality we can appreciate the characteristics of her country: rebustness of spirit, depth of feeling, sincerity of heart, love for the Church. She lived in a glorious age of saints and masters who made their times outstanding for development of spirituality. She listened to them with a disciple's humility, but at the same time could judge them with the perspicacity of a great mistress of the spiritual life. They regarded her as such.

The violent tempest of the Reformation was raging inside and outside the country, setting children of the Church against each other. Through her love of the truth and her intimacy with the Master, she had to face bitter experiences and misunderstandings of all kinds. She could not let her mind be at peace at the sight of such a rupture of unity. " I suffered much ", she wrote, " and, as if I could do something or were something, I wept and begged the Lord to repair so much evil " (*Camino de perfección*, ch. 1, No. 2; BAC, 1962, 185). Her power of feeling for the Church was tried by sorrow at the sight of so much wasted energies; it led her to react with all her strong Castilian spirit, in her yearning to build up the kingdom of God. She resolved to penetrate the world about her with a reforming vision, so as to give that world Christian meaning, harmony and a Christian soul.

Now, five centuries later, Saint Teresa of Avila continues to imprint the form of her spiritual mission, of the nobility to her heart which thirsted for the truth of the Catholic faith, of her love which was free from earthly affection in order to be able to give itself totally to the Church. Before she breathed her last breath, she was well able to utter, as it were, the epilogue of her own life, " At last, I am a daughter of the Church! ".

This saying was a happy presage of the glory of the blessed which awaited Teresa, and in it We like to see a spiritual legacy which is linked to all Spain. We also like to see it as an invitation to all of us to echo her voice, to make it the programme of our own lives, so as to be able to say with her: We are children of the Church.

With Our Apostolic Blessing.

PLAN FOR AUTHENTIC CHRISTIANITY

" **N** ot everyone who says to me, Lord, Lord, shall enter into the kingdom of heaven, but he who does the will of my Father who is in heaven ". These are celebrated words of Jesus Christ, Our Lord. We choose them today as the theme for Our brief reflection, remaining always attentive to that great event, the Council. It should not have been in vain that this event occurred in our days, but it ought to imprint a moral renewal upon our Christian living.

This was the predominant thought in the mind of Our venerated Predecessor when he summoned the Council: " The Christian, Catholic and Apostolic spirit of the entire world ", he said, " awaits a leap forward towards doctrinal penetration and the formation of consciences, from renewed, serene and tranquil assent to the whole of the Church's teaching in its entirety and precision, such as still shines forth from the Council acts of Trent and the I Vatican Council, and in the most perfect correspondence to the fidelity of authentic doctrine. This can, however, be studied and expounded through the forms of enquiry and literary formulation of modern thought " (*AAS*, 1962, p. 792). For this reason the Council wished to assume the character of a mainly pastoral magisterium.

Need to act

The thought behind the Council's moral intention often recurs in its teachings. For example, in the Decree on Ecumenism. This might seem in itself to be remote from directly personal and moral themes, but in it we find: " There is no true ecumenism without interior conversion " (*Unit. redint.* 7). In the Constitution on the Liturgy we find conversion and penitence spoken of as the conditions for arriving at contact with Christ in celebration of the holy mysteries (N. 9). This link between doctrine and morality occurs throughout the gospel. The Lord was Teacher of truth and life at the same time. He instructed us with his words and his example. He left us no books, but he did leave us a new form of existence, which is transmitted and guided by a magisterium and a ministry each an authentic successor of his redeeming mission. It consists in supernatural vivification in grace, that is, in the Holy Spirit.

Interior conversion

Consequently, if we wish to receive the Council's influence, we have to ask ourselves what we want to do with it. Knowing is not enough: it is necessary to act. There are two ways of understanding the application of that knowledge. The first is that of extension, that is, by means of doctrinal and canonical deductions. We will not speak about these now, partly because, if not guided by the Magisterium of the Church, this course can carry us beyond the Church's teachings and intentions. The second way of putting knowledge of the Council into practice is the way of profundity, that is, by means of interior reforms in our souls and in the Church's life, so that the Council may have a really renewing effect. This will be especially true of our understanding of our membership of Christ and the Church, participation in the Church's life (of prayer and of action), recourse to our consciences, responsible use of our liberty, commitment to our personal sanctification, spread of the Christian spirit and vocation, the effort to get closer to our separated Christian brethren and the confrontation between Christianity and the modern world. All this is to recognize the positive values and needs to which we can devote our service. To sum it all up, we must do everything with increased love for Holy Church, Christ's mystical Body and the historical and vital continuation of it, for which he shed his redeeming blood.

We could distinguish various fields and forms of this application of the Council. We could begin by making the exterior, juridical reforms our own, with filial trust. They are authentically derived from the Council: first, liturgical reform, without harassing criticisms and arbitrary alterations: likewise, the structural reforms of the ecclesial community. It would already be a great result of the Council if we were all to give prompt and precise assent to these exterior innovations, which are so closely linked with renewal of ourselves and of the Church. This is the canonical application.

Theological application

The other kind of application is the spiritual one. The volume containing the Council's Constitutions and Decrees can serve as a book of spiritual reading and meditation. It has beautiful passages, full of wisdom and historical and human experience. They deserve meditation and can become food for the soul. God's Word is so widespread now and so responsive to the human requirements of our age, that we can all go to school to it. Its lesson ought not to be missed, for it can well lead Christians of today towards the call of a listening silence, the vocation of the heart which allows the Lord's Truth to become the spirit and life of its existence. The simple, plain, authoritative form of the Council's teachings is itself a lesson in evangelical temperament, pastoral style and imitation of the Lord. He made himself our model: " Learn of me, for I am meek and humble of heart " (*Mt.* 11, 29). This is the spiritual application.

And there is another application, still in the moral field. It is the theological application. Action follows being. Being is known to us from study of the truth. Theological truth presides over the moral order. That concept of life which is presented to us by the plan of salvation and was outlined by the Council's theology, contains the higher law which we ought to follow. From the concept of what we are as Christians arises the imperative of what we ought to be in order to correspond to our definition. From being comes ought to be, that " doing the will of the heavenly Father ", according to Jesus' command which we have mentioned. It is obligatory over and above religious expression itself, when this is devoid of any content that is in conformity with the divine will.

This is how we ought to look for a basis for moral life such as the Council expounded to us, reflecting the gospel. We ought to

335

do this if we wish to apply renewal, *aggiornamento*, faithfully and happily. This call back to theological principles subordinates the precepts of the moral life to them. It puts them under examination, on several grounds. There is the ground of priority: " we must obey God rather than men " (*Ac.* 5, 29)—whence the value of martyrdom. Then there is the ground of abrogation: as when the purely legal prescriptions of the Mosaic law were repealed, as we learn from the teaching of the early Church, especially of Saint Paul (cf. *Ac.* 15; *Gal.* 2, 16). Then there is possible reform of civil, or canonical law, when it is not an expression of the natural law, which is itself divine law inscribed in the human being (cf. *Mt.* 5, 17-20; *Rom.* 2, 14). Finally, there remains the obligation of obedience to the prevailing order in civil society (*Rom.* 13, 7) and in ecclesiastical society (*He.* 13, 17; *Lk.* 16, 10).

But did not the Lord say, " The truth shall make you free "? (*Jn.* 8, 32; *Gal.* 5, 6). Yes. But this truth which liberates from the errors and arbitrariness of human lack of wisdom and love of force, binds the will that knows it in conscience, in a stronger, more logical and more responsible way. It brings man under the law of the Spirit, that is, the law of grace and charity, from which comes that higher call to union with Christ, to imitation of him, to love of God and one's neighbour (*Mt.* 22, 39; *Rom.* 13, 9; *Gal.* 5, 14), to self-abnegation, to service of one's nieghbour, to sacrifice, to sanctity. The Council quite strongly recommends us to reflect on this plan for authentic Christian moral life (cf. *Lumen gentium*, 40; *Optatam totius* 16, etc.). If we do this and make this life our own, then the Council will have some of its best results. It will not be a short-term undertaking, but it will be a salutary one. With Our Apostolic Blessing.

ST. CATHERINE—
DOCTOR OF THE CHURCH

The Holy Father presided in St. Peter's at the ceremony of proclaiming Saint Catherine of Siena a Doctor of the Church, on Sunday October 4th, the feast of Saint Francis of Assisi. The ceremony was attended by festive crowds from Siena and all Tuscany, who celebrated the occasion with music and dancing in St. Peter's Square and all around Rome. The Holy Father spoke as follows in the Basilica.

Spiritual exaltation bursts into Our soul as We proclaim the humble and wise Dominican virgin a Doctor of the Church. The loftiest comparison which We can make (and where its justification may be found) is with the purest joy which Our Lord felt when he " rejoiced in spirit ", as the Evangelist Saint Luke tells us, and said, *I thank thee, Father of heaven and earth, that thou hast hid these things from the wise and prudent, and hast revealed them to the simple. Yes, Father, for so did it please thee* (*Lk.* 10, 21; cf. *Mt.* 11, 25-26).

The truth is that when Jesus thanked his Father for having revealed the secrets of his divine wisdom to the humble, he was not thinking only of the Twelve whom he had chosen from among the uneducated people and whom he would one day send out as his apostles to instruct all peoples and teach them what he had commanded (cf. *Mt.* 28, 19-20). He was also thinking of those who would believe in him. Among those innumerable souls there would be the least cultivated in the eyes of the world.

The Apostle of the Gentiles took pleasure in making this observation when writing to the community of the Greek city of Corinth, which was swarming with people who were infatuated with human wisdom. *For consider your calling, brethren,* he wrote, *how not many who are wise in earthly estimation, not many powerful people, and not many noble have been called by*

337

God. But God has chosen that which is foolish to the world in order to confound the wise; he has chosen that which is weak in order to confound the strong. He has chosen that which is not, in order to bring that which is to nothing, so that no creature may glory in his presence (1 Cor. 1, 26-29).

Exterior activity of Catherine

The Master had already foretold God's preferential choice of what is negligible or even despicable in the world's eyes. He foretold it when he went sharply against earthly evaluations and called blessed the poor, the afflicted, the meek, those hungering for justice, the pure of heart and peacemakers (cf. *Mt.* 5, 3-10).

It is not Our intention to linger over showing how the evangelical Beatitudes found a model of superlative truthand beauty in Catherine's life and exterior activity.

In any case, you all know how she was free of all earthly cupidity, how much she loved virginity consecrated to the heavenly spouse, Christ Jesus, how she hungered for justice and was filled with mercy as she strove to brings peace to families and cities which were torn by rivalries and atrocious hatreds, how she did wonders to reconcile the Republic of Florence with the Supreme Pontiff Gregory XI, and even went so far as to expose her life to vengeance from the rebels. Nor will we stop to admire those exceptional mystical graces with which the Lord chose to endow her and which included the mystical marriage and the sacred stigmata. We think that these are not the circumstances to recall the story of her great-hearted efforts to induce the Pope to return to his rightful place, Rome. The success which she finally achieved in this was truly the masterpiece of her work. For centuries it will be remembered as her greatest glory and will constitute a quite special claim to everlasting thankfulness on the part of the Church.

But We do think that this is the right moment to throw some light, though only briefly, on the second of her titles justifying the conferring of this Doctorate on this daughter of the illustrious city of Siena, in accordance with the Church's judgement. This second title is the peculiar excellence of her doctrine.

The first title is the title of sanctity. This was solemnly

acknowledged, in ample measure and in the unmistakable style of the humanist-that he was, by Pope Pius II, her fellow townsman. He did this in the Bull of Canonization *Misericordias Domini*, which he himself wrote (cf. M.-H. LAURENT, O.P., *Proc. Castel.*, pp. 521-530; Italian translation by I. TAURISANO O.P., *S. Caterina da Siena*, Rome 1948, pp. 665-673). The special liturgical ceremony for it took place in St. Peter's Basilica on June 29th, 1461.

What then shall We say of the eminence of Catherine's teaching? In her writings, that is, her *Letters*, a large number of which have been preserved, in her *Dialogue of Divine Providence* or *Book of Divine Doctrine*, and in her *orationes* we shall certainly not find the apologetic vigour and the theological boldness which mark the works of the great lights of the ancient Church both in East and West. Nor can we expect the uncultivated virgin of Fontebranda to give us lofty speculations which belong to systematic theology and which made the Doctors of the scholastic middle ages immortal. It is true that her writings reflect the theology of the Angelic Doctor in a surprising degree, yet that theology appears there bare of any scientific clothing.

But what strikes us most about the Saint is her infused wisdom. That is to say, lucid, profound and inebriating absorption of the divine truths and the mysteries of the faith contained in the Holy Books of the Old and New Testaments. That assimilation was certainly favoured by most singular natural gifts, but it was also evidently something prodigious, due to a charism of wisdom from the Holy Spirit, a mystic charism.

In her writings Catherine of Siena provides us with one of the most splendid examples of those charisms of *exhortation*, of *the word of wisdom* and the *word of knowledge* which Saint Paul describes as being in operation in some faithful belonging to early Christian communities. He desired that use of them should be well disciplined, and pointed out that such gifts are not so much for the benefit of those endowed with them, as for the whole body of the Church. In that body, he went on to explain, " the Spirit who distributes his gifts to each one as he wills (is) one and the same " (*1 Cor.* 12, 11). Hence the benefit of the spiritual treasures which his Spirit distributes ought to devolve to all the members of the mystical organism of Christ (cf. *1 Cor.* 11, 5; *Rom.* 12, 8; *1 Tim.* 6, 2; *Tit.* 2, 15).

Doctrina eius (scilicet Catherinae) acquisita fuit; prius magistra visa est quam discipula (Proc. Cast. 1, c.). Her doctrine was not acquired: she was a teacher even before she was a pupil. This is what Pius II said in his Bull of Canonization. Indeed, how many rays of superhuman wisdom, how many urgent calls to imitation of Christ in all the mysteries of his life and his suffering, how many efficacious teachings about the practice of the virtues proper to the various states in life, are scattered through the Saint's works! Her Letters are like so many sparks from a mysterious fire, lit in her ardent heart by Infinite Love, that is, the Holy Spirit.

Mystic of the Incarnate Word

But what were the main features, the dominant themes of her ascetical and mystical teaching? It seems to Us that Catherine is the mystic of the Incarnate Word, above all of Jesus Crucified. In this she was in imitation of " glorious Paul " (*Dialogues* c. XI, ed. G. Cavallini, 1968, p. 27), whose bounding and impetuous style she sometimes reflects. She was one who exalted the redeeming power of the adorable Blood of the Son of God, shed on the wood of the cross in expanding love, for the salvation of all generations of mankind (cf. *Dialogue,* c. CXXVII, ed cit. p. 325).

The Saint saw that Blood of the Saviour continually flowing in the Sacrifice of the Mass and in the Sacraments, thanks to the ministry of the sacred ministers and for purification and embellishment of the whole mystical Body of Christ. We may therefore say that Catherine was the *mystic of the mystical Body of Christ,* that is, *of the Church.*

And the Church for her part was for Catherine a genuine *mother* to whom there is a duty to submit and to give reverence and obedience. " The Church ", she dared to say, " is nothing else but Christ himself " (*Letter 171,* ed. P. Misciatelli, III, 89).

What deep respect then and passionate love did the Saint not have for the Roman Pontiff! We Ourself, the least of the servants of God, personally owe Catherine immense gratitude today, certainly not because of the honour that might redound to our humble person, but because of the mystical apologia which she made for the apostolic office of Peter's Successor. Who does not remember? In him she saw *il dolce Cristo in terra*—sweet Christ on earth

(*Lett. 196*, ed. cit. III, 211). To him is due filial affection and obedience, because " Whoever is disobedient to Christ on earth, who represents Christ in heaven, does not share in the fruit of the Blood of the Son of God " (*Lett. 207*, ed. cit., III, *270*).

Almost anticipating not only the doctrine but also the language of the II Vatican Council itself (*Lumen gentium*, 23) she wrote to Pope Urban VI: " Most holy Father ... you know the great necessity for you and for holy Church to keep this people (of Florence), in obedience and reverence to Your Holiness, since here is the head and beginning of our faith " (*Lett. 170*, ed. cit. III, 75).

She also addressed pressing exhortations to Cardinals and to many Bishops and priests; nor did she spare them strong reproaches, but always with deep humility and respect for their dignity as ministers of the Blood of Christ.

Catherine could not forget that she was the daughter of a religious Order, one of the most glorious and active in the Church. She therefore had singular esteem for what she called " the holy religions ". She considered them as a bond of union between the mystical Body, constituted by representatives of Christ (according to a description of her own) and the universal body of the Christian religion, that is, the ordinary faithful. She demanded that religious should have fidelity to their lofty calling, through generous practice of the virtues and observance of their respective rules.

The laity were not last in her maternal solicitude. She sent numerous lively letters to lay people, calling on them to be prompt to practise the Christian virtues and the duties of their state, and to be inspired with ardent love of God and their neighbour, for these too are living members of the mystical Body. " She " (the Church), the Saint said, " is founded on love and is love itself " (*Lett. 103*, ed. G. Gigli).

Her role in Church reform

And how could we forget the intense work she did for reform of the Church? She addressed her exhortations principally to sacred Pastors, for she was disgusted and had holy scorn for the indolence of more than a few of them, and she fumed at their silence while the flock entrusted to them was lost and ruined. " Alas, be silent no longer! Cry with a hundred thousand tongues ", she write to a high prelate; " I see that the world is spoilt through refusal to speak out, Christ's Spouse is pallid; her colour has been taken from her because her blood has been sucked out of her, that blood which is the Blood of Christ " (*Lett. 16 to the Cardinal of Ostia*, ed. L. Ferretti, I, 85).

And what did she mean by renewal and reform of the Church? Certainly not the overthrow of its basic structures, rebellion against the Pastors, a free rein for personal charisms, arbitrary innovations in worship and discipline, such as some would like in our day. On the contrary, she repeatedly affirms that beauty would be given back to the Spouse of Christ and it would be necessary to make reforms " not with war, but with peace and quiet, with the humble and continuous prayers, sweat and tears of the servants of God " (cf. *Dialogue* chs. XV, LXXXVI, ed cit., pp. 44, 197). For the Saint, therefore it was a matter above all of interior reform, then exterior reform, but always in communion and filial obedience to Christ's rightful representatives.

Was our most devoted Virgin also a politician? Yes, undoubtedly? And in an excptional way, in a wholly spiritual acceptance of the word. But she scornfully rejected the accusation of being a political meddler, which some of her fellow townspeople made against her. She wrote to one of them: " ... And my fellow citizens believe that negotiations are going on by means of me or the company that I have with me: they are telling the truth; but they do not know it, and they are prophesying; for I do not wish, and I do not wish those who are with me, to do anything but what is concerned with defeating the demon and depriving him of the lordship which he has seized over man through mortal sin, and to take the hatred out of his heart and bring him to peace with Christ Crucified and with his neighour " (*Letter 122*, ed. cit. II, 235).

Offering her life

The lesson which this political woman *sui generis* gives us still keeps its meaning and values, even though there is a more strongly felt need today to make the due distinction between the things that are Caesar's and the things that are God's, between

Church and State. The Saint's political magisterium had its most genuine and perfect expression in this lapidary sentence of hers: " No state can be preserved in civil law and divine law in a state of grace without holy justice " (*Dialogue*, ch. XIX, ed. cit. p. 291).

Catherine was not content with having carried out an intense and most vast work of truth and goodness in word and in writing. She desired to seal it all with the final offer of her life, for the mystical Body of Christ, which is the Church, at the still youthful age of 33 years. From her deathbed, surrounded by faithful disciples in a little cell by the church of Santa Maria sopra Minerva at Rome, she addressed this moving prayer to the Lord. It is a true testament of faith and most ardent love: *O eternal God, receive the sacrifice of my life for (the sake of) this mystical body of holy Church. I have nothing other to give but what thou hast given me. Take my heart, therefore, and press it out over the face of this spouse* (*Lett. 371*, ed. L. Ferretti, V. pp. 301-302).

This was a message of a most pure faith, of an ardent love, of a humble and generous dedication to the Catholic Church, as the mystical Body and Spouse of the divine Redeemer. This message was typical of the new Doctor of the Church, Catherine of Siena, to enlighten and give example to all who glory in belonging to the Church. Let us receive this message in a grateful and generous spirit, that it may be a light for our earthly life and pledge of future secure membership of the Church triumphant in heaven. So may it be!

MESSAGE OF HIS HOLINESS POPE PAUL VI
ON THE 25th ANNIVERSARY
OF THE UNITED NATIONS

To His Excellency U Thant
Secretary-General of the United Nations Organization

At this time when the United Nations Organization is celebrating the twenty-fifth anniversary of its foundation, we are happy to convey to it, through your good offices, our confident good wishes, and the assurance of our good-will and our support for its worldwide mission. Today we wish once more to repeat the words which we had the honour to pronounce on 4th October 1965 from the tribune of your Assembly " This Organization represents the path that has to be taken for modern civilization and for world peace (*AAS*, vol. LVII, 1965, p. 878).

Is not an anniversary such as this a propitious occasion for assessing and reflecting upon the results which it has been possible to achieve in the course of this first quarter of a century? If it has not been possible to fulfil the expectations and hopes which were raised when your institution came into being, it must at least be recognized that it is within the United Nations Organization that the desire of governments and peoples to work together efficaciously for the establishment of brotherly unity is most surely followed up. Where else, moreover, could these governments and peoples better find a bridge to link them, a table round which they can gather, and a tribunal where they may plead the cause of justice and peace? Even if the sources of violence still smoulder, flaring up here and there into fresh conflagrations, the conscience of humanity still makes itself heard no less clearly in this privileged forum where, going beyond selfish rivalries, men find once more that inalienable part of themselves which unites them all—the human element in man.

Is it not so as to assure, ever more firmly, respect for this human element that your Assembly has rightly taken pains to lay down in appropriate texts, pacts or declarations, the conditions of dignity, of freedom and of security which must be guaranteed " by all, in all places and for all? " (*Message to the Teheran Conference, AAS*, vol. LX, 1968, p. 285). At this agonizing hour of their history, the peoples are more vividly aware than ever of the gap which separates these generous resolutions from their effective implementation. In the face of so many inextricable situations, conflicting interests, deeply rooted prejudices and the tragic series of conflicts, discouragement lies in wait for even the best, as they witness the collapse of the hope of peaceful coexistence by obstinately hostile forces. Let us presume to say this: there will be no lasting peace until a new spirit impels individuals, social groups and nations to true reconciliation. That is why we must strive untiringly to substitute relationships based on force with relationships of deep understanding, mutual respect and creative collaboration.

Proclaimed more than twenty years ago by your Assembly, the Charter of Human Rights remains in our view one of its greatest claims to fame. To ask that all, without distinction of race, age, sex or religion should be able to enjoy human dignity and the conditions necessary for its exercise—is not this to express strongly and clearly the unanimous aspiration of men's hearts and the universal witness of their consciences? No violation in practice can stifle the recognition of this inalienable right. But in circumstances of prolonged oppression, who will prevent those who are humiliated from succumbing to the temptation of what seems to them to be the solution of despair?

In spite of inevitable checks and the many obstacles placed in the way of such a vast body by its very complexity, it must be the honoured task of your Assembly to lend its voice to those who are not able to make themselves heard, to denounce, without care for ideologies, all oppression, whatever its source, and to ensure that cries of distress receive a hearing, just requests be taken into consideration, the weak be protected against the violence of the strong and the flame of hope thus be kept burning in the breast of the most humiliated section of mankind (Cf. *Discourse to the I.L.O., AAS*, vol. LXI, 1969, pp. 479 and 499). It is to the heart of each man—" for the real danger comes from man "—(*Speech to the United Nations, AAS*, vol. LVII, 1965, p. 885). that it is necessary to repeat untiringly: " What have you done to your brother? » (cf. *Gen.* 4, 10), that brother who, for so many be- livers throughout the world, is marked with the indelible im- print of the living God, Father of all men (cf. *Gen.* 1, 26).

For nations just as for men, to speak of rights involves the spelling out of duties. This is what we said to you here five years ago: your purpose is to understand one another, to go for- ward together, to reject the domination of some by others, to en- sure that never again will some fight against others but that all work for each other. This is a vast enterprise, truly worthy of uniting the good will of all in one immense and irrestible effort for that integral development of man and that interdependent de- velopment of mankind to which we have boldly invited them, in the name of a " full-bodied humanism ", in our Encyclical *Populorum progressio*, 42.

As the Second Development Decade dawns, who better than the United Nations Organization and its specialized agencies will be able to take up the challenge presented to all mankind? It is a question of ensuring that the nations, while preserving their identity and original way of life, shall agree at least on the means to be taken to support their common will to live, and, in the case of some of them, to assure their survival. Let us recognize this fact: the common good of the nations, be they large or small, demands that states should rise above their merely nationalistic interests, so that the most brillant schemes may not remain a dead letter and that well-ordered dialogue structures may not be dislocated by plans capable of putting all mankind in peril. Is it not surrendering mankind to an uncertain and perhaps catastro- phic future to continue to throw away on war budgets the most astonishing opportunities for progress that mankind has ever known? Has not the hour struck for reason to take stock of that terrifying future which so much wasted energy risks preparing for the world? " They will hammer their swords into ploughshares, their spears into sickles " (*Is.* 2, 4). May your untiring per- severance, placed at the service of all plans for reciprocal and controlled disarmament, ensure in our industrial age the realization of those words of this ancient prophet of the agricultural era. May it ensure that the resources thus made available are employed for scientific progress, for the harnessing of the immense resources of land and sea and for the sustenance of the ever growing numbers of the members of the human race. May the work of the living never be used against life; on the contrary, let it be used to feed that life and to make it truly human. With imagination, courage and perseverance, you will thus enable all peoples peacefully to take their rightful place in the concord of nations.

To move forward this new dynamism requires, it must be said, a radical change of attitude, in order to acquire " a new way of thinking about the pathways of history and the destinies of the world " (*Speech to the United Nations, AAS,* vol. LVII, 1965, p. 884). There is scarcely need to emphasize the fact that spiritual progress does not stem from material progress—to which however it alone gives true meaning—as the effect from its cause. Technical achievements, however admirable, do not of themselves bring moral advance. When science advances from success to success, its use places ever greater demands upon the conscience of the man who sets it to work. The modern world, troubled in its most dynamic and most youthful elements by the gravest question that has ever assailed it, the question of its survival, hesitates between fear and hope, and desperately searches for a meaning to give its arduous ascent, to make it genuinely human.

It is thus of capital importance that your Organization has recognized among the fundamental rights of the human person what our venerable predecessor John XXIII called man's right " of being able to worship God in accordance with the right dictates of his own conscience, and to profess his religion both in private and in public " (*Pacem in Terris, AAS,* vol. LV, 1963, p. 260): this is religious freedom, the complete value of which was fully affirmed by the Church in the Ecumenical Council ". But alas, this most sacred of all rights is for millions of men, innocent victims of intolerant religious descrimination, ridiculed with impunity (Declaration *Dignitatis humanae,* 2). And so we turn with confidence towards your distinguished Assembly, in the hope that it will be able to promote, in a domain so fundamental to the life of man, an attitude in conformity with the insuppressible voice of conscience, and to ostracize conduct incompatible with the dignity of mankind.

How great is the hope reposed in your Organization that it may achieve that community of free men which is the ideal of humanity; how great is the vigour it must show to bring such a programme to fulfilment. But, as a great contemporary thinker has so rightly observed, " The more difficult this immense task, the more it must attract men. People are not moved to act except for difficult things " (J. MARITAIN, *Christianisme et Démocratie*, Paris, Hartmann 1947, p. 71).

There exists in effect a common good of man, and it is up to your Organization, because of its dedication to universality, which is its reason for being, to promote it untiringly. In spite of permanent tensions and unceasingly recurring oppositions, the unity of the human family shows itself more and more in the very rejection of injustice and war and in the very hope of a world of fraternity where people and communities can freely develop themselves accordong to their material, intellectual and spiritual potentialities. In the midst of the worst confrontations there appears ever more strongly the aspiration towards a world where force —especially that of the strongest—no longer dominates with its blind and selfish weight, but where force is the exercise of a larger and higher responsibility at the service of a free and healthy cooperation among all human groups, in mutual respect for their own proper values.

Is not the task of the United Nations that of strengthening states against the temptations and helping peoples on the road towards a society where each one may be recognized, respected, and supported in his efforts to achieve spiritual growth towards a greater command of self in genuine freedom? Yes, the work of men and the conquests of human genius meet the design of God the Creator and Redeemer provided that his intelligence and his heart rise to the level of his science and his technology and are able to eliminate the forces of division, that is of dissolution, which are always at work in the human race.

So we renew our confidence that your Organization will be able to meeting the immense hope of a world fraternal community in which each one can live a really human life. As disciples of him who gave his life to reunite the scattered children of God, Christians for their part, buoyed up by the hope, which is drawn from the message of Christ, intend to take an energetic part in this great work in collaboration with all men of good will.

May the United Nations, in the unique position it occupies, apply itself resolutely to this task and go forward with confidence and courage. Upon this generous future in the service of all men and of all peoples, we invoke from our heart the blessing of the Almighty.

From the Vatican, 4th October 1970.

PAULUS PP. VI

MAN'S MORAL CONSCIENCE
MUST BE STRENGTHENED

One of the fundamental questions involving the whole human life, especially today, is the question concerning principles of action, criteria of the moral order, rules on what to do. The question is such a basic one that many questions arise during discussions of the problems. People ask: Is there an order, a rule, a law which governs, preordains, and obliges man to act in a certain manner? Is not man free? This question becomes so pressing and so oversimplified that it seems to turn into another: in the last analysis, is not man's real " law " moral indifference, that is to say, anarchy? These and similar questions are posed not only by the thinker who, by dint of destructive criticism, denies the absolute reasons of thought and being. He succeeds in demolishing the basis of every moral obligation and abolishes every so-called " repression "; he grants his disciples a licence to do everything and to do nothing, to live completely according to their instincts. These questions are also posed intuitively by not a small part of the new generation, and are expressed in practice by hatitual attitudes of contestation, rebellion, revolution. And all for one purpose: change, without having any clear idea of how, or why, with the net result: to enjoy oneself.

When Paul, then known as Saul, was thunderstruck at the gates of Damascus by the unexpected vision of Jesus in heaven, he asked two questions: " Who art thou, Lord? " and " What wilt thou have me do? " (*Ac.* 9, 3-5). We refer to this miraculous event as the conversion of Saint Paul, who was thus destined to convert the world to Christianity. Notice the two queries: they are concerned with the knowledge of Christ and a new line of action. Once we know Christ, an imperative need and a command to act arise, immediately and logically. A Christian is a man who acts in conformity with this new nature of his. He has a style of his own, he has a life-plan, and, if he be truly faithful to his Christian vocation, he also has the strength and the grace to carry it out.

The Council's Teachings

The Council summons us again to this renewal of human activity: the Christian moral order (cf. *Inter mirifica*, 6; *Gaudium et spes*, 87, etc.). We thus once more refer to the great teaching which the Church providentially expounded to our time. The formula which the Council gives is a simple one, but the reality to which it refers is quite complex. It involves a number of elements which belong to an organic plan of truth: truth about God, about man, about revelation and the story of salvation. More, it tells us particularly about the existence of a moral obligation, a responsibility, a duty, which commits the whole of life; it tells us about law and the authority which interprets and promulgates it, about liberty, about conscience, about natural law, about grace, about sin, about virtue, about merit, sanctions, and so on. This being so, our first impression is a discouraging one. This concept of Christian morality appears too complicated!

It is all a system, and today it is easy to be against " systems ". Especially in the practical field, there is a desire for simple ideas, clear formulas, elementary language. This develops into weighty volumes of law codes, full of prohibitions and precepts; it ends up in casuistry and legalism. But modern man wants a modern morality.

This is a quite widespread and important assertion. It is something to think about. It needs to be thought about because it is true that today we need to reflect about moral problems and strengthen our moral conscience. We ought to go back to first principles in order to acquire sure, working convictions. We should try to see how the progress made in the modern sciences—especially psychology, medicine and sociolgy—enter the framework of knowledge of man, what we call anthropology. The science of action, that is, morality, derives from that picture, and we have to see whether many ways of behaving and many forms of conduct are reasonable today or not. We should try to see how to apply constant moral principles to new needs and aspirations belonging to our time. The Council desires that studies in moral theology should be perfected (*Optatam totius*, 16).

Tendencies to simplification

And we ought to reflect that in this field of morality, whether theoretical or practical, there is a general tendency to simplify. It would be possible to make a study of the various aspects of this simplification. They often end up by mutilating the moral order. By so doing they go against that wise old adage: *bonum ex integra causa*: good results from the integrity of its component parts. A quite fashionable simplification today, for example, is one regarding the moral laws, both positive and natural. There are some who even challenge the existence of a stable and objective natural law. Progressive permissivenes is triumphant. But we shall have to look and see whether this permissiveness is based on reasonable acceptance of the modern trend. We have to ask whether it does not go against inviolable rules, and whether it produces good fruit—" by their fruits you shall know them ", Jesus said (*Mt.* 7, 20). Whether it eliminates the notion of good and evil, whether it does not deprive the human personality of that vigour which comes from self-mastery, respect for others, and the measure which is due to the requirements of life in society. We must finally ask whether it does not forget a fundamental criterion of progress. Progress does not always consist in abolishing working rules, but lies rather in discovering new rules. It is from observance of these that true progress and human perfection come, from rules which favour social justice and those which hinder certain forms of moral degeneration, such as war, polygamy, breaking one's given word, violating treaties, and so on. Permissiveness may degenerate into licentiousness.

The Higher Precept

Another simplification consists in maintaining that conduct is governed by the situation in which we find ourselves. You have all heard of this. Certainly, the circumstances, the situation, are an element which conditions the human act. But this act may not prescind from higher and objective moral norms, though the situation tells us whether and how they are applicable to the concrete case. Limiting the judgment which directs an action to the situation itself can mean justifying opportunism, inconsistency, cowardice. So forget about character, heroism and true moral law! Man's existence may not overlook his essence (cf. *The Holy Office's Intruction* of February 2nd, 1956, *AAS*, pp. 144-145; Pius XII, *Allocution of April 18th*, 1952, *Discorsi* XIV, p. 69 sq.). Not to mention that conscience, to which situation morality appeals, conscience, alone and unenlightened by transcendent principles, unguided by an authoritative magisterium, cannot be the infallible arbiter of the morality of an action. The conscience is an eye which needs light.

We might go on in this vein, but We prefer to conclude with a consoling response to that rightful desire to have the whole of the moral law summed up in a simple and comprehensive synthesis. That response was given by Christ himself. He was asked what is the first and highest precept of the whole divine law, which was expressed in the Mosaic Law and had developed into all the legal formalism of the time. You know the answer he gave. It was twofold, and it sums up " all the Law and the Prophets ". One part of it is vertical, as we say today, and it is the source of the other, which is horizontal. That law is: Love God and love your neighbour (*Mt*. 22, 36 sqq.). This is the synthesis, with all its implications. This is the Gospel. This is life: " Do this and thou shalt live " (*Lk*. 10, 28), we conclude with Jesus. With Our Apostolic Benediction.

SOLIDARITY AND PRAYER
FOR CATHOLIC MISSIONS

" Mission Day ", which will be celebrated on Sunday next, October 18th, brings back to our minds the great theme of the Catholic Missions.

There is a great deal of talk about the Missions, nearly everywhere; it seems a subject that has been exhausted, and is now reserved for oratorical and conventional propaganda. We are not of this opinion. The missionary fact always seems to Us so profound in the doctrine it presupposes and actualizes; so complex in the forms in which it is carried on; so dramatic in the activity which it invents and demands; so great in the Christian and human virtues on which it is nourished; so vast in the geographical and ethnical dimensions to which it is addressed; so modern on account of the human problems upon which it is grafted; so evangelical in the mysterious and concrete vision it gives us of Christ's presence; such a personal matter, because of the responsibility with which it invests each of us (cf. *Lumen gentium*, 17) and the whole Church (*ib.*, 1 and 5) that it seems to Us, this missionary fact, a subject of inexhaustible study, which we can never promote enough. For these and other reasons, We will speak to you about it briefly.

The conciliar Decree " Ad Gentes "

We will just ask you two questions. The first one: what do you know about the Catholic Missions? This question branches off into many other questions, which are not superfluous, or indiscreet, but intend to honour your conscience and your ecclesial formation. For example: have you ever read and considered the conciliar Decree on missionary activity, entitled *Ad Gentes*? It is a great document, which sums up the doctrine and experience

354

of the past, and which opens great visions on one of the essential characteristics of the Church. " During the Council—writes a distinguished living missionary, who took part in drawing up the Decree—the Church discovered, by actual experience, that she is missionary, in a way that she had never done before " (Fr. Schütte).

This entails moving on from the empirical, episodic, geographical and sociological knowledge of the Missions, of which we have all some idea, if only from the pictures and the adventures which so many fine missionary reviews continually present to our curious glance and our facile interest, moving on to an overall knowledge, to a panoramic vision both of the history of the Church and of her nature. Here missionary activity is seen to be, as it were, the *raison d'être*, the purpose of the Church herself. " This is, the Council says, a supremely great and sacred task of the Church " (*Ad Gentes*, 29).

And why is this so? Our inquiry now crosses the threshold of the mystery, and goes in search of the origin of the Missions in God's plan (*1 Cor.* 2, 7; *Ep.* 3, 9; *Rom.* 16, 25), carried out by Christ, for the salvation of mankind: Christ, the Son of God, was sent by the Father " to bring the good news " (*Lk.* 4, 18). Christ is the first and true missionary, the messenger and mediator of the new and supernatural relationship of men with the Father. He " came to seek and to save the lost " (*Lk.* 19, 10). He came as a man, visible, to our earth and part of our history. And after Him and from Him there followed another divine mission, invisible in itself, this time, a spiritual one, in the heart of men, that of the Holy Spirit, who had already " spoken through the Prophets ", and who was to animate the whole mystical Body of Christ. The mystery of the Blessed Trinity, revealed to us by these divine missions, is therefore at the source of the missionary economy of our salvation.

It is the Holy Spirit that gives rise to the apostolate, another mission, an exterior institution this time. This mission is a ministerial one, connected with the designation of the Apostles and with Pentecost. It is a mission that is intended to be the distributing channel of faith and grace in time and in the world, and to act as an instrument for building the Church (*Jn.* 20, 21; *Gal.* 4, 4; 4, 6; cf. CONGAR, *Esquisse du mystère de l'Eglise*, Cerf 1953; p. 129 f.; and the vol. *Ecclesia Spiritu Sancto edocta*,

Mélanges théol., hommage à Mgr. Philips; Duculot, Gembloux, Belgium 1970).

You see what an origin the missions have! A divine origin, evangelical, apostolic and theological (cf. *Ad Gentes*, 2-3), which shines out over the world with two great ideas: the universality of revelation, of redemption and of the Church, which is not in vain called catholic, that is universal (*Mk.* 16, 15; *Mt.* 28, 19); and the necessity of salvation by means of Christ (*Mk.* 16, 16; *Jn.* 3, 18; *Ac.* 16, 30-31). The missions are the epiphany of faith and charity, brought about by the ministry of the Church. A ministry that is closely bound to its original and authorized authenticity; but also a free ministry, in its choice and its apostolic course.

And the latter aspect, its free option, its dependence on human collaboration, interests us directly. It concerns the human history of evangelization, it documents its deeds of daring and its hesitations, it concerns its efficiency and its weakness, it describes its adventures, its undertakings, its sufferings, it presents to us its characters. They are the Missionaries, the heroes of the Gospel, the preachers, the martyrs, the saints for the expansion of the economy of salvation, the witnesses to the Church as the sacrament of salvation, the workers responsible for the first implantation of the Church and its early development, the heralds of Christian civilizations, the prophets of supreme human destinies.

University of revelation

We believe that one of the reason why our people feel and love the cause of the missions is just this: they know intuitively that there the Gospel is born in men, there is the living Christ, there is the Church in her most genuine and generous attitude. It might be thought that the mission appeal to the people of ancient Christian tradition because of their exotic aspects, their adventurous stories, their unknown landscapes; in a word, because of their phenomenology which impresses the imagination, curiosity, and sentiment. But this attractive and entertaining figuration does not hold attention for itself, but at once introduces it into the understanding of missionary reality; a reality made sublime by the Christian announcement that shines through it and by the human sacrifice it makes evident.

October 14th, 1970

For a more brotherly humanity

Do you know the missions, we were asking? Perhaps they deserve (don't they?) to be better known! If only because they represent one of the greatest, most persevering, most interesting, most free and gratuitous efforts to make of men, scattered, divided or founded on temporal civilizations, a truer, more brotherly, Christian humanity, straining towards hopes that go beyond time. The missions should be better known!

And we have another question to ask you, beloved sons and brothers: what are you doing for the Catholic missions? For this colossal and unarmed enterprise of the offering of Christ to the world which still does not know him? For this heroic tension of the Church bearing the faith and peace all over the earth? Are we not all jointly responsible for the spreading of the Gospel among all men? Do we not see who these men and women missionaries are, our brothers and sisters, giving their lives unstintingly out of pure love for Christ and for distant and unknown peoples? Shall we remain indifferent to these paradoxical examples? Shall we remain amused and selfish onlookers at this spectacle of superhuman realism and incomparable importance, when other causes, which may be good and interesting, but certainly do not deserve human and Christian passion as this does, find so many " fans "?

Answer: let us endeavour to feel solidarity with the cause of the missions. It is the cause of the Gospel, it is the cause of the easy and sure salvation of innumerable men, it is the cause of the promotion of the rights of man and of true civilization, temporal and moral, it is the cause of our very Christian conscience. That is what we must do in the first place. Missionaries must not feel they are alone and abandoned by the charity of their brothers who are already in normal possession of religious and civil life.

That is the first thing. The rest follows naturally: prayer, imitation, offerings.

And with these sentiments in Our heart, from this central point of the earthly Church, the tomb of the Apostle Peter, We send a brotherly thought and affectionate greeting to all valiant men and women missionaries, to all catechists, to all the Catholic communities of the newborn Church, together with Our Apostolic Blessing for you and for them.

PAUL VI CONDEMNS POLICE TORTURE, VIOLENCE AND TERRORISM

Faithful to the duty placed upon us by the Council, we are seeking to remind people of certain general ideas proclaimed by the Council teachings concerning human activity, in the certainty that we are linking our words on the one hand to the teaching of Christ, and on the other hand to the problems and needs of today's world. It is our duty to favour the formation of a way of thinking and behaving that will better correspond to the true moral progress of mankind and society, even if we express ourselves in these weekly meetings in a manner that is informal, popular, very simple and in no way exhaustive. But we wish you to know that the exercise of this humble ministry gives us an awareness of our apostolic responsibility. We feel constrained to express our judgment, not because of a direct and specific competence, which we do not claim to have in the questions proper to this world, but because of the connection that every human question has with the global concept of life and its supreme purpose, and also because of the critical gaze that from every side, including the profane, fixes itself upon us, in order to see if we really do have a universal function of doctrinal and moral magisterium. To the surprise of not a few there reappears, strangely vindicated, the saying of St. Paul: " The spiritual man judges all things " (*1 Cor.* 2, 15), a saying that found an echo, with the force proper to the Middle Ages, in the famous and disputed statement of Boniface VIII, who said that " ratione peccati ", that is, under the transcendent moral aspect, in relation to God, " every human thing is subject " to the power of the keys of Peter (cf. DENZINGER, *Enchiridion Symbol.* 873-874). Recently, for example, following a criminal abuse of power which occurred on a pagan island in the Pacific, a local newspaper asked, " What does the Pope say about it? ".

Torture not to be tolerated

These introductory words will convince you that it is our painful duty to call upon men of good will to reflect upon certain happenings in today's world, happenings which of themselves, through their extraordinary nature and their seriousness, and through the fact that they are repeated—which goes beyond the individual episode and seem to indicate an unexpected moral decline—outrage the sensibilities of all. What happenings? Cases of torture, for example. They are spoken of as a widespread epidemic in many parts of the world; their centre is said, perhaps not without certain political intentions, to be in a great country, which is undergoing the stresses and strains of economic and social development, and which has hitherto been honoured by all and considered free and wise. Now torture, that is, cruel and inhumane police methods, used to extort confessions from the lips of prisoners, is to be openly condemned. In the present age it is inadmissible, even though it be used for the purpose of exercising justice and defending public order. It is not to be tolerated, even if it is used by subordinate bodies without the mandate and permission of the higher authorities, upon which may fall the responsibility for such illegal and dishonouring oppression. It must be disowned and abolished. It offends not only the physical integrity but also the dignity of the human person. It degrades the sense and the majesty of justice. It arouses implacable and contagious feeling of hatred and revenge. Where it has been possible, we have deplored and sought to dissuade from recourse to such barbaric methods. The Church authorities and Catholic public opinion have raised their voice against such iniquitous abuse of power. These categorical affirmations are expressed as a basic principle, because we have no right to express ourselves on the authenticity of certain facts, especially since there have been denials and corrections, issued on several occasions by qualified bodies and special enquiries.

October 21st, 1970

" Theology of Revolution "

Likewise, these affirmations are not intended to justify individual or collective violation of public order, which may have given the guardians of that order a pretext for such excesses. Indeed we find here another category of misdeeds which the Christian sense of social life cannot admit as licit. We speak of violence and terrorism employed as normal means for the overthrow of the established order, when the latter is not itself invested with the open, violent and unjust pattern of an ubearable oppression which is not otherwise capable of being reformed. This mentality and these methods are also to be deplored. They cause unjust harm and provoke sentiments and methods that are destructive of community life, and they lead logically to the lessening and loss of liberty and of social love. The so-called theology of revolution is not in accord with the Gospel spirit. To see Christ, who reformed and renewed human conscience, as a radical subverter of temporal and juridical institutions is not an exact interpretation of the Bible texts, nor of the history of the Church and of the Saints. The Council spirit places man in relationship with the world in completely different terms (cf. *Gaudium et spes; Dignitatis humanae*, 11-12; also the rich bibliography on the question, e.g. LE GUILLON, in *Evangile et Révolution; La violenza, Settimana degli Intellettuali cattolici francesi*, 1967; *Violenza o non Violenza*, ed. Ekklesia; SCHUTZ, *Violence des pacifiques*, Taizé 1968; CULLMAN, *Jesus et les révolutionnaires*, 1970; *La tentazione della violenza*, in *Civiltà Cattolica*, May 1968; etc.).

Murderous repression

What shall we say of murderous repressions, not only against armed rebel formations, but with regard to the unarmed and innocent populace? What shall we say about heavy-handed, intimidating oppressions of whole countries? Everyone sees that warfare is continuing in the world. A judgment becomes all the more difficult and qualified the further it is removed from adequate knowledge by the complexity of the happenings and of their component elements. But here too condemnation, at least in principle,

360

cannot be passed over in silence. We are not for war, even if it can still alas today sometimes be forced on a country by supreme necessities of defence. We are for peace. We are for love. We continue to hope for the liberation of the world from every destructive, murderous conflict. It is always and increasingly our wish that the the aspirations for justice, right and progress will find peaceful, human and Christian ways within the international institutions founded or yet to be founded for that purpose.

Hijackings, kidnappings, drugs

The list of the things we deplore is not yet finished: aircraft hijackings, kidnappings, armed robbery, clandestine trading in drugs, and so many other criminal actions which fill our daily news would call for denunciation and moral condemnation by us. It is a comfort to us to sense the solidarity of public opinion in deploring these happenings. Would that public opinion were likewise of one mind in seeking out logically the causes of such aberrations! We are also sustained by the love we have even for the man who does wrong, and we keep in our heart an unquenchable trust in the restoration to humanity of every countenance that bears the reflection of the face of God. We believe, in fact, in the goodness and mercy of God and in the redemption of Christ.

To all of you we give our Apostolic Blessing.

PAUL VI'S HOMILY
AT CANONIZATION OF THE FORTY MARTYRS

> *On Sunday, October 25th, thousands of pilgrims from England and Wales were present in St. Peter's for the Canonization of the 40 Martyrs of England and Wales. After the Gospel the Holy Father delivered the following homily. He began in English, continued in Italian, and reverted into English for the conclusion.*

We extend our greeting first of all to our venerable brother Cardinal John Carmel Heenan, Archbishop of Westiminster, who is present here today. Together with him we greet our brother bishops of England and Wales and of all the other countries, those who have come here for this great ceremony. We extend our greeting also to the English priests, religious, students and faithful. We are filled with joy and happiness to have them near us today; for us they represent all English Catholics scattered throughout the world. Thanks to them we are celebrating Christ's glory made manifest in the holy Martyrs, whom we have just canonized, with such keen and brotherly feelings that we are able to experience in a very special spiritual way the mystery of the oneness and love of the Church. We offer you our greetings, brothers, sons and daughters; we thank you and we bless you.

While we are particularly pleased to note the presence of the official representative of the Archbishop of Canterbury, the Reverend Doctor Harry Smythe, we also extend our respectful and affectionate greeting to all the members of the Anglican Church who have likewise come to take part in this ceremony. We indeed feel very close to them, We would like them to read in our heart the humility, the gratitude and the hope with which we welcome them. We wish also to greet the authorities and those personages who have come here to represent Great Britain, and together with them all the other representatives of other countries and other religions. With all our heart we welcome them, as we celebrate the freedom and the fortitude of men who had, at the same time, spiritual faith and loyal respect for the sovereignty of civil society.

The solemn canonization of the 40 Martyrs of England and Wales that we have just carried out, gives us the welcome opportunity to speak to you, though briefly, on the significance of their existence, and on the importance that their lives and their deaths have had and continue to have not only for the Church in England and Wales but also for the Universal Church, for each of us and for every man of goodwill.

Our times need Saints, and particularly the example of those who gave the supreme testimony of their love for Christ and his Church. " Greater love has no man than this, that a man lay down his life for his friends " (*Jn.* 15, 13). These words of the Divine Master, which refer in the first instance to the sacrifice that He himself made on the cross, offering himself for the salvation of the whole of mankind, can also be applied to the great and elect host of martyrs of all times, from the first persecution of the new-born Church to those of our days, perhaps less overt, but equally cruel.

The Church of Christ was born from the sacrifice of Christ on the Cross and she continues to grow and develop in virtue of the heroic love of her most authentic sons and daughters. " Semen est sanguis Christianorum " (TERTULLIANUS, *Apologeticus*, 50; *PL* 1, 534). Like the shedding of Christ's blood, so the martyrs' oblation of their lives becomes in virtue of their union with Christ's Sacrifice a source of life and spiritual fertility for the Church and for the whole world. " By martyrdom a disciple is transformed into an image of his Master, who freely accepted death on behalf of the world's salvation; he perfects that image even to the shedding of blood. The Church, therefore, considers martyrdom as an exceptional gift and as the highest proof of love "—the Constitution *Lumen gentium*, 42, reminds us.

A great deal has been said and written about that mysterious being, man: about the resources of his intellect, capable of penetrating the secrets of the universe and of subjugating material things, utilizing them for his own purposes; about the grandeur of the human spirit, manifested in the admirable works of science and art; about his nobility and his weakness; his triumphs and his wretchedness. But that which characterizes man, that which is the most intimate element in his being and his personality, is the capacity to love, to love to the end, to give himself with that love that is stronger than death and extends into eternity.

The martyrdom of Christians is the most sublime expression and sign of this love, not only because the martyr remains faithful to his love to the extent of shedding his blood, but also because this sacrifice is performed out of the loftiest and noblest love that can exist, namely love for Him who created and redeemed us, who loves us as only He can love, and expects from us a response of total and unconditioned donation, that is, a love worthy of our God.

Sign of love

In its long and glorious history, Great Britain, island of saints, has given the world many men and women who loved God with this sincere, loyal love. For this reason we are glad to have been able today to number 40 other sons and daughters of this noble land among those that the Church publicly recognizes as Saints. By so doing she proposes them to the veneration of her faithful, in order that the latter may draw a vivid example from their lives.

To anyone who reads, moved and admiring, the records of their martyrdom, it is clear, we would like to say evident, that they are worthy emulators of the greatest martyrs of past times, owing to the great humility, fearlessness, simplicity and serenity with which they accepted their sentence and their death, nay, even more, with spiritual joy and an admirable and radiant charity.

It is just this deep, spiritual attitude that brackets together and unites these man and women, who in other respects differed from one another in everything that can distinguish such a large group of persons, that is, age and sex, culture and education, state and social condition of life, character and temperament, natural and supernatural dispositions, the external circumstances of their existence. Among the 40 Holy Martyrs we have, in fact, secular and regular priests, religious of various Orders and of different rank, we have laymen of noble birth and of humble origins, we have women who were married and mothers of a family. What unites all of them is that spiritual attitude of unshakable loyalty to the call of God which asked them, as a response of love, for for the sacrifice of their lives.

And the martyrs' response was unanimous. " I cannot forbear to tell you again that I die for God and religion's sake "—St. Philip Evans said—" and I think myself so happy that if I had never so many lives, I would willingly give them all for so good a cause ".

Loyalty and faithfulness

And, like many others, St. Philip Howard, Earl of Arundel, also asserted: " I am sorry I have only one life to offer for this noble cause ". And St. Margaret Clitherow expressed synthetically and with moving simplicity the meaning of her life and of her death: " I am dying for love of my Lord Jesus ". " What a little thing this is, if compared with the far crueller death that Christ suffered for me "—exclaimed St. Alban Roe.

Like many of their fellow-countrymen who died in similar circumstances, these forty men and women of England and Wales wanted to be, and were until the end, loyal to their country which they loved with all their heart. They wanted to be, and were, faithful subjects of the Crown which they all—without any exception—recognized up to the moment of their death as the legitimate authority in everything pertaining to civil and political matters. But this was the drama of the lives of these Martyrs, namely, that their honest and sincere loyalty to the civil authority came into conflict with loyalty to God and with what, according to the dictates of their conscience illuminated by Catholic faith they knew involved revealed truths, especially on the Holy Eucharist and on the inalienable prerogatives of Peter's successor who is, by God's will the universal Pastor of the Church of Christ.

Placed before the choice of remaining faithful to their faith and therefore dying for it, or saving their lives by denying their faith, they rallied to God without a moment's hesitation and with a really supernatural strength, and joyfully faced martyrdom. But so great was their spirit, so noble were their sentiments, so Christian was the inspiration of their lives that many of them died praying for their beloved country, for the King or for the Queen, and even for those who had been directly responsible for their capture, tortures and the ignominious circumstances of their atrocious death.

The last words and the last prayer of St. John Plessington were, in fact, as follows: " God bless the King and the royal family and grant His Majesty a prosperous reign here, and a crown of glory hereafter. God grant peace to the subjects and that they live and die in true faith, hope and charity ".

Industry and sacrifice

Thus St. Alban Roe, just before he was hanged, prayed: " Forgive me, my God, my countless offences, as I forgive my persecutors "; and, like him, St. Thomas Garnet who—after naming individually and forgiving those who had betrayed, arrested and condemned him—besought God: " May all attain salvation and with me reach Heaven ".

On reading the records of their martyrdom and meditating on the rich material collected so carefully on the historical circumstances of their lives and their martyrdom, we are struck above all by that which shines forth unmistakably and luminously in their lives. By its very nature, this is such as to transcend the centuries, and therefore is always fully relevant and, particularly in our days, of vital importance. We are referring to the fact that these heroic sons and daughters of England and Wales took their faith really seriously. This means that they accepted it as the only norm of life and of their whole conduct, a norm from which they received great serenity and deep spiritual joy. With a freshness and spontaneity not lacking in humour, that precious gift characteristic of their people, with an attachment to their duty averse from all ostentation, and with the sincerity typical of those who live with deep and well-rooted convictions, these Martyr Saints are a radiant example of the Christian who really lives his baptismal consecration, and grows in that life that was given to him in the sacrament of initiation and strengthened in that of confirmation. In this way religion is not a marginal factor for him, but the very essence of all his being and acting, so that divine charity becomes the inspiring, active and operating force of an existence straining towards the union of love with God and with all men of goodwill, which will find its fullness in eternity.

The Church and the world of today greatly need such men and women, from all walks of life, priests, religious and laymen. Only persons of such stature and such holiness will be able to change our tormented world and restore to it, together with peace, that spiritual and truly Christian orientation for which every man longs at heart—even sometimes without being aware of it—and which we all need so much.

May our gratitude rise to God for having, in his providential goodness, raised up these Holy Martyrs. Their industry and sacrifice have contributed to the preservation of the Catholic faith in England and Wales.

May the Lord continue to raise up in the Church laymen, religious and priests who are worthy emulators of these heralds of the faith.

May God grant, in his love, that centres of study, formation and prayer may flourish and develop today, too, to prepare, in today's conditions, holy priests and missionaries. Such were, in those times, the Venerable Colleges of Rome and Valladolid and the glorious Seminaries of St. Omer and Douai, from the ranks of which many of the Forty Martyrs came. One of them, a great personality, St. Edmund Campion, said: " This Church will never weaken as long as there are priests and pastors to attend to their flock ".

May the Lord grant us the grace that, in the times of growing religious indifferentism and theoretical and practical materialism, the example and intercession of the Forty Holy Martyrs may encourage us in faith and strengthen our authentic love for God, for his Church and for all men.

May the blood of these Martyrs be able to heal the great wound inflicted upon God's Church by reason of the separation of the Anglican Church from the Catholic Church. It it not one—these Martyrs say to us—the Church founded by Christ? Is not this their witness? Their devotion to their nation gives us the assurance that on the day when—God willing—the unity of the faith and of Christian life is restored, no offence will be inflicted on the honour and sovereignty of a great country such as England. There will be no seeking to lessen the legitimate prestige and the worthy patrimony of piety and usage proper to the Anglican Church when the Roman Catholic Church—this humble " Servant of the Servants of God "— is able to embrace her ever beloved Sister in the one authentic communion of the family of Christ: a communion of origin and of faith, a communion of priesthood and of rule, a communion of the Saints in the freedom and love of Spirit of Jesus.

Perhaps we shall have to go on, waiting and watching in prayer, in order to deserve that blessed day. But already we are strengthened in this hope by the heavenly friendship of the Forty Martyrs of England and Wales who are canonized today. Amen.

THE CHURCH
IN A CHANGING WORLD

W e propose to you a thought, the motif of which each of you can continually find within you, in your own consciousness. This thought concerns the great phenomenon, which we may call universal, of the changes that we witness and in which we ourselves participate, in the order of things.

Everything changes, everything evolves before our eyes, in the social, cultural, practical, economic fields; in every field, we can say. Ordinary life is caught up in these changes, which we meet with in the usual instruments of home and work, in the customs of the family and of the school, in relations with the world transformed by news belonging to everyone and coming from everywhere, in travelling, in behaviour, in ways of thinking, in business and in culture, even in religious life. Everything is moving, changing, evolving, everything is racing towards a future in which we are already living in our dreams. The Council too reminded us of this (cf. *Gaudium et spes*, 5, ss.).

The vanity of life

This is a fact of general order, which arouses in us many thoughts, each of which may become an outlook, philosophical or practical, of great interest, and based on unquestionable facts, and therefore rich in a respectable wisdom of its own. For example, is it not true that, if everything changes, then everything declines, everything passes, everything dies? Our times give us a magnificent and at the same time heart-rending vision of the precariousness of things and men; and therefore, after so much legitimate pride in the achievements of progress, do they not offer us a distressing lesson on the vanity of life?

Do you know that book of the Bible which is entitled " Ec-
clesiastes ", that is, the preacher? It is one of the Sapiental Books,
which literary tradition attributed to Solomon, but which was
actually written at a later date.   This book, without reaching
absolute pessimism, looks at wordly things with pitiless sincerity,
seeing them all to be disappointingly short-lived, beginning with
the famous words: " Vanity of vanities, all is vanity.   What does
man gain by all the toil at which he toils under the sun? " (*Eccl.*
1, 2-3).

And have you ever considered to what an extent reflection on
time and on history has penetrated modern thought, presenting
a variety of philosophical and scientific systems, by which our
culture is fascinated and tormented? Take, for example, evolution
historicism, relativism, and so on (cf. J. MOURAUX, *Le mystère du
temps*).   The importance attached in practice to this primary and
elusive value, time, emphasizes the appeal of modernity, fashion,
novelty, the cult of speed, for the man of today ... We live in time;
and time begets and devours all its children.   Time is money,
it is said.   Times conditions everything.   It is the master of everything.

Consistent and constructive renewal

So it seems, at least.   Hence an extreme conclusion, applied
to the human and religious field: to man, too, changes? So religious truths, the dogmas, change? So nothing permanent exists?
And those who support the claims of stability are living in a
dream-world? Tradition is old age? And so-called progressivism,
youth? Therefore a law handed down from the past, though
rational and " natural ", could be repealed and declared absolete?
And a faith, presenting us with dogmas formulated in the times
and language of ancient cultures, dogmas to be accepted as unquestionable truths, would be intolerable in our days? And
ecclesiastical structures, which count their age in centuries, could
be replaced by others of new and brilliant invention?

You see how many questions there are.   And you certainly see,
too, what repercussions they have in post-conciliar discussions.
Many of them make use of a word, the famous *aggiornamento*,
not as a principle of consistent and constructive renewal, but as

a destructive pickaxe, which has usurped the force of the free-dom " with which Christ has set us free " (*Gal.* 5, 1).

We do not claim to answer these aggressive questions now. We venture to submit them for your consideration merely to stimulate you to seek some adequate answers, if only to avoid the catastrophic consequences that would result from the conclusion that no norm and no doctrine is qualified to endure in time, and that any change, however radical it may be, may very well be adopted as a norm of progress, contestation or revolution. They are extremely complex questions, but not unanswerable.

The pilgrim Church victorious over time

We all realize, we believers particularly, that something re-mains in the succession of time, and must remain, if civilization is not to be transformed into chaos, and Christianity is not to lose all *raison d'être* in modern life.

Let two remarks suffice for the present. First: whence does human and social progress draw the strength to attract the conviction of men, especially its promoters and supporters, if not from an appeal to a demand for justice, for ideal human per-fection, inborn and higher than the law itself, a demand that we find inscribed in the very being of man, as a " natural law ", which must be given a juridical expression, binding on the whole community? Second: Can we ignore the Christ of the past, the historical Christ, Christ the teacher, if we wish to profess an authentic Christianity? Christianity is anchored to the Gospel, where we read, among the other words of Christ: " Heaven and earth will pass away, but my words will not pass away! " (*Mt.* 24, 35). And again, as if spanning the centuries with a bridge which is called tradition, the imperative and prophetic voice of Jesus rings out: " Do this in remembrance of me " ... " For as often as you eat this bread and drink the cup, you proclaim the Lord's death until he comes " (*1 Cor.* 11, 25-26). And what is this institution, which keeps alive the memory of the historical Christ to wait for him at the end of the future centuries, if not the Catholic Church, a pilgrim in time, but victorious over time?

These are profound thoughts, to restore stability and progress to our times. With our Apostolic Blessing.

PAUL VI TO PRIESTS OF ROME

On Wednesday afternoon, October 28th, the Holy Father went to the Lateran Basilica and addressed the first Convention of the Roman Presbytery, during a Liturgy of the Word. He spoke as follows.

We accepted with pleasure the invitation from Our venerated Cardinal Vicar to attend the conclusion of this pastoral Convention. We did so above all because of the opportunity to be among you Priests and Religious of Rome who are engaged in the care of souls, to meet you, and to feel and to show that I am your Bishop. What can more meet the desires and feelings of a Bishop than to be among his Priests, to know they are near him, and to let them know and feel that they are not without assistance from and living communion with their bishop?

This is the first time that it has been given to Us to meet and greet the Roman Clergy constituted in a Presbytery, in accordance with the recent Council prescriptions (cf. *Christus Dominus*, 28). We are sincerely delighted to see this new institution immediately engaged in matters of high and common interest. So We can express with Our presence and Our voice the pleasure We feel in this kind of initiative, which aims at attempting and promoting that greater fellowship of thought and word in the Clergy of a diocese, about which the Council teaches us.

Such exchange of studies and experiences, quickening of pastoral work, comparison and sharing of experiences, and construction of fresh programmes, in cooperation but also in emulation, are to Our mind some of the best of the Council's effects.

It is not an ostentation of empty words at the expense of real work. It is thoughtful, joint effort to get beyond daily routine, which becomes slothful and superficial with time, in order to infuse pastoral charity—the ministry—with that liveliness which it ought to have; to go back to the theological basis and requirements of the ministry itself and apply new norms trustingly, unanimously and punctiliously as issued by ecclesiastical authority; and to profit with apostolic talent from the margin of discretional liberty, left by law to the zeal of the shepherd of souls. Practice of the ministry may thus be adapted to the needs, aspirations and circumstances of differing places.

So, here is Our greeting, Our encouragement and Our blessing. Perhaps you will ask: Will you not say a few words about the theme of the Convention?

Theme pleases Pope

We hesitate to go to the quick of the specific theme of the meeting, which We understand, is: A New Mentality for Renewed Celebration of the Sacraments. We hesitate because of the breadth of this theme and the papers which you have heard. We think they have been marked by knowledge and competence, and We prefer to pay Our respects to them, rather than add anything further.

But if you wish Us to express a simple opinion about the title proposing the object of this Convention, then We will say that We like it. The concept of newness appears in it twice. This word cuts two ways, because it has two sides, one positive and the other negative. The positive side points to growth, vital development, and that characteristic sign of authentically Christian values, namely being always the same, always fruitful, like a tree which is always itself, and grows and buds and become fruitful every spring.

The negative side repudiates that which tradition offers us, even its intangible elements, and trusts in change as such, introducing heterogenous and deforming elements into the principles of the Church's authentic teaching and constitutional forms.

But in this case the recourse to the idea of newness is undoubtedly positive, legitimate and rightful. Right when it refers to our mentality which, we are told, should be new. It seems offensive at first sight to tell Churchmen that they ought to renew their state of mind, almost as if they were off the track or bent down under the weight of moral senility. And it also seems a dangerous thing to do, almost as if the expected renewal of mentality gave authorization to denounce the training one has received as invalid, and to abandon oneself to caprice in thought and experimentation.

No. The new mentality does not mean repudiation of training received, but it does mean stacking off the lazy habit of staying to facile but stale formulas in thought and conduct in order to avoid the effort needed to think about theological truths and external reality.

The density and profundity of the content of those theological truths are such that they should never leave at peace anyone who has made their contemplation, study and praise the light of his spiritual life. External reality means the world's condition and its pastoral needs, and we all know that that reality is undergoing profound and continuous change. New mentality means a wide-awake and open mind and obedience to Christ's precept concerning the obligation of vigilance. We are thinking of that capacity to stay young, about which Saint Paul spoke when he exhorted us " never to lose heart, for though our outer nature is wasting away, our inner nature is being renewed every day " (cf. *2 Cor.* 4, 16). He also tells us, even more precisely and almost as if referring to our own case, that we ought to be " renewed in the spirit of our minds " (cf. *Ep.* 4, 23).

We should be really very glad if the Roman Clergy were to take on a state of mind fitted for the time, following on the Council. The Council's importance and the responsibility it places upon us have perhaps not yet been fully grasped. It is not a question of recklessly throwing away the heritage of good ideas and local usages which we have received through our upbringing and education. It is not a question of accepting ideas and innovations of outside origin and doubtful tendencies, with our eyes shut and servile assent in our minds. Rather is it a question of drawing new, authentic spirituality from our own Roman-ness, a spirituality in which faith—with its certainty and its call to perennial meditation—and charity—with its urgency and universality—may infuse in the sacerdotal soul, the soul of the Priest, especially the one with care of souls, with a way of thinking, a mentality which we may describe as characteristic, because shaped " on the model and from the root of the Catholic Church ", as Saint Cyprian says (*Ep.* 48, 3). And that Catholic Church is precisely this Roman Church, upon which there is stamped mystically and historically a divine plan. Far from arousing pride and vanity, commonplace egoisms and earthly interests, that plan ought to make us who belong to the Roman Clergy more aware of our duty to give example and service, and have zeal and incomparable love for Christ the Lord and his Church. Yes, let us see whether we can endow with a deep interior spirituality this state in life of ours, which grafts us into the mystery of Catholic Rome.

Theological consistency

Once we are persuaded of this, we can easily reflect on the other innovation proposed by the theme of your convention, that of the new Pastorate of the Sacraments. The renewal is here chiefly derived from liturgical reform. You know what that is. But, apart from the purely ritual aspect, two other aspects contribute to this renewal: one concerns theological consistency, the other pastoral fruitfulness. Theological rethinking is clearly desirable, indeed necessary, above all because of the concept of Sacrament itself, which is a divine action accomplished through a human action; the former is the principal cause of grace, the latter is its instrument and condition (Cr. A. Ciappi, O.P., *De sacramentis in communi*, Berruti 1957).

This mysterious meeting of God's transcendent activity with man's ministerial activity deserves to be continually meditated upon and regarded with ever fresh wonder and constantly lively feeling. Its existential character and the fact that it is aways being repeated demand an ever watchful attention, and an attitude of ever new discovery, otherwise the sacramental action will be debased into an exterior and almost superstitious formalism. Secondly, this doctrinal reflection is demanded by the nature of the sacrament, for we know that a sacrament is a symbol, a sign of an intervention and of efficacious conferment of divine grace. A sign is a language. This means that through the element perceptible to the senses the sacrament presents the theme chosen by Christ, that of inexhaustible meditation, leading to a meeting with a divine thought by means of which Christ desires to make us understand something of the mystery to which he wishes to associate us.

So this means that in regard to sacramental life our mentality ought to be one of continual effort to enter into the meaning of the sacramental symbol. Take baptism, for example. St. Paul exhorts us to pass from the exterior experience of the sensible sign to the understanding of its meaning, which is actualized in a specific conferring of grace, that is of the mysterious divine Life, into our humble human life. " Do you not know ", he asked, " that as many of us as were baptized into Jesus Christ were baptized into his death? Therefore we are buried with him through baptism into death, so that, just as Christ was raised up from the dead by the glory of the Father, so we also should walk in newness of life " (*Rom.* 6, 3-4).

What thoughts about the deep and stupendous supernatural truths are aroused in us by the Eucharistic symbol of bread and wine! The chief of such truths is the unity of the mystical Body (S. TH. 73, 3). To what thoughts of fullness of love does matrimony stir us, since it has been made the sign of the charity which links Christ and the Church for which he immolated himself (*Ep.* 5, 25)! And so on.

This means that the new mentality with which we ought to celebrate the Sacraments, consists in an extremely worthy manner of celebration, one in which the minister's reverent and happy faith should shine through (is it always so in practice?). Apart from that, it consists in appropriate instruction for each Sacrament. It may be said that in our usual religious practice and habits, only First Communion receives such care.

Renewed pastoral work

Renewed pastoral efforts should therefore be directed towards applying much more careful methods to preparation for the other Sacraments also. Sacramental pedagogy needs to be more developed in pastoral work. The efficacious cause of grace is first and above all God working in the sacramental act itself (*ex opere operato*, as the theologians say), but the instrumental and conditioning cause of this mysterious divine action depends on man (*ex opere operantis*). It depends on the minister of the Sacrament and on the recipient, as well as on the ecclesial community, which participates in celebration and conferment of the Sacraments (cf. *Presbyterorum Ordinis*, 13).

So, what is required, that the pastorate of the Sacraments may be renewed? Better catechetical and spiritual preparation is desirable, more perfect ritual and community celebration by both ministers and faithful, and more conscientious adoption of the sacramental fact into our lives, for the Sacrament tends to have permanent moral effects. You know all this quite well.

But your Convention will have borne excellent fruit if your pastoral practice is built upon the sacramental ministry. This year you wish to concentrate attention on the Sacrament of Matrimony. What a wide new fields for the ministry the Christian family is, especially before it is actually founded, then in its religious beginnings and later development! The pastoral care of the family is today the most timely, the most demanding and the most producttive of lasting results. Of course it can require much delicate labour from the shepherd of souls, but it can also give greatest satisfaction and draw the greatest merits.

We wish this with all Our heart.

MISSIONARY ASPECT OF POPE'S TRIP

Have you heard about Our journey to the Far East? Perhaps you would like to know something about it. The purpose of this long trip is in accordance with the purposes of Our apostolic mission, and We should like to offer you a few ideas about the Church's life in this age of ours. In this way We hope to have your spiritual company and your prayers for success in Our apostolic travelling.

When is it going to be? God willing, it will begin at the end of this month, on November 26th, and We hope to be back in Rome on December 5th. And where is this journey going to take Us? The list of places has now been published. The first is Manila in the Philippine Islands, between the Chinese Sea and the Pacific Ocean. But We also have to halt for a few hours at Teheran (old Persia). Why are We going to Manila? Because a meeting of the Bishops of East Asia is to held there. The first purpose of Our journey is to meet the Episcopate of the Philippines and that of the countries of that immense part of the world. It is several years since We first received an invitation to visit that nation, the population of which is mainly Catholic. We owe it to that People that We have been invited to make this visit which it so much desires, and which has been asked for by means of courteous but insistent pressure from both the ecclesiastical and the civil authorities, and from so many pilgrims who have come to Rome and told Us of the expectation which calls Us there. We shall remain three days. They will be days crowded with meetings, with gatherings, and religious ceremonies, particularly a priestly ordination of numerous deacons coming from Asian countries. It will also be the occasion of the opening of a Catholic Radio Station, known as *Radio Veritas*, from which We hope to send out a special greeting to all East Asia. This is the pastoral stage.

November 4th, 1970

From Manila to Sydney

From Manila We shall make a rapid journey to one of the distant islands of Polynesia in the midst of the Pacific, in order to pay symbolic respect to the peoples scattered over that immense ocean, and in order to greet one of the most typical of Catholic missions in the independent State of Western Samoa in the Samoa archipelago. That is the missionary stage.

From there to Sydney in Australia. This will be a civic and apostolic stage of Our journey. We shall meet the Episcopate of that big continent, the Episcopates of New Zealand and of other countries in Oceania, and We shall meet the civil authorities and the Austrialian people. Three days. Besides the particularly religious purposes of our trip, there is a special one, which is to associate Ourself with bi-centenary celebrations going on this year in Australia, where Western civilization has accomplished magnificent development. There too are flourshing Catholic communities, many of them largely composed of immigrants from Europe.

From Sydney to Djakarta. A day full of meetings, with the Bishops, the civil authorities, the Catholic communities and the people of Indonesia. How could We fail to take this unrepeatable and desired opportunity?

From Djakarta a flight to Hong Kong; for a few hours only, but We hope they will be enough to give the great Chinese People without distinction testimony of the Catholic Church's and Our own personal appreciation and love.

Djakarta, Hong Kong, Colombo

Then, hastening on, to Colombo in Ceylon. A few hours there, but they too will be full of meetings and ceremonies. Finally, back to Rome, with God's aid, bringing in Our heart many memories, experiences and matters for Us to think about and for Our apostolic ministry.

What is the reason for this journey? We have just mentioned two important meetings of Bishops which are the principal motives of Our going there. We desire to be with Our Brothers in the Episcopate, among them and with them, in this post-conciliar period when Episcopal Conferences have grown up and been organized, and have begun to meet on the continental scale. That seemed to Us to be reason enough for undertaking this extraordinary expedition. Other reasons have since arisen, and have stimulated and encouraged Us. We are also certainly drawn by the desire to make personal contact with new countries and new communities, both national and ecclesial. But We must say at once that, like the other journeys which We have made, this one has nothing touristic about it and has no political purpose of any kind. We indeed desire to admire the panorama of peoples and landscapes whic hwill be presented to Our gaze, as We quickly pass by, obtaining glimpses as it were; and We desire to pay Our respects to civil authorities, who will receive Us with hospitable deference.

But the character of Our pilgrimage is meant to be exclusively apostolic, hence religious, ecclesial, spiritual and missionary: no external festivities, no worldly receptions, no official honours. We are going as a modest and hasty pilgrim. As is now Our custom, We shall have no lodging but in the residences of the local Papal representatives. We shall try to enjoy one sole thing: human and spiritual contact with as many as possible groups of churchmen, faithful, and representative citizens. We will seek some purposeful meetings with churchmen, the ordinary people, students, workers, the poor and suffering, humble families and children, and We shall have a word and a blessing for every meeting.

A Clarification

Who will be with Us? The names of those in Our official suite have been published. Six persons in all, and a few other trusted persons will accompany us for the practical tasks on the journey. We have to make a number of clarifications in this regard in order to dissipate unfounded rumours which have been spread in the last few days. We shall not have Our Cardinal Villot with Us. In order not to leave such delicate offices as are the Secretariat of State and the Council for the Public Affairs of the Church too long without responsible guidance and to be ready for every eventuality, he spontaneously offered to forgo the journey and to stay at his post. We owe him thanks for this exemplary decision to remain at this post where the work is not light.

But We shall be accompanied by Cardinal Agnelo Rossi, until lately the excellent and zealous Archbishop of São Paulo in Brazil. After Cardinal Agagianian had resigned, because of age and ill health, from his office as Prefect of the Sacred Congregation for the Evangelization of Peoples, We appointed Cardinal Rossi in his place. Suppositions have been made by some for consumption by public opinion, according to which Cardinal Rossi was removed from his archiepiscopal see because of positions which he might have taken up—favourable, according to some, the opposite, according to others—in regard to the Brazilian Authorities; or that he was called to Rome because of his particular attitudes favourable to or against certain tendencies in the Church's life; or again, in regard to certain facts in the Brazilian political situation.

We chose to have Cardinal Rossi at the head of that great Roman Congregation; in choosing him We had the counsel of experienced and prudent persons, and there was no hidden intention. That Roman Congregation looks after enormous and complex work for the Catholic Missions, and We desired to have as a collaborator near Us a Cardinal from a continent which is to such a great degree still a mission territory. He is a Cardinal qualified by his wisdom and zeal to direct that celebrated Sacred Congregation (once known as " Propaganda Fide ") both wisely and impartially.

Concluding thought

By coincidence, and perhaps not without some providential meaning, his summons to the Curia came just when Our visit to the Far East was about to begin. The Sacred Congregation for the Evangelization of the Peoples has many regions under its direct guidance out there, and the new Prefect of " Propaganda " will be able to obtain information and experiences which can be of the greatest usefulness in his subsequent service in the Curia.

But We cannot refrain from a general observation about this journey of Ours. It will bring Us into direct contact with peoples who are most distant from this Roman See. Because of this, the see of Rome stands out more clearly than before as the visible earthly centre of the Catholic Church. It is not only the geographical and legal centre, but also the symbolical and spiritual centre of what the Catholic Church is, in its deep and mysterious theological aspects and in those prodigious exterior " marks ". These give the world and the Church itself an excellent account of itself: the apologetic which says that is " one, holy, catholic and apostolic ", the true Church of Christ.

May He, Christ the Lord, be blessed in this fresh episode in the Church's centuries of history. And let honour be done to human genius, which dominates time and space through its most modern means of transport, and makes is possible for the humble itinerant apostle to take the announcement and the confirmation of the message of the Gospel to the ends of the earth.

Dearest Brethren and Children, come with Us in your prayers, and We shall have Our Apostolic Benediction for you too.

TOURISM CAN BECOME BASIS
OF FRATERNITY AMONG MEN

On November 7th the Holy Father received the delegates of the Episcopal Conferences for the Pastoral Care of Tourists which held its IV International Congress in Rome at the initiative of the " Pontifical Commission for the Spiritual Care of Migrants and Itinerants ". Among the delegates were 20 Archbishops and Bishops from 63 countries who were led by Cardinal Carlo Confalonieri, Prefect of the Sacred Congregation of Bishops and President of the Pontifical Commission, and by Archbishop Emanuele Clarizio, Pro-President. Also present were Mons. Giuseppe Zagon, Secretary of the Commission, Father Arrighi O.P., Secretary of the Congress, and the representatives of three Patriarchates of the Oriental Churches. After an address of homage delivered by Cardinal Confalonieri, the Holy Father gave the following discourses.

Dear Friends and dear Sons,

We are very pleased to welcome this morning the delegates of the Episcopal Conferences for the pastoral care of itinerant people. Your symposium is situated within the framework of the " Pontifical Commission for the Spiritual Care of Migrants " which We have recently established in the Congregation for Bishops (Motu Proprio *Apostolicae caritatis* of March 19, 1970, *AAS*, vol. LXII, p. 193), to respond to a particular need of our times. We desired to set up this organism of collaboration in order to help solve the pastoral problems inherent in the ever increasing number of itinerant people without wishing to encroach upon the rights of the National Episcopal Conferences which are so earnestly striving to carry out the practical applications (see *ib.*, 2).

The truly international character of your group shows clearly the universality, the magnitude and the urgency of the problems posed by the movement of these hundreds of millions of tourists who travel from one region, country or continent to another for reasons of recreation, education or business. Your task is to study in common all the facts of this social phenomenon of tourism, to examine its repercussions on the tourist and on those who receive them, and to work together so that the inventive zeal of pastors may deliberately find new opportunities to spread the word of God.

Need to adapt structures

Many changes are to be expected, especially in regions undergoing development and which experience the influx of tourists. The risk of abandoning fine traditions, the irregular conditions of work, and the shocking contrasts are tests for the tourists and for the people who receive them, but they can also help provide the means for new opportunities, social advancement, fraternal dialogue, mutual understanding and openness to other civilizations and cultures. Let us have enough creative imagination, apostolic daring and hope to face this phenomenon of tourism so that, with the grace of God, these ever more complex and important migrations may become the basis for a new fraternity among men and enlarge the witness to the Gospel throughout the world.

We must adapt the present pastoral structures to this dynamism of modern life. The Instruction of the Congregation for Bishops on the spiritual care of migrants (August 22, 1969, *AAS*, vol. LXI, p. 614) had underlined the initial responsibility of the Churches who welcome tourists, but these Churches will not be able to respond to the ever growing and diversified needs of mass tourism: convenient places of worship, more extensive and specialized collaboration. The Church is present in these masses on the move. All Christian communities therefore should be concerned.

In a practical way, many pastoral possibilities are open to us: a clergy prepared for this task should be placed at the disposition of migrants, at least during the high season of tourism; convenient places of worship ought to be set up; the welcome extended to tourists and the preaching should be such that Catholics feel at home anywhere in the world, being received as the children of God in a community of brothers. Furthermore, we should pro-

mote centres for meetings, exchange, dialogue and activities that
are both fruitful and restful for leisure hours. The Christian laity
ought to be assured of a solid personal formation so that they
may be witnesses and " journeying heralds of Christ " (*Apostolicam Actuositatem*, 14), according to one of the themes of your symposium. We ought to promote the responsibility of Catholic
action movements in which the Church militant would have much
to do for the spiritual animation of tourist centres. Particular
attention should be given to what could be called religious
tourism, visits to shrines which could and should be the providential occasion for discovering the Church through her rich artistic
heritage acquired in the course of her two thousand years of
history.

All this reveals the unlimited field open to the zeal of pastors.
It pertains to you to consider the initiatives to be taken and supported, to pool your experiences and suggestions, to alert your
respective countries to these grave problems, and to act in concert
on the major aspects of a common pastoral activity. No doubt it
will take a long time to implement all this, many difficulties will
arise and your means will be limited. But like the Apostle, " the
love of Christ urges us on " (*2 Cor.* 5, 14) and impels us to
announce the Good News of the Gospel in all avenues of the
apostolate, leaving no group like sheep without a shepherd (see *Mt.*
9, 36). With these sentiments We assure you of Our paternal
encouragement and heartily impart to you a special Apostolic
Blessing.

OUR JOURNEY IS AN APOSTOLIC WITNESS

E ver since Our forthcoming journey to the Far East was announced, the question is being asked on all sides: Why this journey? So many suppositions are being made, and some of them aimed at depriving the journey of all real importance. It is suggested that it is just a tourist trip, a journey to gather information, a concession to the modern taste for travelling and moving around, a pretext for propaganda, and so on. Other speculations attribute to the journey hidden motives, polemical or political, or interests of all kinds, diplomatic influences both active and passive, or an intention to serve certain ideological and social movements, and so forth.

Certainly the Pope does not travel without having special and important reasons. He has neither the time, the means or the strength for making such trips just the sake of diversion or rest. There must be some good reason, and the fact that other journeys have been made is not sufficient reason for making another—and such a long and complicated one at that. So, why? Before We took this decision We Ourself put the same question to Our own conscience: Why? Is this journey necessary. Isn't it enough to exercise the apostolic ministry from the See of Rome? Is not this a useless complication which former popes avoided?

A Mission to Travel

The anwers, the first reply, which We are confiding to you today, arose from Our very apostolic consciousness. What does apostle mean? It means one who has been sent, an envoy, an ambassador, a messenger. This is the original meaning of the word, and it has since taken on a much fuller meaning in concrete and historical reality. In the Gospel it took the place of the term chosen disciple (cf. *Lk.* 6, 13), and acquired other functions and meanings, such as witness (*Ac.* 1, 8; 2, 32; 5, 32; 10, 39), teacher (cf. *Mt.* 28, 19-20), minister of the faith (*1 Cor.* 3, 5), one vested with liturgical powers (*1 Cor.* 4, 1), the office of pastor (*Jn.* 21, 15; *1 Pt.* 5, 2), and of bishops (*Ac.* 20, 28).

So we can say that the apostolic office includes that of a travelling mission aimed at expanding and consolidating the Church (cf. *Ac.* 15, 41; 16, 4). But that mission does not exhaust all the many-sided fullness of the apostolic office. Hence the title of apostle may refer to three distinct things: investiture of persons, chosen by Christ and whom he himself called " apostles ", with his specific mandate; the spread of the Gospel and of the Church—what we call the apostolate; finally, the authentic derivation of the permanent work of the Spirit of Christ in the Church—what we call apostolicity.

But the fact remains that the apostle is in fact or by right a pilgrim on the paths of the world, which extend " to the ends of the earth " (*Ac.* 13, 47). It is also a fact that the economy of the Gospel (its proclamation to men, from man to man, and its expansion in the world and in time) is the work of the Holy Spirit. Yes, but not without collaboration from people who consecrate themselves to that great and arduous ministry. " We are God's fellow workers ", St. Paul said (*1 Cor.* 3, 9). St. Augustine confirmed this commenting on the same idea, expressed in the first epistle of the apostle St. John (*1 Jn.* 1, 3): " God willed to have men as his witnesses: *Deus testes habere voluit homines* " (*In Jn. Ep. ad Parthos*, 1, 2; *PL* 35, 1979).

This well-known doctrine has a compelling influence on Us for two other reason (not to mention for the moment other incidental and decisive ones). On the one hand, there is the technical possibility of making very long and rapid journeys without physical fatigue (St. Francis Xavier and missionaries of other times certainly did not have such attractive comfort). On the other hand, there is in the Church a new awareness of its missionary vocation. This was re-awakened by the Council by its presentation of a broad theological vision and its call to every faithful Christian to play a personal part in the Church's missionary activity. Possibility and duty have enkindled the will.

" Sollicitudo omnium ecclesiarum "

We do not wish to give any symbolic or prophetical importance to Our undertaking, a thing which is becoming easy and habitual for modern man. But We did not wish to forgo recourse to means now available for social communications and personal travel in order at least to give an example of loyalty to the apostolic concern which pertains to Our ministry—that *sollicitudo omnium ecclesiarum*, care for, love and duty towards all the Churches (*2 Cor.* 11, 28). Our journey is intended, insofar as it can, as an apostolic witness, an encouragement of missionary efforts, a proof of the supreme interest which the successor of the Roman Apostles and Martyrs, Peter and Paul, takes in attesting and spreading the Gospel of Christ in the world.

This is " the reason why ". Today many challenges, contestations, are afflicting the Church both within and without; strange voices are heard daring to call into question the necessity of putting so much effort into converting to the Catholic faith peoples and persons who are without the light of Christ; some presume to open up the ways of salvation by means of their own arbitrary charisms, without reference to the hierarchy and the ecclesial sign, deriving from the will of Christ. But We, with humble confidence, wish to testify to the need today for the apostolic Church, and to ask all its good children, and you, dearly beloved, to associate yourselves spiritually with Us in this singular and active invocation to the heavenly Father: Thy Kingdom come.

POPE PAUL'S " DAY OF PEACE " MESSAGE

L isten to Us. It is worthwhile. Yes, as usual, Our word is: peace. But it is the word of which the world is in need urgently in need, and that makes it new.

Let us open our eyes at the dawn of this new year, let us observe two orders of general facts and events, which affect the world, its peoples, families and individuals. These facts, it seems to Us, influence our destinies deeply and directly. Each one of us can be their horoscope.

Observe the first order. In truth it is not an order, but a disorder. For the facts which We assemble in this category all indicate a return to thoughts and needs which, it seemed, the tragic experience of war had, or should have, wiped away. At the end of the war everyone said: Enough! Enough of what? Of everything that gave rise to the human butchery and the appalling devastation. Immediately after the war, at the beginning of this generation, humanity became suddenly conscious that it was not enough to bury the dead, heal the wounds, rebuild what was destroyed and renew and improve the face of the earth; the cause of the conflagration we had undergone must be removed. The causes: this was the wise plan: to look for the causes and to eliminate them. The world breathed again. Indeed it seemed that a new era was about to open, the era of universal peace.[1] Everyone seemed ready to accept radical changes, in order to avoid new conflicts. For the political, social and economic structures a perspective of wonderful moral and social innovations was presented. There was talk of justice, of human rights, of betterment of the weak, of orderly co-existence, of organized collaboration, of world union. Great gestures were made: the victors,

---

[1] Cf. VERGIL, *Bucolicon* IV, 2: " magnus ab integro saeculorum nascitur ordo ".

for example, came to the aid of the vanquished. Great institutions were founded. The world began to organize itself on principles of effective union and common prosperity. The way to peace, as a normal and fundamental condition of life in the world, seemed to have been finally planned.

Wars still rage

And yet, what do we see after twenty-five wears of this material and idyllic progress? We see, first of all, that, here and there, wars still rage, and seem to be incurable plagues, which threaten to spread and grow worse. We see a continuation of, and in places an increase in, social, racial and religious discrimination. We see a return of the old mentality; man seems to entrench himself in situations of the past, first psychological and then political. The demons of yesterday rise up again. The supremacy of economic interest, with the all too easy exploitation of the weak, once more return; [2] so does class hatred [3] and class warfare, and thus is born again international and civil strife. The struggle for national prestige and political power is back; the inflexible conflict of opposing ambitions, and of the rooted and uncompromising prejudices of races and ideologies had returned; recourse is had to torture and terrorism; recourse is had to crime and violence, as a burning ideal, heedless of the conflagration that may ensue. Peace is again thought of as no more than a balance of mighty forces and of terrifying armaments. Once again people feel a a tremor of fear lest some catastrophic imprudence might lead to incredible and uncontrollable holocausts. What is happening? Where are we going? What has gone wrong? Or what has been lacking? Must we resign ourselves to doubting that man is capable of achieving a just and lasting peace, and to renouncing the task of implanting into the education of the new generations the hope for, and the mentality of, peace? [4]

---

[2] " ... en acceptant la primauté de valeurs matérielles, nous rendons la guerre inévitable ... ". ZUNDEL, *Le poème de la sainte liturgie*, p. 76.

[3] " ... ci sono poche cose che corrompono tanto un popolo, quanto l'abitudine dell'odio ". MANZONI, *Morale cattolica*, I, VII.

[4] On the evils of war, cf. SAINT AUGUSTINE, *De Civitate Dei* XIX, 7: " whoever tolerates them and thinks of them without anguish of spirit, is much more despicable in his belief that he has found satisfaction, for he has lost even his human feeling: *Et humanum perdidit sensum* ".

Progressive Peace

Fortunately another set of ideals and facts appears before our gaze; and it is that of progressive peace. For, notwithstanding everything, peace marches on. There are breaks in continuity, there are inconsistencies and difficulties. But all the same peace marches on and is establishing itself in the world with a certain invincibility. Every man is conscious of it: peace is necessary. It has in its favour the moral progress of humanity, which is indisputably directed towards unity. Unity and peace, when freedom unites them, are sisters. Peace benefits from the growing favour of public opinion, which is convinced of the absurdity of war pursued for its own sake and believed to be the only and unavoidable means of settling controversies among men. Peace avails itself on the ever closer network of human relations in the fields of culture, economics, commerce, sport and tourism. We must live together, and it is good to know each other, and to respect and help one another. A fundamental cohesion is taking shape in the world. This favours peace. International relations are increasingly developing, and they form the premise and also the guarantee of a certain concord.

The great international and supranational institutions are seen to be providential, at the source as well as at the perfection of humanity's peaceful coexistence.

Twofold question

Before this double picture, on which are superimposed phenomena contrary to the purpose closest to Our heart—that is, peace—it seems to Us that a single, ambivalent observation can be drawn. Let us ask a two-fold question, concerning two aspects of the ambiguous scene the world presents today:

— why, today, does peace recede?

— and why, today, does peace progress?

What is the element which emerges, in a negative sense or indeed in a positive sense, from this simple analysis? The element is always man. Man abased in the first case, man upraised in the second. Let us venture to use a word, which may itself appear ambiguous, but which, given the thought its deep significance demands, is ever splendid and supreme. The world is " love ": love for man, as the highest principle of the terrestrial order. Love and peace are correlative entities. Peace is a product of love: true love, human love.[5] Peace supposes a certain " identity of choice ": this is friendship. If we want peace, we must recognize the necessity of building it upon foundations more substantial than the non-existence of relations (relations among men are inevitable; they grow and become necessary), or the existence of relations of self-interest (these are precarious and often deceptive), or the web of purely cultural or fortuitous relations (these can be double-edged, for peace or for combat).

Founded on justice

True peace must be founded upon justice, upon a sense of the intangible dignity of man, upon the recognition of an abiding and happy equality between men, upon the basic principle of human brotherhood, that is, of the respect and love due to each man, because he is man. The victorious word springs forth: because he is a brother. My brother, our brother.

This consciousness of a universal human brotherhood is also happily developing in our world, at least in principle. Whoever works to educate the rising generations in the conviction that every man is our brother, is building from the foundation the edifice of peace. Whoever implants in public opinion the sentiments of human brotherhood without reserve, is preparing better days for the world. Whoever conceives of the protection of political interests without the incitement of hate and combat amongst men, as a logical and indispensable necessity of social life, is opening to human society the ever effective advancement of the common good. Whoever helps in discovering in every man, beyond his physical, ethnic and racial characteristics, the existence of a being equal to his own, is transforming the earth from an epicentre of division, antagonism, treachery and revenge into a field of vital work for civil collaboration. Where brotherhood amongst men is at root disregarded, peace is at root destroyed.

[5] Cf. *Summa Theologica*, II-IIae, 29, 3.

And yet peace is the mirror of the real, authentic, modern humanity, victorious over every anachronistic self-injury. Peace is the great concept extolling love amongst men who discover that they are brothers and decide to live as such.

Spirit of brotherhood

This then is Our message for the year 1971. It echoes, as a voice arising anew from the conscience of civil society, the Declaration of Human Rights: " All human beings are born free and equal in dignity and rights. They are endowed with reason and should act towards one another in a spirit of brotherhood ". This is the summit reached by the teaching of civilization. Let us not turn back. Let us not lose the treasures of this axiomatic conquest. Rather let us all give rational and resolute attention to this formula, this goal of human progress: " Every man is my brother ". This is peace, in being and in the making. And it avails for all!

For us, brothers of faith in Christ, it is especially valid. To the human wisdom, which, with great effort, has reached such an eminent and difficult conclusion, we believers can add a needed support—before all, the support of certitude (for doubts of all kinds may besiege it, weaken it, destroy it), that of our certitude in the divine word of Christ our Master, as inscribed in his Gospel: " You are all brothers " (*Mt.* 23, 8). We can offer encouragement as to the possibility of applying it (for, in practical reality, how difficult it is to be truly brothers to everybody!). We can do this by turning to another of Christ's fundamental teachings, as to a practical and standard rule of action: " Treat others as you would like them to treat you; that is the meaning of the Law and the Prophets " (*Mt.* 7, 12). How philosophers and saints have meditated on this maxim, which implants the universality of the precept of brotherhood into the individual and positive actions of social morality! And so, finally, we are in a position to provide the supreme argument: the concept of God's Fatherhood, among all men, proclaimed to all believers. A true brotherhood, among men, to be authentic and binding presupposes and demands a transcendental Fatherhood overflowing with metaphysical love, with supernatural charity. We can teach human brotherhood, that is peace, by teaching men to acknowledge, to love, to invoke our Father in heaven. We know that we shall find the way to God's altar barred if we have not first removed the obstacle to reconciliation with our brother man (*Mt.* 5, 23 ff., 6, 14-15). And we know that if we are Promoters of peace, then we can be called sons of God, and be among those whom the Gospel calls blessed (*Mt.* 5, 9).

What strength, what fruitfulness, what confidence the Christian religion bestows on the equation of brotherhood and peace. What joy it is for us to find, at the meeting point of these two terms, the crossing of the paths of our faith with those of the hopes of humanity and civilization.

14 November 1970.

PAULUS PP. VI

BROTHERLY LOVE AND SOLIDARITY CAN BRING ABOUT A NEW WORLD ...

Pope Paul gave the following address to delegates of more than 100 countries at the Rome-held Conference of the Food and Agriculture Organization, Monday, November 16th.

Mr. President,
Mr. Director General,
Gentlemen,

It is a profound joy for us—and also an honour—to bring in our turn to this rostrum the debt of gratitude and the cry of anguish and hope of millions of men and women, on this twenty-fifth anniversary of FAO. What a road has been travelled since that far-off day, the syxteenth of October 1945, when the representatives of forty-four States were invited to sign the act which set up the United Nations Organization for Food and Agriculture. Historians will point out the remarkable accomplishments of FAO, its progressive influence, its unflagging dynamism, the boldness of its views, the variety and breadth of its activities —since " it is above all else an institution orientated to action " [1]— the courage of its pioneers and finally the love of man and the universal sense of brotherhood which are the driving force behind its undertakings. They will point out also the extraordinary challenge thrust at you today: as your efforts increase and become organized, so the number of men multiplies, the misery of many is intensified and while a small number of people is sated with ever-increasing and ever-diversified resources, an ever greater part of mankind continues to hunger for bread and education and to thirst for dignity. The first decade of development—it would

---

[1] *FAO, son rôle, sa structure, ses activités*, Rome, Pub. FAO 1970.

be vain to conceal it—was marked by a certain disenchantment of public opinion in the face of frustrated hopes. Would it thus be the case, as with Sisyphus, to grow tired of rolling the heavy stone and give in to despair?

The Pope's and the Church's support for the aims of FAO

Such an idea could not be expressed in these precincts, in this meeting of persons who face the future with the aims of harnessing it for the service of mankind, notwithstanding the obstacles which may present themselves along the way. From the time of his first meeting with FAO, our predecessor Pope Pius XII, highly praised the deep insight " of your institution, specialized for food and agriculture, the magnanimity which characterizes its economy and application, and finally the wisdom and the circumspect method which determine its realization ".[2] His successor, good Pope John XXIII, would seize every opportunity to express to you his sincere admiration.[3] For our part, we first knew the International Institute of Agriculture in its modest quarters in Villa Borghese, before seeing FAO " traverse the entire road which has led it to the magnificent developments which it knows today ".[4] From that time on we have not ceased to follow with sympathetic interest your generous and disinterested initiatives —particularly the campaign against hunger—to render homage to your many activities and to call upon the Catholics of the entire world to collaborate generously therein, together with all men of good will.[5] Today we are happy to come to the headquarters of your Organization, situated within the very territory of our Diocese of Rome, and thus to return to FAO the many visits which the members of your working sessions have paid to the Vatican.

[2] Allocution of 21 February 1948, *Discorsi e Radiomessaggi di S. S. Pio XII*, vol. IX, Tipografia Poliglotta Vaticana, p. 461.

[3] Cf. in particular, Encyclical *Mater et Magistra*, 15 May 1961, AAS 53 (1961), p. 439.

[4] Allocution of 23 November 1963 at the 12th International Conference of FAO; *Insegnamenti di Paolo VI*, vol. I, Tip. Pol. Vaticana, 1963, p. 343; cf. *Documentation catholique*, vol. 61, Paris, 1964, col. 19.

[5] Cf., in particular, Encyclical *Populorum Progressio*, 26 March 1967, p. 46, AAS 59 (1967), p. 280.

How could the Church, solicitous for the true good of men, not be interested in an activity so clearly orientated as is yours to the alleviation of the greatest distress? How could the Church not be interested in your activity, which is engaged in a merciless combat to provide each man with enough to live—to live a truly human life, to be capable by his own work of guaranteeing the upkeep of his family and to be able through the exercise of his intelligence to share in the common goods of society by a commitment freely agreed to and by an activity voluntarily assumed?[6] It is at this higher level that the Church intends to give you her disinterested support for the great and complex work which you carry out. Your work consists in stimulating international action for providing each person with the nourishment he needs, both in amount and quality, and thus promoting the progressive lessening of hunger, undernourishment and malnutrition.[7] It means eliminating the cause of many epidemics, preparing trained labour and finding for it necessary employment so that economic growth may be accompanied by social progress without which there is no true development.

A courageous and complex undertaking. The environment

By what means do you intend to attain these goals, which we approve with all our heart? The absorbing study—as we can well describe it—of the many dossiers furnished us on your multiple activities have revealed to us the extraordinary and growing complexity of your efforts organized on a world-wide scale. A more intelligent utilization of basic physical resources, a better use of land and water, forest and oceans, an increased productivity from farming, livestock raising and fishing—all this certainly provides commodities in greater quantity and better quality. At the same time nutritional needs grow under the double pressure of a demographic increase—at times very swift—and of a consumption whose graphic curve follows the progression of income. The improvement of soil fertility, the intelligent

---

[6] Cf., for example, Rev. L.-J. LEBRET, O.P., *Développement - Révolution solidaire*, Paris, Editions Ouvrières 1967.
[7] Cf., for example, JOSUÉ DE CASTRO, *Le livre noir de la faim*, Paris, Ed. Ouvrières 1961.

use of irrigation, the redivision of plots of lands, the reclaiming of marshes, the effort at plant selection and the introduction of high-yield grain varieties almost seem to fulfil the vision of the ancient prophet of the agricultural era: " The desert shall rejoice and blossom ".[8] But the carrying out of these technical possibilities at an accelerated pace is not accomplished without dangerous repercussions on the balance of our natural surroundings. The progressive deterioration of that which has generally come to be called the environment risks provoking a veritable ecological catastrophe. Already we see the pollution of the air we breathe, the water we drink. We see the pollution of rivers, lakes, even oceans—to the point of inspiring fear of a true " biological death " in the near future, if energetic measures are not immediately and courageously taken and rigorously put into practice. It is a formidable prospect which you must diligently explore in order to save from destruction the fruit of millions of years of natural and human selection.[9] In brief, everything is bound up together. You must be attentive to the great consequences which follow on every intervention by man in the balance of nature, whose harmonious richness has been placed at his disposal in accordance with the living design of the Creator.[10]

The control of growth: a moral problem

These problems surely are familier to you. We have wished to evoke them briefly before you only in order to underline better the urgent need of a radical change in the conduct of humanity if it wishes to assure its survival. It took millennia for man to learn how to dominate, " to subdue the earth " according to the inspired word of the first book of the Bible.[11] The hour has now come for him to dominate his domination; this essential undertaking requires no less courage and dauntlessness than the conquest of nature itself. Will the prodigious progressive mastery of plant, animal and human life and the discovery of even the secrets of matter lead to anti-matter and to the explosion of death?

[8] Cf. *Is.* 35, 1.
[9] Cf. *Cérès*, Revue FAO, vol. 3, Rome, May-June 1970: *Environnement: les raisons de l'alarme.*
[10] Cf., for example, *Ps.* 64, 10-14.
[11] *Gen.* 1, 28.

November 16th, 1970

In this decisive moment of its history, humanity hesitates, uncertain before fear and hope. Who still does nor see this? The most extraordinary scientific progress, the most astounding technical feats and the most amazing economic growth, unless accompanied by authentic moral and social progress, will in the long run go against man.

An essential acquisition: international solidarity

Well-being is within our grasp but we must want to build it together: individuals for others, individuals with others and, never again, individuals against others. Over and above the magnificent achievements of these twenty-five years of activity is not the essential acquisition of your Organization this: the consciousness acquired by peoples and their governments of international solidarity? Are you not, sometimes without knowing it, the heirs of Christ's compassion before suffering humanity: " I feel sorry for all these people "? [12] Do you not constitute by your very existence an effective denial of the discredited thought of ancient wisdom " Homo homini lupus "? [13] No, man is not a wolf to his fellowman; he is his compassionate and loving brother. Never in the millennial course of the inspiring adventure of man have so many peoples, so many men and women, delegated such a number of representatives with the unique mission of aiding men—all men—to live and to survive. For us this is one of the greatest motives of hope amidst the many threats that weigh upon the world. Those who in the year 2000 will bear the responsibility of the destiny of the great human family are being born into a world which has discovered, more to its advantage than to its disadvantage, its solidarity in good as well as evil, its desire to unite in order not to perish and, in brief, to work together to build a common future for humanity ".[14] We hope that soon the circle of your family will widen and that the peoples that are now absent from this meeting may also sit down at your table so that finally all may contribute together to the same unselfish goal.

[12] *Mt.* 15, 32.
[13] PLAUTUS, *Asinaria*, II, 4, 88.
[14] Cf. appeal in Bombay, 3 December 1964, *AAS* 57 (1965), p. 132; repeated in *Populorum progressio*, 43, *AAS* 59 (1967), pp. 278-279.

Always at the service of man: the demographic problem

Certainly in the face of the difficulties to be overcome there is a great temptation to use one's authority to diminish the number of guests rather than to multiply the bread that is to be shared. We are not at all unaware o fthe opinions held in international organizations which extol planned birth control which, it is believed, will bring a radical solution to the problems of developing countries. We must repeat this today: the Church, on her part, in every domain of human action encourages scientific and technical progress, but always claiming respect for the inviolable right of the human person whose primary guarantors are the public authorities. Being firmly opposed to a birth control which according to the just expression of our venerable predecessor Pope John XXIII would be in accordance with " methods and means which are unworthy of man ",[15] the Church calls all those responsible to work with fearlessness and generosity for the development of the whole man and every man; this, among other effects will undoubtedly favour a rational control of birth by couples who are capable of freely assuming their destiny.[16] On your part, it is man whom you help and whom you support. And how would you ever be able to act against him, because you do not exist except through him and for him and since you cannot succeed without him?

Encouraging the free cooperation of all those involved

One of the best assured invariable principles of your action is that the finest technical achievements and the greatest economic progress cannot effect by themselves the development of a people. However necessary they may be, planning and money are not enough. Their indispensable contribution, like that of the technol-

---

[15] *Mater et Magistra*, AAS 53 (1961), p. 447.
[16] Cf. for example, J.-M. ALBERTINI, *Famine, contrôle des naissances et responsabilités internationales*, in *Economie et Humanisme*, 171, Lyons, 1966, pp. 1-10; P. PRAVERDAND, *Les pays nantis et la limitation des naissances dans le Tiers-Monde* in *Développement et Civilisation*, 39-40, Paris 1970, pp. 1-40.

ogy which they sponsor, would be sterile were it not made fruitful by men's confidence and their progressive conviction that
they can little by little get away from their miserable condition
through work made possible with means at their disposal. The
immediate evidence of results creates, as well as legitimate satisfaction, the decisive commitment to the great work of development. In the long run, if nothing can be done without man,
with him everything can be undertaken and accomplished; it is
truly the spirit and the heart that first achieve true victories. As
soon as those concerned have the will to better their lot, without
doubting their tbility to do it, they give themselves fully to this
great cause, with all the gifts of intellect and courage, all the
virtues of abnegation and self-sacrifice, all the efforts of perseverance and mutual help of which they are capable.

Presenting an ideal to youth: a fruitful earth for all men

The young in particular are the first to give themselves with
all their typical enthusiasm and earnestness to an undertaking
which fits their capabilities and their generosity. The youth of
the rich countries, bored because they lack an ideal worthy of
claiming their support and galvanizing their energies, the youth
of the poor countries, in despair at not being able to work in
a useful way, because they lack the proper knowledge and the
required professional training: there can be no doubt that the
combination of these young resources can change the future of the
world, if we adults can prepare them for this great task, show
them how to approach it and furnish them with the means to
give themselves to it with success. Is not this a plan that will
claim the support of all young people, rich and poor, transform
their outlooks, overcome enmity between nations, heal sterile
divisions and finally bring about a new world: a world that will
know brotherly love and solidarity in effort because it will be
united in the pursuit of the same ideal—a fruitful world for all
men?

Putting an end to scandals:
armaments, wastage, commercial malpractices

A lot of money would be necessary, certainly. But will the world not finally grasp that it is a question of its future? " When so many peoples are hungry, when so many families are destitute, when so many men remain steeped in ignorance, when so many schools, hospitals, and homes worthy of the name remain to be built, all public and private expenditures of a wasteful nature, all expenditures prompted by motives of national or personal ostentation, every debilitating armaments' race becomes an intolerable scandal. It is our duty to denounce it. Would that those in authority would listen to us, before it is too late! ".[17] How is it possible not to experience a deep feeling of distress in face of the tragic absurdity which impels men—and whole nations—to devote vast sums to armaments, to fostering centres of discord and rivaly, to carrying out undertakings of pure prestige, when the enormous sums thus wasted would have been enough, if better employed, to rescue numbers of countries from poverty? It is a sad fate which weighs so heavily upon the human race: the poor and the rich are for once treading the same path. Exaggerated nationalism, racism engendering hate, the lust for unlimited power, the unbridled thirst for domination: who will convince men to emerge from such aberrations? Who will be the first to break the circle of the armaments' race, ever more ruinous and vain? Who will have the good sense to put an end to such nonsensical practices as the brake sometimes applied to certain agricultural products because of badly organized transport and markets? Will man, who has learned how to harness the atom and conquer space, finally succeed in conquering his selfishness? UNCTAD—we like to hope—will succeed in putting an end to the scandal of rich countries buying at the lowest possible prices the produce of poor countries, and selling their own produce to these poor countries at a very high price. There is a whole economy, too often tainted by power, waste and fear, which must be transformed into an economy of service and brotherhood.

---

[17] *Populorum Progressio*, 53, AAS 59 (1967), p. 283.

Need for an effective world authority and international law

In view of the worldwide scale of the problem, there can be no fitting solution except on the international level. In saying this we do not in any way mean to belittle the many generous initiatives both private and public—suffice it to mention our indefatigable *Caritas Internationalis*—whose spontaneous appearance keeps alert and stimulates so much disinterested good will. Quite the contrary. But, as we said in New York, with the same conviction as our reverend predecessor John XXIII in his encyclical *Pacem in Terris*: " Who can fail to see the need and importance of thus gradually coming to the establishment of a world authority capable of taking effective action in the juridical and moral spheres? ".[18] This you have in fact understood, and you have undertaken this World Indicative Plan for agricultural development (PIM), which in intended to integrate in one worldwide view all the various factors in this sphere.[19] There is no doubt that freely entered into agreements between states will assist its being put into practice. Nor is there any doubt that the transition from selfish and exclusive profit-based economies to an economy which will voluntarily undertake the satisfaction of mutual needs calls for the adoption of an international law based on justice and equity, at the service of a truly human universal order.[20]

It is therefore necessary to be brave, bold, preserving and energetic. So many lands still lie fallow, so many possibilities remain unexplored, so many human resources are as yet untapped, so many young people stand idle, so much energy is squandered. Your task, your responsibility and your honour will be to make these latent resources bear fruit, to awaken their powers and to direct them to the service of the common good. Here lie the breadth, the vastness, the urgency and the necessity of your role. Among responsible statesmen, publicists, educators, scientists, civil servants—indeed among all men—you must untiringly pro-

---

[18] Address to the General Assembly of the UN, 4 October 1965, *AAS* 57, (1965), p. 880.

[19] Cf. *Une stratégie de l'abondance*, Collection FAO, L'alimentation mondiale, Cahier, 11, Rome 1970.

[20] Cf. M. F. Perroux, *De l'avarice des nations à une économie du genre humain*, in 39.e Semaine Sociale de France, *Richesse et Misère*, Paris, Gabalda 1952, pp. 195-212.

mote study and action on a world scale, while all believing men
add their prayers to " God who gives the growth ".[21]   Already
there are appearing important results, which yesterday were still
unhoped for, but which today are the guarantee of solid hope.
In these recent days who has not acclaimed as a symbol the
award of the Nobel Prize for Peace to Norman Borlaug, " the father
of the green revolution ", as he is called? How true it is that if all
men of good will throughout the world could be mobilized in
a concerted effort for peace, the tragic temptation to resort to
violence could then be overcome.

**Final appeal: brotherly love.
The suffering Christ**

More than one, perhaps, will shake his read at such prospects. Yet, permit us to say it plainly, on the human, moral and
spiritual level which is ours: no strategy of a commercial or ideological nature will soothe the complaint which rises from those
who are suffering from " undeserved misery ",[22] as the young,
whose " protest resounds like a signal of suffering and an appeal
for justice ".[23] If need and self-interest are powerful and often
decisive motives for men's actions, the present crisis can only be
surmounted by love. For, if " social justice makes us respect the
common good, social charity makes us love it ".[24] " Charity, that is
to say brotherly love, is the driving force behind all social
progress ".[25] Preoccupations of a military nature and motives of
the economic order will never permit the satisfaction of the grave
demands of the men of our time. There must be love for man:
man devotes himself to the service of his fellowmen, because he
recognizes him as his brother, as the son of the same Father; and
the Christian will add: as the image of the suffering Christ, whose

[21] *1 Cor.* 3, 6-7.
[22] *Populorum Progressio*, 9, AAS 59 (1967), p. 261.
[23] Speech made at Geneva, for the 50th anniversary of ILO, 10 June 1969,
AAS 61 (1969), p. 502.
[24] Rev. J. T. DELOS, O.P., *Le bien commun international*, in 24.e Semaine Sociale de France, *Le désordre de l'économie internationale et la pensée chrétienne*,
Paris, Gabalda 1932, p. 210.
[25] Cardinal P.-E. LÉGER, *Le pauvre Lazare est à notre porte*, Paris-Montreal,
SOS-Fides 1967, p. 13.

word moves man in his most hidden depths: " I was hungry and you gave me to eat ... ".[26] This word of love is ours. We present it to you as your most precious treasure, the lamp of charity whose burning fire consumes hearts, whose shining flame lights the way of brotherhood and guides our steps along the paths of justice and of peace.[27]

[26] *Mt.* 25, 35.
[27] *Ps.* 85, 11-14.

POPE PAUL EXPLAINS SPIRITUAL PURPOSE
OF TRIP TO FAR EAST

We once more wish to draw the attention of the veekly Audience to the journey which We are about to make to the Far East. Rather, We want to draw attention to the ecclesial character which it is intended to have and which is its deliberate purpose.

We will not repeat the itinerary or the programme of Our long pilgrimage, but will once more put the question of the reason why before you. Last week We said something about the motives for going, that is, the personal motives for this long excursion. This week We will say something about the motives which will bring Us there—the objective purpose: What are We going to do there?

Discovering the Church

If We tried to tell you about every day of the journey and its doings, We should have a lot to say. But you have heard something, and the newspapers and radio will have more to say about it all when the time comes. At present We wish to emphasize this event as something that ought to stimulate all minds to the discovery of the Church. Discovery of the Church? Surely it has been discovered! It is known, well known to all, whether faithful or not! Did not the Council give us an abundant description of it?

Yes, yes, but the Church is above all something that can never be known well enough. Let us not forget it is a mystery, that is to say a reality which, under its visible, institutional forms, presents itself as a sacrament—that is to say, a sign and instrument of a divine plan in the world. It will never be sufficiently well explored and known. It has been compared to all sorts of things; to a seed which grows and develops—which means a history, a becoming which is full of diverse events and adventures. It has been likened to a building going up according to a plan which, as regards us, has not been fully worked out yet in accordance with the intentions of the divine architect, Christ; it has been compared to a sheepfold, into which the Good Shepherd is leading and gathering his scattered flock (cf. *Jn.* 11, 52). And so on. The Church is the Mystical Body, the People of God, the Kingdom, the Family, the Bride ... (cf. *Lumen gentium*, 6).

The true and complete concept of the Church is so deep, complex, and involved with the destinies of individuals and the whole of mankind, that we shall never succeed in grasping it adequately. So we must be always exploring it.

Today, in fact, after the Council told us so much about the Church, we are experiencing a certain sense of conceptual dizziness. This is to say, if we do not take care to remain attached to what the Church taught us about herself in the hour of fullness of the Spirit and her own authority (cf. *Ac.* 15, 28), we may go off the rails. This largely comes from having a partial, isolated and subjective view of some aspect of the Church. We are aware of a number of happenings which are capable of giving rise to a one-sided, personal concept, darkening the true face of the Church, which shines with authenticity, beauty and mystery. This brings us back to that idea of having a duty to discover or rediscover the Church.

To take an example. It is fashionable to consider the Church in its sociological aspect, that is, those forms and phenomena which its life produces on the human, institutional, statistical, economic and historical planes. This is done with scientific exactitude and leads finally to the conviction that it is a description of the reality of the Church. But it does not always consider the causes which are certainly not all human and measureable. Anyone who dwells on this picture as if it were a sufficient means of studying the Church, ought sooner or later feel the need to rediscover the Church.

A similar observation may be made about the spiritualistic and charismatic concept of the Church which is professed nowadays by some, disciples of by gone Protestant schools of thought, as if this purely " pneumatic ", that is, spiritual value were the sole really interesting one, the one supported by Scripture and the one which constitutes the Church (cf. ALLO, *Première Epître aux Corinthiens*, pp. 87 sq.).

A rediscovery of the Church's true reality is to be recommended here too.

Will it be enough for this purpose to go to books of sound doctrine or go to listen to purely oral exposition of orthodox teaching?

This can certainly be enough to rectify the concept of the Church, if such rectification were needed; it would also be enough to deepen our always insufficient knowledge of it.

But We believe that the witness which Our journey shall provide is not superfluous to our modern need of an experimental, existential knowledge of the Church.

Active and Efficacious Collegiality

What sort of testimony? As We have said, evidence of its mysterious inner qualities and prodigious outer marks: the Church is one, holy, catholic and apostolic. Just think how these characteristic features of the Church can be brought out in stronger relief through this simple but singular episode in this history! Just think of the concrete forms which this event is going to take on! Our journey is chiefly meant to be a meeting, a human and spiritual meeting among persons who already know each other, who understand each other deeply and who love other. We can call it a meeting among Brethren. It not the Church a fraternity? (cf. *Rom.* 12, 10; *1 Th.* 4, 9; *1 Pet.* 2, 17; *1 Pet.* 5, 9, etc.). It will be a genuinely ecclesial joy to discover how many and what kind of Brethren We have in unknown, distant lands. It will be a meeting among Bishops, which will have priority over the other meetings. We shall once more discover how Collegiality is effective and working. It will be a meeting with spirited peoples such as those of the countries We are going to visit.

Will not this stupendous experience be a confirmation and a rediscovery of the Church, which We might say, is accomplishing an historical and spiritual prodigy of the victory over time, and doing it all by herself, as it were? Is it not a victory won through that characteristic effect of passing time, its transcience, not through revolution or death, but through the secret vitality which in characteristic of the Church and which makes its past a source of perennial rebirth and motion towards the future, through the living and active fidelity of her tradition?

We shall discover the footprints of heroic missionaries who first preached the Gospel there and planted the cross. We shall discover the original vocation of those Christianities, which now have the possibility of affirming themselves with the energies and values of their old cultures and give the ancient tree of the Church new leaves, new flowers, and new fruit—exactly what We wish to discover ...

Our discovery has nothing extraordinary or heroic about it—not like those discoveries which are so often made in the world of nature. But We think that, especially if shared by the faithful children of the whole Church, it will have a value of wonder, certainly, and hope, such as many bring the world a moment of light, comfort, and joy.

May God will that it shall be so for you too. With Our Apostolic Blessing.

POPE PAUL'S JOURNEY
AS PASTOR AND MISSIONARY

I t seems to Us that, on the eve of Our journey to the Far East, We can hardly speak to you of anything else, even though you may already know all about it, and such journeys are today technically simple (the wonders of modern progress!) common, and available to all.

It is no longer a novelty for the Pope to go off on a journey. The only novelty there may be is in the practical circumstances, the itinerary, the halts, the duration. But does the material side of it deserve so much attention? We for Our part do not wish to be overcome by fantasy and emotion, yet We cannot refrain from meditating even now on the meaning of these things, and the religious and human value of this undertaking, because of the fact that We are carrying it out in virtue of Our apostolic mission. We are going there as Pope, not as a private traveller, and not even as the chief figure in feasts and ceremonies. But We are going as Bishop, head of the Episcopal College, as Pastor and missionary, as a fisher of men (cf. *Mt.* 4, 19), that is, as a seeker of people of this world, in this time. We are going in order to have a series of meetings—which seem to Us to reflect scenes and words from the Gospel—to visit brethren and children, to get near people and institutions, to honour persons who deserve honour most: those with responsibility, the poor, the young, those who hunger for justice and peace, the suffering, the distant.

The Christian Plan of Salvation

We will confide to you, dearly beloved, that We are aware how Our initiative is taking on big dimensions—much bigger than Our very lowly person. In it We seem to descry as it were in relief, and in a measure difficult to calculate, the picture of the economy of God's kingdom, that is, the Church, which is accomplishing the Christian design for salvation almost without

knowing it. We might perhaps call this the drama of disproportions, for, when God enters upon the scene of our earthly and
historical humanity, what equilibrium of proportions can we find?
If man himself is a tangle of disproportions (cf. PASCAL, *Pensées*,
72), what will his stature be when he comes into comparison
and combination with God, even though God made himself man
in order to be with us at our level? (cf. *Bar.* 3, 38).

Just for convenience in thinking about it, we can image the
picture to be as follows: The scene is history, our own history,
our own time, today, in which we are looking for " the signs of
the times ". It is an uneven scene, for it is full of light and
darkness, and is devastated by the blasts of apparently irresistible
hurricanes: modern ideologies; yet there are also a few spring
breezes—the breath of the Spirit, who " blows where he will " (*Jn.*
3, 8). There are three actors on this stage: one, filling it completely, is the incalculable number of the people of today, growing,
rising, aware as never before, equipped with formidable tools that
give them power which has something prodigious, angelical,
diabolical, salutary and murderous about it. It makes them lords
of the earth and sky, and often slaves to themselves. They are
giants, yet they totter weakly and blindly, in agitation and fury,
in search of rest and order. They know obout everything, and
are sceptical about everything and their own destiny. They are
unbridled in the flesh and foolish in the mind ... One feature
seems to be common to all of them: they are unhappy, something
essential is lacking. Who can get near them? Who can instruct
them about the things that are necessary for life, when they
know so many superfluous things? Who can interpret them and,
through truth, resolve the doubts which are tormenting them?
Who can reveal to them the call which they have implicity in their
hearts? Thes crowds are an ocean—they are humanity. They hold
the stage, and are passing slowly but tumultuously across it. It
is mankind that makes history ...

The Apostle and the Word

But there enters another character. He is small, like an ant,
weak, unarmed, as tiny as a *quantité négligeable*. He tries to
make his way through the throng of peoples; he is trying to say

something. He becomes unyielding, and tries to make himself heard; he assumes the appearance of a teacher, a prophet. He assures them that what he is saying does not come from himself, but is a secret and infallible word, a word with a thousand echoes, resounding in the thousand languages of mankind. But what strikes us most in the comparison we make between this personage and his surroundings, is disproportion: in number, in quality, in power, in means, in topicality ... But that little man—you will have guessed who he is: the apostle, the messenger of the Gospel—is the witness. In this case it is the Pope, daring to pit himself against mankind. David and Goliath? Others will say Don Quixote ... A scene irrelevant outmoded, embarrassing, dangerous, ridiculous. This is what one hears said: and the appearances seem to justify these comments. But, when he manages to obtain a little silence and attract a listener, the little man speaks in a tone of certainty which is all his own. He utters inconceivable things, mysteries of an invisible world which is yet near us, the divine world, the Christian world, but mysteries ... Some laugh; others say to him: we will hear you another time, as they said to Saint Paul in the Aeropagus at Athens (*Ac.* 17, 32-33).

However, someone there has listened, and always listens, and has perceived that in that plaintive but assured voice there can be distinguished two singular and most sweet accents, which resound wonderfully in the depths of their spirits: one is the accent of truth and the other is the accent of love. They perceive that the word is the speaker's only in the sense that he is an instrument: it is a Word in its own right, the Word of Another. Where was that Other, and where is he now? He could not and cannot be other than a living Being, a Person who is essentially a Word, a Word made man, the Word of God. Where was and where is the Word of God made man? For it was and is now clear that he was and is now present! And this is the third actor on the world stage: the actor who stands above it all and fills the whole stage wherever he is welcomed, by a distinct yet not uncustomary way for human knowledge: the way of faith.

Oh Christ, is it You? You, the Truth? You, Love? Are you here, here with us? In this so much developed, so confused world? This world so corrupt and cruel when it decides to be content

412

with itself, and so innocent and so lovable when it is evangelically childlike? This world, so intelligent, but so profane, and often deliberately blind and deaf to Your signs? This world which You, fountain of Love, loved unto death; You, who revealed yourself in Love? You, salvation, You the joy of the human race. You are here with the Church, Your sacrament and instrument (cf. *Lumen gentium*, 1, 48; *Gaudium et spes*, 45). Does it proclaim You and convey you?

This is the perennial drama which develops over the centuries, and which finds in our journey an instant of indescribable reality.

Let us spiritually take part in it all together, dearest Brethren and children. With Our Apostolic Benediction.

DISCUSSES APOSTOLIC NATURE
OF THE CHURCH

*The Holy Father delivered the following ad-
dress to the Assembly of Asian Bishops in
Manila on 28 November.*

V enerable Brothers: Bishops of the Philippines, Bishops of
Asia. Greetings to you in Christ our Lord. Greetings to
you, Cardinal Rufino Santos, Archbishops of this Church of Manila, host to this extraordinary assembly. To each of you, brothers,
our greetings of faith and love. For your Churches, your countries,
our good wishes full of respect, friendship and peace.

Here we are together at last. This meeting makes us very
happy. It is something new, but it corresponds to the profound
nature of the Church. The Church has always been the same;
it is the family of those who believe in Christ, " composed of
every nation under heaven " (*Ac.* 2, 5). The scene at Pentecost
comes to mind and from our hearts there arises and finds expression on our lips the invocation to the Holy Spirit: Veni Sancte
Spiritus. To savor this moment with you, a moment that seems
to us historic and full of mystery, we have made the long journey
from Rome to Manila. We have come to meet you, dear brothers,
to know you better, to pay honour to this assembly of yours, to
encourage your work, to sustain your resolves. You are the
reason for our presence here today and at this moment the subject
of our words. On this our visit to your vast continent, you are,
moreover, the prime object of our love.

Even more worthy of our immediate attention than the novelty
and singularity of this meeting are, it seems to us, the theological
meaning that it manifests and the mystery that it makes present:
Christ is here. He is here through the reality, ever repeated: a
gathering in his name (*Mt.* 18-20). He is here through the faith
that makes him live in each one of us (*Ep.* 3, 17). He is here also
through the coming of our humble person, to whom, as a lowly

successor of Peter, is applied in a very special way the title of Vicar of Christ. And Christ our Lord is here through the apostolic ministry entrusted to each of us (cf. *Lumen Gentium*, 21), and through the collegial relationship that joins us together (*ib.* 22). We, the successors of the Apostles and the pastors of the Church of God, are invested with the power not only of representing Christ, but also of making present on earth and in time his voice (*Lk.* 10, 16) and his saving action (*Mt.* 28, 19). Christ is here.

The mark of Apostolicity

Let us take notice of this mysterious reality, with an act of faith both conscious and strong. It is true: we firmly believe that the Lord's promise, " Behold, I am with you always, to the close of the age " (*Mt.* 28, 20), is fulfilled now, at this moment of history, in a singular and marvellous way. Christ is with us.

How is this promise fulfilled at this moment? It is fulfilled in the countenance of the Church, herself the " sign and sacrament " of Christ (cf. *Lumen gentium*, 1; DE LUBAC, *Méditation sur l'Eglise*, 157 ff.). This countenance seems here to reflect with brilliant clarity the characteristic marks of the Church: one, holy, catholic and apostolic. This last mark, apostolicity, concerns us now in a particular way. Let us think about it for a moment.

All of us meeting here are successors of the Apostles. We have received from Christ himself the mandate, the power, his Spirit to carry on and to spread his mission. We are the heirs of the Apostles; we are Christ working in history and the world; we are the ministers of his pastoral government of the Church; we are the institutional organ, entrusted with dispensing the mysteries of God (cf. *1 Cor.* 4, 1; *2 Cor.* 6, 4; *Lumen gentium*, 20).

You know that the Council has clearly proclaimed this doctrine, which forms part of the divine and unchanging constitution of the Church. You know too there have sprung up many discussions about this doctrine; not all of them are useful for confirming and expounding it, as they should, but sometimes indeed more apt to confuse the doctrine and weaken it. This seems to us a suitable occasion for restating our firm support of the doctrine of the apostolic nature of the Church. We must realize that this doctrine establishes the permanence and the authenticity of the foundation of the Church by Christ; it marks the boundaries of ecclesial communion (cf. *Lk.* 10, 16; 11, 23; *Unitatis Redintegratio,* 2); it qualifies our persons with a sacramental character for the ministry that is entrusted to us; it makes us members of a single Apostolic College, under the leadership of Peter, establishing between us bonds of unity, love, peace, solidarity and collaboration; it vindicates the importance and the fidelity of tradition. Besides this it demonstrates the present vitality and ever-renewed youth of the Church; it explains its organic hierarchy and the vital capacity of the Mystical Body to function; it safeguards the existence and the exercise of the ministerial powers proper to the Christian priesthood, which shares in the single priesthood of Christ; it is the prime source, authorized and responsible, of missionary activity (cf. JOURNET, *L'Eglise du Verbe Incarné,* II, 1208, 2). The fact that it derives its authority not from " below " but from Christ does not mean that it sets up a privileged caste, but rather it makes of the Episcopate an organ for the benefit and service of all the individual churches, and of the entire Catholic Church, one which works from love, to the very point of sacrifice (cf. *Christus Dominus,* 6).

We remind you of all this, brothers, that your confidence may be great in Christ's assistance for you and your labours, for your sufferings and your hopes. You must be aware of your vocation, the fact of your having been chosen and of your responsibility. You must ever hear re-echoing in the depths of your souls the words of Saint Paul: " Be on your guard for yourselves and for all the flock of which the Holy Spirit has made you the overseers, to feed the Church of God which he bought with his own blood " (*Ac.* 20, 28). Be strong, be patient. You have before you an immense field for your apostolate; its very geographical vastness and the enormous multitudes that inhabit it would suffice to fire your apostolic zeal.

Here we should cast our glance over that human panorama in which your ministry must be exercised, although we know that you have already had experience in theory and in practice.

You have before you an immense field for your apostolate. It is difficult to speak of Asia as a whole since more than half of mankind lives here. One can however point to a certain network of common interests, a certain identity in the way of looking at life and a certain harmony of aspirations. Young in its peoples but rich in civilizations often thousands of years old, Asia is impelled as by an irresistible desire to occupy her rightful place in the world, and her influence is effectively increasing. The attraction to change and the desire for progress are present everywhere, and we see is them a fresh chance for the man of today.

" Our hope is great "

It is certainly true that—except for certain regions such as the Philippines—the Church, in spite of a history which is already long, is represented in Asia only by small minorities. Yet who can say how much heroic devotion, as well as faith in the men of Asia, has guided from the first beginnings the destiny of the missions of this continent? Who could ever fully describe the journeyings—often, even up to our own times, painful and tragic—of a missionary apostolate upheld by only one support, that coming from on high! There fore our hope is great, based as it is upon the command of the Lord to go to all nations, and upon his promises conveyed in the parables of the mustard seed and the leaven in the dough (*Lk.* 13, 18-20).

We shall limit ourself to indicating a few points which seem to us to be of capital importance for your present mission. Nothing of what we say is new to you; but we hope that you will take comfort in hearing your thoughts and intentions confirmed by our words.

The first thing that we would propose to you is this: let us make an effort to take as our guide the teaching of the recent Ecumenical Council. This teaching sums up and ratifies the heritage of Catholic tradition and opens the way for a renewal of the Church according to the needs and possibilities of modern times. This adherence to the teachings of the Council can establish a wonderful harmony throughout the Church, and this harmony can enhance the effectiveness of our pastoral activity and preserve us from the errors and weaknesses of the present time. This is especially true in one particular field, the field of faith. It seems to us that the defence and the spreading of the faith must take first place in our spiritual expression, and that it must be the prime object of our pastoral care. We bishops are the teachers of the faith. We are the preachers, the promoters of instruction in the faith. This is our main task and commitment. From this duty flows everything that we do to encourage study of the faith, catechesis, knowledge and meditation of the Word of God, Catholic teaching and Catholic schools, our press, the use of social communications and ecumenical dialogue. We cannot keep silent. We must not lose the truth and unity of the faith. We must strive to make the faith the fundamental driving principle of the Christian life of our communities.

A plea for Prayer

To this plea for the affirmation and the orthodoxy of the faith permit us to add a plea for prayer. In our day we are witnessing the decline of prayer, and you know the causes of this. Yet in favour of prayer we have two great—though different—resources: the first is the liturgical reform promoted by the recent Council. The Council has not only renewed the outward form of ritual, always according to certain traditional norms, but it has also given fresh life to the sources—doctrinal, sacramental, communal and pastoral—of the Church's prayer. We must take advantage of this providential teaching, if we wish prayer always to be the living and sincere expression of the faithful and always to retain in the Church a place of honour among religious values. The second resource of prayer is the natural inclination of the Asiatic spirit. We must honour and cultivate this deep and innate religious sense, which is the hallmark of the soul of the Eastern world. We must defend the spirituality proper to these peoples and ensure that their contact with materialistic modern secular civilization does not suffocate the inner aspirations of this spirituality. We are certain that the Church possesses the secret of true conversation with God; and you have the duty of opening the hearts of your people to the mysterious and true Word of God and to the intense filial expression of religious dialogue to which Christ authorized us and which the Spirit gives us the power to direct to the heavenly Father.

In this regard there arises another fundamental point, which concerns not only the languages of prayer and religious instruction but the genius and style of evangelization which, as the Council says, must "be adapted to the particular way of thinking and acting" of the peoples to which it is directed (cf. *Ad Gentes*, 16-18, etc.).

If, in the past, an insufficient knowledge of the hidden riches of the various civilizations hindered the spread of the Gospel message and gave the Church a certain foreign aspect, it is for you to show that the salvation brought by Jesus Christ is offered to all, without distinction of condition, without any privileged link with one race, continent or civilization. Far from wishing to stifle "the seeds of good in men's hearts and minds or in their own rites and culture", the Gospel heals, raises and perfects them for the glory of God (cf. *Lumen gentium*, 17; *Ad Gentes*, 22). Just as Jesus Christ shared the condition of those who were his own, so the man of Asia can be a Catholic and remain fully Asian. As we declared a year ago in Africa, if the Church must above all be Catholic, a pluralism is legitimate and even desirable in the manner of professing one common faith in the same Jesus Christ.

Respect for human person

And this, brothers, is also the foundation of your particular responsibility as you continue to proclaim Jesus Christ to the men of Asia. None better than an Asian can speak to an Asian. None better than he should know how to draw from the treasures of your rich cultures the elements for the building up in Asia of a Church which vill be one and catholic, founded upon the Apostles and yet different in its life styles. Should we not note, to the praise of your peoples and for the strengthening of your pastoral activity, the natural disposition of the peoples of the East for this religious mystery, which seems a prophetic sign of their call to Christian revelation?

Your individual churches would certainly lack an essential aspect of maturity if missionary vocations did not develop within them. It is for the bishops of Asia, for their priests, their religious brothers and sisters and their lay people engaged in the apostolate to be the first apostles of their Asian brothers, with the cooperation of missionaries from abroad, whose merits are so great, and whose efforts—God grant—will continue and grow, in the name of the unchangeable solidarity that is the duty of the whole Church in this sphere.

One of the aspects of the present adaptation of missionary activity, which we stressed in our last Message for Mission Sunday, is the importance it accords to the action of development. Is not the Gospel, which is the good news preached to the poor (*Lk*. 4, 18), the source of development? The Church, conscious of human aspirations towards dignity and well-being, pained by the unjust inequalities which still exist and often become more acute between nations and within nations, while respecting the competence of States, must offer her assistance for promoting " a fuller humanism ", that is to say, " the full development of the whole man and of every man " (*Populorum progressio*, 42). It is a logical consequence of our Christian faith. The hierarchy of the Philippines recalled it quite recently: " Christianity and democracy have one basic principle in common: the respect for the dignity and value of the human person, the respect of those means which man requires to make himself fully human " (9 July 1970). It is in the name of this principle that the Church must support as best she can the struggle against ignorance, hunger, disease and social insecurity. Taking her place in the vanguard of social action, she must bend all her efforts to support, encourage and push forward initiatives working for the full promotion of man. Since she is the witness of human conscience and of divine love for men, she must take up the defence of the poor and the weak against every form of social injustice.

An authentic and lasting peace

We know that much has been done by you in this regard, on the level both of study and action. We are convinced that in this way you are contributing to the maintaining of peace: " Christian faith, as well as the intimate link that should exist between the promotion of human rights and the socio-economic progress of man are the true basis for authentic and lasting peace ", as the Philippine episcopate likewise declared (1 May 1970).

As we utter that world " peace " how can we fail to raise up anew our heart to implore from the Lord that the peoples so painfully and for so long afflicted by war be able at last, in justice and in peace, to lead a happy and peaceful life!

Finally, we pray to Christ that he will grant that this journey may be for all the peoples of Asia a confirmation of the invitation offered them by him to accept his message, charged with truth and love, divinely conceived for them, for each of them, in his own language and in harmony with his own civilization, as it has been received and as it continues to be welcomed still by the people of the Philippines!

May Mary, Mother of the Word made flesh, mother of the Apostles, preside still over this Pentecost.

ASIA MUST NOT SUCCUMB
TO GODLESSNESS

*On 29th November the Holy Father went to
the Auditorium of " Radio Veritas ", the Catholic Broadcasting Station of Manila. There
he took part in the final session of the Symposium of the Bishops of Asia. Afterwards he
broadcasted over " Radio Veritas " his Message
to the Peoples of Asia.*

1. To you the countless millions of men and women, our brothers and sisters who live in Asia, this crossroads of cultures ancient and modern, and in a special manner to those among you who are our own children in Christ—the blessing of God, abiding peace and fraternity.

We are happy to address these words to you on the occasion of the inauguration of Radio Veritas, to which we desire to offer our encouragement for an ever more enlightened, generous and fruitful activity. We also express our appreciation to all those who have made possible the realization of this important work. It is our fervent wish that through it there may reach you the echo of the teachings of Christ, to raise your hearts to the God of love and truth. We hope that it will knit among you, its listeners, bonds of evangelical love, so that, made conscious of " the joys and hopes, the griefs and the anxieties of the men of this age, especially those who are poor " (*Gaudium et spes*, 1), you may together undertake the construction of a more just and more united society.

Brethren, this is the first time the head of the Catholic Church has come to this part of your continent, and providence has decreed that it should be in our humble person. We are grateful, for we regard Asia with love and reverence for the venerable antiquity and richness of its millennial culture. This immense land is the source of great civilizations, the birthplace of world religions, the treasure-house of ancient wisdom. We are now in a region where the cultural currents of the East and the more recent ones from the West have merged in mutual enrichment.

Hope for the future

2. As we address our words to you, we cannot, omit mention of a consideration which is as obvious as it is worthy of being kept constantly in mind. Your continent, stretching from the limits of ancient Europe and Africa to the Pacific and covering very nearly a third of the lands given to man for his home, is inhabited by more than a half of all mankind. This fact alone gives some idea of the magnitude of the problems that face your people. At the same time it shows the importance—we might say the weight—that Asia has for the present, and, ever more so, for the future of the entire world. This double aspect we regard with great interest, and with respect for those whose task it is to ensure with far-sighted wisdom, that development takes place with the necessary speed and care, not with clamorous and dangerous disorder, but in a beneficial and rational way. Our interest also goes hand in hand with our good wishes and with our willingness to contribute all that we can to this end. Our interest is mingled too with great hope.

No one more than ourself sincerely wishes to see you take your rightful place in the world and receive your legitimate share in the means and opportunities of economic and social welfare. No one more than ourself is aware of and deplores the situations of incomplete development or of unequal distribution that still exist among you, in the relations of one nation with another or among citizens of one and the same nation. No one more than ourself —because of justice and out of affection for your peoples, without distinction or preference except for the weakest and the most needy, through the very interest we have in peaceful coexistence and in good and fruitful cooperation within your countries, throughout your vast regions and also outside and beyond them— expresses the fervent wish that such situations may be eliminated at the earliest possible moment and as completely as possible, in conformity with the natural rights of individuals, of the various social groups and of all peoples.

We are aware that the difficulties are many, also in the technical sphere. These difficulties cannot be bypassed without worldwide cooperation and mutual and disinterested assistance. Happily the consciousness of this necessity is gaining ground and the realization of the duty of solidarity is growing among the nations of the world. We exhort you to act generously in this great movement. We exhort also those outside the continent of Asia who have the ability and the duty to do so, to offer ever more generous cooperation for the integral development of all.

To combat injustices

In like manner we feel the pressing duty to exhort all those in positions of responsibility to deal decisively with injustice in situations and in relations among various social groups, wherever such injustices are found. We exhort them further to give an ever stronger impulse, with open minds and hearts and with a firm hand, to the human betterment of all citizens, giving particular attention to the needs and rights of the most impoverished and abandoned among those citizens: from the workers who aspire to just wages to those who work on the land, where there is often a crying need for wise agrarian reform.

3. As we utter these exhortations we are sustained by a great hope. This hope, we would like you to know, is based not only on the help of God and on the responsible commitment of all of you— from the most humble to the most exalted in your respective functions—but also on awareness of the virtues and natural qualities which, in spite of the countless differences between one people and another, are common to all your peoples and of which certain ones constitute for those people a characteristic mark.

In fact, contemplating the past history of your nations, brethren, we are impressed most of all by sense of spiritual values dominating the thoughts of your sages and the lives of your vast multitudes. The discipline of your ascetics, the deep religious spirit of your peoples, your filial piety and attachment to the family, your veneration of ancestors—all of these point to the primacy of the spirit; all reveal your interminable quest for God, your hunger for the supernatural.

These characteristics are not of value for your spiritual life alone. Taken together, they not only do not constitute an obstacle to the attainment of that technical, economic and social progress to which your numberless peoples rightly aspire; but indeed, they offer a foundation of incalculable value to favour full progress in such a way so as not to sacrifice those deepest and most precious values which constitute man as the being that is directed by the influence of the spiritual—the master, at least potentially, of the cosmos and of its forces, and likewise the subduer of himself.

In the shade of materialism

Science and technology are proof of the conquest of the material order by the spirit of man. And yet it is under the shadow of these achievements that materialism has taken shelter. Wherever technology is introduced on a large scale, there materialism also tries to insinuate itself. With your traditional spiritual outlook, however, your sense of discipline and morality, and the integrity of your family life, you must be able to counter materialism and even help Western civilization to overcome the dangers that its very progress brings in its wake.

4. But materialism with all its negative consequences is only the outward symptom of a deeper malaise now afflicting large sections of the human family: a weakening of faith in God, or even the total loss of it. And when atheism turns militant and aggressive, as it has done, it becomes immensely more dangerous to individuals and nations. All the God-fearing peoples of your continent and their religious leaders have to face this common danger. Asia where great world religions were born must not succumb to godlessness. We pray, and invite you all to pray with us, that God's light and love may preserve your peoples from such a danger.

5. Here it is our duty to say a word about the presence and action of the Catholic Church in your midst. We do so all the more willingly from this land of the Philippines, in which the Catholic Church has for centuries been fully at home. The Church feels at home not only here but in all your nations. What she has to bring to you also, that is the message of Christ, is not imposed upon its hearers but rather proclaimed in open and friendly words. It is offered for your instruction and meditation, and it is not such as in any way to cancel out or lessen the cultural and spiritual values that constitute your priceless heritage.

Christ is light and truth and life. And we proclaim him to you as he appears to our unshakeable faith. We are obedient to his charge, his command: Go, preach to all nations the good, the happy news, instructing them in my teaching of love and life. This we do, brothers and life. This we do, brothers and sisters, with humble love for you, with deep respect for yourselves and for your ancient and venerable traditions.

To those still suffering from war

In fact, the Church, by virtue of her essential catholicity, cannot be alien to any country or people; she is bound to make herself native to every clime, culture and race. Wherever she is, she must strike her roots deep into the spiritual and cultural ground of the place and assimilate all that is of genuine value.

Our predecessors, the Second Vatican Council, and we ourself, have not only encouraged this movement but also furnished the necessary guidelines for it. Thus, while preserving the cultural excellence and individuality of each nation, the Catholic Church will be able to communicate what is of universal value in each of them to all the others, for their mutual enrichment.

Christ and his message certainly have a divine charm which the deeply religious East can appreciate. Your faith and love, overflowing into your daily life and activity, can make this message, and Christ himself, visible and acceptable to your countrymen as no preaching can do.

6. This mission of bringing Christ and his Church close to the men and women of Asia belongs not only to the hierarchy, the priests and the religious brothers and sisters, but to each one of you, our dear Catholic sons and daughters of the different nations which we are now addressing.

Together you make up the People of God. Together you must show forth Christ to others. In imitation of Jesus Christ who went about doing good (cf. *Ac.* 10, 39), Christians are the best friends of their fellowmen. Their faith must impel them to work for the sanctification of the world (cf. *Lumen gentium*, 31) and to take the lead in that indispensable movement of brotherly solidarity. It is this which must satisfy all men in their hunger for bread, employment, shelter and education; this movement must bring a response to men's yearnings for responsibility, freedom, justice, the moral virtues, and in a word, a " complete humanism " (*Populorum progressio*, 42).

7. We cannot bring our words to a close without directing a heartfelt and particularly affectionate greeting to those peoples of your continent who are still oppressed by the tragedy of war. Our heart is heavy at the thought of the thousands of victims of the conflicts now taking place, at the thought of the orphans and widows abandoned, of the homes and villages destroyed, at the thought of the hate which is spread abroad and which often explodes, even today, in acts of war and terrorism, affecting also many innocent and defenceless people.

Freedom for all

We have not ceased—nor shall we cease—in urgent appeals, both in public and in our meetings with leaders, that an unflagging search be carried out, with wise and persistent goodwill, for the means to suspend hostilities and to reach at last a just and honourable peace, which will ensure for all the peoples involved freedom from disturbance, liberty and the chance for a serene and fitting existence.

This appeal, this fervent plea, we wish solemnly to renew here and now. And to all those who are suffering, to all those who are seeking to alleviate their sufferings and to all those who are working for peace we send our most sincere good wishes.

8. At the same time we renew from our heart the expression of our profound sharing in the bitter grief that in these recent weeks has struck a great and dear land Pakistan which has been the victim of a natural disaster, the like of which probably does not exist in human memory.

9. Upon everyone, finally, upon all the peoples of Asia, upon their heads of state and rulers, whom we greet with respect, we invoke from on high wisdom and the will and sufficient strength to ensure the happy and rapid development of their respective nations throughout this entire continent. To the heads of the religions of Asia and to their faithful we express our esteem for the religious sense which they foster with such great concern for the well-being of their brothers. To our dear Catholic sons and daughters, whom we once more recall with paternal affection, we extend our good wishes and impart our Blessing.

EPISCOPAL CONFERENCE IN SIDNEY

Early in the morning of 1st December the Holy Father, accompanied by Cardinal Gilroy, boarded a motor launch near the Apostolic Delegation, and disembarked at a point near the Cathedral. There he attended a three-hour session of the joint Episcopal Conferences of Australia and Oceania, meeting in the crypt of the Cathedral, and delivered the following address.

We have come among you not only to talk to you, but also, and especially, to listen to you. And gladly we have listened to you, devoting our attention to the conclusions of your assembly. It will be, moreover, a pleasant duty for us to recall your discourses and reflect on your discussions and deliberations, storing up for ourself and for the whole Church your experience and wisdom, in relation both to the Church's doctrine and her pastoral guidance; and so we abstain now from commenting on the themes which you have dealt with in your meeting.

We do not, however, wish to deprive ourself of the pleasure, or release ourself from the duty, of saying a fraternal word to you on so exceptional and favourable an occasion. Thus we return to the theme of unity within the Church and the unity of the Church. This very encounter is a celebration of this external distinguishing mark of the Church of Christ; it likewise celebrates the internal mystical characteristic of the same Church of Christ, which he founded in unity, manifesting in a supremely clear way his wish " that they may be one " (*Jn.* 17, 11; 21-23).

Let us reflect together a moment on unity in the Church. We shall do well to consider how much theological thought was given to this theme down the centuries: from the unforgettable and prophetic words of the " Didachè " (cf. 9, 4; 10, 5), and of the letters of Saint Ignatius of Antioch (cf. *Philad* 4; *Ep.* 20, 2; *Smyrn* 1, 2; etc.), to the treatise of Saint Cyprian (*De Catholicae Ecclesiae Unitate*), to the thought of Saint Ambrose (cf. *Ep.* 11, 4; *PL* 16, 986), of

Saint Augustine especially, of Saint Leo, and to the great theologians of the Middle Ages (cf. S. Tн. 11, 8) and of the Renascence (cf. Cajetan, Bellarmine, Suarez etc.), and down to the modern writers (cf. J. Adam Moehler in particular, Newman, Scheeben, Perrone, Clérissac, Congar, Hamer, Cardinal Journet in his great synthesis on *l'Eglise du Verbe Incarné*), and finally to the post-conciliar theologians (cf., among the many, Philips, etc.). We must not forget the great encyclical " Mystici Corporis " of Pope Pius XII. And we must always keep before us the documents of the Second Vatican Council, in particular two constitutions *Lumen gentium* and *Gaudium et spes*, in which the Church's doctrinal awareness of herself and of her historical and concrete position in the modern world is expressed in an incomparable manner.

We permit ourself to remind you of this great cultural fact of the Church of today, on account of its first-rank importance for ecclesial life, and on account of the obligation springing from it for us bishops, witnesses of the faith and shepherds of the People of God—the obligation to take up a secure position on the teaching concerning the Church, and especially on her unity. It is her unity which must give to the Church's countenance her divinely—reflected radiance, the sign of her authenticity and her symbolic exemplarity also for the contemporary world which is orientated towards temporal unification in a peaceful civilization.

It is for you, venerable brothers, to accept this obvious recommendation and to pursue in depth a study so attractive, so vast, so complex as is that of our dearly loved Catholic Church, for which Christ shed his blood (cf. *Ep.* 5, 25).

It is for us, on the other hand, barely to touch on two aspects of this intimate communion of the Church within herself.

The first communion, the first unity, is that of faith.

Unity in faith is necessary and fundamental, as you know. On this demand there can be no compromise. No matter how different are the subjective conditions of the believer, we cannot admit uncertainty, doubt or ambiguity concerning the supreme gift, which Revelation has given us, about God the Father, the almighty, Creator of all things, the immanent Principle of all that exists, the transcendental and inexpressible Being, worthy of unlimited adoration and love on the part of us who have the indescribable good fortune to be raised from the level of creatures to that of children of God. Likewise we can have no hesitation about recognizing in Jesus Christ the Word made man, the Teacher of supreme truths about man's destinies, the sacrificed and risen Saviour of mankind, the head under whom everything is brought together (cf. *Ep.* 1, 10), and the one who by his Cross draws all men to himself (*Jn.* 12, 32) and makes of men who are faithful one mystical Body (cf. *Ep.* 4, 4). We can have no doubts about the Holy Spirit, who gives life and bears witness of himself within our hearts (cf. *Jn.* 15, 26; 16, 13; *Rom.* 8, 16; etc.), and who gives the Church qualified ministers for decisive witness on religious truths (cf. *2 Cor.* 10, 5-6). We cannot prescind from the great reality emanating from Christ, his continuation, his social and historical Body, visible and mystical, his Church, the sign and instrument for the salvation of mankind. In this regard we cannot forget the lapidary words of Saint Augustine: " The Christian has nothing to fear so much as being separated from the body of Christ " (In *Io. Tr.* 27, 6; *PL* 35, 1618). In a word, the Creed, our Creed, is for us inalienable. It is our riches. It is our life.

Human reality of Catholicism

With this security—for the confirming of which, as Peter's humble but authentic successor, we have been given special power by Christ the Lord (*Lk.* 22, 32)—we look at the human reality of Catholicism. By its very definition, it is for all men, for all races, for all nations, for all the earth.

How can Catholicism, so firm and so jealous about its unity, embrace all men, who are so different from each other? Does it perhaps demand absolute uniformity in all manifestations of life? Is there perhaps only one practical and historical way of interpreting the true and unique faith of Christ?

You know, brothers, how easy and clear is the answer to this disturbing question. It was given by the Holy Spirit himself on the day of Pentcost, when those who had been filled by the divine outpouring sent from heaven by Christ in fire and in wind began to speak foreign languages so that each of their listeners heard them " in his own native language " (*Ac.* 2, 6), although they belonged to different races. Then too the reply is given by the recent Council, amply and repeatedly, especially in the now famous Decree *Ad Gentes*, where the unity which marks Catholicism is shown in harmony with its apostolicity. Far from smothering what is good and original in every form of human culture it accepts, respects and puts to use the genius of each people, endowing with variety and beauty the one seamless garment (*Jn.* 19, 23) of the Church of Christ (cf. *Ps.* 44, 10; *Ad Gentes* 22; etc.).

So, one may ask, is " pluralism " admitted? Yes, but the significance of this word must be well understood. It must on no account contradict the substantial unity of Christianity (cf. *Ep.* 4, 3-6). You are acquainted with some dangers that lie hidden in pluralism. These occur when it is not limited to the contingent forms of religious life, but presumes to authorize individual and arbitrary interpretations of Catholic dogma, or to set up as a criterion of truth the popular mentality, or to prescind in theological study from authentic tradition and from the responsible magisterium of the Church.

The second aspect of the Catholic communion is that of charity. You know what supreme importance charity has in the whole of the divine design of the Catholic religion, and what particular place charity has in the connecting fabric of ecclesial unity. We must practice in its ecclesial aspects, which the Council has emphasized, a more conscious and active charity. The People of God must accordingly be progressively educated in mutual love for each of its members; the whole community of the Church must by means of charity feel itself united within itself, undivided, living in solidarity and therefore distinct (cf. *1 Cor.* 1, 10; 12, 25-26; *2 Cor.* 6, 14-18). Hierarchical relationships, pastoral ones (as is well known), collegial relationships, those between different ministerial functions, social ones, domestic ones—all must have running through them an ever active stream of charity, having for its immediate effects service—that is, self-sacrifice and selfgiving— and unity. The Church is charity; the Church is unity.

This, it seems to us, is the principal virtue demanded of the Catholic Church, at this moment of history, for it is a time that is spiritually very disturbed, to the point of inspiring fear of great and ruinous upheavals. The Church will be solid and strong if she is united within herself in faith and by charity. Many ask what must the Church do to draw close to her the hostile and unbelieving world. Unity in faith and love will be the witness which will have a salutary action on the world, in accordance with the word which Jesus left to us (*Jn.* 17, 21).

This, venerable brothers, is the message which we leave you in the name of Christ in memory of this encounter: " that all may be one ". With our fraternal Apostolic Blessing.

SPOTLIGHT ON YOUTH IN AUSTRALIA

*At 11.30 a.m., on 2nd December, Pope Paul ce-
lebrated an open-air Mass at Randwick Race-
course. It was estimated that 150,000 boys
and girls from Catholic schools all over Australia were present at the Mass. They presented a colourful spectacle in their variegated
uniforms. The schools in Australia were granted a holiday for the occasion.
During the Mass His Holiness preached the
following homily.*

Dear son and daughters,

I t was our wish to include in the programme of our meetings
this special contact with your world: that of the young people
of Australia. It was not that you are not a part of the Catholic
community—of course you are, since you share in the one baptism
and the one faith (*Ep.* 4, 5). But it seemed to us that within this
people, itself so young, you are the young amid the young, and
you have a right to a special message.

We would like you to see this talk as a sign of the special
liking the Church has for youth. It is not that the Church feels
ol and looks for support in the strength of the young and vigorous. Certainly she can be glad of her long history, and the rich
experience she has gained from contact with many generations of
all races and cultures. We do not think that this is any hindrance
to her taking an interest in the rising generation of today, or seeking their support. Her reason for existence and her justification
is to extend the presence of Jesus Christ among men, to spread his
Word and to communicate his life. Did Christ not call himself
" the Way, the Truth and the Life " (*Jn.* 14, 6)? Is he not the Light
for all man (*Jn.* 1, 9)? He is the new and perfect man, eternally
young because he has mastery over the changing events of time.
In our time just as in the first ages of Christianity he is the one
who fully reveals man to himself and makes it possible for man

to be completely fulfilled. The Council rightly called Christ " the goal of human history, the focal point of the longings of history and of civilization, the centre of the human race, the joy of every heart, and the answers to all its yearnings " (*Gaudium et spes*, 45).

The ray of light

The Church's mission is directly related to Christ's will to go towards each person, in order to help him fully to develop his inmost being in accordance with his talents, and in order to raise him up and save him by making him a son of God. It is from Christ that the Church receives a power beyond that of any merely human society, the power to be the full answer for your young hearts; for she is " the real youth of the world " (The Council's Message to Youth, 8 December 1965). She renews herself unceasingly, offering each new generation and each new people the good news which saves them, as she draws from the infinite treasure of the Word of God the answer to the most puzzling situations.

That is why the Church comes to you in complete honesty and simplicity. She knows what values you possess—your enthusiasm for the future, your strength in numbers, your thirst for what is just and true, and your aversion for hatred and its worst expression which is war, even your rejection of the out-of-date elements in present-day civilization. God placed these virtues in you so that you might meet a new situation with a new attitude. He who created life, he who wished by his Incarnation to share fully—except for sin—in our human condition, has likewise the ability to make human history go forward towards its goal. He can save this world from division and chaos by leading it, with the free cooperation of each individual, towards the wonderful destiny of the Kingdom of God.

There is an intimate connection, dear young people, between your faith and your life. In the very dissatisfaction that torments you and in your criticism of that society—which today is rightly called a permissive society—there is a ray of light.

In that society there are unfortunately every day more aggressive acts, new attitudes and behaviour patterns which are not Christian. When you denounce them and ask that society eliminate them and replace them with values authentically based on real justice, real sincerity, real moral rectitude and real brotherhood, you are indeed right. You have not only the approbation but the full support of the Church.

Sharing man's advance

But be attentive to the maner in which you treat this matter and make this effort, for if you turn back on yourselves, if you set yourselves up as supreme judges of your truth, if you reject the past wholesale—that is to say, if you reject what has been built up by the efforts of representatives of the same human race to which you belong, people with fundamentally the same qualities and defects— then the world of tomorrow will not be noticeably better, even if it is different; the root of the trouble will not have been extirpated: namely, man's pride. " Man can organize the world apart from God ", we said in our encyclical *Populorum progressio,* " but without God man can organize it in the end only to man's detriment. An isolated humanism is an inhuman humanism " (42).

If on the other hand you agree to encounter the one who more than all others gave proof of his love for man by delivering himself up to death to save him, then you will light the flame of your ideals at the fire of his infinite love: in that case you will share in man's advance towards the light. " For of all the names in the world given to men, this is the only one by which we can be saved " (*Ac.* 4, 12).

For or against

That is your vocation, dear sons and daughters. That is where your duty lies. You must make the choice: you will be either for man with Jesus Christ, or against man. It is not a matter of a sentimental or superficial choice. It is a matter of your lives and those of others.

It is up to you, with the help of your parents, educators and friends, among yourselves and within organizations suited to your age and your studies, to deepen your knowledge and understanding of these realities of your faith. It must not be that your lives as young people should now depend on the light of the faith you had as children.

Besides, it is not a matter of you alone, it is matter of all your brothers and sisters of Australia. It is a matter that goes beyond your frontiers; it is a matter of the world's salvation. It was not as isolated individuals that God saved us; his plan for us was to form a united and peaceful people. You will find your happiness essentially in sharing it with others. There is no lack of opportunity to do so. They come from among your own numbers, from your companions in the same course. They come from your parishes, from the poor, from the sick. They come from beyond the seas, from the world which surrounds you and which is trying to find the real reasons of living.

With great fervour and affection we beg the Lord to enlighten those who doubt, to comfort those who suffer and to reveal himself to all of you. We pray that he who is so good and so close to each of you will give peace and joy to your will hearts. With very deep affection we give our special apostolic blessing to you who are gathered here and to all the youth of Australia.

LOVE, WHICH WILL BE FOREVER

On 4th December Paul VI concelebrated Mass with several bishops and about 200 local priests, at Hong Kong. After the reading of the Gospel, he delivered the following homily.

Dear brothers and sons and daughters,

I t is with joy that we have accepted the gracious invitation extended to us by your zealous shepherd, our brother, Bishop Hsu. We are pleased to take the occasion of the apostolic yourney that has brought us to Asia and Australia for meetings with the Episcopal Conferences to make a visit, howsoever brief, to the largest Chinese diocese in the world. We are very happy to be with you, dear sons and daughters of Hong Kong. We want to thank you personally for the affection and devotion that you have manifested to the Holy See in many different ways. We want to congratulate you on the many accomplishments of your so vital Catholic community. We want to encourage you to persevere firmly in the faith of your baptism and confirmation and to exhort you to an ever greater commitment in searching the most apt means of rendering the Christian message of love more understandable in the world in which you live. Thus you will contribute effectively in showing to all your brothers and sisters the perennial youth and reforming power of the Gospel of Christ and so give them a hope for the building up in love of a more fraternal society.

We are now in prayer.

Twofold relationship

May each one of us be conscious of the twofold relationship that this prayer, our Holy Mass, produces in our souls. We are in relationship with Christ, and we are in relationship with men, our brothers.

Yes, gathered here together in the name of Christ, we are with him. Rather, he is with us. He himself has assured us of it. Where you meet in my name, he said, I shall be there with you (cf. *Mt.* 18, 20). Moreover, to our humble person is entrusted the ministry of representing him, Jesus Christ, the one Head, though now invisible, of the Church (cf. *Summa Theologica* III, 8, 1), the supreme " Shepherd and Guardian " of our souls (cf. *1 Pet.* 2, 25). It is a joy to us that our office as his Vicar makes his presence in this sacred assembly more deeply felt, makes his divine power more effective and his spiritual consolation more immediate. The rite that we are celebrating will shortly become even more realistic and mystical: then it will be the sacrificial meal which Christ himself instituted that it might recall and sacramentally renew his redeeming Passion; and he will give himself to us as the food of eternal life.

Fullness of meaning

Brethren, let us all join in giving to this celebration the fullness of its meaning. Let us endeavour to adhere to it, each and every one of us, with the most firm assent of our minds. Let us give it the humble, resolute, and total profession of our faith, that we may have an everlasting memory to sum up this extraordinary and happy moment. In a short time we shall be saying: " Let us proclaim the mystery of faith ". That is the first relationship that this liturgical action of ours should make active now and for ever: faith. We proclaim this faith to you all and we confirm you in it.

There is a second relationship, as you know, which is produced by our celebration: it is produced first in our consciousness, then in our hearts, and finally in our exterior life.

The Eucharist is a sign and a bond of unity (cf. *Summa Theologica* III, 73, 2 and 3). It is a sacrament of communion. In the very act whereby the Eucharist puts us in real communion with Christ it puts us in spiritual, mystical, moral and social communion with all those who eat the same bread (cf. *1 Cor.* 10, 17). It is the sacrament of ecclesial unity. It is the supreme uniting element of the community of the faithful. It is the sacrament which contains the real Body of Christ and which has as its purpose to produce the Mystical Body of Christ, which is the Church.

We pause and draw the conclusion. The Church is then the unifying effect of the love of Christ for us. It can itself be considered a living sign, a sacrament of unity and of love. To love is her mission. While we are saying these simple and sublime words, we have around us—we almost feel it—all the Chinese people wherever they may be.

There comes to this far eastern land, for the first time in history, the humble apostle of Christ that we are. And what does he say? Why does he come? To sum it up in one word: Love. Christ is a teacher, a shepherd and a loving redeemer for China too. The Church cannot leave unsaid this good word: love, which will be forever.

POPE'S DISCOURSE
TO COLLEGE OF CARDINALS

On the morning of December 22nd, Pope Paul received in audience the Sacred College, the Pontifical Family and Roman Prelates who expressed to the Holy Father their good wishes for Christmas. The Pope addressed them as follows.

Venerable Brothers,

T he passing of time brings us once more to this meeting, in which hearts overflow with expressions of good wishes for an ordered and happy unfolding of the coming days of our life here on earth; it is a moment when, taking a wider and more lofty perspective, they turn to the divine Ruler of our destinies to beg that fulness of wisdom and merit which alone can give to our lives their true meaning and their highest value. This moment, as it comes round once again, truly has an eschatological significance endowed with a mysterious purpose of which none of us is unaware. The reason for this we know well: if this exchange of good wishes seeks the motive for its spontaneity and sincerity, it finds it in the fact that it is the celebration of a memory a great memory, that of the birth of Our Lord into the world nineteen hundred and seventy years ago, according to the common reckoning. Thus it is that our hearts, having expressed fervent and optimistic wishes for the future, turn once more towards the past. They turn towards that event which lit up and determined the course of history—the entry of the Word of God into human kind; from this the Church took its origin, its reason for existence and its final goal. This yearly audience therefore leads us to make the effort, not easy yet inspiring, to place before our mind's eye the total panorama of time, in which our religion finds its setting, as it were the river bed along which it courses through the changing scene of history. In order not to lose, in the little time available to us and in face of such a vast historical panorama, the sense of the concrete and immediate, our reflection pauses for a moment at the present and we ask with special concentration: what is the present hour for us, for the Church? Even reduced to these restricted limits the question could have an answer of ample proportions, too great for a talk such as this; moreover the words of the Cardinal Dean have already touched upon several facts and several aspects of the Church's present hour. It is sufficient for us at this time to pick out a few characteristic points of this historical moment of the Church herself, in order subsequently to draw from them, with you, resolutions and wishes befitting the hour now marked upon the clockface of our time, at this blessed and propitious anniversary of the birth of Christ Our Lord.

The long voyage

This traditional meeting takes on today special significance in view of the long journey that we have carried out (accompanied in particular, with his habitual intrepidity, by the Cardinal Dean, the spokesman today of the Sacred College's good wishes, and by the new Prefect of the Congregation for the Evangelization of Peoples).

Indeed, the first point worthy of a certain reflection is our journey to the Far East. So much has been said about it by the mass media of the press, radio and television, that there is no need for us now to describe it once more. We would like rather to express our praise and thanks to all who gave accurate and detailed accounts of the event and who made objective, informed and friendly comments upon it. Even greater gratitude must be expressed to those who made this expedition possible and facilitated it. We cannot forget their thoughtfulness and their welcome; this is not so much because they were shown towards our lowly person, but because the intention was to honour thereby the ministry entrusted to us, and in a special way the fact that we represent the Lord. To him is due from us, more than from anyone else, the homage of our faith and love. Because we represent the Lord, the intention was therefore to honour also the sign and principle of the unity and universality of our Church. Our journey was thus a singular celebration of the Church, to which novelty alone gave pious and curious interest, without its simple and genuine religious and informal character being in any way obscured by any studied exterior show. Thus, without any artificiality, it was made a part of the now normal life of the Church. As is well known, our journey was made in response to local invitations. The two main ones were those from the Philippines and from Australia. Both took shape from the pressing requests of the ecclesiastical hierarchies and the civil authorities of the two countries. To these were added other invitations, likewise from the chruch and civil authorities, invitations that we felt we should accept; moreover, we did not wish to lose the occasion of giving proof to Indonesia and the Island of Ceylon of our equal and respectful interest. Other invitations we had regretfully to decline, invitations of themselves equally worthy of our consideration, but our programme could not be extended beyond certain limits. We now feel the obligation of this solemn occasion to renew the expression of our thanks, our homage and our good wishes for the courteous welcome extended to us in their respective lands by the civil authorities of the various countries we visited. We shall never forget their noble courtesy. May the Lord reward them for their kind and thoughtful hospitality.

Episcopal conferences

But, as we say, the stopping-places of our itinerary were ecclesiastical in nature. The two main ones were the meeting of the representatives of the Episcopal Conferences of Eastern Asia at Manila, and that of the representatives of the Episcopal Conferences of Oceania in Sydney. We took part in the closing sessions of which shares with us the toil and responsibility of our service to the entire Church. The merit is not ours but yours; it belongs to all those who work with you to facilitate this service. We are consoled to give witness to this excellent activity of yours —witness to its diligence, its intensity, its fidelity, its commitment to the loyal application of the recent Council. We feel an obligation to express our sincere gratitude for the help and assistance which the Sacred College gives to our work in the pastoral government of the Church. The daily labour at the service of this Apostolic See performed by you, venerable brothers, with disinterestedness and generosity, with dignity and firmness, coupled with profound humility, constitutes a singular merit, the value of which we fully appreciate. We cannot pass over in silence the exemplary spirit of abnegation which animates the members of the College of Cardinals especially when the higher good of the Church demands from them renunciation and sacrifice. May God reward in abundant measure such unfailing dedication and may he turn these sentiments of ours—sentiments of esteem for and gratitude towards each one of you—into copious graces for your venerable persons.

With two last thoughts we end our address.

" Pope John XXIII " Prize

The first of these refers to the awarding of the peace prize, named after our venerable Predecessor, Pope John XXIII. It is the first time that this prize is being given. After long consultations and reflections—the credit for which we give especially to the Council of the respective Commission—the award has been made to a Religious. She is a modest and silent person but not unknown to those who observe the courage which charity exerts in the world of the poor. Her name is Mother Teresa; she is the Superior General of the Congregation of the Missionaries of Charity who for twenty years along the byways of India has been performing a magnificent mission of love in favour of those suffering from leprosy, in favour of the old, the children, those abandoned. This award is meant to be a public recognition of her apostolate of charity which is no longer restricted to the needy of India. It already extends to three continents—reaching at our invitation the very outskirts of Rome—thus mobilizing an immense army of living forces at the service of the world of suffering. We hold up to the admiration of all this intrepid messenger of the love of Christ; we do this so that by her example the number of those who expend themselves for their brethren may grow and that there may be better established in the world the sense of solidarity and human brotherhood.

December 22nd, 1970

Bishops' Synod

The second thing which we intend to say to you regards the General Synod of Bishops which opens next September 30th and which will have as its subject: " The Ministerial Priesthood " and " Justice in the World ". We were led to this by the importance which we attach to the active collaboration of the representatives of the Catholic episcopate in the government of the universal Church. We believe that their wise views, with the help of God, will again make an efficacious contribution to the solution of questions of such gravity, which at the present moment seem to demand with greater urgency the attention and care of pastors and of the faithful.

And now we terminate our address by formulating for each of you fervent good wishes of joy, prosperity and peace for the coming Chrismas feast. We offer our respectful good wishes to the Oriental Churches, especially those in communion with this Apostolic See, and also to those with whom the bonds of perfect unity in faith and love are being revived and strengthened. We pray to the Divine Redeemer that the new year which approaches may find us all ever responding fully and fervently to our respective duties.

Counting, as always, on your prayers and on your willing collaboration, we impart with affection to you and to all your dear ones, in pledge of divine graces, our Apostolic Blessing.

POPE REMINISCES ON TWO ASPECTS
OF RECENT JOURNEY

Here We are, back again after Our great journey to the lands of the Far East, enjoying the always fresh and uplifting encounter of these General Audiences. It seems to Us that We hear an affectionate and curious question arise from you: " Tell us something about your trip ... ". Dearest children, it is not possible in this place and at this moment, for there would be too much to say. In any case, you already know what happened, the places We visited, the meetings, the scenes that occurred ... on that long and rapid pilgrimage. But We will give you a few fleeting general impressions.

The world's wonder

The first concerns you directly: it is what was at the root of the wonder with which the world followed this event. In itself such an event has nothing exceptional about it, for who does not travel today? Who has not been overcome by the fascination exercised by these magnificent modern means of transport? It seems to Us that the wonder was expressed in two respects. The first is the association of the Pope with travel, as if this were hard to do, as if travel were not part of the history of the popes. This is because the Pope is regarded as a fixed point, he who stands steadfast at the Church's centre, clearly fulfilling the function of maintaining and representing unity. Other Popes made journeys away from Rome in other times, and away from Italy, but when we look at those journeys closely we find that they were motivated by particular and contingent purposes. It does not appear that those popes spontaneously took the decision to make journeys based on another principle, also personified in the papacy's function, its catholicity, the universality of the ministry which was en-

445

trusted to Peter, to the Pastor of Pastors, to the missionary par excellence, Saint Paul (cf. *1 Tim.* 2, 7; *2 Tim.* 1, 11; *Gal.* 2, 7).

But it seemed to Us, to Our conscience, in spite of Our awareness of our personal littleness, to be a perfectly normal thing to exercise this function of being open to all peoples and all countries, which are spiritually as near to the Church's heart as they are distant in terms of geography and race. It seemed to Us to be the way of carrying out a vocation which belongs to Our apostolic office; it was like a reawakening caused by the world's historical maturity, of Our office's innate mission to be present to all, to serve all, to be the friend of all and an apostle to all, and the central link in the chain of universal communion.

It is easy to see that all this may well produce, who knows, what other acts of witness in the future!

Thus it was that We met the distant Churches of Asia and Australia especially. It is difficult for Us to express with what fullness of emotion We came into contact with the Bishops of East Asia gathered at Manila, and those of Oceania, gathered at Sydney. And what joy it was—almost like a family reunion— to find multitudes of brethren amongst those populations, especially in the Philippines, to experience the mystery of the mystical Body almost physically, and to find its reality again in islands scattered upon the Pacific Ocean, and in the very modern communities of Australia.

True role of Church

And the priests—the brave and excellent priests, true labourers of the kingdom of God, the men and women religious, who are above all praise, and the immense crowds of faithful, flocks of lay people engaged in building up the Church, as a vision, as an experience, as a means of praising God and of giving thanks for those who yesterday planted those Churches, and for those who are today cultivating them with tireless ardor and causing them to grow in loyalty to the Gospel and service to mankind! And what strength and consolation for the hope and the victory of the faith and charity We found, when We saw so many Christians, brethren who are still separated from Us, but who, like Us, are hungry for full reconciliation!

We will say no more. Be glad with Us; deepen your Catholic and missionary consciousness; become aware of the clash which spontaneously shows itself between the Church and the world, that contrast which the now famous Constitution *Gaudium et spes* sets forth in such grave, clear, but such trusting terms. Thus convince yourselves that the Church's duty today is certainly not to torment itself with criticism and bitter challenges, nor to conform to the amoral tendencies of such a great part of modern society, nor again to eliminate the mysterious truths and difficult duties of Christianity, but rather to be coherent with itself and show what it is, to be strong in faith, and to rejoice in the songs of its prayer, to be wholly concerned with promoting justice and peace in the world, in view of the sole Saviour, Jesus Christ.

WISDOM ALONE LIBERATES THE WORLD

On Christmas Day, 25th December, the Holy Father delivered the following address before giving his blessing "Urbi et Orbi".

T his encounter for the exchange of Christmas greetings between you, who are listening to us here and far away, and us, who are a witness of Christ born into the world, raises a porovcative question. The question arises in our heart as it certainly does in yours. It concerns our apostolic ministry in its entirety and stirs in a fundamental way your conscience as men of today. The question that confronts us all is this: Does Christianity still have today something relevant to say to the modern world? Does the Gospel message still correspond to what modern man is capable of receiving? Can it make itself understood? Above all, can it truly constitute the salvation, the fulfilment and the joy of the new generations?

We kept asking ourself this complex and fundamental question during our recent journey to distant countries, as we stood before unnumbered multitudes of festive and curious persons. All of them secretly were eager to have from us a revealing message, one that would liberate and orientate. The answer welled up spontaneously from the inner certitude of our faith: Yes, we do have this ever new and vital message, because we have the Gospel, because we have Christ. That answer recurs to us with exuberant certitude on this occasion. It recurs in such a way that it becomes a proclamation full of the power of the Spirit and of prophetic hope for you who are listening to us and for the entire world: the Child whose birth we commemorate in the history of mankind, Jesus the Son of the Virgin Mary, is also the Son of the living God; he is the Messiah, the Christ, the Saviour; he is the one on whom all the destinies of men depend because he has linked them with himself with a mysterious bond of infinite love—our lot is bound up with him.

We have need of Christ

We would like to raise our voice today and be heard in the secret recesses of every single conscience and in the immense context of the modern world: Christ is that truth which we are seeking, Christ is that life of which we have need.

But it is at this point that we are confronted with an inner fear, a dramatic doubt: Who will listen to us? Who will understand? Will the clash of the divine plan with the deafness of so many men not occur again, as the Evangelist John expresses it by a quotation from Isaiah: " Lord, who could believe what we have heard said, and to whom has the power of the Lord been revelade? " (*Jn.* 13, 38; *Is.* 53, 1; *Rom.* 10, 16).

There is always difficulty in understanding Christ as the principle and the cause of salvation. How can the world which is used to measuring the truth of life according to a scale of temporal values accept such a teacher, such a leader? Not only is he himself humble, weak and poor, but he preaches humility, meekness and poverty for others.

The Sermon on the Mount—in which the poor, the meek, the pure, those who mourn, those who thirst for justice and the persecuted are called happy—is made by him into the programme of a new kingdom, a kingdom whose symbol is the great emblem of the cross, and which is founded on the law of dying in order to live, that is, of duty and of sacrifice. Moreover, how can the world of today, so profane and secularized and allergic to whatever is of a sacred character and linked up with the transcendental and religious world, accept Christ and have a liking for him?

Faith discovers

And yet we are sure that our effort is not in vain. The paradox of Christ who is little, unarmed and crucified, yet, as the Word of God, is radiant, full of grace and truth, and living again in the victory of the Resurrection, is resolved in our day too in a marvellous act of faith. This act of faith can discover in him, in Christ, the one who came down from heaven to earth, who became the brother of all and who brought himself down to the level of low and suffering humanity. It can discover in him the one who aligned himself with those rebelling against hypocrisy and injustice and who breathed sentiments of goodness and love into the exasperated hearts of men. This act of faith can discover the one who reached out to encounter men of modern progress, informed of everything, endowed with everything, capable of everything, yet unknowledgeable and erring about the highest reasons of life and not able to acquire its fullness and happiness; the one who said to them simply and solemnly: I am the way and the truth and the life, what are you looking for?

We want to be liberated from those illusions, frustrations, injustices and repressions to which the modern world has subjected us in violation of its promises—this is what the young are saying, the disinherited, the automatons of modern technology: we want to be free persons, real men, people rescued from hunger and from the spiral of incurable inferiority. Yes, answers the Man of men: come to me all you who are in tribulation and I will console you. I am with you, with the power of the spirit, not with the violence of force and passion. Wisdom alone liberates the world.

We want to make the world into a single family—say the sociologists and statesmen; everything leads us to knock down the barriers which separate nations from each other and to reduce them to simple shelters of values proper to each people and each culture, not allowing them to be obstacles to communications, which are now of worldwide dimensions, much less bastions of the formidable devices of war and destruction. Yes, responds the Master, but you must free yourselves of the centuries-old poison which you carry in your blood, that of selfishness and hate, of conflict as a system, of exclusiveness, of pride and personal or class interest. You must come to my school where one learns to look upon every man as his brother, not a rival nor an enemy. It makes hearts human and sensitive to the needs of others; it makes them respectful of others' dignity. I am the teacher of brotherhood and friendship; I am the axis of a higher unity because I am the source of charity and the love which has God as its principle, its power and its goal. In me all of you can and must become a single entity; humanity redeemed and reconciled with itself and with God the Father of all.

Every man a brother

We would like—implore the men of today, at times with the anguish of despair—we would like to have true hope, hope that does not die with the passage of time, hope that guarantees real and total satisfaction to the natural aspirations of the heart; and these are the greater and more demanding in proportion to the culture and advancement of the man of today. Yes, Christ answers once more, I am the bread of life; he who eats this bread will live forever.

It is the small Child of Bethlehem who is spreading today his silent and irresistible message. Who will listen to it? Who will accept it?

You who are poor, you who are suffering, you who are prisoners, you who are refugees, you who are bewildered by the darkness of evil—you are the prime candidates to listen to this message.

And you, no less: young people, disturbed and impatient in regard to the times we live in, yet even more desirous and capable of building up a new society in which moral and spiritual values have top priority.

And also you: men of science and intellectuals; you who belong to the economic and political world—do you not notice by the very shadows that are fearfully projected in front of us that we often have our backs turned on Christ?

And it is thus that we again this year proclaim Christ. This is the meaning of the good wishes which we extend to you and to the whole world in our greeting of " Happy Christmas ".

APPENDIX

LETTER OF POPE PAUL VI
ON PRIESTLY CELIBACY

Your Eminence,

The declarations about ecclesiastical celibacy which were published in Holland recently have profoundly saddened Us and raised many questions in Our mind: because of the reasons for such a grave stand, which is contrary to the sacrosanct norm in force in our Latin Church, because of the repercussions upon the whole People of God, especially on the clergy and young men preparing for the priesthood, because of the disturbing consequences in the life of the entire Church, and the echoes which it is arousing among all Christians, also among other members of the human family.

In view of these queries, We feel the need to open Our mind to you, Lord Cardinal, who so closely share the cares of Our Apostolic Office.

First of all We ask Ourself with humble and absolute interior sincerity whether there was any responsibility on Our part in regard to those unfortunate resolutions, which are so out of keeping with Our attitude and, We believe, with that of the whole Church.

The Lord is Our witness of the feelings of esteem, affection and trust which We have always had for Holland which is such a well-deserving part of Christ's Mystical Body. You, Lord Cardinal, well know how deferential and friendly We were in Our personal conversation and letters and in the action taken by the Organs of this Apostolic See to ward off the declarations in question.

* * *

Those declarations give rise to much uncertainty and confusion. Consequently, it is a grave and compelling duty for Us to state Our attitude with all clarity: the attitude of him to whom a mysterious design of divine providence has in this difficult hour entrusted the care of all the Churches (cf. *2 Cor.* 11, 28).

The reasons adopted to justify such a radical change in the centuries-old norm of the Latin Church, which has been the means of so many fruits of grace, holiness and missionary apostolate, are well known. But We must say without equivocation that they do not appear convincing to Us. They seem to overlook a fundamental and essential consideration which must never be forgotten and which belongs to the supernatural order. That is to say, they represent a breakdown of the genuine concept of the priesthood.

The only perspective to be kept in mind is that of the mission of the Gospel, of which we are the heralds and witnesses, with faith and in hope of the Kingdom. The Bishop and the priest have the mission of announcing the Gospel of grace and truth (cf. *Jn.* 1, 14), to bring the message of salvation to the world, to make it aware of its sin and at the same time of its redemption, to call it to hope, to win it away from idols which are always reappearing, and convert it to Christ the Saviour. The evangelical values cannot be understood and lived except in faith, in prayer, in penance, in charity, not without struggle and mortification, not without arousing at times the scorn, incomprehension and even persecution of the world, as in the case of Christ and the Apostles.

It is the ever deeper understanding of these considerations which has led the Latin Church to make renunciation of the right to found a family a condition for admission to the priesthood. That understanding has been matured in a providential way during the course of history which has known many efforts and many struggles to affirm the Christian ideal; and that renunciation has been spontaneously made by many servants of the Gospel. The considerations mentioned are still valid, perhaps more today than at any time. Are we, who have been called to follow Jesus, incapable of accepting a law which has been tried and proved by such long experience, and of abandoning all, family, nets, to follow Him and bring the Good News of the Saviour (cf. *Mk.* 1). Considering everything before God, before Christ and the Church, and before the world, We therefore feel it is Our duty clearly to reaffirm what We have already declared and several times repeated: that the link between priesthood and celibacy, as established for centuries by the Latin Church, constitutes for it a supremely precious and irreplaceable good. It would be extremely rash to undervalue it or even to let it fall into disuse. It has been consecrated by tradition and is an incomparable sign of total dedication to the love of Christ (cf. *Mt.* 12, 29). It is a bright demonstration of the missionary demand which is essential in every priestly life, in service of the risen Christ, who lives for ever and to whom the priest has consecrated himself in total readiness for the sake of the Kingdom of God.

There are priests who, for reasons recognized as valid, have unfortunately found themselves radically unable to persevere. We know they are only a small number, whereas the great majority wishes, with the help of grace, to remain faithful to the sacred pledges made before God and the Church. It is with great sorrow that We agree to accept their insistent request to be released from their promises and dispensed from their obligations. We do this only after careful examination of every single case. However, the profound understanding which We have for persons, in a spirit of paternal charity, must not hinder Us from deploring an attitude which is so little in accord with what the Church rightfully expects from those who have definitely consecrated themselves to its exclusive service.

The Church will therefore continue in the future as in the past to entrust the divine ministry of the word, of the faith and of the sacraments of grace only to priests who remain faithful to their obligations.

The same many-sided contestation manifested today against such a holy institution as sacred celibacy, makes more imperious than ever Our duty to sustain and encourage in every way the innumerable ranks of priests who have remained loyal to their pledge. Our thoughts and blessing go out to them with most special affection.

For this reason, after mature examination of the matter, We clearly affirm it Our duty not to permit the priestly ministry to be exercised by those who have turned back after having put their hand to the plough (cf. *Lk.* 9, 62).

In any case, is not this the constant tradition of the venerable Oriental Churches, to which reference is so often made in this regard?

At all events, We hardly dare to think of the incalculable consequences which a different decision would entail for the People of God on the spiritual and pastoral planes.

While We feel it Our duty to reaffirm the norm of sacred celibacy in this way with so much clarity, We are not forgetting a question which has been insistently raised with Us by some Bishops, whose zeal, attachment to the venerable tradition of the priesthood in the Latin Church and the very eminent values which it expresses, are known to Us. We also know their pastoral anxieties in view of certain quite special needs of their apostolic ministry. They ask Us whether it might not be possible to consider ordaining to the priesthood men of advanced age who have given proof of exemplary family and professional life in their social circumstances, in a situation of extreme shortage of priests, and limited to regions in such a situation.

We cannot conceal that such an eventuality arouses grave reservations on Our part. Would it not be, amongst other things, a very dangerous illusion to believe that such a change in traditional discipline could be restricted in practice to local cases of true and extreme necessity? And would it not also be a temptation to others to look to it for an apparently easier answer to the present lack of sufficient vocations?

In any case, the consequences would be so grave and would pose such new questions for the Church's life, that they would, if considered, need to be given attentive previous examination, by Our Brothers in the Episcopate in union with Us. Account would have to be taken before God of the good of the universal Church, which could not be separated from that of the local Churches.

* * *

These problems which come under Our pastoral responsibility are truly grave, and, Lord Cardinal, We have wished to confide them to you.

You together with Us are witness of the appeals which come to Us from all sides. Many of Our Brothers and Children implore Us not to make any change in such a venerable tradition. They, together with Us hope that Our Venerable Brothers, the Bishops of Holland, will reflect further about the matter with the Apostolic See, through trusting and fraternal contacts. Such further reflection will need to be matured in prayer and charity. We for Our part desire more than ever to seek together with the Pastors of the dioceses of the Netherlands for means of solving their problems in a suitable way, in common consideration for the good of the whole Church. We therefore believe it to be above all necessary to assure the Bishops, the priests and all the members of the Dutch Catholic Community of Our constant affection, but at the same time to assure them that it is Our conviction that it is indispensable to reconsider the desires expressed and the stand taken in a question of such grave importance and scope for the universal Church. These ought to be reconsidered in the light of the reflections stated above and in a spirit of authentic ecclesial communion.

We count particularly, Lord Cardinal, on your valuable collaboration in the work which the Holy See will have to do in this connection.

Your aid will also be valuable for the contacts which will have to be made with the Bishops of the entire world, in order that all Episcopal Conferences, maintaining perfect communion with Us and the universal Church in absolute respect for its laws, may assure their priests, Our fellow workers, that We are following and will continue to follow with Our paternal affection their anxieties in the apostolate and their problems; that the Episcopal Conferences may remind them at the same time of the beauty of the grace which the Lord has granted them, also of their sacred pledges and the missionary demand of their ministry. In these circumstances Our thoughts cannot but go out most cordially to those young men who are preparing themselves with the generosity of their apostolic drive to serve Christ and their fellows in the priesthood with all their hearts. They are really the Church's hope for the evangelization of the world: always provided that they commit themselves irrevocably and without reserve to the form of life which the Church puts before them.

Finally, Lord Cardinal, it will be necessary to make insistent calls to the multitude of faithful souls, who are still silent but do not therefore suffer less in this time of trial, and ask them for generous prayers.

May the Lord grant all, Pastors and faithful, the power of hope and the ardour of charity: " may grace be with all those who love Our Lord Jesus Christ with unchanging love " (*Ep.* 6, 24).

With these sentiments, We impart to you Our Apostolic Blessing. From the Vatican, February 2nd 1970, the Feast of the Presentation of Jesus to the Temple.

PAUL PP. VI

APOSTOLIC LETTER

ISSUED " MOTU PROPRIO " BY POPE PAUL VI
ESTABLISHING AN AGE LIMIT FOR THE EXERCISE
OF MAJOR FUNCTIONS BY CARDINALS
PAULUS PP. VI

The natural relationship between the increasing burden of age and the ability to perform certain major offices, such as those of diocesan bishop and parish priest, was dealt with by the Second Vatican Ecumenical Council in the Decree *Christus Dominus* (21 and 31). Implementing the wishes of the Council Fathers, we, by our Apostolic Letter *Ecclesiae Sanctae* of 6 August 1966, called on bishops and parish priests voluntarily to submit their resignation not later than their seventy-fifth birthday (11 and 20, para. 3).

The same question of age was touched on by the general regulations of the Roman Curia, issued under the title *Regolamento Generale della Curia Romana*, which we approved and ordered to be published on 22 February 1968. It is laid down therein that major and minor officials should retire from office on the completion of their seventieth year, and higher prelates at the beginning of their seventy-fifth year of age (art. 101, para. 1).

It seems to us now that the good of the Church demands that the increasing burden of age should be taken into consideration also for the illustrious office of the cardinalate, to which we have on several occasions given special attention. It is in fact a particularly important office which demands great prudence, both for its quite unique connection with our supreme office at the service of the whole Church and because of the high importance it has for all the Church when the Apostolic See falls vacant.

Accordingly, after long and mature consideration of the whole question, and continuing to trust for the future in the unceasing counsel and prayers of all the cardinals without distinction, we decree:

I

Cardinals in charge of departments of the Roman Curia (listed in art. 1 of the *Regolamento Generale*) or to the other permanent institutions of the Apostolic See and Vatican City are requested to submit their resignation voluntarily to the Pope on the completion of their seventy-fifth year of age. After due consideration of all the circumstances of each case, he will judge whether it is fitting to accept the resignation immediately.

II

On the completion of eighty years of age, cardinals
1. cease to the members of the departments of the Roman Curia and of the other institutions mentioned in the above article:
2. lose the right to elect the Pope and consequently also that of entering the conclave. If, however, a cardinal completes his eightieth year after the beginning of the conclave, he continues to enjoy the right of electing the Pope on that occasion.

III

The arrangements in articles I and II, 1 take effect even when the five-year term dealt with in article 2, para. 5, of the Apostolic Constitution *Regimini Ecclesiae Universae* is not yet completed.

IV

What is laid down in article II above applies no less to cardinals who, by exception, continue in charge of a diocese, or keep its title without the function of governing it, after their eightieth year.

V

Even after completing their eightieth year, cardinals continue to be member of the Sacred College in all other respects. They retain all the other rights and prerogatives connected with the office of cardinal, including the faculty of taking part in any General or Special Congregation which may be held during a vacancy of the Apostolic See before the beginning of the conclave.

VI

If it should happen, because of unusual circumstances, that the Cardinal Camerlengo of the Cardinal Major Penitentiary should continue in office until his eightieth year, the following procedure is decreed:

1. If he completes his eightieth year before the death of a Pope and if a successor has not been appointed by then, or if he should do so between a Pope's death and the beginning of a conclave, then, during the vacancy of the Apostolic See, a regular Congregation of the Sacred College will vote to elect a successor to remain in office until the new Pope's election;

2. If he completes his eightieth year after the beginning of the conclave, his term of office is by law extended up to the election of the new Pope.

VII

If the Dean of the Sacred College is not present at the conclave because of having completed his eightieth year, the duties of his office are performed within the conclave by the Subdean, or, if he too should be absent, by another of the more senior cardinals in accordance with the general order of precedence.

VIII

A system similar to that laid down in article VII is to be followed, if necessary in the performance of the duties in the conclave assigned by law to the three cardinals who are at the head of the orders.

Interim Arrangement

Those who are now members of the Sacred College and have completed their eightieth year of age on the date of coming into force of this Apostolic Letter may continue, if they so wish, to take part, with voting rights, in the Plenary and Ordinary Congregations of departments of the Roman Curia.

Appendix

We decree that what is laid down by this Apostolic Letter should come into force on 1 January 1971.

We order that all the things decreed in this letter issued " Motu proprio " be regarded as established and ratified, notwithstanding anything to the contrary, even if worthy of very special notice.

Given in Rome at Saint Peter's on the twenty-first day of November in the year 1970, the eighth of our pontificate.

PAULUS PP. VI

APOSTOLIC EXHORTATION

TO ALL THE BISHOPS IN PEACE AND COMMUNION WITH THE APOSTOLIC SEE, ON THE FIFTH ANNIVERSARY OF THE CLOSE OF THE SECOND VATICAN COUNCIL

Beloved brothers, health and our Apostolic Blessing.

It is now five full years since, after intense working sessions lived in prayer, study and fraternal exchange of thought and opinion the bishops of the whole world returned to their dioceses, resolved to ensure " that nothing would block the great river whose streams of heavenly graces today refresh the city of God '[1] and that there would be no lessening of the vital spirit which the Church now possesses ".[2]

Thanking God for the work accomplished, each bishop took back with him from the Council not only the experience he had of collegiality, but also the doctrinal and pastoral texts which had been painstakingly perfected.   These texts were spiritual riches to be shared with our co-workers in the priesthood, with the religious and with all the members of the People of God.   They were sure guides for proclaiming the word of God to our age and for internally renewing the Christian communities.

That fervour has known no slackening.   The successors of the apostles have worked unreservedly to apply the teaching and directives of the Council to the Church's life, each of them where the Holy Spirit has placed him to feed the Church of God,[3] and all of them together in many ways, but especially in the episcopal conferences and synods of bishops.   In accordance with the hope

---

[1] *Ps.* 45, 5.
[2] Apostolic Exhortation *Postrema Sessio*, 4 November 1965, in *AAS* 57, 1965, p. 867.
[3] *Ac.* 20, 28.

expressed in our first encyclical " Ecclesiam Suam "[4] the council deepened the Church's awareness of herself. It shed more light on the demands of her apostolic mission in the world of today. It helped her to engage in the dialogue of salvation with a genuinely ecumenical and missionary spirit.

I

But it is not our intention here to try to draw up a balance sheet of the researches, undertakings and reforms, which have been so numerous since the Council ended. Devoting our attention to reading the signs of the times, we would like, in a fraternal spirit, to make together with you an examination of our fidelity to the commitment we bishops undertook in our message to humanity at the beginning of the Council: " We shall take pains so to present to the men of this age God's truth in its integrity and purity that they may understand it and gladly assent to it ".[5]

This commitment was made unambiguously clear by the pastoral constitution " Gaudium et spes ", truly the Council's charter of the presence of the Church in the world: " The Church of Christ takes her stand in the midst of the anxieties of this age, and does not cease to hope with the utmost confidence. She intends to propose to our age over and over again, in season and out of season, the apostolic message ".[6]

It is of course true that the shepherds of the Church have always had this duty of handing on the faith in its fulness and in a manner suited to men of their time. That means trying to use a language easily accessible to them, answering their questions, arousing their interest and helping them to discover, through poor human speech, the whole message of salvation brought to us by Jesus Christ. It is in fact the episcopal college which with Peter and under his authority, guarantees the authentic handing on of the deposit of faith, and for that purpose it has received, as Saint Irenaeus expressed it, " a sure charism of truth ".[7] The faithfulness of its witness, rooted in

---

[4] *AAS* 56, 1964, pp. 609-659.
[5] 20 October 1962, *AAS* 54, 1962, p. 822.
[6] 82; *AAS* 58, 1966, pp. 1106-1107.
[7] *Adversus Haereses* IV, 26; 2, 2; *PG* 7, 1053.

Appendix

Sacred Tradition and Holy Scripture and nourished by the ecclesial life of the whole People of God is what empowers the Church, through the unfailing assistance of the Holy Spirit, to teach without ceasing the word of God and to make it progressively unfold.

Increased effort needed

Nevertheless, the present position of the faith demands of us an increased effort in order that this word may reach our contemporaries in its fulness and that the works performed by God may be presented to them without falsification and with all the intensity of the love of the truth which can save them.[8] In fact, at the very moment when the reading of God's word in the liturgy is enjoying a wonderful renewal, thanks to the Council; when use of the Bible is spreading among the Christian people; when advances in catechesis, pursued in accordance with the Council's guidelines, are making possible an evangelization in depth; when biblical, patristic and theological research often makes a precious contribution to a more meaningful expression of the data of revelation—at this very moment many of the faithful are troubled in their faith by an accumulation of ambiguities, uncertainties and doubts about its essentials. Such are the Trinitarian and Christological dogmas, the mystery of the Eucharist and the Real Presence, the Church as the institution of salvation, the priestly ministry in the midst of the People of God, the value of prayer and the sacraments, and the moral requirements concerning, for instance, the indissolubility of marriage or respect for life. Even the divine authority of Scripture is not left unquestioned by a radical demythologization.

Bishops are authentic teachers

While silence gradually obscures certain fundamental mysteries of Christianity, we see manifestations of a tendency to reconstruct from psychological and sociological data a Christianity cut off from the unbroken Tradition which links it to the faith of the

[8] Cf. 2 *Th.* 2, 10.

apostles, and a tendency to extol a Christian life deprived of religious elements.

All of us, therefore, who through the laying on of hands have received the responsibility of keeping pure and entire the faith entrusted to us and the mission of proclaiming the Gospel unceasingly, are called upon to witness to the obedience we all give the Lord. It is an inalienable and sacred right of the people in our charge to receive the word of God, the whole word of God, of which the Church has not ceased to acquire deeper comprehension. It is a grave and urgent duty for us to proclaim it untiringly, that the people may grow in faith and understanding of the Christian message and may bear witness throughout their lives to salvation in Jesus Christ.

The Council reminded us forcefully of this: " Among the principal duties of bishops, the preaching of the Gospel occupies an eminent place. For bishops are preachers of the faith who lead new disciples to Christ. They are authentic teachers, that is, teachers endowed with the authority of Christ, who preach to the people committed to them the faith they must believe and put into practice. By the light of the Holy Spirit, they make that faith clear, bringing forth from the treasury of revelation new things and old,[9] making faith bear fruit and vigilantly warding off any errors which threaten their flock.[10] Bishops, teaching in communion with the Roman Pontiff, are to be respected by all as witnesses to divine and Catholic truth. In matters of faith and morals, the bishops speak in the name of Christ and the faithful are to accept their teaching and adhere to it with a religious assent ... ".[11]

Certainly, faith is always an assent given because of the authority of God himself. But the teaching office of the bishops is for the believer the sign and channel which enable him to receive and recognize the word of God. Each bishop, in his diocese, is united by his office with the episcopal college which, in succession to the apostolic college, has been entrusted with the charge of watching over the purity of faith and the unity of the Church.

[9] Cf. *Mt.* 13, 52.
[10] Cf. *2 Tim.* 4, 1-4.
[11] Dogmatic Constitution *Lumen Gentium*, 25; *AAS* 57, 1965, pp. 29-30.

II

Let us unhesitatingly recognize that in the present circumstances the urgently needed fulfilment of this preeminent task encounters more difficulties than it has known in past centuries.

In fact, while the exercise of the episcopal teaching office was relatively easy when the Church lived in close association with contemporary society, inspiring its culture and sharing its modes of expression, nowadays a serious effort is required of us to ensure that the teaching of the faith should keep the fulness of its meaning and scope, while expressing itself in a form which allows it to reach the spirit and the heart of all men, to whom it is addressed. No one has better shown the duty laid upon us in this regard than our Predecessor Pope John XXIII in his discourse at the opening of the Council: " In response to the deep desire of all who are sincerely attached to what is Christian, Catholic and apostolic, this teaching must be more widely and more deeply known, and minds must be more fully permeated and shaped by it. While this sure and unchangeable teaching must command faithful respect, it should be studied and presented in a way demanded by our age. The deposit of faith itself—that is to say the truths contained in our venerable teaching—is one thing; the way in which these truths are presented is another, although they must keep the same sense and signification. The manner of presentation is to be regarded as of great importance and, if necessary, patient work must be devoted to perfecting it. In other words there must be introduced methods of presentation more in keeping with a magisterium which is predominantly pastoral in character ".[12]

Safeguard the truth

In the present crisis of language and thought, each bishop in his diocese, each synod and each episcopal conference must be attentive lest this necessary effort should ever betray the truth and continuity of the teaching of the faith. We must beware, in particular, lest an arbitrary selection should reduce God's design to the limits of our human views and restrict the proclaiming of his word to what

[12] *AAS* 54, 1962, p. 792.

our ears like to hear, excluding on purely natural criteria what does not please contemporary taste. " If anyone ", Saint Paul warns us, " preaches a version of the Good News different from the one we have already preached to you, whether it be ourselves or an angel from heaven, he is to be condemned ".[13]

In fact it is not we who are judges of the word of God. It is his word which judges us and exposes our habit of conforming to this world. " The weakness and insufficiency of Christians, even of those who have the function of preaching, will never be a reason for the Church to water down the absolute nature of the word. The edge of the sword [14] can never be dulled thereby. The Church can never speak otherwise than as Christ did of holiness, virginity, poverty and obedience ".[15]

In passing, let us remember this: if sociological surveys are useful for better discovering the thought patterns of the people of a particular place, the anxieties and needs of those to whom we proclaim the word of God, and also the opposition made to it by modern reasoning through the widespread notion that outside science there exists no legitimate form of knowledge, still the conclusions drawn from such surveys could not of themselves constitute a determining criterion of truth.

All the same, we must not be deaf to the questions which today face a believer rightly anxious to acquire a more profound understanding of his faith. We must lend and ear to these questions, not in order to cast suspicion on what is well-founded, nor to deny their postulates, but so that we may do justice to their legitimate demands within our own proper field which is that of faith. This holds true for modern man's great questions concerning his origins, the meaning of life, the happiness to which he aspires and the destiny of the human family. But it is no less true of the questions posed today by scholars, historians, psychologists and sociologists; these questions are so many invitations to us to proclaim better, in its incarnate transcendence, the Good News of Christ the Saviour, a message which in no way contradicts the discoveries

---

[13] *Gal.* 1, 8.
[14] *Heb.* 4, 12; *Rev.* 1, 16; 2, 16.
[15] Hans Urs von Balthasar, *Das Ganze im Fragment*, Einsiedeln, Benzinger 1963, p. 296.

of the human mind but which rather raises that mind to the level of divine realities, to the point of allowing it to share, in a still inarticulate and incipient yet very real way, in that mystery of love which the Apostle tells us " is beyond all knowledge ".[16]

Encourage theologians, exegetes

To those in the Church who undertake the responsible task of studying more deeply the unfathomable riches of this mystery, namely theologians and in particular exegetes, we shall manifest encouragement and support in order to help them to pursue their work in fidelity to the great stream of Christian Tradition.[17] In the recent past it has quite rightly been said: " Theology, being the science of the faith, can only find its norm in the Church, the community of the believers. When theology rejects its postulates and understands its norm in a different way, it loses its basis and its object. The religious freedom affirmed by the Council and which rests upon freedom of conscience is valid for the personal decision in relation to faith, but it has nothing to do with determining the content and scope of divine revelation ".[18] In like manner, the utilization of human scientific knowledge in research in hermeneutics is a way of investigating the revealed data, but these data cannot be reduced to the analyses thus provided, because they transcend them both in origin and content.

In this period which follows a Council which was prepared by the rich attainments of biblical and theological knowledge, a considerable amount of work remains to be done, particularly in the field of developing the theology of the Church and working out a Christian anthropology taking into account progress made in human sciences and the questions the latter pose to the mind of the believer. We all recognize, not only how important this work is, but also that is makes particular demands; we understand the

---

[16] *Eph.* 3, 19.
[17] Cf. *Relatio Commissionis in Synodo Episcoporum Constitutae*, Rome, October 1967, pp. 10-11.
[18] Declaration of the German Bishops, Fulda, 27 December 1968, in Herder *Korrespondenz*, Freiburg im Breisgau, January 1969, p. 75.

inevitable waverings. But in face of the ravages being inflicted upon the Christian people by the diffusion of venturesome hypotheses and of opinions that disturb faith, we have the duty to recall, with the Council, that true theology " rests upon the written word of God, together with sacred Tradition, as its perpetual foundation ".[19]

Dearly beloved brothers, let us not be reduced to silence for fear of criticism, which is always possible and may at times be well-founded. However necessary the function of theologians, it is not to the learned that God has confided the duty of authentically interpreting the faith of the Church: that faith is borne by the life of the people whose bishops are responsible for them before God. It is for the bishops to tell the people what God asks them to believe.

This demands much courage of each one of us; for, even though we are assisted by exercising this responsibility in community, within the framework of the synods of bishops and the episcopal conferences, it is none the less a question of a personal and absolutely inalienable responsibility for us to meet the immediate daily needs of the People of God. This is not the time to ask ourselves, as some would have us do, whether it is really useful, opportune and necessary to speak; rather it is the time for us to take the means to make ourselves heard. For it is to us bishops that Saint Paul's exhortation to Timothy is addressed: " Before God and before Christ Jesus who is to be judge of the living and the dead, I put this duty to you, in the name of his Appearing and of his Kingdom: proclaim the message and, welcome or unwelcome, insist on it. Refute falsehood, correct error, call to obedience—but do all with patience and with the intention of teaching. The time is sure to come when, far from being content with sound teaching, people will be avid for the latest novelty and collect themselves a whole series of teachers according to their own tastes; and then, instead of listening to the truth, they will turn to myths. Be careful always to choose the right course; be brave under trials; make the preaching of the Good News your life's work, in thoroughgoing service ".[20]

[19] Dogmatic Constitution *Dei verbum*, 24; *AAS* 58, 1966, p. 828.
[20] *2 Tim.* 4, 1-5.

472

III

Therefore, dearly beloved brothers, let each of us examine himself on the way in which he carries out this sacred duty: it demands from us assiduous study of the revealed word and constant attention to the life of men.

How in fact shall we be able to proclaim fruitfully the word of God, if it is not familiar to us through being the subject of our daily meditation and prayer? And how can it be received unless it is supported by a life of deep faith, active charity, total obedience, fervent prayer and humble penance? Having insisted, as is our duty, on teaching the doctrine of the faith, we must add that what is often most needed is not so much an abundance of words as speech in harmony with a more evangelical life. Yes, it is the witness of saints that the world needs, for, as the Council reminds us, God " speaks to us in them, and gives us a sign of his kingdom, to to which we are powerfully drawn ".[21]

Teach them Jesus Christ

Let us be attentive to the questions that are expressed through the life of men, especially of the young: " What father among you ", Jesus says to us, " would hand his son a stone when he asked for bread? ".[22] Let us listen willingly to the questionings that come to disturb our peace and quiet. Let us bear patiently the hesitations of those who are groping for the light. Let us know how to walk in brotherly friendship with all those who, lacking the light we ourselves enjoy, are nevertheless seeking through the mists of doubt to reach their Father's house. But, if we share in their distress, let it be in order to try to heal it. If we hold up to them Christ Jesus, let it be as the Son of God made man to save us and to make us sharers in his life and not as a merely human figure, however wonderful and attractive.[23]

In being thus faithful to God and to the men to whom he sends us, we shall then be able, with prudence and tact, but also with

---

[21] Dogmatic Constitution *Lumen Gentium* 50; *AAS* 57, 1965, p. 56.
[22] *Lk.* 11, 11.
[23] Cf. *2 Jn.* 7-9.

clears vision and firmness, to make a correct assessment of opinions. This is, beyond any doubt, one of the most difficult tasks
for the episcopates, but also one of the most necessary today. In
fact, in the clash of conflicting ideas, the greatest generosity runs
the risk of going hand-in-hand with the most questionable statements. " Even from your own ranks ", as in the time of Saint
Paul, " there will be men coming forward with a travesty of the
truth on their lips to induce the disciples to follow them "; [24] and
those who speak in this way are often convinced of doing so in the
name of God, deluding themselves about the spirit that animates them. In the matter of discerning the word of faith, do we
take sufficient note of the fruits that it brings? Could God be the
source of a word that would make Christians lose the sense of
evangelical self-denial or which would proclaim justice while
forgetting to be the herald of meekness, mercy and purity? Could
God be the source of a word which would set brothers against
brothers? Jesus warns us of this: " You will be able to tell them
by their fruits ".[25]

Let us demand the same from those co-workers who share with
us the task of proclaiming the word of God. Let their witness
always be that of the Gospel; let their word always be that of the
Word who stirs up faith and, together with faith, love of our
brothers, bringing all the disciples of Christ to imbue with his
spirit the mentality, the manners and the life of the terrestrial
city.[26] It is in this way that, to quote the admirable expression
of Saint Augustine, " God, not men, brought you this; thus even
through the ministry of timid men God speaks in full freedom ".[27]

Dearly beloved brothers, these are some of the thoughts suggested to us by the anniversary of the Council, that " providential
instrument for the true renewal of the Church ".[28] In joining
with you in all fraternal simplicity to examine our fidelity to
this fundamental mission of proclaiming the word of God, we have
been aware of responding to an imperative duty. Someone per-

[24] *Ac.* 20, 30.
[25] *Mt.* 7, 15-20.
[26] Cf. Decree *Apostolicam Actuositatem*, 7, 13, 24; *AAS* 58, 1966, pp. 843-844,
849-850, 856-857.
[27] *Enarratio in Psalmos*, 103; *Sermo*, 1, 19; *PL* 37, 1351.
[28] Cf. Apostolic Exhortation *Postrema Sessio*, in *AAS* 57, 1965, p. 865.

haps will be surprised, may even protest. In the serenity of our soul we call upon you to witness to the necessity that urges us on to be faithful to our charge as shepherd; we call upon you likewise to witness to our desire to join with you in taking the means most adapted to our days and at the same time most in conformity with the Council's teaching, the better to ensure its fruitfulness. As we join you in entrusting ourselves to the sweet motherly care of the Virgin Mary, we invoke with all our heart upon you and your pastoral mission the abundant graces of " him whose power, working in us, can do infinitely more than we ask or imagine; glory be to him from generation to generation in the Church and in Christ Jesus for ever and ever. Amen ".[29]

May these wishes be supported by our Apostolic Blessing, which we impart to you with affection.

Given in Rome, at Saint Peter's, on the eighth day of December, the solemnity of the Immaculate Conception of the Blessed Virgin Mary, in the year nineteen hundred and seventy, the eighth of our pontificate.

PAULUS PP. VI

[29] *Eph.* 3, 20-21.

INDEX

ANALYTICAL INDEX

AD GENTES

– Vatican II decree on mission (see Missions) 1, 2, 6, 28; 238; (60; 242).

AGGIORNAMENTO

– (also see Council, renewal, reform and Church in modern world).
– Aggiornamento of Church's exterior structures and interior life, 71; 974.
– To bring Gospel to modern world, 263.
– To be regarded as a principle for consistent and constructive renewal; 370.

ALPHONSUS (St.)

– Theologia Moralis 1, p. 3; 133.

AMBROSE (St.)

– De officiis); 81.
– De Spiritu Sancto I, 12, 126; 205.
– De Spiritu Sancto I, 7, 89; 207.

ANSELM (St.)

– 309.

APOSTOLICAE ACTUOSITATEM

– N. 14; 385.

APOSTLES (Apostolic ministry and ministers)

– Apostles and their successors, enjoy the charisms of the spirit promised to them; 126. – Have the right and duty to teach truth of faith; 126. – Authoritative channels of the truths of faith, missionary investiture of 131; 387.

ASIA (Asian faithful; situation in Asia)

– Asian hierarchy; church in Asia: crossroad of cultures, ancient and modern; 422. – Birth place of world religions; 422. – Treasure house of ancient wisdom; 422. – Its decisive place in the world on account of its population; 423. – Its races united with a network of interests; 416. – A certain identity of outlook on life and harmony of aspirations; 416. – A people rich in civilization and culture; 417, 422.
– Spiritual values and religious spirit of (the Asiatics); 424. – Filial piety and attachment to family; and veneration for ancestors; 424. – Primacy of spirit: quest and hunger for God; 424.
– Spiritual sense of A., to provide basis for full progress (in technical, economic and social spheres); 424.
– (Asians, to hold fast to) their spiritual sense and values to counter materialism; 425.
– Asia must not succumb to atheism; 425.
– Church in Asia, missionary apostolate, in; 417.
– Church in Asia to be Asian in style, but Catholic in its teaching in communion with the See of Peter; 419. – An Asian can be true Catholic and remain fully Asian; 419. – (Need to develop) missionary vocation in A.; 419. – Natural inclination of Asiatic to prayer; 417. – Deep innate religious sense of Asiatic spirit, to be fortified by Gospel spirit; 418. – Catholic Church (feels) at home in Asia; 425. – Need to defend spirituality proper to Asian people from materialistic civilization; 418.
– Episcopal Conference of Asian Bishops; 378 (see papal trip to Far East).
– Duty of Asian Bishops: to adapt evangelization to thinking culture of people of the places; 419. – To show that the message of salvation and Church are for all races; 419.

- Radio Veritas, inauguration of (see papal trip to the Far East).
- Situations of incomplete development; and unequal distribution among Asian people, to be set right; 423; peaceful co-existence; and fruitful cooperation among countries of Asia, desirable; 423.
- Need for a movement of brotherly solidarity in Asia to satisfy the legitimate aspirations of freedom and justice and complete humanism; 426.
- Task of those responsible, to deal firmly and decisively with injustice among social groups; 424. – To ensure far-sighted wisdom in development; 423. – To heed to labour problems and agrariam reforms; 424. – To give particular attention to the impoverished and abandoned; 424.
- Continent of Asia, oppressed by tragedy of war; 427. – Acts of terrorism and war; 427. – Misery caused by the natural tragedy in East Pakistan; 427. – Suspension of hostilities and reaching honourable peace, need of the hour 427.

AUGUSTINE (St.)

- Phil. 2, 1. – Societas Spiritus; 29. – Ep. ad Diognetum V-IV; 30. – Serm. 138; 30. – Sermo V, 3; 115. – In Ep. Contr. Joannis ad Pathos 1, 2, 3; 131. – Contr. Man. V; 134. – Conf. I, XI. c. 4n. 6; 140. – De moribus ecclesiae 1, 30, 130. – City of God. 18, 51; 2; 189. – Conf. XI, 14; 190. – In Ps. 137; 190. – Miscellanea augustiniana; 205. – Conf. I, 1; 214. – Enarr. in Ps. 73; 266. – Conf. 1, 1; 300. – Contra Faustum; 309. – De civ. Dei. XV, 6; 317. – Enarr. in Ps. 49; 323.

AUSTRALIA

- Episcopal conference of Australia in Sydney (see papal trip to Far East).
- Pope Paul's discourse to Australian youth; 432.

AUTHORITY

- Authority originates grom a positive intervention of Lord's will to goyern and judge; 51. – The responsibility a. of church's pastors; 13.
- A. in church derived from the original institution of Christ; 44.
- A. indisputable to society; 43.

- Gospel institutes and establishes authority; 51.
- Gospel authority, at the service and good of others; 51.
- Church authority, for service of guidance and order; 22.
- A. of church over exterior and interior acts of her faithful; 44.
- Exercise of A. in due form and measure enters the sphere of charity; 53-373. – Should be made with delicacy and understanding; 53; 373. – Need to revise the manner of, a; 128. – Through restriction of liberty of action not desirable; 128. – Should be made by assisting people to act in a free responsible manner, in keeping with the nature and purpose of A. in church; 128.
- Ecclesiastical A. is not constituted democratically; 62; 253.
- Divine A. of Church questioned by radical demythologization; 467.
- Tendency to devaluate A. in the name of lberty; 48.
- Exclusive stress laid on the function of the spirit at expense of authority; 49.

BAPTISM

- Baptism elevates human beings to supernatural order; 72; 116. – Calls us to live as sons of God in holiness and perfection; 72; 323. – A sacrament of initiation into Christian life; 110. – Produces in the Christian Christ's death and resurrection; 110. – Faith, prerequisite condition for the reception of B; 115. – Incorporates us into Christ and Church in faith; 115. – The true ecclesial sacramental birth in Holy Spirit; 130.
- Common baptismal priesthood of the faithful; involves responsibility in the framework of salvation; 277.

BELIEVER and BELIEF

- Believer: accused as a man with static psychology; 212. – One living in the past, distrusting changes in every field of human life; 212. – Not a " man of our time "; 212. – Basically apathetic and afraid; 212.
- The Believer not a professional quietist; 214. – Not an enemy of renewal and progress; 215. – A ready and intelligent promoter of re-

newal and progress; 215. – Does not avoid the demands of the present; 212; – Does not flee from the fascination of progress; 212. – Lives by the inheritance of the traditional faith and grace; 213. – His link with the past and transcendent supernatural does not cut him off from the present and future; 213. – His faith links him to hope; 213.

– Being afraid of believing, an evil that attacks the foundations; 209.

– Putting trust in purely naturalistic and utilitarian and philanthropic belief; 210 (see modernism).

BENEDICT'S (St.)

– Way to God; 187.

BETTI (Il magisterium del Romano Pontefice)

– 133.

BENEDICT XIV, Pope, (Servorum Dei Beatificationis)

– 327.

BONIFACE II, Pope (Ratione Peccati)

– 358.

BISHOP (as pastor, Episcopate, order, function)

– Episcopal authority comes from Christ; 416. – For the service of all the faithful and church; 416.

– Exercise of magisterium, rendered difficult to the episcopal ministry by the complexity of modern times; 126; 469.

– Bishops as successors of Apostles, preachers and promoters of instruction in faith; 415; 418. – To encourage the study of faith and catechesis; 418. – To promote Catholic education and institutions; 418. – To promote use of the means of social communication; 418. – To undertake ecumenical dialogue; 418. – Are entrusted with) their mission of announcing the Gospel of grace and truth; 456. – To examine their fidelity to their commitments to the teachings of Council; 456. – Duty and responsibility of keeping faith entire and pure; 468. – Hand the faith in its fullness to the people in manner and language accessible to them; 466. – To be vigilant to ward off errors threatening faith. – Their faithful; 468. – To teach in communion with the Roman Pontiff in matters of morals and faith; 468.

– Episcopal function demands courage; 472.

– Bishops: to be attentive in the face of the present crisis of language and thought; 469. – To see that God's design is not reduced to the limits of human view by arbitrary selection; 469. – Not to be deaf to the vital questions disturbing the modern believer; 469. – To encourage and support theologians and exegetes; 472. – Not to keep silent for fear of criticism in the face of seeming errors and deviations; 472. – Duty to proclaim the message, refute falsehood, correct error, call to obedience, patience and charity 472. – To choose the right course in the midst of myths and novel opinions; 472; 474. – To be brave in trials; 472. – To make preaching of Good News, their life's work in thorough-going service; 472. – To learn how to walk in brotherly friendship with those not having faith; 473. – In sharing their distress the aim should be to heal it; 473. – In leading them to Jesus, as the Son of God, and not to Jesus as merely human figure; 473. – To have prudence and tact, clear vision and firmness; 474. – To be watchful of false prophets who mislead people with a travesty of truth; 474.

BROTHERHOOD

– See: Problem of World Peace.

CATHERINE OF SIENA (St.)

– Conferring of the title of Doctor of the Church, justified; 338. – Outstanding sanctity and peculiar excellence of St. C.'s doctrine merits the title; 338. – God's preferential choice of the weak and foolish in the eyes of the world to reveal the secret of divine wisdom; 337; 338.

– St. Catherine's life and achievements a life lived in the practice of evangelical beatitudes 338; 340; 342; 343.

- Eminence of St. C.'s doctrine: her writings reflect the theology of St. Thomas; 340; 341. – Mystical apologia made by her for the apostolic office of Peter's successor; 338; 340. – Political magisterium of the St. C.; 343.

CARDINAL (Sacred College of C.)

- Assistance of C. in the government of the Church; 442.
  Office of the Cardinalate requires prudence regarding election of Pope; 461.
- C. lose the right to elect Pope on 80th year of age; 462. – Cease to be in charge of Roman Curia departments and institutions of Apostolic See; 462. – To submit resignation voluntarily on completion of 75th year of age; 462. – Continue to remain members of S. C.; 463.
- Motu Proprio of Pope Paul VI; 461-463.
- Regolamento Generale della Curia Romana; 461.
- Ecclesiae Sanctae, age-limit for Bishops to exercise their office; 461.

CANON LAW

- International Congress on C. L.; 25.
- Canon Law. – Rome, home of law both civil and ecclesiastical; 25. – C. L., a juridical science dealing with church's life as society; 25. – Its importance for spiritual life and civil progress of humanity; 25. – Requirements of free and honest probity in C. L.; 26. – Place of tradition and innovation in C. L.; 26. – Divine and human law in church; 26. – Origin of church law found in (St. Paul's organization of the) first Christian communities; 27. – Canonists to base teaching of C. L. on Holy Scripture and theology; 27. – Need for Lex Fundamentalis in church; 28. – Pope Gregorius IX decretum on C. L.; 28. – Code of C. L. derived from the essence of God, 28. – C. L. not an expression of autocratic power; nor a despotic and arbitrary iussum; 29. – C. L. a norm for interpretation of divine law and interior law of conscience; 29. – Provides a balance between rights and duties; 29. – Between

liberty and responsibility, dignity of the individual and demands of common good; 29. – C. L. provides a balance between church's immutable constitution and her (versatile) adaptability to the demands of modern system; 28. – Tradition providing wisdom and authenticity to C. L.; 28. – Separation between Church and state in temporal affairs; 30. – Church laws are directed to the reign of charity; 47. – Ubi societas ibi ius: the law of church's external structures; 51. – C. L. and salvation of man; 52. – C. L. concerned with spiritual values; protects and regulates administration of sacraments; 52.
- Canonical order, a constitutional law of church willed by Christ; 52. – Legitimacy of juridical power in the church; 53. – Accusations of legalism and formalism; juridical positivism or juridical historicism; 30. – Claim of charismatic voice to emancipate people's consciences from church's normative power; 27.
- Revision of church's code of C. L.; 53; 257. – Necessitated to bring church law in line with modern sociological reality; 53. – A new codification in the context of ecclesiology of Vatican II. – Of its pastoral effects on the world to-day; and development and progress of juridical science, 258. – Reform of C. L. and civil law, when not based on natural law, desirable; 336.

CELIBACY

- Celibacy and recruitment; 63. – Ascetic and mystic struggle of Latin Church; 63. – C. together with freely chosen priesthood can achieve interior fullness of charity; 124. – Easing canon law prescribing total C. not desirable; 64. – Priestly C., a sacrosanct norm in Latin church; 455. – Consecrated by tradition as a sign of total dedication; 456; 63. – A constant tradition in the oriental church; 458. – A bright demonstration of the missionary demand; 457. – Accepted spontaneously by the servants of Gospel; 456. – A law tried and proved by long historical experience; 456. – An answer to the call of Christ to follow him,

abandoning all, family and nets; 456.
- Renunciation to found family, a condition for admission for priesthood in the Latin Church; 456. - Before God and Church; 457.
- Exercise of the ministry of priesthood only by priests remaining faithful to their pledges and obligations; 458.
- Ordaining married men to priesthood; 458.
- Probem of C. to be solved in a way in common consideration for the good of the whole church; 459.
- Grace and joy of celibate priesthood; 459.
- Declaration on eccl. celibacy by Dutch hierarchy; 455. - Repercussions on the people of God, clergy and aspirants for priest-hood; 455.
- Disturbing consequences in the life of entire church; 455. - Echoes aroused by it among all Christians and the members of the human family; 455. - Causing much uncertainty and confusion in the church; 456. - Radical change in C. breakdown of the genuine concept of the priesthood; 456.
- Evangelical values understood and lived only in faith and prayer, penance and charity, struggle and mortification; amidst scorn and persecution of the world; 456.

CHARITY (also see love)

- Charity: hallmark of Christian life; 14. - Nobility and fruitfulness of Christian C.; 47. - C. frees yoke of constraint; 49. - C. a movement towards God; 56. - Divine C. and fraternal C. necessary for the life of the church; 65. - Practice of C. in the liturgy of the word; 66. - C. gives church its specific quality of the Mystical Body of Christ; 100. - Paradox of C., to give to others in order to obtain Christ; 324. - Its supreme importance in Catholic communion; 431. - C., its immediate effects-service, self-sacrifice, self-giving and unity; 431.

CHRIST

- C. the centre and source of Christian life; 14. - Master and bread of our personal life; 14. - The sole, supreme and eternal Head and generator in the church; 29. - Refused to be a political Messiah and preferred the name of Son of Man; 49. - Revealed us the mystery of divine sonship; 90. - Christ's life, a narrow way, a life of cross; 72. - Bread of Life, Light of the world, the Good Shepherd, the Way, Truth and Life, 90. - C., life and truth of the existence of individual and community of believers; 91; 433. - C. the highest degree of tension in the liberty of conscious life; 91. - C. the supreme answer to the tempestuous questionings of inner voice; 93; 434. - C. defender of the poor, the little, oppressed and the suffering; 107. - C. dominates history, thought, concept of man and human salvation; 151; 434. - C. came to this world to free us from all idols; 204. - Fidelity to C. for he has the words of eternal life; 281. - C. the Teacher, revealer, the Light and joy of every heart; 309; 334. - The destinies of mankind depend on C.; 448. - C., Man of men; the new and perfect man inviting and consoling those in tribulations; 433; 450. - C. axis of unity, (as he is the) source of love and charity; 450. - C. the Bread of Life guaranteeing those who eat it, eternal life; 451.

CHRISTIANITY (Christian living and life)

- Christianity: Profession of C.; 12. - Problem and necessity of choice in C. life; 14. - Christian's obligation to do the will of God; 335. - C. acts in conformity with Christian vocation; 351. - Christians, the best friends of their fellowmen: to work for the sanctification of the world; 426. - Christianity and its message still valid to the world of to-day; 448. - Renewal of C. does not need the formation of a new C; 296. - Christianity's stability of existence and consistency, its continuity in development and movement not obscurantist, archaic or bourgeois or clerical; 296. - Tendency to reconstruct a new C. from psychological and sociological data; 467. - A C. cut off from tradition linking the faith of the Apostles; 467. – Tendency to extol Christian life deprived of religious element; 468.

CHRISTMAS

– Commemoration of the birth of Jesus; 448. – Silent and irresistible message of the child of Bethlehem; 451. – Message of C. for poor suffering, prisoners and refugees; young and disturbed; men of science and intellectuals and those belonging to the political and economic world; 451.

CHURCH

– C. not invented for new times; 12. – Church's mission of salvation and peace; 12; 178; 434. – Consistency a preliminary criteria in the C.; 13. – Confidence in the C.; 13; 281. – Faithful, the vital members of the Mystical Body of Christ, the C.; 281. – Church's twofold basic purpose: to be and to do Christ's will; to infuse faith and grace; 22; 178. – C. founded by Christ is a visible society; 27; 406. – C., people of God constituted as an organic body; 27; 407. – C. her mystico-ethical introspection; 29. – The sole demand of C., free exercise of moral and spiritual mission; 30. – C. the sacrament of salvation; 30; 178; 189; 406; 412; 439. – C. as our mother, and teacher of the faith of the Lord; 30; 108. – C. essentially a communion; 31 (see communion). – C. a liberation obedience; 42. – C. a bridge between God and man; 43. – C. an organized social communion governed pastorally; 43. – Finding peace in belonging to the C. Newman's example; 45. – Church's hierarchical structure; 51. – Jesus willed his teaching to be entrusted to a qualified power, and not to be subjected to individual's interpretation; 51. – C. complex comprising human and divine element; 51. – C. pillar and mainstay of truth erected for all ages; 52. – C. is Christ's body, a family of believers, of one heart and one mind; 60; 118; 178. – C. is prayer association; 143. – C. is not a kind of philanthropical humanism; 144. – Nor a temporal sociological organization; 144. – An organism teaching men to communi-

cate with God; 144. – C. a mystical edifice built on Peter by Christ; 154; 407. – C. a summons from God to mankind; 177. – C. its story, a passage from the Old Testament giving into the New; 177. – C. constitutes a relationship, a dialogue, communnion, salvation and blessedness; 178. – mankind responding to God's call in Christ; 178. – C. is Lumen Gentium like Christ; 178. – C., an offering of Saving Truth and an outstretched hand of redemption and happiness; 179. – Church's call is not offensive, does not reproach; 180. – Church's voice, a liberating one, of prayer, of hope; 180. – The concept of C. invisible as utopian – a purely spiritualist and liberal interpretation of Christianity; 27. – Fidelity to C. betrayed, minimized, debated and interpreted acc. to private views; 281. – C. not a wall of division; 296. – C. bearer of Christ's paradoxical cross; 318. – C. a sheepfold into which the Good Shepherd is leading and gathering his scattered flock; 407. – Need to discover and rediscover the mysteries of the church; 407; 408. – C. is not separated from the world but lives in it breathing its culture; 262. – Temptation of considering C. in her time-bound sociological and historical aspects; 262. – Which gives only onesided and subjective view of her; 407. – Spiritualistic and charismatic concept of church; 407. – C. alone can instruct men about the truths of this life, interpret history, resolve doubts, and reveal men the call implicit in them; 411.
– The sameness of the C. in history; 414. – The presence of Christ in the sign and sacrament of the Church; 415. – C. is one holy, Catholic and Apostolic; 415; 381.
– Church's part in social action and progress; 420.
– C. cannot be alien to any country or people; 426.
– C. can never speak otherwise than as Christ did of holiness, virginity, poverty and obedience; 470.
– Doctrine of the Apostolic nature of the C; 416. – C. established authenticity of the C. of Christ; 416. – C. importance and fidelity of tra-

dition; 416. – C. apostolic college under the primacy of the successor of Peter; 416. – C. vitality and ever-renewed youth of the church; 416. – C. ministerial powers proper to Christian priesthood; 416.

Pilgrim Church in history and time:
– C. exists in the changeability of time; 189. – Habitual illusions of making this earth a fixed point, a resting place; 190. – Fulfilment of the divine plan; 191. – In the fullness of time safeguard of the depositum of faith and values in time; 191. – Guarantee that the adversities of time and history cannot prevail against her; 191. – The fixed goal of P. C. is meeting Christ; 191. – The meaning and direction of history in reaching salvation; 192. – Christians responsible participants in the life and progress of the world; 192. – The relation between Christians and the world is one of balance and synthesis between immobility and relativism; 192.
– Catholic Church pilgrim in time, but victorious over time; 371. – Guarantees a synthetic combination of stability and progress; 371.
– God, starting and reaching point of Pilgrim church; 4; 5.

CIVILIZATION
– Human C. and society must develop in Christian and human values; 82.
– C's movement towards total secularization; 290. – Autonomy of temporal values; 290. – Liberation from the alleged link with religion restricting man's knowledge and interests to the scope of earthly realities exclusively; 290.
– C's growth, development and progress; its task of averting world destruction; 7; 9.

CICERO (pro cluento)
– 51.

COMMUNICATIONS, SOCIAL
– World Day of S. C.; 112.
– Worrld Year of Education – UN enterprise for promotion of mass C.; 113.
– S. C. media: responsibility of all in the use of S. C. m.; formation of

youth to live up to their calling as individuals and Christians; 112. – to be used to bring out the real problems of the world; 112; 236. – To seek authentic values of life; 112. – A reality capable fostering equality and fraternity; 234. – A means to enriched convergence of culture and unity; 234. – A means for broadening one's outlook and establishing contacts and communications; for sharing the experiences of life; 113.
– S. C. M. open beginnings of education and provide wealth of information; 113; 234. – Means at the service of mankind and of the whole man; 113. – Provide youth access to culture of quality, taste for authentic values of brotherhood peace, and justice and general welfare; 113; 234. – Can bring home message of true life; 114. – To bring youth to experience the participation in the life of living God; 114. – A means to announce the new language of the Good News; 114; 235. – Can bring us Christ, the wisdom, sanctification and redemption as answer to radical and disquieting questionings of youth; 114 – Can keep the seekers of Christ remain young; 114. – Involves sciences of man and of nature; 233. – Its world-scale influenc challenging the whole man; 233. – Sets up tensions within the vital duality of society and person; 233; 234.
– Task of parents and educators to help youth to choose, judge and assimilate; 113.
– S. C. to aid the development of man in his personal and social values; 234.
– S. C. m. entail danger of hiding and supplanting true value of traditional vehicles of culture; 113. – Dragging into the pitfalls of eroticism and violence; 113. – Leading into the perilous paths of incertitude and anxiety; 113. – Risk of alienation, conformism; passive and unchecked acceptance of models of thought and behaviour; 234.
– Need to put an end to the corrupting enterprises of S. C. m.; 113.
– Problem of the S. C. influencing family, school and young without prior formation; 234.

- S. C. a phenomenon to be analysed philosophically and critically; 234.
- Facts presented by S. C. must be in conformity with the moral imperatives; 234.
- Correct use of the methods for transmitting the content and message; 234.
- Pontifical commission for S. C.; 232.
- Pastoral and apostolic responsibility in S. C.; 232.
- Inter Mirifica document on to giving wider expression to Episcopal Collegiality; 233. - To give just and due recognition to local fields of competence; 233.
- Church activity in S. C. based on structures central and local, regulated by complete and upto-date norms; 233.
- Renewal of catechesis, preaching, religious symbolism through S. C. m.; 179; 237.
- The process of the reform of the language of religion not to be allowed to alter the content of Christ; 180.
- Theology of the phenomenon of S. C. m.; 235.
- Doctrinal point of view of S. C. importance of the thorough study of it; need to foster and encourage it.; 233.
- Necessity of spreading the doctrinal implications of S. C. to develop a vast movement of public opinion; 235.
- Formation of consciences in the light of the doctrinal implications of S. C.; 236.
- Good use of press, radio, cinema, television and other audio-visual aids for spread of Gospel; 236.
- Lay apostleship movements in S. C. m.; 236.
- Need of specialized courses, training centres; 237.
- Direct pastoral use of S. C. m.; 237.
- Effective presentation of the church's news through S. C. about her.; 237.
  - communication between men and contact of different cultures tending towards unity of mankind; 239.

COMMUNION (also see Unity; Ecumenism; community spirit)

- Internal ecclesial community consists in perfect C. of minds and purposes of work; 60.

- Fraternal community unity in Christ; 61.
- Communitarian nature mankind willed by divine plan; 61.
- C. in the church hierarchical; 61.
- Intrinsic relationship between personal spirituality and community spirit; 65.
- Community spirit to be linked with deep punctual interior religiousness; 65.
- Externalism and legalism; 65.

C. SPIRIT

- In the Communion of the Church. Jesus willed that his community be hierarchical in structure, a social spiritual organism; 51; 230.
- Ecclesial community; 11.
- Sense of C. among the People of God; 228.
- C. spirit has its origins in the common baptismal priesthood of the faithful; 229. - Among organized religious groups practising evangelical counsels; 229.
- Work of ecumenism based on communion; 229 (see ecumenism).
- Communitarian spirit of the postconciliar church; 230.
- Church, a communion by intrinsic and constitutional necessity; 230.
- Church Communion involves a basis of equality, personal dignity, common brotherhood, progressive solidarity, disciplined obedience; 230.
- Genuine community spirit follows the truth in love and grows in charity, 231.

CONFERENCE, Episcopal: collegiality

- Relationship of Collegiality and pastoral function of the Pope with the E. C.; 119; 193.
- Principle of E. C. can become a living reality in dialogue and collaboration; 194.
- Establishment of E. C. with the mandate to adapt liturgy to the needs of local situation; 257.
  Coordination and advancement of local churches in communion with the church of Rome through E. C.; 257.
- Pope's confidence in the establishment of the E. C.; 126.
- Papal trip to the Far East to make

the reality of E. C. more effective;
408.
- Pastoral function of Episcopate of
the Episcopate of Asia; 417.
- E. College with Peter and under his
authority guarantees fidelity to the
depositum of faith; 466.

CONFESSION

- Sincere reconciliation wth God
through the sacrament of C.; 96.

CONFIDENCE

- Need to battle with confidence contra in spem in all situations; 121.
- Personal, total and deep confidence
in Christ is willed by himself; 122.
- Need to have C. in the unchallengeable power of divine mandate of
church to teach and guide; 127.
- C. in the goodness of the great
majority of Christians towards hierarchy; 127.
- C. in the wise and patient renewal
of the art of exercising authority
by Bishops; 128.

CONFLICT (see Violence)

Y. Congar: (Pour une Eglise servante
et pauvre).
- 267.

CONSCIENCE

- Conscience: a theme of discussion
begun by Socrates, reawakened principally by Christianity; 322. - Psychological consciousness, man's inner perception of himself becomes
moral C.; 322. - Law written by God
within man's heart is a voice from
the depth of his C; 322. - Voice of
C. calls for obedience for its dictates;
322. - C. shrine of man's encounter
with God; 322. - Man's dignity
consists in his obedience to the law
of his conscience; 322. - Exercise
of the reflective act gives rise
to a sense of responsibility and
personality; 322. - C. perfects itself
when bound by charity; 51. - C. operates in liberty bound by truth and
animated by charisms of the Holy
Spirit; 51. - Jesus, the honest search
of inner personal voice of life, 92.
- Believer's C. receives infallible security in the fundamental truths
from Church's magisterium; 133. -

C., the proximate rule of action,
ought not to prescind from the
higher and moral law; 133. - C. on
its own right not enough to give
knowledge of the reality of things
or of the morality of action; 133;
352. - Church recognizes and acknowledges rights and priority of C. in
formulating a moral judgment about
individual and immediate acts; 133.
- Examination of C. set in motion
by Council; 23. - Restricting the
field of moral sensitivity to personal
consciences cannot be approved; 97.
- Claim of modern groups to the
power of emancipating conscience
(see modernisms). - Liberty of C., argument advanced in favour of emancipation of Church's magisterium;
133. - C. enlightened by grace becomes vocation demanding total response; 323. - C. of the pious is the
altar and seat of God; 323.

COUNCIL VATICAN II

- Convocation of C. to bring modern
world with the perennial energies
of the Gospel; 225; 333.
- Fulfilment of C. teachings requires
painful revisions and timely re-
straints; 11; 256.
- C. brought about disciplinary innovations modifyng those of Trent and
of Clement XI; 270.
- Council, pastoral in nature; 274; 333.
- C.'s legacy, a process of development;
279.
- Voice of C., undoubted voice of
Christ, a lamp to light our road
of pilgrimage; 23.
- C. deepened the doctrine of Church,
highlighting her mystical aspect; 27;
156.
- C.'s fashioning of moral and religious ideas; 42.
- C. teaching on perfection of man;
- ennobled anthropology giving it
its due and right place, but not to
the detriment of Christology and
theology; 42.
- C., the most perfect gift of the Holy
Spirit; 195.
- C. teaching, an authentic compendium of doctrine; 55.
- C. 's moral renewal on Christian
living; 11; 333.
- C. acknowledges frailty of her members and institutions in history; 56.

- C. stresses positive values; its method being pointing out of divine goodness in everything; 56; 58.
- C. teaching can educate us in good will infusing an attitude of good spirit; 57.
- Richest result of post-conciliar period-coordination and collaboration between Holy See and Episcopal Conferences; 257.
- Post-conciliar period in the church only transitory; 279.
- Need for vigilance and prayer in the post-conciliar period; 280.
- Council documents provide nourishment and law both individual and community; 280.
- Fidelity to C. by adhering to its exhortations, and fulfilling its tasks; 280.
- Applicaton of the knowledge of c. by means of doctrinal and canonical deductions; 334. - Doctrinal application involves understanding of our membership of the Body of Christ and church; 334. - Participation in the church's life of prayer and apostolate; - Recourse to our consciences; responsible use of liberty; commitment to our personal sanctification: spread of Christian spirit and vocation; effort to get closer to our Separated Brethren; confrontation between church and modern world; 334. - Canonical application of the knowledge of Council: acceptance of the juridical reforms of the church; liturgical and structural reforms of the ecclesial community; 335. - Spiritual and theological application of the knowledge of C.: by devoted study and meditation of its decrees and teaching; 335.
- C. deepened awareness of herself and her ecumenical, apostolic and missionary vocation; 466.

COURAGE OF TRUTH

- Courage of Truth: a moral and psychological virtue; 211. - Implies a mature mind, boldness of will, capacity for love and sacrifice; 211. - Required of teachers and champions of Truth and all baptized and confirmed Christians; 211. - Implies profession of dutiful fidelity to Christ; 211.

CROSS

- Cross: spes unica of Christians; 97. - Offers Christian hope to the suffering world; 98. - Christian believer to follow the Lord, " a target of contradiction " and carry his own crosses; 158. - Sermon of the Mount, a programme wth the emblem of the cross; 449.

CULLMEN

- " Jesus et les Révolutionnaires "; 360.

CYPRIAN (St.)

- " De Cath. Unit. c. 6 "; 30.

DANIELOU (Card.)

- "L'avenir de la religion "; 315.

DANTE

- (Par. 6, 12; 28, 3; (Par. 33, 9); 152.

DAWSON

- " Progress and Religion "; 212.

DEI VERBUM

- N. 5, 118; n. 5-10, 133.

DE LUBAC H.

- " Méditation sur l'Eglise "; 178.
- " Sur les chemins de Dieu "; 308; 138; 139.

DE MORÉ, PONTIGIBAUD

- " Du fini à l'infini "; 139.

DEPUY B. D.

- " La rev. div. "; 270.

DENZINGER, H. - A. SCHÖNMETZER

- 137.
- " Ench. Sym. 873-874 "; 358.

DEVELOPMENT

- See Mission; FAO.

DEVIATIONS

- Post-conciliar D. in the church.
- Intolerance and depreciation of church traditions and past system; 12.
- Facile sympathy for everything outside the church; 12.

- Formation of hypothesis and innovation of new systems in church; 12; 45.
- Obedience to authority as troublesome bonds; 12; 21.
- Seeking for excessive personal freedom; 12.
- Errors of confusing custom with tradition and excess love for church customs; 13.
- Innovations deriving from the Council; 13; 22.
- Errors of relativism, historicism and existentialism; 21.
- Putting hope in radical metamorphosis of inheritance; 22.
- Indolence and laziness in Christian life with regard to Council's teaching; 22.
- Spirit of corrosive and destructive criticism of church and council; 22; 12; 240.
- Individual judment to fashion a convenient concept of church; 23.
- Spirit of criticism of church in conformity with the spirit and morals of the world; 23.
- Criticism of the magnanimous choice of the religious life; 45.
- Arbitrary interpretation of the church doctrine with a display of erudition; 45 (also see modernism and its tendencies) church; faith etc).

DIALOGUE

- Ecclesial style in D.; 128. – D. with God in one's interior life; 323. – D. used properly can be a good means of exercising pastoral authority; 128. – D. developed with various representatives of modern humanism; 259. – Secretariat for the D. with non-christian religions and humanisms; 259 (also see Ecumenism, Unity etc.).

DIGNITATIS HUMANAE

- (N. 8). 49; 54; (n. 11, 12)
- 360; 347.

DIPLOMACY

- (Church's relations wth states); also see Uno, FAO.
- Diplomatic Corps accredited to Holy See, a synthesis of the world; 15.
- Church Diplomacy: mission of church in the world of diplomacy; 15; 245.

- fulfilment of responsibilities of the Apostolic See; 15. – Diplomatic activity of the Holy See sanctioned by centuries-old historical experience; 16. – Church relations with institutes and organisms of temporal order; 16. – Church's essential role in diplomatic world is religious; 16. – Holy See's D. aimed at fostering mutual dialogue between nations; 16. – Recognizing rights and duties of each nation; 16; 245. – Modern Roman Pontiff's action in fostering respect for basic principles of civil and international life, justice, concord and peaceful cooperation; 16. – Church's activity in the service of peace in the education of communities and families; 17. – Pope's task to intervene on concrete plan of action for Int. peace; 18. – Pope Pius XII's efforts for peace during world war II; 18. – Pope John XXIII – offer of mediation in situations of int. tensions; 18. – Ethical and spiritual content of papal diplomatic activity; 18. – Ethical and spiritual content of papal diplomatic activity; 18.
- Council call on church to fortify the unity of human family; 16.
- Church's relations with Int. organisms for the spiritual salvation of men; 18. – For promotion of dignity of human person; 18. – For progress of nations in justice and peace; 18; 244; 245. – Holy See's D. activity, a total dedication to the problem of human life; 18; 245. – H. S. dialogue with world states for recognition of rights and freedom of the church; 18. – Church's diplomatic contacts for promotion of authentic humanism open to transcendence; 18. – For promotion of human personal and social values; 19. – War, horror, and tragedy in the Nigerian conflict; 20. – Church's respect for international law; 20.
- Holy See's D. relations with various countries not established on conflict; 245. – Not founded on interests opposed to those of the countries; 345.
- Holy See seeks to collaborate in the welfare of various peoples in their integral development and moral progress; 245.

DOGMA AND DOCTRINE

- Trinitarian and Christological dogmas; 467.
- Dogma of the mystery of the Eucharist and Real Presence; 000. - Of Church as the institution of salvation and priestly ministry; 467.
- Ambiguities and uncertainties and doubts about Doctrine and Dogmas of Church in post-conciliar times; 467.

DOSTOYEVSKI

- If there be no God everything becomes licit; 96.

DRUGS

- Drugs: a poison to physical psychical and moral health; 98. - Clandestine and organized traffic of Drugs, to be condemned; 98. - Drugged hedonism; 95 (see hedonism).

ECCLESIAM SUAM

- 262.

ECONOMIC

- Economic and civic wants of developing peoples.
- Third World's cry fo help for E. D.

ECUMENISM
AND ECUMENICAL UNITY

- Spiritual and moral unity in the church; 13. - Week of prayer for church unity; 31. - Reintegration of all Christians into one church; 31. - Christian's fundamental duty of preserving unity; 31. - Unity of faith, of spirit, in the bond of peace; 31. - Unity by one Baptism in one God, Father of all; 31. - Division caused by abnormal historical situations by the principle of " cuius regio eius religio " 31; 32. - Rise of diverse Christian confessions and churches; 32. - Principle of private judgment, cause of division; 32. - Personal and arbitrary interpretation of Bible; 32. - Intercommunion by Catholics and dissidents not permissible; 32. - Unity not possible without the same faith and the valid priesthood; 32. - authoritative notification by Vatican E. Secretariat for union of Christians; 32 - Oneness of Christianity, a happy outcome of E.

fostered by Vatican II; 33. - Unity willed by Christ, is the need and in interest of Christians and Catholic religion; 33. - Must be expressed by a single Church; 33. - Movement and steps taken towards eccl. and universal communion; 33. - Fraternal and sincere collaboration between Catholics and non-Catholics; 000. - Common efforts in cultural, social and charitable fields; 33. - Sincere possibility of integration of good, true and beatiful aspects of differing expressions of Christianity in one ecclesial communion; 34. - Existence of positive and progressive ecumenism; 34. - Need of individual effort to help the Gospel cause of one fold and one Shepherd; 34.
- Real-ecumenism can come from true interior conversion; 333. - Necessary to be true and convinced, firm and good Catholics; 34. - A watered-down camouflaged Catholicism cannot help Ecumenism; 34. - Easier and questionable forms of Christian life depreciate the cause of Christ and unity in church; 34. - Unity among Catholics, the first step towards genuine Ecumenism; 34; 61. - Need for rooting out all egoism and dissensions within Catholic communion; 34.
- Requirements for Ecumenism, firmness and simplicity of faith nourished by God's word and Eucharist; 35. - Spirit of service and sacrifice, prayer and love of Christ crucified; 35.
- Visit of Vasken I, supreme Catholicos of Armenians to Roman Pontiff, in the cause of furthering unity; 181; 258.
- Ecumenism in post-conciliar period: fraternal relations developed with Separate Brethren; 258. - Meetings with Catholic and non-Catholc ecclesial communities; 258.
- Ecumenism in pastoral dimensions being developed by working commissions of theologians; 258.
- Establishment of Jerusalem Ecumenical Institute for the History of Salvation; 258. - Frequent contacts with non-Christan religions, like Moslems, Buddhists, Jews, made through dialogue; 259.

Analytical index

EUCHARIST

- " Sacrificial meal; Real Presence " also see Holy Mass.
- Eucharist: most definitive act of Christian religion; 32. – Institution of the sacraments of Holy Orders and of E.; – A matter of confidence not permitting elusive exegesis (of the authentic reality) of the words of Christ; 101. – Faith in E. drives away objections brought about by ignorance and refined dialects of profane thought; 102. – In E. mystery of faith opens as mystery of love; 219. – Nobis natus nobis datus, mystery of Incarnation and Redemption manifested in E.; 219. – Jesus' giving of himself in E.; 219. – E. a sacrament of unity; 220. – In E. Jesus wishes to be the principle of life and love in the communicant; 220. – E. a sacrifice, a renewal of Jesus' death on the cross; 221. – Corpus Christi, a feast of Christ's love for us and our love for him and love for one another; 221.
- E. mystery of truth, an example, a testament, commandment and teaching; 221.
- E. willed by Christ as a means of overcoming solitude in personal life; 248. – Overcoming distance between generations, between history and geography; 248.
- Individual and collective participation in the E. 299.
- E. sign and bond of unity; 438. – Puts us in real communion with Christ, and spiritual, mystical and moral communion with those sharing the same bread; 438.
- **Real Presence:** Presence of Christ in the church, personal, true, real, and is sacramental; 218. – Established in church through the legacy of Christ's word; preserved by ministerial tradition; 218. – Jesus conceals himself in the E. but reveals in it.; 219. – Christ in the E. contains the true body and blood of Jesus; soul and divinity under the species of bread and wine; 218; 220; 101. – Real and sacramental Presence of Jesus multiplied by him in time and number to give himself to each of us; 219; – Real Presence, ambiguities, uncertainties and doubts by novel opinions; 467.

EVANGELIZATION

- See Missions.

EVIL (also see SIN)

- Consciousness of evil in us and in us and in the world, a realism, a diagnosis for the cure of salvation; 94.
- Goodness, a means for breaking the chain of evil; 10.

EVOLUTION

- (Also see TIME, "Pilgrim Church in Time ").
- Man's continuous evolution to become morally perfect; 81.
- E. in history, the secret of the metamorphosis of the modern world; 29.
- Modern philosophical systems of E. historicism, relativism; 370.
- (See Progress, Modernisms).

EXISTENTIALISM

- Modern society in confusion and anxiety-ridden pessimism arising from existentialism; 95.
- (Also see modernisms).

FAITH

- Faith, an act of reflection by reason on the science of God; 309. – Services of reason required by E.; 309. – Does not suffocate reason nor takes its place; 309. – Joins reason with the acceptance of the word of God. – Exalts it.; 309. – Search for God by faith supported by reason; 309. – Its liberating and redeeming experience in the person having it. 315. – F. made for man of the modern times; 315. – F. for time is the same faith marked by religious truth and religious fidelity to the depositum of faith; 318. – Act of F. can discover Christ in the suffering humanity; 450. – The Christ who rebelled against hypocricy and injustice; 450.
- Faith: basic principle of Christian living; 14. – Realistic vision of F.; 73. – F. in Christ Jesus Son of God and a sincere confession of it obtains eternal life; 116. – F. a free and full response to God revealing and speaking; 117; 130. – F. a vital

supposition for membership of Christ's Mystical Body; 118. – Profession of F. entails sacrifice and moral courage; 158. – Pauline credo an explicit profession of F. of church's authoritative teaching and authentic tradition; 209.

– Man without F. betrays his moral insufficiency and despair; 73.
– Loss of F. in church's magisterium and tradition; 45.
– Selective criterion in the acceptance of the dogma deprives F. of its objective consistency; 117; 210.
– Independent judgments of the truths of faith takes away unity and charity; 000.
– Firmness and purity of F. threatened to-day by opposing thoughts and morals of the world; 126. – By weariness of Catholic truth; 000. – By excessive and incautious pluralism inside church; 126. – By weakening of orthodoxy and content of the doctrine of F.; 000.
– Prayers and good will are required to fortify our threatened faith; 290.
– Objective faith, not a personal opinion, but a fixed and defined doctrine based on the testimony of the magisterium. – The church; 133.
– Cult of man in preference to divine worship; 210.
– Legitimizing ambiguous and uncertain expressions of F.; 210.
– Shield of F. to withstand dangers of modernism; 211.
– F. undergoing an eclipse (owing to unfavourable subjective conditions) in modern man; 304; 315.

FAMILY

– Equipes Notre-Dame (whose members devote themselves to weave with Christ the daily thread of conjugal love); 166. – Church's apparent questioning of human love in the past deplored; 166. – God not an enemy to the human realities of family love; 166. – Good News of Christ is good news for human love; 166.
– Family: The Saviour began the work of salvation in the sanctuary of F. love; 169. – F. a domestic sanctuary of the church; 167; 170. – Christian and human vocation of the F.; 167. – Council's reaffirmation of the call to holiness to the spouses; 167. – Need to foster in F. an education that builds in child and adolescent a sexually mature personality; 168. – F. a community life of the spouses; 170. – A veritable cell of the church; 170. – A basic germinal cell and the most fundamental organism; 170. – Spouses find in their child "an infinite mystery and love", 170. – Duty of spouses to watch over the physical and moral growth of their children; 171. – Parental education to their children, a real service to Christ; 171. – God's authority and love is exercised through those of the parents; 171. – God's providence is respected through the devotedness of the parents; 171. – Homes that experience the trial of not having children; 172. – Hospitality in the home and welcome given to every newborn; 172. – Gospel good news is also for families which while making demands also liberates them; 174. – Peace in the home of loving spouses; 176. – Happy and faithful homes prepare for the church and the world a new springtime; 176.
– Apostolate of the home formation of the betrothed; assistance to the newlyweds; help to homes in distress; 172.
– Pastors to respect the demands of the consciences of the married; 174. – To educate and form their consciences according to moral laws; 174.

F.A.O. (UNO)

– Its progressive influence and dynamism; 395. – Variety and breadth of its activities; 395. – Drivng force behind its undertakings are love of man and universal sense of brotherhood; 395.
– Holy See's interest in the past in the activities of F.; manifested in the discourses of: Pope Pius XII and Pope John XXIII's encyclical "Mater Magistra"; 396 – Pope Paul's active and personal solicitude in official and unofficial ways; 396.
– Church's solicitude and interest in

the initiatives by FAO and her disinterested support to its undertakings; 397.
- FAO's tasks: to stimulate international action to provide each man nourishment both in quantity and quality required; 397. - Promoting progressive lessening of hunger; undernourishment and malnutrition; 397. - Eliminating the cause of epidemics; 397. - Preparing trained labour; 397. - Finding necessary employment for trained labour; 397.
- Scope a more intelligent utilization of basic physical resources; 397. - a better use of land and other natural resources; 397. - An increased productivity from farming, livestock raising, fisheries; 397. - Improvement of soil fertility; 397. - Intelligent use of irrigation; 397. - Redivision of plot lands; 398. - reclaiming marshes; 398. - Effort at plant selection and introduction of high-yield grain varieties; 398.
- Risks involved: dangerous repercussions resulting from imbalance of natural surroundings by accelerated technical progress; 398. - Progressive deterioration of environment; 398. - Ecological catastrophe; 398. - Pollution of air, water of rivers and oceans leading to biological death; 398.
- Survival of man: need for radical change in the conduct of humanity; 398. - Prodigious victories of science and technology not to be allowed to lead to explosion of death; 398. - Moral and social progress to accompany and balance that of science technology and economy; 399. - Well-being to be built upon the principle of individuals for others and with others and not against others; 399.
- FAO-its achievements and place in history; 399. - Heirs of Christ's compassion before suffering humanity; 399. - FAO, a unique adventure in the history of man; a mission of aiding all men to live and survive; 399. - Fruit of humanity's desire to unite in order not to perish; 399.
- To work together to build a common future for humanity; 399.
- Temptations in FAO's undertakings; 400. - Using its authority to diminish the number of guests rather than multiply the bread to be shared; 400. - Accepting opinions extolling planned birth control, believed to be a radical solution to developing countries; 400.
- Church encourages scientific and technical progress; 400. - claims respect for the inviolable rights for human person; 400.
- Public authorities, primary guarantors of the inviolable rights of the human person; 400.
- Church opposes a birth control unworthy of the dignity of man; 400.
- Church accepts a rational control of birth by couples responsible; 400.
- Youth of rich and poor countries, combination and harnessing of the energies of youth and support to achieve human solidarity; 401.
- scandals: public and private expenditure of a wasteful nature; 402. - Expenditure motivated by national and personal prestige; 402. - Vast expenditure for armaments fostering centres of discord and rivalry; 402. - Enormous sums wasted on prestigious undertakings, which could be better utilized for helping to feed poor countries; 402. - Exaggerated nationalism, racism, unlimited thirst for power and domination; 402. - Strikes disrupting transport of agricultural products and markets; 402. - Rich countries buying raw products of poor countries at the lowest prices possible and selling finished products at very high price; 402. - Economy tainted by power, waste and fear; 402.
- World-wide food problem to be solved on an international level and initiatives; 403.
- World indicative plan of agricultural development; 403.
- Establishment of world authority; 403.
- Need for transformation of the selfish and exclusively profit-based economy into an economy of service; 403.
- FAO's task of honour: to make the latent land and human resources to bear fruit; and direct it to the service of common good; 403. - Promote study and action wth re-

gard to food and agricultural problems and solutions; 404.
- Norman Borlaug, father of green revolution, an example worthy of emulation; 404.
- FAO, to make brotherly love driving force of its mission of social justice and progress; 404.

FATALISM

- (See modernisms and tendencies).
- Resigned F., cause of unhappiness of human living; 95.

FEAR OF GOD

- Fear of God, essence of the natural religious sense, is the beginning of wisdom; 251. - Logical and ontological principle of Bibles's philosophy; 251.

FIDEI DONUM

- 242.

FORTITUDE

- Fortitude presupposes principles, logic, personal freedom; 22. - Involves unpopolarity, sacrifice, and fidelity to an irrevocable choice; 22. - Fidelity to an unquestionable law; 22. - A virtue of pre-eminence in post- conciliar period, 22.

FRANCIS DE SALES (St.)

- Theotimus II, IX.
- 56.
- Intr. to Devout Life.
- 170.

FUCHS

- Teologia e vita morale alla luce del Vaticano II.
- 81.

GARRONE (Card.)

- Le Concile, p. 78.
- 61.

GAUDIUM ET SPES

- Vatican II document on Church in the Modern world.
- 270; 274; 466.
- 30; (23-24). - 61; (36) - 72; 80; (30) - 81; (38) - 106; (59 par. 3) - 137;

(4-10) - 164; (49) - 167; (1, 47-52) - 167; (45) - 189; (3) - 254; (88) - 267; (8) - 351; 360.

GOD

- Creator of all things; 429. - Immanent principle of all existence; 429. - Transcendental and inexpressible Being worthy of unlimited adoration; 429. - Incomprehensibility of God's nature; 284. - Theology and religion are for the conquest of G.,; 283. - Reason and faith, roads leading to the knowledge of G.; 283. - Common sense directs us to know G.; 284 - Vatican I defence of reason's capacity to reach to the knowledge of the Supreme Truth; 284; 308. - Existence of G. can be known with certainty; 284. - Nature of G. can be known by way of analogy and negation; 284; 308; 312. - G. remains a positive mystery; 284. - knowledge of G. can be deepened by evidence of reason joined with that of faith; 285. - G. to be sought in the Book of His creation; 285. - In the study of his word, in the school of his Church; 285. - G. can be seen in the depth of one's own conscience; 285. - Existence of G., the constitutional law of the universe; 288. - Man created to know love and serve G.; 287; 303. - G. is light to our thought, true good of our action, and love in our life; 289. - No ethics can be maintained without G.; 289. - We cannot know G. without G.; 293; 308. - Recognition of G., in no way hostile to man's dignity; 293. - Through his relation with G. man is freed from all servitude of history and society; 298. - Regeneration of the idea of G. in manifold aspects of faith and charity; 293. - G. our beginning and end; 302. - Modern life is a search for values; 303. - God is the real object of every search; true value worth being looked for; 303. - Man has an irreplaceable need for G. 300. - Man's dependence on G. is free but morally necessary; 251. - Blind acceptance and belief in G. without thinking and discussion; 282.
- Death of God: a philosophy arising from the absurdity and sickness of human mind; 210; 283 - Doubting

about the existence of God; 282. – Practical scepticism, a pseudo-superior modern attitude; 282. – Atheism, a declared anti-God attitude; 282. – " G. is dead " – a blasphemous and sacrilegious negation, referring to a false concept of G.; 283. – an idol set up by modern man to suit his own religious ideas and sentiments; 286; 303. – Lack of confidence in the possibility of knowing G.; 283. – An agnostic acknowledgment of the unreachable transcendence of God; 283; 290. – Preoccupation in empirical and scientific matters obscured metaphysical rationality from man in knowing G.; 283; 287; 299. – Temptation of the practical negation and abandonment of the search of G.; 286; 298; 307. – Of giving up the practice of religion; 286; 298. – Of acquirement of an easy-going conscience; 286.

– " No more need of God " – axiom of liberty and discovery for the modern man. 286; 291; 303. – Uselessness of G., religion, faith, and prayer; 286. – Confrontation of one's own conscience with the demands of divine law; 287. – Annoying " bonds of convention " and superstition of and religion; 287. – Anthropocentric trend in to-days progressive man; 288. – Man's judgments are measured by egoist and utilitarian considerations; 288. – Tendency to reject God and religion as obsolete ideas; 290. – G. described as mystical, as mystical, imaginary and unreal; 291. – Modern form of atheism; fascination of modern form of atheism on youth; 291. – Due to the supposed openmindedness which it fosters and authorizes; 291. – Projects as a sign of mental progress; 291. – As cause and effect of scientific and technical social and cutural progress; 291; 299. – Modernity of doctrine not enough in itself to endow it with credibility; 292. – Replacing G. with modern materialism and immanent idealism does injury to G. and man 301.

– Modern Apostolate consists in creating conditions for attaining an authentic humanism; 306. – To establish a connatural way of getting beyond man's one-dimensional materialist

and positive level; 305. – Modern idols of noble and lofty concepts and values, not justifiable substitute for God and religion; 299.
– Seeking God: alternative to s. G. is falling into despair; 310. – Condemning our thought to mediocre and conventional electicism; 310. – Our search for G. to be endless until we join him; 310. – G. present in him already, who looks for him; 311. – We cannot seek G. the way we seek earthly things; 311. – Knowledge of God's nature by via remotionis and via excellentiae; 312. – Finding G. in modern times in literary testimonies, philosophical writings and religious experiences; 314.

GOOD OPTIMISM

– See Optimism.

GOOD SPIRIT

– See Optimism.

GOOD WILL

– See Will.

GRACE

– Law of grace; 80.
– Church introduces mankind into the realm of G. and educates in it.; 80.
– Relation between law of nature and law of G.; 80.
– G. of acceptance of God's word; 316
– G. a gift which cooperates with responsible liberty; 316.
– Preaching the truth is useless unless there be grace; 317.

GRAVISSIMUM EDUCATIONIS

– 171; 297; 317.

GREGORY THE GREAT

– 87.
– Regula Pastoralis; 276.

HAGIOGRAPHY

– The study of, is made with modern methods of historical criticism psychological analysis and Church's judgment; 37.

HAMER

– L'Eglise est une Communion.
– 31.

HEDONISM
- Hedonistic mentality leads to illusion and pessimism; 75. - In the Christian conception of contemporary life; 74.
- Secular concept of the world; 58. - Also see God, Time. - Drugged hedonism; 95.

HISTORY
- See " Pilgrim church in time and history "; also evolution.
- History of our day, of men equipped with prodigious power and capacities for salutary progress of the world, and also for destruction; 411.

HOPE
- Essential relation of faith with H.; 213. - A theological virtue, a moving force of Christian and human dynamism; 213. - Existence of the element of H. in modern mentality for the attainment of some future good; 213. - Critical and pessimistic psychology of the young often leads them into despair when their hopes belie; 214. - Christian, a man of hope, not knowing despair; 214. - Christian. H. aims at attaining at Supreme Good; 214. - Modern secular man's hope conditioned to the instinct of enjoyment; 214. - Short-termed hopes, tangible and economic; 214. - Christian hope absorb all the truly human and honest tension in secular hope; 214. - Escatological hope does not reduce the importance of man's earthly commitments, but supports and accomplishes it.; 293. - True hope does not die with the passage of time; 451. - Guarantees real and total satisfaction to the natural aspirations of heart; 451.

HUMANAE VITAE
- (n. 9). - 169; (n. 1). - 141.

HUMANAE SALUTIS
- Bull of Pope John XXIII.
- 255.

HUMANISM
- An isolated humanism, is an inhuman humanism (also see Missions, Bishops, UNO etc.).

INTERNATIONAL SITUATION
- Order, peace and justice (see violence and conflict in the world).
- Order cannot be brought about by violation of human rights; 207.
- Mankind's right to peace can be realized by elimination of the causes of conflicts within and among nations; 207.
- Search for a just and equitable negotiated settlement of the armed conflict; 206; 262; 319.
- Papal voice of intervention is veiled in discretion and aimed against violation of human rights; 207. - Aimed at evoking a hearing to justice and human brotherhood; 207.
- Pope's appeal for concrete work for peace: that the normal principles of humanity and brotherhood prevail over every other criterion; 262.
- Need for evangelical sincerity towards all men; 261.
- Equitable solution required to attain balance of justice; 261.
- Efforts to bring relief and to reawaken feelings of humanity in areas of conflict; 319.
- Credibility of words spoken and actions performed, at stake; 262.
- Mere words of speech, not believed by the youth of to-day; 262.
- Church speaks of truth, justice and liberty, progress and concord; peace and civilization; 263. - Brings the message of universal brotherhood to people; 263.

ITALY
- Italian church; episcopate; priests:
- IV General Assembly of Episcopal Conference; 119.
- Life of church in Italy, a unique blend of history and tradition; 119. - Shaped by male ecclesial structures; 119.

IRENEUS (St.)
- Adv. Haereses. iv, 28, 4.; 173.
- Adv Haereses. iv, 5, 1.; 293.
- Adv. Haereses. iv, 6, 4.; 308.

IVO OF CHARTRES
- Prol. in Decretum; 47.

IGNATIUS OF ANTIOCH (St.)
- 108.

IGNATIUS OF LOYOLA (St.)

- Spiritual exercises; 288.

IMMANENTISM

- Replacing God with modern materialism and immanent idealism; 301 (see God).

INEQUALITY

- Poverty, antagonisms and selfishness of classes give rise to inequality among peoples; 207. – Inequality among world powers; 207. – I. In the Third world and its cry for help; 260. – The danger of growing inequalities between wealthy and developing nations; 260. – Imbalance growing between profitholders and exploited labourers; 261. – Problem of unequal distribution of wealth between nations; 261.

INTELLIGENCE

- Intelligence: a power of assimilation and assent; 139. – The sense of the divine; avid and skilful faculty of recognizing the traces of God; 139. – Passionate involvement in scientific knowledge; 305. – Use of intelligence and polarization of will in the context of man's positive development, cause of negation of religion; 305. – Mastery obtained by science not enough for the insatiable demand of mind; 307. – Intellectus quaerens fidem; 308.

INTER MIRIFICA

- N. 6; 351.

JEROME (St.)

- In Eph.; 178; (comm. in Is. Prol.; 272.

JOHN OF AVILA (St.)

- St. John of Avila: canonization of; 222. – Apostle of Andalusia. – Patron of the diocesan clergy of Spain; 222. – An exemplary model to the modern priests of our day; 223.
- Life, sanctity and significance; 224; 227.

JOHN OF THE CROSS

- Canticle, verse. 5; 140.

JOHN XXIII (Pope)

- Addresses. I. p. 298; 170; 469.

JOURNET (Card.)

- L'Eglise III. 590-594; 115; 139.
- L'Eglise III.; 191; 416.

JOY

- Alleluia: a cry of praise full of joy and enthusiasm to the Lord; 154. – Sustains and accompanies us to the eternal life; 154.
- Joy: of being within the fold of Christ the centre of religion, faith and grace of the spirit; 155. – J. must be perennial in the constant meeting with the Risen Christ; 155.

JUDGE

- Justice; court; law.
- Court of Sacred Roman Rota; 46.
- Image of judge in Church to-day; 46.
- Judge: calm and impartial interpreter of law; and one who discharges his office with lofty Christian conscience; 46; 54. – Sense of duty and responsibility in his functions; 46. – Qualities of discretion and clemency joined with dutiful strictness; 46. – Objective interpreter of ius through his subjective ius; 47. – Moral sensitivity, lofty and indispensable prerogative of judge; 47. – Potestas et libertas eminent requirements of judge; 47. – Moral uprightness and disinterestedness, prerequisites of a judge; 48. – Need for solitude for the cause of justice in a judge; 48. – Impartiality presupposes profound and unshakable integrity; 48. – Aequitas of judgment a special attribute of Roman law; 47. – Aequitas, a quality of priestly moderation in the spirit of Gospel; 47.
- Exercise of judicial power in the church criticized; 48. – Considered as vestiges of absolute power; 53. – Use of coercive power in church; 53. – Pastoral significance of the exercise of coercive measure: for the moral and spiritual integrty of the church and for the good of the guilty; 53.

JUSTICE

- Concept of the God of justice in the Sacred Scriptures; 48.

- Justice: a service to God; 48. -
Cause of justice and liberty makes
us yearn for a life of brotherly
love; 24. - The church's principles
are hinges and not blocks for justice
and liberty; 24. - Justice and law
stem from a sacred ethical principle
of life both of individuas and peoples; 245. - Justice and law have
their origin and strength in the religious faith; 245.

KIDNAPPING

- (And other criminal aberrations).
- Kidnapping persons through threats
and for venal and vindictive ends,
a degrading phenomenon of civilized
society; 98.
- Air-craft hijacking, kidnappings,
armed robbery, clandestine trading
in drugs call for denunciation from
church; 34.
- Public opinion to stand opposed to
these criminal aberrations; 34.

LAGRANGE GARRIGOU

- " Le sens commun "; 284.

LAITY

- Council of Laity: papal commission
established to trasform tension between L. and clergy into dialogue;
83.
- Lay Apostolate in the modern world;
84.
- Threefold dimensions of the L.: human person created in the image of
God; 84. - Rendered Christian by
baptism; 84. - As Catholic, a member
of the Mystical Body of Christ; 85.
- Laity, an active subject in the church;
85. - Specific character of the L. to
share in the multiform activities
and progress of the world; 84. -
Promotion of dignity and responsibility in the church; 85.
- Laity Council: to stimulate cultural
apostolate to deepen the message of
the Gospel, wth fidelity to the See
of Peter; 85. - Mutual exchange of
views between laity and clergy is
imperative in the apostolate; 86. -
Role of coordination of the laity
with the hierarchy; 85; 86. - To be
qualified interpreters and faithful
spokesman of papal pastoral preoc-

cupations for the faithful; 86. - Task
of christianizing the world of to-day;
87. - Vocation of C. L. in the common
baptismal priesthood; 121. - Call to
attain christian perfection; 121.
- Catholic Laity: to give obedience to
and collaboration with church's pastors in the mission of salvation. -
Pastoral magisterium of the Holy See
affirms and confirms confidence; 121.
- In the Catholic laity; 121. - Owes
fidelity and trust to church; 121. -
Required to undertake relative participation and corresponsibility; 122. -
Its ecclesial character and its secular
autonomy acknowedged by Council;
122. - Witnesses and " journeying heralds of Christ "; 285.

LAW

- Positive Law, supported by Natural
law; 50. - Safeguards human good; 50.
- Provides for autonomy of the individual; 50. - Gives fruitful expression
to individual personality; 50. - Obligation to give obedience to the prevailing order in civil and eccl. society; 336. - Necessity of a juridical
order in a society; 49.
- Law of Gospel: is the love of God
and of neigbour; 51. - Jesus' condemnation of legalism of his time;
50. - Condemnation of judaizers and
teaching on the L. of G. by St. Paul;
50.
- Ius scriptum: an expression of reason and demand of common good;
48.

LIBERTY AND FREEDOM

- Liberty: Christians are called to liberty; 44. - Teaching on christian liberty by St. Paul, the Apostle of liberty; 44; 50. - Spiritual significance
of law and liberty; 44. - Church as
liberating obedience; 44 - Church order liberates man from ignorance,
sin and death; 44. - Church liberation aids man's capacty of integral
self-development; 44. - Gospel, a call
for freedom of spirit; 49. - Salvation
and freedom achieved by Christ on
cross; 49. - Liberty and authority do
not oppose but complement each
other; 50. - Mutual cooperation of
liberty and authority fosters growth
of community; 50. - Appeal to Gospel

for liberty against law; 49. – Current anti-hierarchical attitude by appeal to liberty against authority; 51.
– Liberty of science, argument advanced in favour of emancipation from eccl. magisterium; 133. – Church recognizes liberty in the field of scientific truth; 133. – Religious freedom based on freedom of conscience is valid for personal decision to faith (is affirmed by Council); 471. – But cannot determine the content and scope of divine revelation; 471.

LIFE

– Life, respect for, and doubts and uncertainty about; 467.
Constitution on Sacred Liturgy.
– N. 2; 189. – Stresses the need of conversion and penitence as prerequisites for contact with Christ; 333.

LITURGY

– Liturgical reforms willed by council and worked out for pastoral needs; 144; 256; 317. – Introduction of spoken languages into worship and in the studies of theology made with a view to adapt religion to the age and nature of times; 317. – Participation in the liturgical life an eminent preparation for union with God; 229.

LOVE

– Also see love in marriage, charity.
– Love: interior principle of church; 28.
– Code of love, stranger to all impositions; 50. – Essence of moral life and perfection; 71.

LUMEN GENTIUM

– Constitution on the Church; 270.
– L. G. – (n. 48); 30. – (n. 8); 51, 5. – (n. 28); 61. – (n. 40); 72. – (n. 53); 94. – (23); 119. – (25); 134. – (53-56); 152. – (11); 173. – (n. 8); 129. – (10-11);; 229. – (9); 238. – (44); 321. – (2, 11); 330. – (40); 336. – (17); 354 – (42); 363.

MAGISTERIUM

– Hierarchical M., intermediary between Christ and its faithful; 131. – Eccl. M. guarantees the genuine

expression of God's word; 131. – Protestant reformation excluded Church's M. and put the believer in direct contact with Scripture leaving it to his private judgment; 132. –Eccl. M. attacked by the very ones who ought to defend it; 126. – Liberty of science and conscience, arguments advanced against the Eccl. M.; 133.

MAN

– M. himself a tangle of disproportions; 411.
– Fundamental principles of human being; 72.
– Man's pride, root of all trouble in society; 435.
– Without God. M. can organize a world which will lead him to his ruin; 435.
– Man's advance towards light by a choice of being for man with Jesus, and not against man; 435.

MARIA SOLEDAD TORRES ACOSTA (St.)

– Canonization of Maria Soledad, foundress of " Servants of Mary "; 36.
– Life of Maria: sanctity; 38; 39; 41.
– Servants of Mary: a provident religious family dedicated to the service of humanity-consecrated to bodily and spiritual charity; 38; 40.

MARIE VICTOIRE THERESE COUDERC (St.)

– Canonization; 181.
– St. Marie: foundress of the Congregation of Our Lady of the Cenacle; 182.
– Life and sanctity; 12; 13; 186.
– Congregation of Our Lady of the Cenacle: modeled on the spiritual line of the Society of Jesus; 185; 186; 187. – A religious institute containing synthesis of contemplative and active life dedicated to Our Lady; 186; 187. – Its interior aspect spiritual exercises, Retreats, seeking to apply the teachings of the encyclical of " Mens Nostra " of Pius XII; 187.

MARITAIN JAQUES:

– Liturgie et Contemplation; 229. – Christianisme et Democratie; 348.

MARRIAGE

- Christian and human vocation in marriage; 167.
- Duality of sexes willed by God, created by Him to His own image to be a source of life like Him; 167-168.
- M. not to be reduced solely to physical desire and genital activity; 167.
- Scripture teaches us to discover in M. complementariness of the values of man and woman: – Creativity, nobility and weaknesses of conjugal love; 167. – Its openness to the mysterious designs of divine love; 167. – Cautions against temptations of eroticism; 168. – Rescuing M. from the enslavement of sensuality; 168. – Union of man and woman in M. constitues a mutual gft of each other in order to give together; 168. – In M. union each party affirms and refines itself; 168. – M., its irrevocable indissolubility; 168. – M., manifest in a community life; 168. – M. a contract by man and woman for an objective bond; 168. – The laws and requirements of M. are a guarantee, protection and a real support in daily conjugal life; 168. – In M. each personality remains distinct, and does not dissolve in fusion; 168.
- Conjugal love: an means towards the infinite; an elan total, faithful, exclusive and creative; 169.
- Conjugal act maintains and strengthens love becoming a source of life; 169.
- Adam and Eve, source of evil unleashed on the world; 169.
- Joseph and Mary, summit whence holiness spreads all over the world; 169.
- Matrimonial union, represents the union of Christ with the church; 170.
- Christian love in conjugal life brings the spouses to their fullness with patient generosity; 170.
- Spouses, free and responsible collaborators with the Creator; 171.
- Married couples not to let themselves carried away by the current and thought of paganized behaviour of the world; 173.
- Sanctity in married life; 173.
- Virtue of conjugal chastity; 174.
- Spouses in M. find Paschal Mystery of death and Resurrection accomplished; 175.
- Demands of conjugal love neither intolerable nor impractical laws: a gift of God to help them come through and beyond their weaknesses to the riches of love fully human and Christian; 175.
- Mixed marriages, church regulations on; 257.
- Doubt and uncertainties in modern mind regarding indissolubility of M.; 467.

MARTYRDOM

- The value of M.; 336.
- Semen est sanguis Christianorum (Tertullian); 363.
- Need of our times, saints from all walks of life, with heroic virtues and testimony of their love for God and church; 363; 367.
- Church was born from the M. of Christ, and grows in virtue of the heroic love of their children; 363.
- M. an exceptional gift and highest proof of love; 364.
- The disciple in M. perfects the image of Christ; 364.
- M. the sublime expression of faithful love for Christ to the extent of shedding blood; 365.

MARTYR SAINTS

- Canonization of the 40 English and Welsh Martyrs; 362.
- Significance of spiritual faith, heroism, loyal respect for the sovereignty of the civil society; 363.
- Drama of the M. S. conflict between sincere loyalty to God and truths of religion and the obedience to civil authority; 364; 365; 366.
- Special characteristics of M. S.; 366.
- Industry and sacrifice of the M. S. contributed to the preservation of Catholic faith in England and Wales; 367.
- Example of M. S., source of strength for our authentic love of God and Church in times of religious indifferentism and materialism; 37.
- Pope prays that the blood of M. S. may heal the wound of separation

between Anglican and Catholic Church; 367.

- Unity of faith between Anglican and Catholic Churches without dishonour to the former's prestige and patrimony; 368.

MARY

- Devotion to Mary, our spiritual Mother reaffirmed by Pope; 150..
- Unchanged value of enlightened renewal of Catholic's veneration of Mary, justified by Council; 151.
- Profane outlook and critical spirit has made the piety and devotion to M. less spontaneous and less convinced; 151.
- M. cooperated in the work of human salvation through free faith and obedience; 152.
- Christ, our Brother, through the maternal ministry of M.; 152.
- M. the most perfect image and likeness to Christ; 152.
- M. excellent exemplar in faith and charity; 152.
- M. personifies kindness, humility and purity of the Gospel; 152.
- M. Prophetess of our redemption; 153.
- Mary's Magnificat reveals the transforming design of Christian economy; 153.
- M. with a mission of pity, goodness intercession for all; 153.
- M. Mother of the Church; 153.

MASS

- Sacrifical meal of Holy Thursday: (also see Eucharist).
- The M. of Holy Thursday: an intimate union with the Lord in the sacramental celebration; 99. – Manifestation of charity of being of one heart and one mind; 100. – Celebration of the commemoration of the commandment of love; 100. – Washing of the feet by Christ, an example of humility; 100.
- Image of Christ presented to the world in eschatological yearnings; 101.
- Ritual and passover meal, the sign and pledge of the old alliance; 101.
- Mystery of Agape, the mystery of Lord's presence; 101.

- Christ's sacramental action, a sacrifice of meal representing immolation and death; 103; 438.
- Mass: produces in the faithful relationship with Christ and relationship with others; 437.
- Christ remains amidst those gathered in his name; 438.
- M. to be given fullness of its meaning by firm assent of mind and profession of faith 438.
- M., the liturgical celebration of Paschal Mystery; 108.

MATERIALISM

- See God.

MESSIAH

- Liturgy of Palm Sunday projects a prologue to Christ's suffering; shows the Messianic character; 89.
- Messiah-means Christ, the Annointed, chosen, the Consecrated one; 89. – Israel's expectation of M. as the king of history; 89.
- Gospel of Palms offers a choice of acceptance or the rejection of M.; 91.
- Christ, the M., defender of the poor, consoler of the suffering; 93. – The key of all past and future history; 90; 434.
- Jesus' refusal to be a political Messiah; 49.

MIRACLES

- M., experience of those signs of the presence and action of the Godhead; 312.
- The exceptional curiosities of the incredulous and unreligious world regarding M., 312; 313.
- M. of Jesus in the Gospel drew interest trust and faith of the people in him; 313.
- Challenge of modern critics of the truth and reality of M.; 313.
- M. are a special way to draw people's attention to the practice of religion; 313.

MOEHLER J. A.

- L'unite dans l'Eglise.
- 229.

MISSIONS

- Evangelization and Development.
- Ad Gentes, council Decree on the M.; 274; 354. - Broad theological vision given to m. activity by council; 387.
- Urgency of missionary apostolate in the post-conciliar era; 238; 239.
- Duty of the Apostolic ministry to preach the Gospel to the world; 238.
- The pilgrim church missionary by nature; 238.
- Modern world offers a wider inviting field for E. to the courage and wisdom of missionaries; 239.
- New approach in the theology of evangelization; 240. - In the missionary activities; of its structural method and activity; 240.
- New Missionary approach consists in evangelization and development; 240.
- Evangelization: strictly religious activity aimed at preaching and building God's kingdom; 240; 242. - Priority of E. in missionary activity both in its concept and its exercise and organization; 241. - Kerygma, focal point of missionary activity, message of Christ, the cross and christian living; 241. - The folly and scandal of preaching Christ is strength and wisdom of Christ's mission; 241; 242.
- Development: aspect of missionary activity enunciated in Populorum progressio; 241. - Duty of resolutely and intelligently fostering the growth of economic cultural, social and spiritual well-being of peoples; 241; 242; 243. - Need of synthesis between E. and D. in which the one complements the other; 241.
- Task of freeing the spiritual character of E. from the fetters of economics; from the suspicion of colonialism; from the inefficiency of naturalism when faced with differing cultures; 242.
- Missionary activity to be conditioned to the needs of different situations keeping faithful to apostolic spirit; 242.
- Pre-evangelization of missionary apostolate, contact with future Christians; 242. - Living with them and giving them the example of good Christian life; 242. - bearing witness to the human validity of Christ's message in various institutions; 242.
- Laity in the field of missionary activity; 243.
- Missionary phenomenon, evangelical in the concrete vision it gives to Christ's presence; 354. - Knowledge of the M. in their empirical geographical and sociological dimensions; 355.
- Christ, the first and true missionary from God, 355. - Visible M. of Christ in history continued by Holy Spirit in invisible manner; 355. - The revelation of the mystery of the Trinity, at the basis and source of M. apostolate; 355. - Evangelical, apostolic and theological origin of missions; 356.
- Missionary actvity, its dependence on human collaboration made evident by self-sacrifice; 356.
- Missionaries, heroes of Gospel and its preachers; martyrs and saints for its cause; 356.
- Catholic Missions, an unarmed enterprise of offering Christ to the world; a spectacle of super-human realism; 357.
- Missions, an epiphany of faith and charity; 356.
- Joint responsibility of all Christians in the spread of Gospel; 357.
- Cause of Gospel, a cause of the promotion of human rights; of true civilization temporal and moral; of Christian conscience; 357.
- Call for assistance to M. and missionaries, both spiritual and material; 357.
- Need to deepen our Catholic and missionary consciousness; 447.
- Questioning voices of validity of church's missionary efforts to convert people; 388.

MODERNISMS

- Modern tendencies.
- Confusion in modern thought; 27.
- Claim of a charismatic voice, to emancipation of people's conscience; 27.
- Modern man's psychological distrust of Catholic doctrine; 45.
- Present-day confusion of the notion of good and evil; licit and illicit; just and unjust; 73.

– Pessimism prevailing in modern psychology; 73.
– Confusion of a-priori-optimism, modern naturalism; anxiety-ridden pessimism arising from existentialism; 95.
– Drugged hedonism, cause of unhappiness in human living; 95.
– Modern psychology makes the way of faith complicated; 117.
– Modern ideologies and public opinion bring confusion in the minds regarding faith; 117.
– Resigning oneself with a stoic long-suffering magnanimity is a mistaken path; 117.
– Tendency to prescind from the existing church and inventing or creating a new one based on ideological and sociological patterns; 123; 204; 210.
– Tendency to secularize everything, an influence even among clergy and religious; 144; 203; 449.
– Destructive forces in the church; 204.
– Scepticism of human intelligence in religious matters; 204.
– Desacralizing and laicizing movements of the modern world and devious currents of thought in the church; 279; 303.
– Driving force of modern tendency evolution, change in ideas arising from progress, from mutation in the realm of life; 449.
– Feeling of insecurity troubling mankind; 23.
– Demoralizing spread of crime and immorality; 73.
– Man's plight in the turmoil of changing world and social evolution, contestation, negation and violence; 203; 369.
– Precariousness of things and men; 369.
– Appeal to modernity, fashion, novelty, cult of speed; 370.
– Modern world in need of Christ, the truth it is seeking for, the life it is in need of; 448.

MORALITY
MORAL PRINCIPLES AND LAWS

– Consistency of morals in the profession of Christianity; 73.
– Uncompromising fidelity to fundamental norms of human honesty; 72.

– Necessity of normative rationality in an evolving society; 73.
– Council teaching on the moral concept of man; 78; 351.
– Existence of original Christian moral law; 78.
– Dynamism of the moral law, both natural and Christian; 81.
– Fundamental principles always remain unchanged; 81.
– Theological truth subordinates the precepts of moral order to it.; 355; 336.
– Moral principles when oversimplified tend to moral indifference and anarchy; 350; 352.
– Trend of modern thinking denial of absolute reasons of thought and being; 350. – Demolishing the very basis of moral obligation; 350. – Seeking licence to do everything or not to do, and living acc. to one's instincts; 350.
– The Council summons to the renewal of the Christian moral order; 351.
– Existence of moral obligation, a responsibility, a commitment of the life; 351.
– Need for serious reflection on progress made in the sciences of psychology, medicine, sociology; 351.
– Application of constant moral principles to new needs and aspirations of our time; 352.
– Situation ethics: simplication of moral rules leads to conduct governed by situation; 352.
– Situation ethics in conduct means justifying opportunism inconsistency, cowardice; 353.
– Appeals to situation morality undermine character, heroism and true moral law; 353.

MORAUX J. (Le mystère du temps)
– 370.

MYSTICISM

– Spiritual and mystical experience of God, a higher stage of union with God; 312.
– Mystical contact with God, an interior manifestation of the Lord's love to those who love him; 313.
– Mystical saints in the church; 313.
– Originality of mystical action, a delicate and complicated psychological phenomenon; 328.

– Mystical experience, a suffering and at the same time enjoyment of spiritual charism; 328.

MYSTICI CORPORIS

– Encyclical of Pius XII.
– 429.

NATURAL LAW

– Natural Law-strict observance of the fundamental criteria of; 48. – An instrinsically just guide for the freedom of man; 50. – Principles and demands of, derived from life itself; 72. – Interpreted by common sense and ordinary reason; 72. – Enunciated in the Ten Commandments, absorbed, confirmed and perfected by Gospel; 72; 50. – Obedience to N. L. makes us true men and Christians; 72. – Uncompromising fidelity to the fundamental norms of human honesty; 72. – Integrity confirms dignity of man; 73. – Observance of natural virtues, a duty of Christians; 81. – Observance of N. L. a profession of rational justice; 73. – Existence of N. L. evident from the immanent sense of conscience and light of reason; 79. – A powerful interior law which demands to be expressed and affirmed; 79. – Christian concept recognizes N. L. in man; 79. – And upholds human personality and dignity; 79. – Church's rightful authority, the law-maker and interpreter of N. L.; 79. – Church's duty to make explicit, formulate and codify N. L. and give sanction; 79. – N. L. and life of grace to be integrated in practice to attain perfection; 81. – N. L. and law of conscience require to be interpreted by Church's divine authority; 351. – Challenge to the existence of objective natural law; 352. – Progress human and social comes from demand of N. L. which claims for justice and human perfection; 371.

NATURALISM

– See " modernism " and its tendencies.

NEW MAN

– Modern man's awareness of his own greatness and his capacity (to cross impassable barriers in all fields); 163.
– Search for New Man: as he is God's plan; 163. – As the creator of tomorrow; 163. – As the arbiter of himself and the world; 163. – As the lord of the cosmos; 163.
– Ambivalence of man to-day; 164.
– Man torn by the crisis of his own finiteness and interior contradictions; 164.
– The N. M. sought after is in Christ; 164. – Regenerated in Baptism, open to the inspiration of the Spirit; 164. – a witness to the eschatological realities; 164.
– The N. M.: committed to infusing in the realm of earthly realities an order of justice, honesty, equilibrium and love; 164.

NEWMAN (Card.)

– Apologia pro vita sua.
– 45; 204.

OBEDIENCE

– Obedience: fundamental moral virtue; 43. – Supreme example given by Mary by her fiat to God's message; 43. – Basis of man's relations with Christ and God; 43. – God's will, a demanding relationship with man; 43. – Economy of salvation needs response of human fiat; 43. – Church's constituent law and her spirituality; 43. – Implies submission to persons in authority; 43; 52. – Hinge of social life and order; 43. – O. to God rather than man; 336. – Loyal observance of the moral prescriptions of Christ; 50. – O. to Christ, St. Paul's teaching on; 44. Lack of O. to church's authority in to-day's world; 22. – Antihierarchical charismatic tendency presents disobedience as rightful, justified and a safeguard of liberty; 49.

OPPRESSION

– Oppression of the weak and defenceless, cause restlessness and tension; 207. – See UNO, FAO, Peace etc.

OPTATAM TOTIUS

– N. 16; 297; 336; 352; 28; 174.

OPTIMISM

- Good spirit, core of healthy optimism; 57.
- Healthy O. not for satirical and destructive criticism; 57.
- Healthy O. does not employ liberty as a cloak for maliciousness; 57.
- Good O. judges evil in frankness; 57.
- Good O. tries to construct and not to demolish; 58.
- Good O. knows to be content with little. Manzoni; 57.

PACEM IN TERRIS

- 163; 347.
- Papal Travel to the Far East.
- Papal travel to the F. E. by Pope's apostolic and ecclesial mission; 378; 386; 387; 406. – Not touristic, or prompted by political purposes, but exclusively apostolic and missionary; 380; 386. – Religious and human value of Pope's journery; 410. – As Bishop and head of the Episcopal College; 410. – As pastor, missionary, fisher of men, seeker of the people; 410. – To sustain the hierarchy of the East in their apostolate; 414. – To show presence and solicitude for the Episcopal Conferences of the post-conciliar period; 380; 388; 408.
- Pastoral stage: to attend Asian Bishop's Conference in Manila; 378. and greet Asian people; 378.
- For the opening of " Radio Veritas "
- Missionary stage: journey to the islands of Polynesia in the Pacific; 379. – Pay symbolic respect to the typical missions in Western Samoa; 379. – Encourage missionary effort in the world; 388.
- Apostolic stage: to meet Episcopate of Australia, New Zealand and Oceania at Sydney; 379; 442. – To meet hierarchy, and faithful, civil authorities of the East (Australia, New Zealand, Oceania, Djakarta, Hong Kong, Ceylon) to show them papal love and church's presence; 379; 381; 442.
- Travel, a part of the history of Popes; 445. – Of Peter and Paul to preach the Gospel to all nations; 446. – Undertaken by Pope Paul to be open to all peoples and all countries; 446. – A way of exercising

vocation of the apostolic office of the Pope; 446. – Afforded a family reunion of the members of the Mystical Body scattered in Asia and Oceania; 446.

PASCAL (Pensees)

- 411.

PASCHAL MYSTERY

- See Resurrection.

PASTOR

- Pastoral ministry; function; power; shepherd (also see Bishop, Priest).
- Pastoral power comes through apostolic transmission; not by election, nor by investment by community;
  – Intended for the good of the church; 253.
- Principal purpose of Vatican II for pastoral nature; its decree, – Christus Dominus — outlining pastoral office of Bishops; 274.
- Meaning of Pastoral: Homer's description of King as shepherd of people; its biblical significance; Jesus as the Good shepherd; 274.
- Pastoral function of Risen Christ conveyed to Peter; 274.
- Proof of Peter's love for his Master in shepherding His flock; 274.
- Pastoral function entails exercise of authority, teaching and guidance;
  – A prerogative, a responsibility, a power of initiative anteceding the flock; 275.
- Pastoral authority, for the benefit and advantage of those on whom exercised; 13; 275. – Its justification is in its implication; 275.
- Ideal pastor's rightful superiority only in service of others; 275.
- Purpose of authority in pastoral function cure and care of souls; 275.
- Concept of shepherding perfected in the care of souls; 275.
- Care of souls implies service done for Love with love; 276.
- Absolute expression of pastoral service, total giving of self and sacrifice; 276.
- Subjective pastoral requisites: solicitude, humility, disinterestedness, tenderness; 276.
- Objective pastoral requisites: study and experience in the care of souls,

pastoral theology, sociology, pastoral psychology; 276.
- Pastorate, not just empiricism and good fellowship applied to community relationship but concrete application of truths in the care of souls; 276.
- Pastoral function proper to laity; 277.
- Defence and spreading of faith, prime object of pastoral care; 417.

PAUL (St.)

- The first historian and first theologian of the Eucharist; 220.
- Saint's sole concern to know Christ crucified; 108.

PAUL VI (Pontificate)

- Pope Paul VI: speech to the UN; 346; 347. - Message to Tehran Conference; 345. - Discourse to the ILO; 346. - 50th anniversary of priestly ordination; 247.
- Pontificate: predominant task to fulfil the tasks set forth by the council; 256. - Ensure renewal willed by the council; reconstitution of the offices of the Holy Office; 256. - Determination to hold fast to the perspectives of Vatican II; 194. - Impart greater efficiency to the council of the synod of Bishops; 193. - His vocation as ressembleur du college apostolique; 194. - His conciliar constancy; 195. - His resolve to dedicate whole of his work for peace; for conserving and establishing harmony among nations; 206.

PEACE

- The new world day of peace 1970; 7. - P. of conscience; 7, 8. - Universality of P.; 7. - Christ's sacrifice, for P. between heaven and earth; 9. - Holy Mass, a memorial of P.; 9. - Education, indispensable for P.; 9. - Uprooting of force and revenge, ingrained prejudice necessary for P.; 9. - Need for order, temporal and otherworldly; 7. - P., a light for world, a light in the experiences of daily life; 8. - Patience and forgiveness for conquering P.; 10. - Policy and spirit of P. a personal responsibility and duty; 8. - P., civilization's demand and no utopia; 9. - Prayer and faith, Christian weapons to conquer P.; 10.

- P., remedy for unsettled and tormenting problems; 7. - P., not weakness nor cowardice; 8. - P. Harmony implanted in society by God, and actualized by men; 17. - Achieved by triumph over egoism, pride, rivalries, ambitions and injustices by evangelical unselfishness; 17. - To be messengers of P., a Gospel demand; 107. - P. begotten of certainty of faith and security of love, hope and confidence in Christ; 107. - Spiritual P. arises from possession of truth and love of prayer; 205.

PROBLEM OF PEACE IN THE WORLD

- P. not absence of war, not brought about by dictatorship; 17.
- Pope's message of P. an echo arising from the conscience of civil liberty; 393.
- Causes of tension and threat to peace; 390. - Increase in social, racial and religious discrimination; 390. - Supremacy of economic interest; easy exploitation of the weak; 390 - Struggle fomational prestige; uncompromising prejudices of races and ideologies;390. - Recourse to torture and terrorism, crime and violence; 390.
- P. thought of as balance of forces and armaments; 17; 390.
- Just and lasting P. achieved by implanting a mentality of P. in new generations; 390.
- Moral progress of humanity favours establishment of P.; 391.
- P. grows in the network of human relations of culture tourism, commerce, sport; 391.
- Public opinion the only means of settling controversies; necessity of implanting sentiments of brotherhood in it.; 9; 391; 392.
- Guarantee of growing P.: cohesion and concord in international relations; peaceful co-existence perfected through supra-national institutions; upholding the value of human dignity; 391; 393.
- Love for man: highest principle of terrestrial order; generates identity of choice, friendship culminating in P.; 392.
- P. cannot come from relations of self-interest, or purely cultural or fortuitous ones; 392.

- True peace must be founded on justice; 17; 392. – On recognition of equality between men; principle of human brotherhood; 392.
- Existence of the consciouness of universal brotherhood; 392.
- Education of rising generations in the conviction of universal brotherhood; 392.
- Protection of political interests without incitement of hate and combat; 392.
- Discovering human equality in every man beyond his physical and ethnic characteristics; 392.
- Human freedom, equality in dignity, rights of man gifted with reason, spirit of brotherhood, nobler achievements of civilization; 8; 393.
- Every man is my brother, a goal worthy of rational and resolute attention; 393.
- Gospel support for human brotherhood deriving from the concept of God's common fatherhood; 393.
- God's altar barred for those not reconciled with their brothermen; 394.
- Promotors of P., the blessed ones, sons of God; 394.

PEACE PRIZE (Pope John XXIII)

- Awarded for works of peace; 442. (See " Mother Theresa ").

PENTECOST

- P. commemoration of the birth of church, Mystcal Body of Christ; 197. – A feast of wisdom, charity, consolation, joy, hope and holiness; 197. – Feast of souls set on fire by divine inward presence; 197. – Feast of the beginning of Christian culture and civilization; 197.

PERFECTION

- Christian perfection; 72; C. P. supposes union of ascetic and mystic on differing levels; 187.

PERFECTAE CARITATIS

- 321.

PERMISSIVENESS

- Triumphalism of progressive P. in modern society; 352.

- P., a degradation of the self-mastery of human personality; 352.
- Morals of P. society: its aggressive acts and attitudes; its non-christian behaviour patterns; 435; need to supplant these with values of moral rectitude and Christan virtues; 435.

PESSIMISM

- See " Modernisms ".

PETER DAMIAN (St.)

- 187.

PETER (the See of Pope)

- Pope visible head of the church; 28; 119.
- Peter's prerogatives, authority and charism; 32.
- See of Peter, sure foundation to build up our life; 106.
- Tribune of Peter, has given witness and certainty of Peter in the Risen Christ; 106.
- Pope, successor of Peter, foundation of the unity of Bishops and the faithful; 119; 431.
- Abode of Peter, centre of faith and charity; symbol of Catholic church, of Christ present and invisible; 143; 381.
- Roman See, visible earthly centre of C. Church; geographical and legal centre; symbolical and spiritual centre; 381.
- Office of apostolic succession to guard the message of Christ, propagate defend and teach it; 131; 431.
  Duty of pope's magisterium, to favour moral progress of mankind; 35.
- Pope not a prisoner or supporter of any given school of theology; 195.
- Pope's primary duty to be head of brother bishops; bear witness to the faith of the church; 195.
- Pope alone is the appointed spokesman of church; authorized to expound conciliar teaching; 195.
- Pope, servant of the servants; 247.
- Spiritual powers of the keys of Peter to judge all things; 358.
- Pope as Peter's successor has the infallible word; 412. – Alone can speak of the invisible world with certainty; 412.

- Peter's successor, represents Christ, the Supreme Shepherd and Head of the Church; 438.

PIUS II
- Bull Misericordias Domini; 339.

PIUS XII
- Discorsi; viii. p. 288); 96.

PLURALISM
- Council encourages P. in human expressions of faith, but not in its contents; 297; 431.
- P. not to give rise to doubts equivocations or contradictions; 397; 431. - Nor legitimize subjectivism of opinions in dogmatic matters; 297.
- Plurality opinions, not accepted by authority of church; 62.

POPULORUM PROGRESSIO
- (N. 54-57); 261. - (n. 14); 113.

POOR OF SPIRIT
- Church of the poor; 265; 267.
- Christ annointed to bring good news to the poor; 265.
- Public opinion expects church and Holy See poor in the spirit of Christ; 268.

POVERTY
- P. evangelical law of Christ; 18; 265. - Theme of P. dominant in the sermon of the Beatitudes; 265. - Evangelical P. entails corrective religious relationship with Christ; 266. - P. puts God as the supreme good in the scale of earthly possessions; 266; - Christ revealed himself socially through P.; his doctrine on P. marked with humbleness of heart, temperance and detachment; 266. - Principle of Christian P. inspires Christian asceticism; 266. - Council exhortation to practice spirit of P.; 267. - Ecclesial P. inspired church to rid of historical habits which go against Ev. poverty; 267. - Ecclesial P. church's proper appearance; 267. - Mystery of Christ revealed in moral and sociological aspect of poverty; 267. - Church aspect of terrestrial power from due to contact with particular cultural conditions; 268.

PRAT
- (La theol. de St. Paul); 109.

PRAYER
- Church, family of worshippers in spirit and truth; 143; 144.
- Catholicism, the praying church; 144.
- Decline in personal prayer, threat to Liturgy; leads to exterior ritualism; 145.
- Interiority and individuality in prayer; 143.
- Need of personal prayer; 145.
- Soul ispired with charity and p., abode of God; 145.
- P. resistance to church's afflictions and evils; 159.
- Sources in favour of P. Liturgical reform, participation of community prayer; 418. - Value of prayer; doubts and uncertainties; 467.

PREACHING
- Themes of Lenten P. not out of date, 130.
- P. requires mandate, investiture, mission from God; 130.

PRESBYTERIUM ORDINIS n. 2, 6, 7.
- 61.

PRESENCE REAL
- See " Eucharist ".

PRIEST
- P. participates, shares and collaborates with Episcopal priesthood; 61. - Priestly order subordinate to E. order; 61. - Council recognition of priestly personality; priest's corresponsibility in the pastorate; 125.
- P. not to isolate their P. from their Bishops nor from church; 200.
- P. his controversial sociological position in modern society; 59. - Crisis of identity in P.; 223. - Crisis exaggerated by public opinion, and aggravated by lack of reverence to tradition; 122.
- Ministerial P. contested and called into question; its depreciation, betrayal and denial; 248. - Open and sacrilegious scandal by P. and religious; violation of pledges made to Christ and church; 124; 248.

- Priestly life: perfect communion in P. L.; 61. – True P. neither sanctimonious nor worldly; lives his p. with wisdom and sacrifice; 63. – Personal spirituality; 65. – Moral fortitude in P.; 63. – Man of meditation and prayer; 65. – A life set apart from worldly care, from family life; distinguished from contemporary society, but engrafted in it as the salt of the earth; 124. – Happiness and beauty in P. L.; its intrinsic relation with cross of Christ; 198. – P. heart closed to every mean ambition; a heart after that of Christ; 201. – life of service at the disposal of community; 248. – Alter Christus; 200.
- Priestly power and function traditio postestatis-divine power belonging per se to Christ; 198. – Indelible character of P. in the chosen; 200. – Choice of priesthood implies specific relationship with God, church and world. - Imposes duties of dedication to life of charity and holiness; 200. – P. Character makes one dispenser of the mysteries of God; 47. – P. principle of charity and unity for the Mystical Body of Christ; 48. – To renew the sacramental miracle of the Eucharist; 248. – To announce and distribute word made flesh; 248. – P. ministry to be adapted to the needs and aspirations of people and places; 373. – Dignity and mission of P. can be ennobled by new findings of spirituality, theology and sociology; 373.

RACE

- Racial intransigence; 97.
- Ethnical and social discriminations, ignoble elements of the past; 97.

REASON

- Man's good cannot but be reasonable; 22.
- The mastery obtained by science not enough for the insatiable demands of reason; 307. – Reason's natural movement to search for the " why " of things; 308.
- Reason's irreplaceable function in religion; 308.
- R. a faculty man ought to be proud of, but as religious, one ought to be watchful and humble with it; 308.

- Reason's role in the direction of progress; 308.
- Man to have boldness of his reason, to learn how to get up in the end to the source; 308.

REFORM AND RENEWAL

- Renewal in the thinking of the church; 11. – R. of church not for disintegration of tested historical reality; 12. – Arbitrary reformers of the church cannot have " pleasure in and love for the church "; 155. – The spirit at work in the church is not of contestation, but of renewal; 203. – Renewal in religious awareness; 294. – Renewal to be operated in the heart of orthodoxy; 294. – Renewed in spirit of mind we need to put on Christ's nature and seek him in all things; 294. – Renewal entails dangers of bringing change for its own sake, to keep up with the transformism of the world; 295. – Unwarranted harmony, out of harmony with the church's inalienable tradition; 295. – Renewal requires theological consistency and pastoral fruitfulness; 375. – Renewal in the pastorate of Sacraments; 375. – Desirable and necessary so as not to let sacramental action debased into an exterior and superstitious formalism; 375. – Continual effort necessary to enter into the meaning of the sacramental symbol; 376. – Need of the development of sacramental pedagogy in pastoral work; 377.
- Renewal in religious teaching: need to renew kerygma; 316. – Renewal in the mode of presenting religion to the modern generation; 316. – Art and wisdom in adopting religious teaching to the learner's receptive abilities; 317. – Multiplication of means and expressions in religious instruction not to change content of faith; 317. – Temptation of doctrinal relativism in teaching the religious truths; 318.

RELIGION

- R. connects man with God; 306.
- R., a bond linking conscience to its source and to its end; 131.

- R. is life of soul in need of continual renewal, purification and growth in a subjective way; 294.
- Jesus' R. did away with law and its observances and called everyone to worship in spirit and truth. Christ did not found an abstract religion, nor a mere school of religious thought; 132. – But a society of believers in him; 132.
- R. exists in the thinking of modern tendency as reinterpreted in a purely humanistic way; 290; 301.
- History said to be the cause of the dissolution of the religious idea; 291.
- R. regarded as an antiquated, indefensible and an unjustifiable survival; 291.
- World of R. appears to be imaginary and superstitious to modern man; 299. – Danger of reducing the benefits of R. to purely human dimensions; 290; 301.

RELIGIOUS LIFE

- Magnanimous choice of R. life criticized in the post-conciliar period; 24.
- R. life cannot be lived as an individualistic expression of the relationship between man and God, between Christian and Christ, between the Catholic and church; 228. – Cannot grow in an autonomous group shut off from universal ecclesial communion; 228.
- R. man, described as a reactionary, an old-fashioned simpleton, an unhappy person unable to free himself from the shackles of an obsolete state mind; 291.
- R. renewal, a continuous process towards perfection; 294.
- Current religious crisis; 315.
- R. institutions a bond of union between the Mystical Body and the universal body of the faithful; 341.

RENUNCIATION

- Renunciation and sacrifice, hallmark of Christian life; 74.
- R., least popular in the comforts of modern life; 74. – Inner greed for possession and enjoyment of the comforts of modern civilization; 75.
- R., choice of serving one sole master; 75.

- R., of Satan, a precondition to the reception of Baptism; 75.
- Moral indifference set up as pedagogical principle as against Christian R; 76.
- Self-R. and normative discipline necessary to be strong and faithful Christians; 76.
- Christian abnegation imposes austere vigilance of thought and morality; 76.
- Christian R., the only authentic way of following Christ; 76. – Gives practice of self-control and establishes Christ's redemptive economy; 76.

RESURRECTION

- Paschal Mystery; Easter drama.
- Easter drama: a combination of divine and human mystery; 94. – Mystery of Christ a victim in justice for the sins of mankind; 94. – Mystery of victory over death and triumphant resurrection; 94. – The disorders and sufferings of modern life remind us the need of confidence in the death and R. of Christ; 97. – Christ's self-immolation and R. our justification of Paschal life; 97. – Church born out of Paschal mystery as a result of redemption; 115. – Peace, Easter message of Christ; 105. – Jesus' R. a historical reality, 105; 154. – Easter peace offers us certainty in thought and sureness in action; 106. – Faith in Risen Christ frees man from fear and doubt; 106. – Mystery of R. continued by Christ animating, purifying and strengthening the noble longings of human family; 106. – The story of redemption, a guiding inspiration for the true emancipation in the modern world; 107. – Easter Mystery, the central, biblical, theological and spiritual theme of our faith; 108. – not an isolated event, but linked with human destiny and salvation; 109. – R. a necessary complement of Passover mystery; 109. – R. of Christ, a means of sustaining our faith and pledge of our hope; 109. – essential consummation and an integral part of Redemption; 109. – Final stage of Paschal mystery, is fullness of salvation; complete immersion of our life with that of God; 111.

RINASCITA CHRISTIANA

- National Congress of the Christian Renewal movement. – Spirit of fraternity, of the movement; 161.
- Rinascita Christiana: Apostolate of R. C.; 162. – Task of taking up church's aggiornamento, with fidelity to church hierarchy and respect for her traditions; 162. – Presence of commitment in the world of to-day; 162. – Its apostolate amidst contradictions between a high degree of material progress and poverty of christian leaven and influence; 163. – to remove causes of rupture in the minds of Christians between religious belief and activity with a temporal content; 163. – Need for restoration of interior unity based on faith and charity; 163. Work and committing oneself to the renewal of modern man through contact with Christ; 163. – The apostolate implies being reborn everyday to newness of life; 164. – By intimate contact with God through grace and liturgy; 164. – In charity for the brotherhood; 164. – Open to the inspiration of the Holy Spirit; 164.

ROMAN PRESBYTERY COUNCIL: ROMAN PRIESTS

- Community spirit among priests in the diocese of Rome; 60.
- Presbyterian Council of Rome, its significance and effectiveness; 62; 372.
- Spiritual and practical concord in joint pastoral action; 62.
- Vicariate of Rome. – Its manifold problems, of priestly ministry, problems material and spiritual; 64.
- Presbyterian Council, a friendly training ground for the new style of episcopal authority; 128.
- Statue of Catholic Action harmonizes and coordinates the relations between laity and hierarchy; 128.
- Convention of R.P.C. an attempt at promoting greater fellowship of thought and word among clergy; 375.
- Responsibility of R.P.C. and its importance: – drawing new authentic spirituality from the Roman-ness; 374. – Not discarding the heritage and local good usages; 374. – Not accepting doubtful tendencies and innovations with servile assent; 374.

ROMAN CURIA

- Also see Cardinals.
- Bishops' fruitful collaboration with R. C.; 257.

SACRED SCRIPTURE

- Word of God; Gospel.
- Papal Documents on S. S.; 271: – **Providentissimus Deus** by Leo XIII in 1893; – **Spiritus Paraclitus** by Benedict XV in 1920; – **Divino afflante Spiritus** by Pius XII in 1943.
- Church has the guarantee of divine inerrancy in preaching and interpreting S. S.; 271.
- Church-recognizes in S. S. unchangeableness of her doctrine; – validity and permanency of God's word; – prophetic value and spiritual nourishment; 271.
- Doctrinal development of S. S. in the economy of salvation; 271. – Jansenist doctrines of Paschese Quesnels; 271. – Protestants took S. S. as the sole guide cutting it off from S. Tradition and Church; 271.
- Differing and contradictory interpretations of S. S. make unity of faith difficult; 132.
- Church approval for translations and editions of SS. in collaboration with Separated Brethren; 271.
- Ignorance of S. S. is ignorance of Christ; 271.
- Vatican II document on S. S.: **Dei Verbum**; 270. – Establishes function of the Holy Spirit in respect to Revelation; 270. – States relation of S. S. to Church's magisterium and the rule of faith; 270. – Confirms that Church venerated Books of S. S. as the supreme rule of faith together with sacred tradition; 271; 461.
- Force and power of the word of God, source of Church's spiritual life and sanctification; 272.
- Church nourished herself and her faithful with the Bread of Life from the table of the w. of G.; 272; 467.
- Liturgical reform, place of honour of the w. of G. in; 273; 467.
- Prayer essential to understand the S. S.
- Economy of the Gospel, work of the Holy Spirit in collaboration of the ministers of the w. of G.; 37.
- W. of G. cannot be received unless supported by a life of deep faith,

active charity, total obedience, fervent prayer and humble penance; 473.

- God cannot be the source of a word which makes Christians lose the sense of evangelical self-denial, 474. – God cannot be the source of a word which proclaims justice without being a herald of meekness mercy and purity; 474. – God cannot be the source of a word which sets brothers against brothers; 474.
- Perennial youth and reforming power of the Gospel; 437.
- G. raises and perfects seeds of good in men's hearts and minds, 419.
- G. message source of hope and certitude to modern man to build tomorrow's world; 256; 420.
- Scriptural warning to those who claim to bringing a different G.; 204.

SACRIFICE

- Sacrifice, supreme act of our religion; 76. – Sign of the Cross that brings death and life at the same time; 76. – Detaches us from useless and harmful desires; 77. – Makes us pleasing to God; 77.

SALVATION

- Salvation, attained through living according to Christ's word and spirit; 80.
- Light of S. shows us the right path and gives us an awareness of evil; 95.
- Divine plan of S. of human race depends on the living a relationship between us and Christ; 110.
- S. requires free assent to the faith; 116.
- Divine plan of S. requires apostolic proclamation of the word of God; 116.
- Dialogue of S. to be conducted on a world-wide scale to realize the objectives of the Council; 265.

SARDINIA

- Pope Paul's visit to Sardinia; 146.
- Our Lady of Bonaria-the Patroness of Sardinia; 146.
- Pope St. Pontian, martyr of the Roman Church and a fellow worker of the miners of S.; 148.

- Shepherds, workers in salt deposits, fishermen of S. bring to mind the scenes of the Gospel. 147; 149.
- Apostolate of the sea for Seafarers; 150.

SANCTITY
AND SANCTIFICATION

- Sanctity reveals fullness of life and boundless happiness; 37. – An immersion in the light of Christ and God; 37. – Exaltation of personality in S.; 37. – Immortal transfiguration of our moral existence; 37. – An inebriating forestate of the Communion of Saints; 37. – Acquires paradise by the upright morality in this life; 37. – Presents to the world its radiating example; 37. – Is the imitation of Christ in the Gospel of Beatitudes; 37. – Is imitation of Christ in his kerosis, his twofold humiliation of Incarnation and Redemption; 37.
- Church's vitality and S. displayed by saints and religious families of the 19th Century; 38.
- Past patterns of S. still valid for modern times; 38.
- Need to combine historical and classical forms of S. with the exigencies and forms of modern times; 38.

SCEPTICISM—see God—MODERNISM
SCIENCE
AND SCIENTIFIC KNOWLEDGE

- Pontifical Academy of Sciences, establishment of; 135.
- Academy of Lincei founded in 1603, revived by Pius IX by the motu proprio **In multis solaciis**; enlarged by Leo XIII under P.A.S.; 135.
- Desirability of disciplines in P.A.S. of positive and humanistic sciences with a view to foster the unity of human spirit; 136.
- True knowledge of things by scientific research, not contradictory to the truths of Christian faith; 136.
- Faith and Sc. knowledge can de integrated in the unity of knowledge while keeping their respective autonomy; 136.
- Church affirms legitimate autonomy of human culture and sciences; 137.
- S. can elevate human family to a sublime understanding of truth and universal values; 137.

- Temptation to agnosticism comes by man's refusal to subordinate himself to God; 138.
- True s. constitutes a spingboard to God; 139.

SCHILLER B., La teologie morale, p. 72.
– 81.

SCHUTZ., Eklesia, violenza o non violenza.
– 360.

SECULARISM: see Modernism.

SECULAR INSTITUTES

- Secular Institutes, world congress of 320.
- Representatives and members of S. I. consecrated to God; 320.
- Members of S. I. living in world, characterized by service to mankind and fidelity to Church; 320.
- Church immersed in profane temporal victories in the past; 32.
- Pluralism, a mark of S. I.; 323; 324.
- Vocation to S. I. is also a vocation to Christian perfection; 324.
- Moral discipline in S. I., always to be in a state of vigilance and personal initiative; 324.
- Members of S. I., to strive for personal sanctification; – to work for **Consecratio Mundi;** 324. – Consecration of, a commitment and compensation of the beatitude of possessing Christ; 324. – Have a mission of salvation to carry to the people of our day; 325. – Belong to the Church by a special title as consecrated seculars; 325.

SEMINARY

- Seminary, the study of the problem of; 64. – Should be a centre of agreement for ecclesial community; 64. – Should be more of pedagogical arena than a school of knowledge; 64. – Continues to be the home of Mother church; 64.

SERVICE

- Concept of s. in scriptures; 251.
- Latria develops into diaconia; 251.
- Redeeming Messiah, as the " servant of the Lord "; 251.

- Christ became slave, obedient unto the death of the cross; 251.
- Spirit of s. and spirit of submission to Father's will in the mission of Christ; 252.
- Council related the authority of the church to the idea of s.; 252.
- Ministry means service for others and sacrifice of self 252.
- The idea of s. in the authority of the church testified and supported by New Testament tradition and patristic theology; 253.
- Idea of s. does not exclude the necessity of hierarchical government in the church; 253.
- Ecclesial order is an order of s.; 253. all members of the church; 254.
- Ecclesial s., the particular task of
- Church at the s. of bringing the message of salvation; 254.
- The idea of s. to be brought in accord with that of liberty; 254.
- S., Lord's commandment to every man in regard to his neighbour; 277.

SHEPHERD (see " Pastor ")

SICK

- Christ mystically personified in sick humanity; 40.
- Caring for s., a message and command of Gospel; 40.
- Caring for physical suffering and spiritual poverty; 40.
- Works of mercy, practice of; 40.
- Visiting suffering neighbour in his home, a new field of refined charity; 40.

SIMON P. H. (question aux savants).
– 138.

SIRI, Card. (La Chiesa).
– 132.

SIN

- Sin, negative aspect of things; 56. – Satan's ambush on man; 56. – Mortal and actual, deadly enemies of true life; 95.
- Consequences inherited through Original Sin; 79.
- O. S. psycho-ethical imbalances disturbing the moral life in us; 95.
- Greatest sin of man to-day is losing the sense of sin; 96.

- Losing the sense of sin, result of losing the sense of God and relationship with him; 96.
- Encounter with Christ gives us consciousness of sin; 96.

HOLY SPIRIT

- Holy Spirit's action in the church; 22. - Principle of Christian's new life of grace; 116. - Inspirer of faith itself; 116. - Animator of the Mystical Body of the Church and its members; 430.
- One possesses the H. S. to the extent one loves the church; 155.
- Relationship between the H. S. and the church in the divine plan of salvation; 155.

SUFFERING

- Church is suffering from the pressures for transformation and conformity; 157. - By individualist contestations and novelties; 157. - Where her ecclesiastical tradition is treated with disrespect; 157. - When her canonical order is criticized as arbitrary and repressive legalism; 157. - When her authority is combatted and dissolved in excessive pluralism; 157. - By the malaise caused in the church by children in her own communion; 157. - By the effect on her from the progress of civil society and its collective malaise; 157.
- Suffering, a more sensitive and evident aspect of the church; 157.
- Silent patience of loyal souls who accept and share church's suffering in her adversity; 158. - Faithful souls firmly attached to the rule of faith and of church's law; 159.
- Loyal faithful suffering with the church, guardians of **sensus ecclesiae**; 159. - Souls, humble and poor in spirit, heirs of tradition, 159.
- We must accept pilgrim and suffering church with virile joy, remembering the sufferings of Christ; 160.

SYNOD

- General Secretariat of the Bishops, a sign of Synod's vitality; 195. - A guarantee of order, of research, of coordination in the problems of the Church government; 195.
- The work of Synodal meeting, an

extention of pastoral solicitude of the Bishops; 196.
- Bonds of perfect in faith and collaboration of the Catholic Episcopate perfected in the Synod; 444.
- Second General Synod of the Episcopate to discuss the themes of ministerial priesthood and Justice in the world; 444.
- Synod's doctrinal and disciplinary impulse on the post-conciliar church; 28.

THEOLOGY

- T. a science of faith having its norm in Church; 471.
- Institution of Pontifical Theological Commission: to promote theological studies; 127. - To help the Holy Office in answering theological incertitudes; 256.
- Post-conciliar T. gives a place of honour to Christian anthropology; 471.
- Use of scientific knowledge in research of hermeneutics; 471.
- True T. rests on the Word of God, together with Sacred Tradition provides a deterrent to venturesome hypotheses and opinions; 472.

THEOLOGY OF REVOLUTION

- T. of R. not in accord with Gospel spirit; 360.
- Council spirit is against T. of R.; 360.
- Christ's reforming and renewing of human conscience not done through radical subversion of temporal and juridical institutions; 360.

TERRORISM

- (see violence and conflict).

TERESA OF AVILA

- Church's conferring of the title of " Doctor of the Church " on St. T.; 326.
- St. T., first woman Doctor of the Church; 330.
- Justification of the title of Doctor on St. Th.: - title conferred taking into account of St. Paul's admonition that women be silent in the Church; 331. - Title of a Doctor does not entail hierarchical function of teaching in the Church; 331.

- St. Teresa of Avila; life and sanctity significance; 326; 329; 331; 332.
- Eminence of St. Teresa's doctrine; 327; 328; 329.

TERESA, Mother

- Superior of the Missionaries of Charity, first recipient - of Pope John XXIII Peace Prize; 442 (see Pope John XXIII Peace Prize).

St. THOMAS

- (**Contr. Gent.** 1, 30); 311. - (**Summ. Theol.** 111, 73); 438. - (I. II; 106; 1 and 108, 1); 28.

TAINE, III, 125

- 322.

TAIZE (violence de Pacifiques)

- 360.

TRESMONTANT, C.

- 139.

TIME

- T. mystery of; 5.
- Determining future and destiny of man in T.; 5.
- Evolution of T.; 5.
- God's kingdom in T.; 5.
- Christians' task in the building and developing od the earthly city and his collaboration with the efforts of unbelievers in its progress and history; 5.
- Beneficent influence of Divine Providence on the factor of T.; 4.
- Forgetfulness of last realities; 5.
- Conciliar teaching on the factor of T. in its decrees; 5.
- Accumulated possessions in T.; 4.
- Singular preoccupation of the present, topicalism, secularization; 5.
- T., a cosmic and historical law; 3. - Irreversible and unrelenting; 3. - Its never-ending scope; 3. - Controller of destiny; 3. - Its obscurity and fatality; 3. - A present gift used intensively and enjoyed wisely; 5. - Not to enjoy it with slothful indifference and anxious hedonism; 190. - Precariousness of, and hence to be used with feverish intensity for salvation; 190; 5.
- Scale of values, true and false; 4.

- Temporal death, terrible frontier; 6.
- Transitoriness of T. G.; 21; 190.
- Optimistic conception of T.; 7.
- Evolution development and progress in T.; 19.
- Ideas that triumph in T. can and do change in T.; 292.
- T. conditions everything, begets and devours all; 370.
- Christian belief in the element of permanency in the succession of T.; 371.
- Norm or Doctrine qualified to endure only in T., a false thinking; 371.
- Pilgrim Church in history and time (see [Pilgrim] Church); 189.

TORTURE

- Phenomenon of T. reflects a moral decline; 359.
- Police t., and inhumane methods to exhort confessions; 359; 98.
- Torture, a phenomenon to be disowned and abolished; 359. - Inadmissible in the present age; 359. - offends physical integrity of man and also his human dignity; 359. - Degrades sense of majesty and justice; 359. - Arouses feelings of hatred and revenge; 359.
- Church-authorities and Catholic Public Opinion voice their abhorrence of the methods of T.; 359.

TOURISM (apostolate of)

- **Apostolicae Caritatis** - motu proprio for establishing of Pontifical Commission for the Spiritual care of Migrants in the Congregation for Bishops; 383.
- Pastoral care for itinerant people; 383.
- Task of the Commission: - to study the facts of the social phenomenon of tourism; 384. - ways of spreading the word of God in this field; 384.
- Problems arising in the field of tourism especially where fine traditions are abandoned; 384.
- Need of creative zeal, apostolic daring and hope to face new changes in the sphere of tourism on the part of the pastors; 384.
- T. can bring about fraternal dialogue, mutual understanding, openness to other civilizations and cultures; 384.

- Pastoral structures to be adapted to the dynamism of T.; 384.
- Responsibility of spiritual care of migrants, a care of all Christian Communities; 384.
- Spiritual animation of tourist centres; 385.

TRADITION

- Ecclesiastical T. is one which identifies with ministry; 252.
- T. in modern current of thought considered as old age; 370.
- The faithful of Church's witness, rooted in Sacred T.; 467.

TRAVEL

- See Papal trip to the Far East.

TRUTH (also see " Courage of Truth ")

- Truth: – Criterion for judging T.; 21; 470. – Measure of T. and integrity; 21. – Church structure of Chrisitanity based on T. of faith; 209. – Involves conscience, facts, history, science, culture, philosophy, faith; 209. – Growing weary of T., a temptation easily accepted by modern man; 45. – T. in crisis to-day - objective T. replaced by subjective T.; 210. – Subjective T. constitutes experience, appeal to conscience, free personal opinion; 210. – Criticism of church's capacity to know T. and think validly; 210. – Philosophic T. giving way to agnosticism, scepticism, snobbery of systematic doubt; 210. – Pretext of pluralism undertaken to express divine T. in a variety of languages and mentalities; 210. – Need to pledge one's life to T., 204. – T. remains but requires purification in its human expressions; 296. – We enter into T. only through charity; 309. – T. liberates from the errors and arbitrariness arising from lack of wisdom and love; 336. – T. brings man under the law of the Spirit of grace and charity; to union with Christ and love of neighbour; to self-abnegation, sacrifice and sanctity; 336.

Unitatis Redintegratio

- 2 (p. 416); 4 (34); 7 (333).

UNITED NATIONS ORGANIZATION

- U.N.O. – represents the path of modern civilization and world peace; – the bridge to link various governments of brotherly unity; 344. – A bridge to link various governments; 344. – A round table for discussions and gathering; – A tribunal for pleading the cause of justice and peace; – A privileged forum where conscience of humanity makes itself heard; in the midst of violence and wars; 544.
- U.N. Charter of human rights: – an expression of the unanimous aspirations of men's hearts and universal witness of their consciences; 345. – a guarantee of enjoying human dignity and the conditions necessary for its exercise without distinction; 345. – Fundamental human rights recognized by the U.N. Charter; 347. – Right to religious freedom – man's right to worship God in accordance with dictates of his conscience; 347.
- U.N. to defend innocent victims of intolerant religious discrimination; 347. – To promote the right to the exercise of the voice of conscience and ostracize conduct incompatible with the dignity of mankind; 348.
- U.N. Assembly – its praiseworthy conditions of dignity of freedom and security in all its undertakings; 345: – its tasks: – to lend voice to those who are not able to make themselves heard; 345. – To denounce all oppressions without care for ideologies; 360; 345. – To ensure that cries of distress receive a hearing; 345. – To denounce all oppressions without care for ideologies; 360; 345. – To ensure that cries of distress receive a hearing; 345. – To ensure that just requests be taken into consideration; 345. – The weak be protected against the violence of the strong; 345. – That the flame of hope be kept burning in the breast of the most humiliated; 346. – To make understand one another and work for each other; 346. – To promote common good of man and achieve community of freedom, the ideal of humanity; 348. – Strengthen states to help their people achieve fullness of their personality and social and spiritual freedom; 348.

- UN's untiring perseverance for inducing reciprocal and controlled disarmament; 347.
- The question of survival of man hesitates between hope and fear; 347.
- Real danger comes from man; 346.
- Nations in preserving their identity and original way of living should agree upon the common will to survive and live; 346.
- Common good of nations demands that states rise above nationalistic interests and international prestige; 347.
- Papal invitation to mankind through " Populorum Progressio " to work for " full-bodied humanism "; 346.
- Great opportunities to be utilized for progress of mankind instead of war budgets; 346.
- Resources from scientific and technical achievements to be utilized to sustain the human race; 347.
- Integral development of man and interdependence of mankind, an enterprise worthy of every effort for its achievement; 346.
- True reconciliation between individuals social groups and nations necessary for lasting peace; 345.
- Relationships based on understanding mutual respect and creative collaboration; 345.
- Work of the living not to be used against life but to feed life and make it grow; 347. - Spiritual progress does not stem from material progress; 347. - Technical achievements of themselves do not bring moral advances; 347; 400. - Advance of science places greater demands on the conscience of man; 347.
- Unity of human family shows itself in the rejection and war; 348. - In the hope of world fraternity in recognizing a brother in every man; by virtue of the indelible imprint of the living God, Father of all men; 346; 348; 404. - In the atmosphere favouring development of material, intellectual and spiritual of persons and communities; 348.
- Work of men and conquests of human genius to meet the design of God; 348.
- Intelligence and heart of man, to rise to the level of his science and technology to be able to eliminate forces of division and dissolution; 348.
- Special task of Christians in the efforts of the UN to bring about world fraternity; 349.
- Modern statesmen and sociologists, to strive to make the world a single community; 450.
- Use of science and technology for peace and social justice; 450.
- U.N.O. Food and Agricultural Organization of the (see F.A.O.).

UNITY

- Didache, unity in the Church; 428.
- U. in Catholic Church, as cultural fact orientated towards temporal unification in a peaceful civilization, 429.
- U. in Catholic faith in Christ in diverse conditions of human culture; 431.
- U. of faith in Church, an intimate communion of church within itself; 430.
- U. by charity in Catholic communion; 431 (see Charity).
- U. in faith and love, a witness in the world; 432.
- Unum sint, Christ's messianic desire expressed to his disciples; 61.
- U. of human spirit; 136.
- Politico-religious compromise, contrary to Christian and Church unity; 31.
- God's plan in the economy of salvation, to form people united in peacefulness; 436.

UNIVERSE

- The word of God existed from the beginning in the U. as the true light enlightening every creature; 137.
- Mysterious beauty of creation; 140.
- The meeting with God, in the quasi-limitless grandeur of his works; 140.
- God the Creator of the U. and Father of men wishes to be sought after, found, adored, and loved by the paths of scientific discoveries and modern techniques; 141.
- The quest of human mind for an explanatory idea of the ensemble; 138 (see intelligence and reason).
- Church encourages the investigation, discovery and conquest of the universe; 137.

- Nuclei of galaxies, significant of Pascal's " this silence of infinite spaces "; 138.

Violence and conflict in the world:

- Violence and reprisals, ideals of liberty cannot be justified by; 98; 261.
- Violence and terrorism employed as normal means for the overthrow of the established order cannot be justified; 360.
- Violence cause unjust harm and provoke sentiments of hatred; destroy community peace and order; 360.
- Vengeful and malicious reprisals resulting in insecurity and food; 262.
- Armed conflict in the Middle East; 97; 206; 262; 319.
- Increasing armaments race and conflicts, an irrational phenomena; 97; 206.
- Acts of terrorism and guerilla warfare directed against legitimate governments and inflicted on unarmed people, condemned; 98; 360.
- Murderous expressions against armed rebel formations; 360.
- Heavy-handed intimidating oppressions of whole countries, condemned; 360.

VOCATION

- Problem of v. in the Church; 63.
- Scarcity of v. depends on family and social conditions; 63.
- Consciences of new generations unresponsive to Xt's voice; 63.
- V. of youth, a call to heroic service of the Kingdom of God; 63.
- Pressing need of v. in the Church; 63.
- V. generated by conscience, a consecration, a total gift of self to God in the practice of evangelical counsels; 323.

WAR

- Sufferings and afflictions of civil, war; 262. – W. even when necessitated by defence, not desirable; 361.

WILL

- Will wholly directed to practical and economic problems, a modern aberration; 305.

GOOD WILL

- Good will depends on moral uprightness and rationality; 56. – And public opinion; 57. – Makes use of good as a weapon to overcome evil; 57. – Profound secret of G. W. is in the Cross of Christ; 58.

WOMEN in Church

- Sublime mission of w. in the People of God; 330. – W. required to profess faith by virtue of baptismal character and common priesthood of the faithful; 330. – Special capacity of w. for mystical prayer; 330. – Council recognition of lofty collaboration of w. with divine grace in establishing the Kingdom of God; 331; Council call on w. to cooperate for peace and salvation of mankind; 331.

YOUTH

- Youth of the world, animated by power of Xt can provide answer to the yearnings of the young hearts; 434. – Church renewal of herself to offer good news by offering answer to the puzzling situations faced by youth; 434.
- Youth and permissive society, and unchristian behaviour patterns; 435.
- Youth disinherited, the automatons of modern technology; 450.
- Youth urgent need for liberation of, from illusions, frustrations, injustices and repressions; 450.